This translation of *The Development of the Monist View of History* is by Andrew Rothstein and was originally published in London, 1947, by Lawrence and Wishart. The translations of Plekhanov's preface to the second and third editions and of his article "A Few Words to Our Opponents," given here as an appendix, were made by A. Fineberg.

The translations have been checked with the latest Russian edition.

CONTENTS

	Page
Publisher's Foreword	5
Preface to the Second and Third Editions	9
Chapter I. French Materialism of the Eighteenth Century	13
Chapter II. French Historians of the Restoration	26
Chapter III. The Utopian Socialists	45
Chapter IV. Idealist German Philosophy	89
Chapter V. Modern Materialism	144
Conclusion	288
Appendix I. Once Again Mr. Mikhailovsky, Once More the "Triad"	328
Appendix II. A Few Words to Our Opponents	339
Notes	389
Name Index	397
Subject Index	402

PUBLISHER'S FOREWORD

The Development of the Monist View of History was written by Plekhanov in 1894 and was first published in St. Petersburg, in 1895, under the pseudonym N. Beltov. He was prompted to write the book by Mikhailovsky's[1] articles in *Russkoye Bogatstvo*[2] directed against the Russian Marxists. But long before the appearance of the articles Plekhanov had been planning to write an extensive work on the materialist conception of history, setting forth the principles of dialectical materialism and criticizing the idealist theory of the Narodniks.

It was the great merit of Plekhanov and the first Russian Marxist group—the Emancipation of Labour Group, which he formed abroad—that they were the first to disseminate Marxism in Russia and to criticize the ideological positions of Narodism. After *Socialism and the Political Struggle* and *Our Differences*, Plekhanov wrote a series of general philosophical works in which the principles of Marxism were brilliantly expounded, and which played a major role in the dissemination of Marxism in Russia and in combating the influence of the Narodniks. His writings paved the way for the triumph of Marxism in Russia. To the futile theories of the Narodniks—in which sighs for the "unhappy muzhik" were combined with a contemptuous regard for the people as a "mob" which was only capable of destruction, and as obedient clay in the hands of "critically minded" individuals—Plekhanov opposed the integral and harmonious philosophy of Marxism, the ideology of the only consistently revolutionary class in history, an ideology infused with a deep faith in the people and the creative power of its vanguard, the proletariat.

The Development of the Monist View of History is one of the most distinguished of Plekhanov's works. Lenin referred to it as a book "which had helped to educate a whole generation of Russian Marxists." (*Works*, 4th Russ. ed., Vol. 16, p. 243.)

In *The Development of the Monist View of History*, Plekhanov shows that the Marxist philosophy was the logical product of the whole past development of science. He analyzes the views of the French materialists, the theories of the French historians of the Restoration, the tenets of the great Utopian Socialists, and German idealist philosophy. While bringing out the contradictions which were inevitably inherent in these theories because of the restricted historical and class outlook of their authors, he reveals what was progressive in each of them.

Plekhanov shows that it was only the genius of Marx which placed philosophy and history on a genuinely scientific basis. Critically reshaping and developing the entire theoretical heritage of the past, Marx had created the greatest of revolutionary theories, which correctly reflected the laws of world development. He had armed the proletariat with a theoretical weapon of tremendous transforming power.

Plekhanov's works of this period dealt a decisive blow to Narodism.

In his writings against the Narodniks, Plekhanov showed that it was absurd to put the question the way the Narodniks did: should capitalism develop in Russia or not? Producing irrefutable facts, he demonstrated that Russia had already entered the path of capitalist development and that there was no force that could divert her from this path.

The task of the revolutionaries was not to arrest the development of capitalism in Russia—that they could not do anyhow. Their task was to secure the support of the powerful revolutionary force brought into being by the development of capitalism, namely, the working class, to develop its class consciousness, to organize it, and to help it to create its own working-class party.

Plekhanov also shattered the second major error of the Narodniks, namely, their denial of the role of the proletariat as the vanguard of the revolutionary struggle. The Narodniks looked upon the rise of the proletariat in Russia as something in the nature of a "historical misfortune," and spoke of the "ulcer of proletarianism." Plekhanov, championing the teachings of Marxism, showed that they were fully applicable to Russia and that in spite of the numerical preponderance of the peasantry and the relative numerical weakness of the proletariat, it was on the proletariat and on its growth that the revolutionaries should base their chief hopes.

Plekhanov shattered the third major error of the Narodniks as well, namely, that "heroes," outstanding individuals, and their ideas played the prime role in social development, and that the role of the masses, the "mob," the people, classes, was insignificant. Plekhanov accused the Narodniks of idealism, and showed that the truth lay not with idealism, but with the materialism of Marx and Engels.

But even after Plekhanov's writings, Narodism was still far from defeated. It had to be definitely smashed ideologically, as the bitterest enemy of Marxism. This task was brilliantly performed by Lenin. Plekhanov was unable to complete the defeat of Narodism. Already at that period, in the 80s and 90s, there were mistaken elements in his views which contained the germs of his future Menshevism: he failed to see the revolutionary role of the peasantry as the ally of the proletariat in the revolution; he wrongly regarded the Russian bourgeoisie as a force that might render assistance, if only unstable assistance, to the revolution. Plekhanov and his group failed to solve the problem of combining Marxism with the working-class movement. That problem was solved by Lenin. Lenin alone measured up to the tasks of developing revolutionary theory and directing the revolutionary movement which were demanded by the era of imperialism and proletarian revolutions.

However, Plekhanov's mistakes and his subsequent political evolution are no reason for forgetting the valuable works he produced in the period when he was still a consistent Marxist.

"... I think it proper," Lenin wrote in 1921, "to observe for the benefit of young members of the Party that one *cannot* become an intelligent, a *real* Communist unless one has studied—I say advisedly, *studied*—everything Plekhanov has written on philosophy, for it is the best in world Marxist literature." (*Works*, 4th Russ. ed., Vol. 32, p. 73.)

And among Plekhanov's philosophical writings, *The Development of the Monist View of History* is the best, a model of militant revolutionary criticism of idealist philosophy.

Two articles by Plekhanov dealing with questions discussed in the book are given as appendixes to this edition: "Once Again Mr. Mikhailovsky, Once Again the 'Triad'" and "A Few Words to Our Opponents."

PREFACE TO THE SECOND AND THIRD EDITIONS

I have here corrected only *slips* and *misprints* which had crept into the first edition. I did not consider it right to make any changes in my *arguments*, since this is a *polemical* work. Making alterations in the substance of a polemical work is like appearing before your adversary with a new weapon, while compelling him to fight with his old weapon. This is impermissible in general, and still less permissible in the present case because my chief adversary, N. K. Mikhailovsky, is no longer alive.

The critics of our views asserted that these views are, first, wrong in themselves; secondly, that they are particularly wrong when applied to Russia, which is destined to follow its own original path in the economic field; thirdly, that they are bad, because they dispose their supporters to impassivity, to "quietism." This last stricture is not likely to be reiterated by anyone nowadays. The second has also been refuted by the whole development of Russian economic life in the past decade. As to the first stricture, it is enough to acquaint oneself with recent *ethnological* literature, if with nothing else, to be convinced of the correctness of *our explanation of history*. Every serious work on "primitive civilization" is obliged to resort to it whenever the question under discussion is the causal connection between manifestations of the social and spiritual life of "savage" peoples. Witness, for example, the classical work of K. Stainen, *Unter der Naturvölkern Zentral-Braziliens*. But I cannot, of course, dilate on this subject here.

I reply to some of my critics in an article appended to this edition, "A Few Words to Our Opponents," which I published under a pseudonym, and therefore refer in it to my book as if it were the work of another person whose views are also my own. But this article says nothing in opposition to Mr. Kudrin,[3] who came out against me in *Russkoye Bogatstvo* after it had appeared. In reference to Mr. Kudrin, I shall say a couple of words here.

It might seem that the most serious of his arguments against historical materialism is the fact he notes that one and the same religion, Buddhism for instance, is sometimes professed by peoples at very different levels of economic development. But this argument may appear sound only at a first glance. Observation has revealed that "one and the same" religion *substantially differs in content* depending on the level of economic development of the peoples professing it.

I should also like to reply to Mr. Kudrin on another point. He found in my book an error in the translation of a Greek text from Plutarch (see footnote, p. 142), and is very scathing about it. Actually, I am "not guilty." Being on a journey at the time the book was published, I sent the manuscript to St. Petersburg without giving the quotation from Plutarch, but only indicating the *paragraphs* from which it should be taken. One of the persons connected with the publication of the book—who, if I am not mistaken, *graduated from the same classical gymnasium* as Mr. Kudrin—translated the paragraphs I had indicated and ... made the mistake Mr. Kudrin points out. That, of course, is a pity. But it should also be said that this mistake was the only blunder our opponents could convict us of. They too had to have some moral satisfaction. So that, "humanly speaking," I am even glad of the error.

N. Beltov

Н. Бельтовъ.

КЪ ВОПРОСУ

О РАЗВИТІИ

МОНИСТИЧЕСКАГО ВЗГЛЯДА НА ИСТОРІЮ

Отвѣтъ гг. Михайловскому, Карѣеву и комп.

Audiatur et altera pars.

С.-ПЕТЕРБУРГЪ.
Типографія И. Н. Скороходова (Надеждинская, 43).
1895.

Title page of the first Russian edition

Chapter I

FRENCH MATERIALISM
OF THE EIGHTEENTH CENTURY

"If you nowadays," says Mr. Mikhailovsky, "meet a young man ... who, even with some unnecessary haste, informs you that he is a 'materialist,' this does not mean that he is a materialist in the general philosophical sense, in which in olden days we had admirers of Büchner and Moleschott. Very often the person with whom you are talking is not in the least interested either in the metaphysical or in the scientific side of materialism, and even has a very vague idea of them. What he wants to say is that he is a follower of the theory of economic materialism, and that in a particular and conditional sense."*

We do not know what kind of young men Mr. Mikhailovsky has been meeting. But his words may give rise to the impression that the teaching of the representatives of "economic materialism" has no connection with materialism "in the general philosophical sense." Is that true? Is "economic materialism" really so narrow and poor in content as it seems to Mr. Mikhailovsky?

A brief sketch of the history of that doctrine will serve as a reply.

What is "materialism in the general philosophical sense"?

Materialism is the direct opposite of *idealism*. Idealism strives to explain all the phenomena of Nature, all the

---
* *Russkoye Bogatstvo*, January 1894, Section II, p. 98.

qualities of matter, by these or those qualities of the *spirit*. Materialism acts in the exactly opposite way. It tries to explain psychic phenomena by these or those qualities of *matter*, by this or that organization of the human or, in more general terms, of the animal *body*. All those philosophers in the eyes of whom the prime factor is *matter* belong to the camp of the *materialists*; and all those who consider such a factor to be the *spirit* are *idealists*.

That is all that can be said about materialism in general, about "materialism in the general philosophical sense": as time built up on its fundamental principle the most varied superstructures, which gave the materialism of one epoch quite a different aspect from the materialism of another.

Materialism and idealism exhaust the most important tendencies of philosophical thought. True, by their side there have almost always existed *dualist* systems of one kind or another, which recognize *spirit* and *matter* as separate and independent *substances. Dualism* was never able to reply satisfactorily to the inevitable question: how could these two separate substances, which have nothing in common between them, influence each other? Therefore the most consistent and most profound thinkers were always inclined to *monism*, i.e., to explaining phenomena with the help of *some one main principle* (monos in Greek means "one"). Every consistent *idealist* is a monist to the same extent as every consistent *materialist*. In *this* respect there is no difference, for example, between Berkeley and Holbach. One was a consistent *idealist*, the other a no less consistent *materialist*, but both were equally *monistic*; both one and the other equally well understood the worthlessness of the *dualist outlook on the world*, which up to this day is still, perhaps, the most widespread.

In the first half of our century philosophy was dominated by *idealistic* monism. In its second half there triumphed *in science*—with which meanwhile *philosophy* had been completely fused—*materialistic* monism, although far from always consistent and frank monism.

We do not require to set forth here all the history of materialism. For our purpose it will be sufficient to consider its development beginning with the second half of last century. And even here it will be important for us to have in view mainly one of its trends—true, the most important—namely, the materialism of Holbach, Helvetius and their supporters.

The materialists of this trend waged a hot polemic against the official thinkers of that time who, appealing to the authority of Descartes (whom they can hardly have well understood), asserted that man has certain *innate ideas*, i.e., such as appear independently of his experience. Contesting this view, the French materialists in fact were only setting forth the teaching of Locke, who at the end of the seventeenth century was already proving that there are "no innate principles." But setting forth his teaching, the French materialists gave it a more consistent form, dotting such "i's" as Locke did not wish to touch upon, being a well-bred English liberal. The French materialists were fearless *sensationalists*, consistent throughout, i.e., they considered all the psychic functions of man to be *transformed sensations*. It would be valueless to examine here to what extent, in this or that particular case, their arguments are satisfactory from the point of view of present-day science. It is self-evident that the French materialists did not know a great deal of what is now known to every schoolboy: it is sufficient to recall the views of Holbach on chemistry and physics, even though he was well acquainted with the natural science of *his* age. But the French materialists' incontestable and indispensable service lies in that they thought consistently from the standpoint of *the science of their age*—and that is all that one can and must demand of thinkers. It is not surprising that the science of our age has advanced beyond the French materialists of last century: what is important is that *the adversaries of those philosophers were backward people even in relation to science of that day*. True, the historians of philosophy usually oppose to the views of the French materialists the view of Kant, whom, of course, it would be strange to reproach with lack of knowledge. But this contraposition is quite unjustified, and it would not be difficult to show that both Kant and the French materialists took, essentially, the same view,* but made use of it differently and therefore arrived at different conclusions, in keeping with the different characteristics of the social relations under the influence of which they lived and thought. We know that this opinion will be found paradoxical by people who are accustomed to believe every word of the historians of philosophy. There is no opportunity to prove it here by circumstantial argument, but we do not refuse to do so, if our opponents should require it.

Be that as it may, everyone knows that the French materialists regarded all the psychic activity of man as transformed *sensations* (sensations transformées). To consider psychic activity from this point of view means to consider all notions, all conceptions and feelings of man to be the result of *the influence of his environment upon him*. The French materialists did adopt this very

---

* Plekhanov's statement about "both Kant and the French materialists taking, essentially, the same view" is erroneous. In contradistinction to Kant's agnosticism and subjective idealism, the French materialists of the eighteenth century believed in cognizability of the external world.—*Ed.*

view. They declared constantly, very ardently and quite categorically that man, with his views and feelings, is what his environment, i.e., in the first place *Nature*, and secondly *society*, make of him. "L'homme est tout éducation" (man depends entirely on education), affirms Helvetius, meaning by the word education the sum-total of social influence. This view of man as the fruit of his environment was the principal theoretical basis for the *progressive demands* of the French materialists. For indeed, if man depends on his environment, if he owes it *all* the qualities of his character, then he owes it also his defects; and consequently if you wish to combat his defects, you must in suitable fashion change his environment, and moreover his *social* environment in particular, because Nature makes man neither bad nor good. Put people in reasonable social relations, i.e., in conditions where the instinct of self-preservation of each of them ceases to impel him to struggle against the remainder: co-ordinate the interests of the individual man with the interests of society as a whole—and virtue will appear of her own accord, just as a stone falls to the earth of its own accord when it loses any support. Virtue requires, not to be *preached*, but to be *prepared* by the reasonable arrangement of social relations. By the light-hearted verdict of the conservatives and reactionaries of last century, the morality of the French materialists is up to the present day considered to be an *egotistical* morality. They themselves gave a much truer definition: in their view it passed entirely into *politics*.

The doctrine that the spiritual world of man represents the fruit of his environment not infrequently led the French materialists to conclusions which they did not expect themselves. Thus, for example, they sometimes said that the views of man have absolutely no influence on his conduct, and that therefore the spreading of one idea or another in society cannot by a hairbreadth change its subsequent fate. Later on we shall show wherein such an opinion was mistaken, but at this stage let us turn our attention to another side of the views of the French materialists.

If the ideas of any particular *man* are determined by his environment, then the ideas of *humanity,* in their historical development, are determined by the development of the social environment, by the *history of social relationships.* Consequently, if we were to think of painting a picture of the "progress of human reason," and if we were not to limit ourselves in doing so to the question of "*how?*" (*in what particular way did the historical advance of reason take place?*), and put to ourselves the quite natural question of "*why?*" (*why did that advance take place just in this fashion, and not otherwise?*), we should have to begin with the history of the environment, the history of the development of social relations. The centre of gravity of our research would thus be shifted, at all events in the first stages, in the direction of studying the laws of social development. The French materialists came right up against this problem, but proved unable not only to solve it but even correctly to state it.

Whenever they began speaking of the historical development of mankind, they forgot their sensationalist view of "man" in general and, like all the philosophers of "enlightenment" of that age, affirmed that *the world* (i.e., the social relations of mankind) *is governed by opinions* (*c'est l'opinion qui gouverne le monde*).* In this lies the

---

* "I mean by opinion the result of the mass of truths and errors diffused in a nation: a result which determines its judgements, its respect or contempt, its love or hate, which forms its inclinations and customs, its vices and virtues—in a word, its manners. This is the opinion of which it must be said that it governs the world." Suard, *Mélanges de Littérature*, Paris, An XII, tome III, p. 400.

radical contradiction from which the materialism of the eighteenth century suffered, and which, in the reasoning of its supporters, was divided into an entire series of secondary and derivative contradictions, just as a banknote is exchanged for small cash.

Thesis. Man, with all his *opinions*, is the product of his *environment*, and mainly of his social environment. This was the inevitable conclusion from the fundamental proposition of Locke: *there are no innate principles.*

Antithesis. Environment, with all its qualities, is the product of *opinions*. This is the inevitable conclusion from the fundamental proposition of the historical philosophy of the French materialists: *c'est l'opinion qui gouverne le monde.*

From this radical contradiction there followed, for example, the following derivative contradictions:

Thesis. Man considers good those social relations which are useful to him. He considers bad those relations which are harmful to him. *The opinions of people are determined by their interests.* "L'opinion chez un peuple est toujours déterminée par un intérêt dominant," says Suard.* What we have here is not even a *conclusion* from the teachings of Locke, it is simply the repetition of his words: "No innate practical principles.... Virtue generally approved; not because innate, but because profitable.... Good and Evil ... are nothing but Pleasure or Pain, or that which occasions or procures Pleasure or Pain, to us."**

Antithesis. The existing relations seem useful or harmful to people, according to the general system of opinions of the people concerned. In the words of the same Suard, every people "ne veut, n'aime, n'approuve, que ce qu'il croit être utile" (every people desires, loves and approves

---
* Suard, tome III, p. 401.
** *Essay Concerning Human Understanding*, Book I, Ch. 3; Book II, Ch. 20, 21, 28.

only what it considers useful). Consequently in the last resort everything again is reduced to the opinions which govern the world.

Thesis. Those are very much mistaken who think that religious morality—for example, the commandment to love one's neighbour—even partially promoted the moral improvement of mankind. Such commandments, as ideas generally, are quite devoid of power over men. Everything depends on social environment and on social relations.*

Antithesis. Historical experience shows us "que les opinions sacrées furent la source véritable des maux du genre humain"—and this is quite understandable, because if opinions generally govern the world, then mistaken opinions govern it like blood-thirsty tyrants.

It would be easy to lengthen the list of similar contradictions of the French materialists, inherited from them by many "materialists in the general philosophical sense" of our own age. But this would be unnecessary. Let us rather look more closely at the general character of these contradictions.

There are contradictions and contradictions. When Mr. V. V.[4] contradicts himself at every step in his *Destinies of Capitalism* or in the first volume of his *Conclu-*

---

* This principle is more than once repeated in Holbach's *Système de la Nature*. It is also expressed by Helvetius when he says: "Let us suppose that I have spread the most stupid opinion, from which follow the most revolting consequences; if I have changed nothing in the laws, I will change nothing in manners either" (*De l'Homme*, Section VII, Ch. 4). The same opinion is frequently expressed in his *Correspondance Littéraire* by Grimm, who lived for long among the French materialists and by Voltaire, who fought the materialists. In his *Philosophe Ignorant*, as in many other works, the "Patriarch of Ferney" endeavoured to demonstrate that not a single philosopher had ever yet influenced the conduct of his neighbours, since they were guided in their acts by customs, not metaphysics.

sions from an Economic Investigation of Russia, his sins against logic can be of importance only as a "human document": the future historian of Russian literature, after pointing out these contradictions, will have to busy himself with the extremely interesting question, in the sense of social psychology, of why, with all their indubitable and obvious character, they remained unnoticed for many and many a reader of Mr. V. V. In the direct sense, the contradictions of the writer mentioned are as barren as the well-known fig-tree. There are contradictions of another character. Just as indubitable as the contradictions of Mr. V. V., they are distinguished from the latter by the fact that they do not send human thought to sleep, they do not retard its development, but push it on further, and sometimes push it so strongly that, in their consequences, they prove more fruitful than the most harmonious theories. Of such contradictions one may say in the words of Hegel: Der Widerspruch ist das Fortleitende (contradiction leads the way forward). It is just among these that the contradictions of French materialism in the eighteenth century must be rightfully placed.

Let us examine their main contradiction: *the opinions of men are determined by their environment; the environment is determined by opinions.* Of this one has to say what Kant said of his "antinomies"—the thesis is just as correct as the *antithesis*. For there can be no doubt that the opinions of men are determined by the social environment surrounding them. It is just as much beyond doubt that not a single people will put up with a social order which contradicts all its views: it will revolt against such an order, and reconstruct it according to its own ideals. Consequently it is also true that opinions govern the world. But then in what way can two propositions, true in themselves, contradict each other? The explanation is very simple. They contradict each other only because we are looking at them from an incorrect point of view. From that point of view it seems—and inevitably must seem—that if the thesis is right, then the antithesis is mistaken, and vice versa. But once you discover a correct point of view, the contradiction will disappear, and each of the propositions which confuse you will assume a new aspect. It will turn out to be supplementing or, more exactly, *conditioning* the other proposition, not excluding it at all; and if *this* proposition were untrue, then equally untrue would be *the other* proposition, which previously seemed to you to be its antagonist. But how is such a correct point of view to be discovered?

Let us take an example. It often used to be said, particularly in the eighteenth century, that the constitution of any given people was conditioned by the manners of that people; and this was quite justified. When the old republican manners of the Romans disappeared, their republic gave way to a monarchy. But on the other hand it used no less frequently to be asserted that the manners of a given people are conditioned by its constitution. This also cannot be doubted in the least. And indeed, how could republican manners appear in the Romans of the time, for example, of Heliogabalus? Is it not patently clear that the manners of the Romans during the Empire were bound to represent something quite opposite to the old republican manners? And if it is clear, then we come to the general conclusion that the constitution is conditioned by manners, and manners—by the constitution. But then this is a contradictory conclusion. Probably we arrived at it on account of the mistaken character of one or the other of our propositions. Which in particular? Rack your brains as you will, you will not discover anything wrong either in one or in the other; they are both irreproachable, as in reality the manners of every given people do influence its constitution, and in this sense are its *cause*, while on the other hand they are conditioned by the constitution, and in this sense are its *consequence*. Where, then, is the way out? Usually, in questions of this kind, people confine themselves to discovering *interaction*: manners influence the constitution and the constitution influences manners. Everything becomes as clear as daylight, and people who are not satisfied with clarity of this kind betray a tendency to *one-sidedness* worthy of every condemnation. That is how almost all our intellectuals argue at the present time. They look at social life *from the point of view of interaction*: each side of life influences all others and, in its turn, experiences the influence of all the others. Only such a view is worthy of a thinking "sociologist," while those who, like the Marxists, keep on seeking for some more profound reasons or other for social development, simply don't see to what degree social life is complicated. The French writers of the Enlightenment were also inclined to this point of view, when they felt the necessity of bringing their views on social life into logical order and of solving the contradictions which were getting the upper hand of them. The most systematic minds among them (we do not refer here to Rousseau, who in general had little in common with the writers of the Enlightenment) did not go any further. Thus, for example, it is this view-point of interaction that is maintained by Montesquieu in his famous works: *Grandeur et Décadence des Romains* and *De l'Esprit des Lois*.*

---

* Holbach in his *Politique naturelle* takes the standpoint of interaction between manners and constitution. But as he has there to deal with practical questions, this point of view leads him into a vicious circle: in order to improve manners one must perfect the constitution, and in order to improve it, one must improve manners. Holbach is rescued from this circle by an imaginary bon prince, who was desired by all the writers of the Enlightenment, and who, appearing like deus ex machina, solved the contradiction, improving both manners and constitution.

And this, of course, is a justifiable point of view. *Interaction undoubtedly exists between all sides of social life.* But unfortunately this justifiable point of view explains very little, for the simple reason that it gives no indication as to *the origin of the interacting forces.* If the constitution itself presupposes the manners which it influences, then obviously it is not to the constitution that those manners owe their first appearance. The same must be said of the manners too: if they already presuppose the constitution which they influence, then it is clear that it is not they which created it. In order to get rid of this muddle we must discover the historical factor which produced both the manners of the given people and its constitution, and thereby *created the very possibility of their interaction.* If we discover such a factor we shall reveal the correct point of view we are seeking, and then we shall solve without difficulty the contradiction which confuses us.

As far as the fundamental contradiction of the French materialists is concerned, this means the following. The French materialists were very mistaken when, contradicting their customary view of history, they said that ideas mean *nothing*, since environment means *everything*. No less mistaken was that customary view of theirs on history (c'est l'opinion qui gouverne le monde), which proclaimed opinions to be the main fundamental reason for the existence of any given social environment. There is undoubted interaction between opinions and environment. But scientific investigation cannot stop at recognizing this interaction, since interaction is far from explaining social phenomena to us. In order to understand the history of mankind, i.e., in the present case the history of its opinions, on the one hand, and the history of those social relations through which it passed in its development, on the other—we must rise above the point of view of interaction, and discover, if possible, that factor which determines both *the development of the social environment* and *the development of opinions*. The problem of social science in the nineteenth century was precisely to discover that factor.

The world is governed by opinions. But then, opinions do not remain unchanged. What conditions their changes? "The spreading of enlightenment," replied, as early as the seventeenth century, La Mothe le Vayer. This is the most abstract and most superficial expression of the idea that opinions dominate the world. The writers of the enlightenment of the eighteenth century held to it firmly, sometimes supplementing it with melancholy reflections that the fate of enlightenment, unfortunately, is in general very unreliable. But the realization that such a view was inadequate could already be noticed among the most talented of them. Helvetius remarked that the development of knowledge is subordinated to certain laws, and that, consequently, there are some hidden and unknown causes on which it depends. He made an attempt of the highest interest, still not assessed at its true value, to explain the social and intellectual development of man by *his material needs*. This attempt ended, and for many reasons could not but end, in failure. But it remained a testament, as it were, for those thinkers of the following century who might wish to continue the work of the French materialists.

CHAPTER II

FRENCH HISTORIANS
OF THE RESTORATION

"One of the most important conclusions which can be drawn from the study of history is that government is the most effective cause of the character of peoples; that the virtues or the vices of nations, their energy or their weakness, their talents, their enlightenment or their ignorance, are hardly ever the consequence of climate or of the qualities of the particular race, but are the work of the laws; that nature has given *all to everyone*, while government preserves or destroys, in the men subjected to it, those qualities which originally constituted the common heritage of the human race." In Italy there occurred no changes either in climate or in race (the influx of the barbarians was too insignificant to alter the latter's quality): "Nature was the same for Italians of all ages; only governments changed—and these changes always preceded or accompanied changes in the national character."

In this way Sismondi contested the doctrine which made the historical fate of peoples depend only on geographical environment.* His objections are not unfounded. In fact, *geography* is far from explaining everything in history, just because the latter is *history*, i.e., because, in Sismondi's words, governments change in spite of the

---

* *Histoire des Républiques italiennes du moyen âge,* Paris, t. I, Introduction, pp. v-vi.

fact that geographical environment remains unchanged. But this in passing: we are interested here in quite a different question.

The reader has probably already noticed that, comparing the unchanging character of geographical environment with the changeability of the historical destinies of peoples, Sismondi links these destinies with one main factor—*"government,"* i.e., with the *political institutions of the given country.* The character of a people is entirely determined by the character of the government. True, having stated this proposition categorically, Sismondi immediately and very essentially modifies it: political changes, he says, preceded changes of the national character *or accompanied them.* Here the character of the government appears to be rather determined by the character of the people. But in this case the historical philosophy of Sismondi encounters the contradiction with which we are already familiar, and which confused the French writers of the Enlightenment: the manners of a given people depend on its constitution; the constitution depends on their manners. Sismondi was just as little able to solve this contradiction as the writers of the Enlightenment: he was forced to found his arguments now upon one, now upon the other branch of this antinomy. But be that as it may, having once decided on one of them—namely that which proclaims that the character of a people depends on its government— he attributed to the conception of government an exaggeratedly wide meaning: in his eyes it embraced *absolutely all the qualities of the given social environment,* all the peculiarities of the social relations concerned. It would be more exact to say that in his view absolutely all the qualities of the social environment concerned were the work of "government," the result of the constitution. This is the point of view of the eighteenth century. When the French materialists wanted briefly and strongly to express their conviction of the omnipotent influence of environment on man, they used to say: c'est la législation qui fait tout (everything depends on legislation). But when they spoke of legislation, they had in mind almost exclusively *political legislation, the system of government.* Among the works of the famous G. B. Vico there is a little article entitled: "Essay of a System of Jurisprudence, in Which the Civil Law of the Romans Is Explained by Their Political Revolutions."* Although this "Essay" was written at the very beginning of the eighteenth century, nevertheless the view it expresses on the relationship between civil law and the system of government prevailed up to the French Restoration. The writers of the Enlightenment reduced everything to "politics."

But the political activity of the "legislator" is in any event a *conscious* activity, although naturally not always expedient. The conscious activity of man depends on his *"opinions."* In this way the French writers of the Enlightenment without noticing it themselves returned to the

---

* We translate the title of the article from the French, and hasten to remark in so doing that the article itself is known to us only from certain French extracts. We were unable to discover the original Italian text, as it was printed, so far as we know, only in one edition of Vico's works (1818); it is already missing from the Milan edition in six volumes of 1835. However what is important in the present case is not *how* Vico performed the task he had set himself, but *what task it was.*

We shall incidentally anticipate here one reproach which shrewd critics will probably hasten to level at us: "You indiscriminately make use of the term 'writers of the Enlightenment' and 'materialists,' yet far from all the 'Enlighteners' were materialists; many of them, for example Voltaire, vigorously combated the materialists." This is so; but on the other hand Hegel demonstrated long ago that the writers of the Enlightenment who rose up against materialism were themselves only *inconsistent materialists,*

idea of the *omnipotence of opinions*, even in those cases when they desired to emphasize the idea of the *omnipotence of environment*.

Sismondi was still adopting the view-point of the eighteenth century.* Younger French historians were already holding different views.

The course and outcome of the French Revolution, with its surprises that nonplussed the most "enlightened" thinkers, proved a refutation, graphic to the highest degree, of the idea that opinions were omnipotent. Then many became quite disillusioned in the power of "reason," while others who did not give way to disillusionment began all the more to incline to acceptance of the idea of the omnipotence of *environment,* and to studying the course of *its* development. But in the era of the Restoration environment too began to be examined from a new point of view. Great historic events had made such a mock, both of *"legislators"* and of political constitutions, that now it already seemed strange to make dependent on the latter, as a basic factor, all the qualities of a particular social environment. Now political constitutions began to be considered as something derivative, as a *consequence* and not as a *cause*.

"The majority of writers, scholars, historians or publicists," says Guizot in his *Essais sur l'histoire de France*,** "have attempted to explain the condition of society, the degree or the nature of its civilization, by the study of its political institutions. It would be wiser to begin with the study of society itself, in order to learn and understand its political institutions. Before becoming a cause, institutions are a consequence; society creates them before it begins to change under their influ-

* He began working at the history of the Italian Republics in 1796.
** Their first edition appeared in 1821.

ence; and instead of judging the condition of a people from the system or the forms of its government, we must first of all investigate the condition of the people, in order to judge what should be and what could be its government.... Society, its composition, the mode of life of individual persons in keeping with their social position, the relations of various classes of persons, in a word, the *civil condition of men* (l'état des personnes)—such, without doubt, is the first question which attracts the attention of the historian who desires to know how peoples lived, and of the publicist who desires to know how they were governed."*

This view is directly opposed to the view of Vico. The latter explained the history of civil law by political revolutions. Guizot explains the political order by civil conditions, i.e., by civil law. But the French historian goes even further in his analysis of "social composition." He states that, among all the peoples who appeared on the historical arena after the fall of the Western Roman Empire, the *"civil condition"* of men was closely connected with *agrarian relations* (état des terres), and therefore the study of their agrarian relations must precede the study of their civil condition. *"In order to understand political institutions, we must study the various strata existing in society and their mutual relationships. In order to understand these various social strata, we must know the nature and the relations of landed property."*** It is from this point of view that Guizot studies the history of France under the first two dynasties. He presents it as the history of the struggle of various social strata at the time. In his history of the English Revolution he makes a new step forward, representing this event as the strug-

---

* *Essais* (10° édition), Paris, 1860, pp. 73-74.
** *Ibid.*, pp. 75-76.

gle of the bourgeoisie against the aristocracy, and tacitly recognizing in this way that to explain the political life of a particular country it is necessary to study not only its agrarian relations, but also all its property relations in general.*

Such a view of the political history of Europe was far from being the exclusive property of Guizot at that time. It was shared by many other historians, among whom we shall refer to Augustin Thierry and Mignet.

In his *Vues des révolutions d'Angleterre* Thierry represents the history of the English revolutions as the struggle of the bourgeoisie against the aristocracy. "Everyone whose ancestors were numbered among the conquerors of England," he writes of the first Revolution, "left his castle and journeyed to the royal camp,

---

* The struggle of religious and political parties in England in the seventeenth century "was a screen for the social question, the struggle of various classes for power and influence. True, in England these classes were not so sharply delimited and not so hostile to one another as in other countries. The people had not forgotten that powerful barons had fought not only for their own but for the people's liberty. The country gentlemen and the town bourgeois for three centuries sat together in parliament in the name of the English Commons. But during the last century great changes had taken place in the relative strength of the various classes of society, which had not been accompanied by corresponding changes in the political system.... The bourgeoisie, country gentry, farmers and small landowners, very numerous at that time, had not an influence on the course of public affairs proportionate to their importance in the country. They had grown, but not been elevated. Hence in this stratum, as in other strata lying below it, there appeared a proud and mighty spirit of ambition, ready to seize upon the first pretext it met to burst forth." *Discours sur l'histoire de la revolution d'Angleterre*, Berlin, 1850, pp. 9-10.

Compare the same author's entire six volumes relating to the history of the first English Revolution, and the sketches of the life of various public men of that time. Guizot there rarely abandons the view-point of the struggle of classes.

where he took up a position appropriate to his rank. The inhabitants of the towns and ports flocked to the opposite camp. Then it might have been said that the armies were gathering, one in the name of *idleness and authority*, the other in the name of *labour and liberty*. All idlers, whatever their origin, all those who sought in life only enjoyment, secured without labour, rallied under the royal banner, defending interests similar to their own interests; and on the contrary, those of the descendants of the former conquerors who were then engaged in industry joined the party of the Commons."*

The religious movement of the time was, in Thierry's opinion, only the reflection of positive lay interests. "On both sides the war was waged for positive interests. Everything else was external or a pretext. The men who defended the cause of the *subjects* were for the most part Presbyterians, i.e., they desired no subjection even in religion. Those who adhered to the opposite party belonged to the Anglican or the Catholic faith; this was because, even in the religious sphere, they strove for authority and for the imposition of taxes on men." Thierry quotes in this connection the following words of Fox in his *History of the Reign of James II*: "The Whigs considered all religious opinions with a view to politics.... Even in their hatred to popery, (they) did not so much regard the superstition, or imputed idolatry of that unpopular sect, as its tendency to establish arbitrary power in the state."**

In Mignet's opinion, "the movement of society is determined by the dominating interests. Amid various obstacles, this movement strives towards its end, halts once that end has been reached, and yields place to

---

* *Dix ans d'études historiques*, the sixth volume of Thierry's Complete Works (10th ed.), p. 66.
** London, 1808, p. 275.—*Tr*.

another movement which at first is imperceptible, and becomes apparent only when it becomes predominant. Such was the course of development of feudalism. Feudalism existed in the needs of man while it still did not exist in fact—the first epoch; in the second epoch it existed in fact, gradually ceasing to correspond to men's needs, wherefore there came to an end, ultimately, its existence in fact. Not a single revolution has yet taken place in any other way."*

In his history of the French Revolution, Mignet regards events precisely from this point of view of the "needs" of various social classes. The struggle of these classes is, in his opinion, the mainspring of political events. Naturally, such a view could not be to the taste of eclectics, even in those good old times when their brains worked much more than they do nowadays. The eclectics reproached the partisans of the new historical theories with *fatalism,* with prejudice in favour of a *system* (esprit de système). As always happens in such cases, the eclectics did not notice at all the really weak sides of the new theories, but in return with the greater energy attacked their unquestionably strong sides. However, this is as old as the world itself, and is therefore of little interest. Much more interesting is the circumstance that these new views were defended by the *Saint-Simonist* Bazard, one of the most brilliant representatives of the socialism of that day.

Bazard did not consider Mignet's book on the French Revolution to be flawless. Its defect was, in his eyes, that among other things it represented the event it described as a separate fact, standing without any connection with "that long chain of efforts which, having overthrown the

---

* *De la féodalité des institutions de St. Louis et de l'influence de la législation de ce prince,* Paris, 1822, pp. 76-77.

old social order, was to facilitate the establishment of the new regime." But the book also has unquestionable merits. "The author has set himself the task of characterizing those parties which, one after the other, direct the revolution, of revealing the connection of these parties with various social classes, of displaying what particular chain of events places them one after the other at the head of the movement, and how finally they disappear." That same "spirit of system and fatalism," which the eclectics put forward as a reproach against the historians of the new tendency, advantageously distinguishes, in Bazard's opinion, the work of Guizot and Mignet from the works "of literary historians (i.e., historians concerned only for beauty of style) who, in spite of all their numbers, have not moved historical science forward one step since the eighteenth century."*

If Augustin Thierry, Guizot or Mignet had been asked, do the manners of a people create its constitution, or, on the contrary, does its constitution create its manners, each of them would have replied that, however great and however unquestionable is the interaction of the manners of a people and its constitution, in the last analysis, both owe their existence to a third factor, lying deeper—*"the civil condition of men, their property relations."*

In this way the contradiction which confused the philosophers of the eighteenth century would have been solved, and every impartial person would recognize that Bazard was right in saying that science had made a step forward, in the person of the representatives of the new views on history.

But we know already that the contradiction mentioned is only a particular case of the fundamental contradiction of the views on society held in the eighteenth cen-

---

* "Considérations sur l'histoire," in *Le Producteur*, Part IV.

tury: (1) man with all his thoughts and feelings is the product of environment; (2) environment is the creation of man, the product of his "opinions." Can it be said that the new views on history had resolved this fundamental contradiction of French materialism? Let us examine how the French historians of the Restoration explained the origin of that civil condition, those property relations, the close study of which alone could, in their opinion, provide the key to the understanding of historical events.

The property relations of men belong to the sphere of their *legal* relations; property is first of all a legal institution. To say that the key to understanding historical phenomena must be sought in the property relations of men means saying that this key lies in institutions of law. But whence do these institutions come? Guizot says quite rightly that political constitutions were a *consequence* before they became a cause; that society first created them and then began to change under their influence. But cannot the same be said of property relations? Were not they in their turn a consequence before they became a cause? Did not society have first to create them before it could experience their decisive influence on itself?

To these quite reasonable questions Guizot gives highly unsatisfactory replies.

The civil condition of the peoples who appeared on the historical arena after the fall of the Western Roman Empire was in the closest causal connection with landownership:* the relation of man to the land determined his

---

* Consequently, of modern peoples *alone*? This restriction is all the more strange that already Greek and Roman writers had seen the close connection between the civil and political life of their countries, and agrarian relations. However, this strange limitation did not prevent Guizot making the fall of the Roman Empire depend upon its state economy. See his first "Essay": *Du régime municipal dans l'empire romain au V-me siècle de l'ère chrétienne.*

social position. Throughout the epoch of feudalism, all institutions of society were determined in the last analysis by agrarian relations. As for those relations they, in the words of the same Guizot, "at first, during the first period after the invasion of the barbarians," were determined by the social position of the landowner: "the land he occupied acquired this or that character, according to the degree of strength of the landowner."* But what then determined the social position of the landowner? What determined "at first, during the first period after the invasion of the barbarians" the greater or lesser degree of liberty, the greater or lesser degree of power of the landowner? Was it previous political relations among the barbarian conquerors? But Guizot has already told us that political relations are a consequence and not a cause. In order to understand the political life of the barbarians in the epoch preceding the fall of the Roman Empire we should have, according to the advice of our author, to study their civil condition, their social order, the relations of various classes in their midst, and so forth; and such a study would once again bring us to the question of what determines the property relations of men, what creates the forms of property existing in a given society. And it is obvious that we should gain nothing if, in order to explain the position of various classes in society, we began referring to the relative degrees of their freedom and power. This would be, not a reply, but a repetition of the question in a new form, with some details.

The question of the origin of property relations is hardly likely even to have arisen in Guizot's mind in

---

* That is, landownership bore this or that *legal* character, or in other words its possession involved a greater or lesser degree of dependence, according to the strength and liberty of the landowner (*loc. cit.*, p. 75).

the shape of a scientific problem, strictly and accurately formulated. We have seen that it was quite impossible for him not to have taken account of the question, but the very confusion of the replies which he gave to it bears witness to the unclarity with which he conceived it. In the last analysis the development of forms of property was explained by Guizot by exceptionally vague references to *human nature*. It is not surprising that this historian, whom the eclectics accused of excessively systematic views, himself turned out to be no mean eclectic, for example in his works on the history of civilization.

Augustin Thierry, who examined the struggle of religious sects and political parties from the view-point of the *"positive interests"* of various social classes and passionately sympathized with the struggle of the third estate against the aristocracy, explained the origin of these classes and ranks in *conquest*. "Tout cela date d'une conquête; il y a une conquête là-dessous" (all this dates from a conquest; there's a conquest at the bottom of it), he says of class and rank relations among the modern peoples, which are exclusively the subject of his writing. He incessantly developed this idea in various ways, both in his articles and in his later learned works. But apart from the fact that "conquest"—an international political act—returned Thierry to the point of view of the eighteenth century, which explained all social life by the activity of the legislator, i.e., of political authority, every fact of conquest inevitably arouses the question: why were its social consequences these, and not those? Before the invasion of the German barbarians Gaul had already lived through a Roman conquest. The social consequences of *that* conquest were very different from those which were produced by the *German* conquest. The social consequences of the conquest of China by the Mongols very little resembled those of the conquest of England by the Normans. Whence do such differences come? To say that they are determined by differences in the social structure of the various peoples which come into conflict at different times means to say nothing, because what determines that social structure remains unknown. To refer in this question to some previous conquests means moving in a vicious circle. However many the conquests you enumerate, you will nevertheless arrive in the long run at the inevitable conclusion that in the social life of peoples, there is some X, some unknown factor, which is not only not determined by conquests, but which on the contrary *itself conditions the consequences* of conquests and even frequently, perhaps always, *the conquests themselves*: and is the fundamental reason for international conflicts. Thierry in his *History of the Conquest of England by the Normans* himself points out, on the basis of old monuments, the motives which guided the Anglo-Saxons in their desperate struggle for their independence. "We must fight," said one of the earls, "whatever may be the danger to us; for what we have to consider is not whether we shall accept and receive a new lord.... The case is quite otherwise. The Duke of Normandy has given our lands to his barons, to his knights and to all his men, the greater part of whom have already done homage to him for them: they will all look for their gift, if their duke become our king; and he himself will be bound to deliver up to them our lands, our wives and our daughters: all this is promised to them beforehand. They come, not only to ruin us, but to ruin our descendants also, and to take from us the country of our ancestors," etc. On his part, William the Conqueror said to his companions: "Fight well and put all to death; for if we conquer we shall all be rich. What I gain, you will gain; if

I conquer, you will conquer; if I take this land, you shall have it."* Here it is abundantly clear that the conquest was not an end in itself, and that "beneath it" lay certain "positive," i.e., *economic interests*. The question is, what gave those interests the form which they then had? Why was it that both natives and conquerors were inclined precisely to the feudal system of landownership, and not to any other? "Conquest" explains nothing in this case.

In Thierry's *Histoire du tiers état*, and in all his sketches of the internal history of France and England, we have already a fairly full picture of the historical advance of the bourgeoisie. It is sufficient to study even this picture to see how unsatisfactory is the view which makes dependent on conquest the origin and development of a given social system: that development progressed quite at variance with the interests and wishes of the feudal aristocracy, i.e., the conquerors and their descendants.

It can be said without any exaggeration that in his historical researches Thierry himself did much to refute his own views on the historical role of conquests.**

---

* *History of the Conquest of England by the Normans* (Eng. ed.), London, 1841, pp. 67, 68.—*Tr.*

** It is interesting that the Saint-Simonists already saw *this* weak side of the historical views of Thierry. Thus, Bazard, in the article quoted earlier, remarks that conquest in reality exercised much less influence on the development of European society than Thierry thought. "Everyone understanding the laws of development of humanity sees that the role of conquest is quite subordinate." But in this case Thierry is closer to the views of his former teacher Saint-Simon than is Bazard: Saint-Simon examines the history of Western Europe from the fifteenth century from the view-point of the development of economic relations, but explains the social order of the Middle Ages merely as the product of conquest.

In Mignet we find the same confusion. He speaks of the influence of landownership on political forms. But what the forms of landownership depend on, why they develop in this or that direction, this Mignet does not know. In the last analysis he, too, makes forms of landownership depend on *conquest*.*

He senses that it is not abstract conceptions such as "conquerors" and "conquered," but people possessing living flesh, having definite rights and social relations that we are dealing with in the history of international conflicts; but here, too, his analysis does not go very far. "When two peoples living on the same soil mingle," he says, "they lose their weak sides and communicate their strong sides to each other."**

This is not profound, nor is it quite clear.

Faced with the question of the origin of property relations, each of the French historians of the time of the Restoration whom we have mentioned would probably have attempted, like Guizot, to escape from the difficulty with the help of more or less ingenious references to "*human nature.*"

The view of "human nature" as the highest authority which decides all "knotty cases" in the sphere of law, morality, politics and economics, was inherited in its entirety by the writers of the nineteenth century from the writers of the Enlightenment of the previous century.

If man, when he appears in the world, does not bring with him a prepared store of innate "practical ideas"; if virtue is respected, not because it is innate in people, but because it is useful, as Locke asserted; if the principle of social utility is the highest law, as Helvetius said; if man is the measure of things wherever there is

---

* *De la féodalité*, p. 50.
** *Ibid.*, p. 212.

a question of mutual human relations—then it is quite natural to draw the conclusion that the nature of man is the view-point from which we should assess given relations as being useful or harmful, rational or irrational. It was from this standpoint that the writers of the Enlightenment of the eighteenth century discussed both the social order then existing and the reforms which they thought desirable. Human nature was for them the most important argument in their discussions with their opponents. How great in their eyes was the importance of this argument is shown excellently, for example, by the following observation of Condorcet: "The ideas of justice and law take shape invariably in an identical form among all beings gifted with the capacity of sensation and of acquiring ideas. Therefore they will be identical." True, it happens that people distort them (les altèrent). "But every man who thinks correctly will just as inevitably arrive at certain ideas in morality as in mathematics. These ideas are the necessary outcome of the irrefutable truth that men are perceptive and rational beings." In reality the views on society of the French writers of the Enlightenment were not deduced, of course, from this more than meagre truth, but were suggested to them by their environment. The "man" whom they had in view was distinguished not only by his capacity to perceive and think: his "nature" demanded a definite bourgeois system of society (the works of Holbach included just those demands which later were put into effect by the Constituent Assembly). His "nature" prescribed free trade, non-interference of the state in the property relations of citizens (laissez faire, laissez passer!),* etc.,

---

* True, not always. Sometimes, in the name of the same nature, the philosophers advised the legislator "to smooth out the inequalities of property." This was one of the numerous contradictions of

etc. The writers of the Enlightenment looked on human nature through the prism of particular social needs and relations. But they did not suspect that history had put some prism before their eyes. They imagined that through their lips "human nature" itself was speaking, understood and assessed at its true value at last, by the enlightened representatives of humanity.

Not all the writers of the eighteenth century had an identical conception of human nature. Sometimes they differed very strongly among themselves on this subject. But all of them were equally convinced that a correct view of that nature alone could provide the key to the explanation of social phenomena.

We said earlier that many French writers of the Enlightenment had already noticed a certain conformity to law in the development of human reason. They were led to the idea of this conformity to law first and foremost by *the history of literature*: "what people," they ask, "was not first a poet and only then a thinker?"* But how is such succession to be explained? By the needs of society, which determine the development of language itself, replied the philosophers. "The art of speech, like all other arts, is the fruit of social needs and interests," asserted the Abbé Arnaud, in the address just mentioned in a footnote. Social needs change, and therefore there changes also the course of development of the "arts."

---

the French writers of the Enlightenment. But we are not concerned with this here. What is important for us is the fact that the abstract *"nature of man"* was in every given case an argument in favour of the quite concrete aspirations of a definite stratum of society, and moreover, of *bourgeois* society.

* Grimm, *Correspondance Littéraire* for August, 1774. In putting this question, Grimm only repeats the idea of the Abbé Arnaud, which the latter developed in a discourse pronounced by him at the French Academy.

But what determines social needs? Social needs, the needs of men who compose society, are determined by the nature of man. Consequently it is in that nature that we must seek the explanation of this, and not that, course of intellectual development.

In order to play the part of the highest criterion, human nature obviously had to be considered as fixed once for all, as *invariable*. The writers of the Enlightenment did in fact regard it as such, as the reader could see from the words of Condorcet quoted above. But if human nature is invariable, how then can it serve to explain the course of the intellectual or social development of mankind? What is the process of any development? A series of changes. Can those changes be explained with the help of something that is invariable, that is fixed once for all? Is this the reason why a variable magnitude changes, that a constant magnitude remains unchanged? The writers of the Enlightenment realized that this could *not* be so, and in order to get out of their difficulty they pointed out that the *constant* magnitude itself proves to be variable, within certain limits. Man goes through different ages: childhood, youth, maturity and so forth. At these various ages his needs are not identical: "In his childhood man has only his feelings, his imagination and memory: he seeks only to be amused and requires only songs and stories. The age of passions succeeds: the soul requires to be moved and agitated. Then the intelligence extends and reason grows stronger: both these faculties in their turn require exercise, and their activity extends to everything that is capable of arousing curiosity."

Thus develops the individual man: these changes are conditioned by his nature; and just because they are in his nature, they are to be noticed in the spiritual development of *all mankind*. It is by these changes that is to be explained the circumstance that peoples begin with epics and end with philosophy.*

It is easy to see that "explanations" of this kind, which did not explain anything at all, only imbued the description of the course of intellectual development of man with a certain picturesqueness (simile always sets off more vividly the quality of the object being described). It is easy to see likewise that, in giving explanations of this kind, the thinkers of the eighteenth century were moving round the above-mentioned vicious circle: environment creates man, man creates environment. For in effect, on the one hand it appeared that the intellectual development of mankind, i.e., in other words the development of human nature, was due to social needs, and on the other it turned out that the development of social needs is to be explained by the development of human nature.

Thus we see that the French historians of the Restoration also failed to eliminate this contradiction: it only took a new form with them.

---

* Suard, *loc. cit.*, p. 383.

Chapter III

THE UTOPIAN SOCIALISTS

If human nature is invariable, and if, knowing its main qualities, we can deduce from them mathematically accurate principles in the sphere of morality and social science, it will not be difficult to invent a social order which would fully correspond to the requirements of human nature, and just for that very reason, would be an *ideal social order*. The materialists of the eighteenth century were already very willing to engage in research on the subject of a *perfect system of laws (législation parfaite)*. These researches represent the *utopian element* in the literature of the Enlightenment.*

The Utopian Socialists of the first half of the nineteenth century devoted themselves to such researches with all their heart.

---

* Helvetius, in his book, *De l'Homme*, has a detailed scheme of such "perfect system of laws." It would be in the highest degree interesting and instructive to compare this utopia with the utopias of the first half of the nineteenth century. But unfortunately both the historians of socialism and the historians of philosophy have not up to now had the slightest idea of any such comparison. As for the historians of philosophy in particular, they, it must be said in passing, treat Helvetius in the most impermissible way. Even the calm and moderate Lange finds no other description for him than "the superficial Helvetius." The absolute idealist Hegel was most just of all in his attitude to the absolute materialist Helvetius.

The Utopian Socialists of this age fully shared the anthropological views of the French materialists. Just like the materialists, they considered man to be the product of the social environment around him,* and just like the materialists they fell into a vicious circle, explaining the variable qualities of the environment of man by the unchanging qualities of *human nature*.

All the numerous utopias of the first half of the present century represent nothing else than attempts to invent a perfect legislation, taking *human nature* as the supreme criterion. Thus, Fourier takes as his point of departure the analysis of human *passions*; thus, Robert Owen in his *Outline of the Rational System of Society* starts from the "*first principles of human nature*," and asserts that "rational government" must first of all "ascertain what human nature is"; thus, the Saint-Simonists declare that their philosophy is founded on a new conception of human nature (sur une nouvelle conception de la nature humaine);** thus, the Fourierists say that the social organization invented by their teacher represents a number of irrefutable deductions from the immutable laws of human nature.***

---

* "Yes, man is only what omnipotent society or omnipotent education make of him, taking this word in its widest sense, i.e., as meaning not only school training or book education, but the education given us by men and things, events and circumstances, the education which begins to influence us from the cradle and does not leave us again for a moment." Cabet, *Voyage en Icarie*, 1848 ed., p. 402.

** See *Le Producteur*, Vol. I, Paris, 1825, Introduction.

*** "Mon but est de donner une *Exposition Elémentaire*, claire et facilement intelligible, de l'organisation sociale, déduite par Fourier des lois de la nature humaine." (V. Considérant, *Destinée Sociale*, t. I, 3e édition, Déclaration.) "Il serait temps enfin de s'accorder sur ce point: est-il à propos, avant de faire des lois, de s'enquérir de la véritable nature de l'homme, afin d'harmoniser la loi, qui est par elle-même modifiable, avec la nature, qui est immuable

Naturally, the view of human nature as the supreme criterion did not prevent the various socialist schools from differing very considerably in defining the qualities of that nature. Thus, in the opinion of the Saint-Simonists, "the plans of Owen contradict to such an extent the inclinations of human nature that the sort of popularity which they, apparently, enjoy at the present time" (this was written in 1825) "seems at first glance to be inexplicable.* In Fourier's polemical pamphlet, *Pièges et charlatanisme des deux sectes Saint-Simon et Owen qui promettent l'association et le progrès*, we can find a number of harsh statements that the Saint-Simonists' teaching also contradicts all the inclinations of human nature. Now, as at the time of Condorcet, it appeared that to agree in the definition of human nature was much more difficult than to define a geometrical figure.

To the extent that the Utopian Socialists of the nineteenth century adhered to the view-point of *human nature*, to that extent they only repeated the mistakes of the thinkers of the eighteenth century—an error which was common, however, to all social science contemporary with them.** But we can see in them an energetic effort

---

et souveraine?" *Notions élémentaires de la science sociale de Fourier, par l'auteur de la Défense du Fouriérisme* (Henri Gorsse, Paris, 1844, p. 35). "My aim is to give an *Elementary Exposition*, clear and easy to understand, of the social organization deduced by Fourier from the laws of human nature (V. Considerant, *Social Destiny*, Vol. I, 3rd ed., Declaration). It is high time we reached agreement on the following point: would not it be better, before making laws, to inquire into the real nature of man in order to bring the law, which is in itself modifiable, into harmony with Nature, which is immutable and supreme?"

* *Le Producteur*, Vol. I, p. 139.

** We have already demonstrated this in relation to the historians of the Restoration. It would be very easy to demonstrate it also in relation to the economists. In defending the bourgeois so-to break out of the narrow confines of an abstract conception, and to take their stand upon solid ground. Saint-Simon's works are especially distinguished for this.

While the writers of the French Enlightenment very frequently regarded the history of humanity as a series of more or less happy, but chance occurrences,* Saint-Simon seeks in history primarily *conformity to law*. The science of human society can and must become just as exact as natural science. We must study the facts of the past life of mankind in order to discover in them the laws of its *progress*. Only he is capable of foreseeing

---

cial order against the reactionaries and the Socialists, the economists defended it precisely as the order most appropriate to human nature. The efforts to discover an abstract "law of population"—whether they came from the Socialists or the bourgeois camp—were closely bound up with the view of "human nature" as the basic conception of social science. In order to be convinced of this, it is sufficient to compare the relevant teaching of Malthus, on the one hand, and the teaching of Godwin or of the author of the *Comments on Mill*,[5] on the other. Both Malthus and his opponents equally seek a single, so to speak absolute, law of population. Our contemporary political economy sees it otherwise: it knows that each phase of social development has *its own, particular*, law of population. But of this later.

* In this respect the reproach addressed by Helvetius to Montesquieu is extremely characteristic: "In his book on the reasons for the grandeur and decadence of Rome, Montesquieu has given insufficient attention to the importance of happy accidents in the history of that state. He has fallen into the mistake too characteristic of thinkers who wish to explain everything, and into the mistake of secluded scholars who, forgetting the nature of men, attribute to the people's representatives invariable political views and uniform principles. Yet often one man directs at his discretion those important assemblies which are called *senates*." *Pensées et Réflexions,* CXL, in the third volume of his *Complete Works*, Paris, MDCCCXVIII. Does not this remind you, reader, of the theory of "heroes and crowd" now fashionable in Russia? Wait a bit: what is set forth further will show more than once how little there is of originality in Russian "sociology."

THE UTOPIAN SOCIALISTS 49

the *future* who has understood the *past*. Expressing the task of social science in this way, Saint-Simon in particular turned to the study of the history of Western Europe since the fall of the Roman Empire. The novelty and scope of his views can be seen from the fact that his pupil Thierry could practically effect a revolution in the study of French history. Saint-Simon was of the opinion that Guizot also borrowed his views from himself. Leaving this question of theoretical property undecided, we shall note that Saint-Simon was able to trace the mainsprings of the internal development of European societies further than his contemporary *specialist historians*. Thus, if both Thierry and Mignet, and likewise Guizot, pointed to property relations as the foundation of any social order, Saint-Simon, who most vividly and for the first time threw light on the history of these relations in modern Europe, went further and asked himself: why is it that precisely these, and no other relations, play such an important part? The answer is to be sought, in his opinion, in the *requirements of industrial development*. "Up to the fifteenth century lay authority was in the hands of the nobility, and this was useful because the nobles were then the most capable industrialists. They directed agricultural works, and agricultural works were then the only kind of important industrial occupation."* To the question of why the needs of industry have such a decisive importance in the history of mankind, Saint-Simon replied that it was because the object of social organization is production (le but de l'organisation sociale c'est la production). He attributed great significance to production identifying the useful with the productive (l'utile c'est la production). He

---

* *Opinions littéraires, philosophiques et industrielles*, Paris 1825, pp. 144-45. Compare also *Catéchisme politique des industriels*.

4—615

categorically declared that "la politique... c'est la science de la production."

It would seem that the logical development of these views should have brought Saint-Simon to the conclusion that the laws of production are those very laws by which in the last analysis social development is determined, and the study of which must be the task of the thinker striving to foresee the future. At times he, as it were, approaches this idea, but that only at times.

For production the implements of labour are necessary. These implements are not provided by nature ready-made, they are invented by man. The invention or even the simple use of a particular implement presupposes in the producer a certain degree of intellectual development. The development of "industry" is, therefore, the unquestionable result of the intellectual development of mankind. It seems as though opinion, "enlightenment" (lumières) here also reign unchallenged over the world. And the more apparent the important role of industry becomes, the more is confirmed, seemingly, this view of the philosophers of the eighteenth century. Saint-Simon holds it even more consistently than the French writers of the Enlightenment, as he considers the question of the origin of ideas in sensations to be settled, and has less grounds for meditation on the influence of environment on man. The development of knowledge is for him the fundamental factor of historical advance.* He tries to

---

* Saint-Simon brings the idealistic view of history to its last and extreme conclusion. For him not only are *ideas* ("principles") the ultimate foundation of *social relations*, but among them "scientific ideas"—the "scientific system of the world"—play the principal part: from these follow religious ideas which, in their turn, condition the *moral conceptions of man*. This is *intellectualism*, which prevailed at the same time also among the German philosophers, but with them took quite a different form.

discover the laws of that development; thus he establishes the law of three stages—*theological, metaphysical and positive*—which later on Auguste Comte very successfully gave out to be his own "discovery."* But these laws, too, Saint-Simon explains in the long run by *the qualities of human nature*. "*Society consists of individuals*," he says. "*Therefore the development of social reason can be only the reproduction of the development of the individual reason on a larger scale.*" Starting from this fundamental principle, he considers his "laws" of social development finally ascertained and proved whenever he succeeds in discovering a successful analogy in the development of the individual confirming them. He holds, for example, that the role of *authority* in so-

---

* Littré strongly contested the statement of Hubbard when the latter pointed out this... borrowing. He attributed to Saint-Simon only "the law of two stages": theological and scientific. Flint, in quoting this opinion of Littré, remarks: "He is correct when he says that the law of three stages is not enunciated in any of Saint-Simon's writings" (*The Philosophy of History in Europe*, Edinburgh and London, MDCCCLXXIV, p. 158). We shall contrast to this observation the following extract from Saint-Simon: "What astronomer, physicist, chemist and physiologist does not know that in every branch of knowledge the human reason, before proceeding from purely theological to positive ideas, for a long time has used metaphysics? Does there not arise in every one who has studied the history of sciences the conviction that this intermediate stage has been useful, and even absolutely indispensable to carry out the transition?" (*Du système industriel*, Paris, MDCCCXXI, Preface, pp. vi-vii). The law of three stages was of such importance in Saint-Simon's eyes that he was ready to explain by this means purely political events, such as the predominance of the "legists and metaphysicians" during the French Revolution. It would have been easy for Flint to "discover" this by carefully reading the works of Saint-Simon. But unfortunately it is *much easier to write a learned history of human thought than to study the actual course of its development*.

cial life will in time be reduced to *zero*.* The gradual but incessant diminution of this role is one of the laws of development of humanity. How then does he prove this law? The main argument in its favour is reference to the individual development of man. In the elementary school the child is obliged unconditionally to obey his elders; in the secondary and higher school, the element of *obedience* gradually falls into the background, in order finally to yield its place to *independent* action in maturity. No matter how anyone may regard the history of "authority," everyone will nowadays agree that here, as everywhere, comparison is not proof. The embryological development of any particular *individual* (*ontogenesis*) presents many analogies with the history of the *species* to which this individual belongs: *ontogenesis* supplies many important indications about *phylogenesis*. But what should we now say of a biologist who would attempt to assert that the ultimate explanation of phylogenesis must be sought in ontogenesis? Modern biology acts in the exactly opposite way: it explains the embryological history of the *individual* by the history of the *species*.

The appeal to human nature gave a very peculiar appearance to all the "laws" of social development formulated both by Saint-Simon himself and by his followers.

It led them into the vicious circle. *The history of mankind is explained by its nature.* But what is the key to the understanding of the nature of man? *History.* Obviously, if we move in this circle, we cannot understand either the nature of man or his history. We can make only some individual, more or less profound, observations concerning this or that sphere of social phe-

---

* This idea was later borrowed from him and distorted by Proudhon, who built on it his theory of *anarchy*.

nomena. Saint-Simon made some very subtle observations, sometimes truly instinct with genius: but his main object—that of discovering a firm scientific foundation for "politics"—remained unattained.

"The supreme law of progress of human reason," says Saint-Simon, "subordinates all to itself, rules over everything: men for it are only tools. And although this force [i.e., this law] arises from ourselves (dérive de nous), we can just as little set ourselves free from its influence or subordinate it to ourselves as we could at our whim change the working of the force which obliges the earth to revolve around the sun.... All we can do is consciously to submit to this law (our true Providence) realizing the direction which it prescribes for us, instead of obeying it blindly. Let us remark in passing that it is just in this that will consist the grand step forward which the philosophical intelligence of our age is destined to accomplish."*

And so humanity is absolutely subordinated to the law of its own intellectual development; it could not escape the influence of that law, should it even desire to do so. Let us examine this statement more closely, and take as an example the law of the three stages. Mankind moved from theological thought to metaphysical, from metaphysical to positive. This law acted with the force of the laws of mechanics.

This may very well be so, but the question arises, how are we to understand the idea that mankind could not alter the workings of this law *should it even desire to do so*? Does this mean that it could not have avoided metaphysics if it had even realized the advantages of positive thinking while still at the end of the theological

---

* *L'Organisateur*, p. 119 (Vol. IV of the *Works* of Saint-Simon, or Vol. XX of the *Complete Works* of Saint-Simon and Enfantin).

period? Evidently no; and if the answer is no, then it is no less evident that there is some lack of clarity in Saint-Simon's view of the conformity of intellectual development to law. Wherein lies this unclarity and how does it come about?

It lies in the *very contrasting of the law with the desire to alter its action*. Once such a desire has made its appearance among mankind, it becomes itself a fact in the history of mankind's intellectual development, and the law must embrace this fact, not come into conflict with it. So long as we admit the possibility of such a conflict, we have not yet made clear to ourselves the conception of law itself, and we shall inevitably fall into one of two extremes: either we shall abandon the standpoint of conformity to law and will be taking up the viewpoint of what is *desirable*, or we shall completely let the desirable—or more truly what was *desired* by the people of the given epoch—fall out of our field of vision, and thereby shall be attributing to *law* some mystical shade of significance, transforming it into a kind of Fate. "Law" in the writings of Saint-Simon and of the Utopians generally, to the extent that they speak of conformity to law, is just such a Fate. We may remark in passing that when the Russian "subjective sociologists" rise up in defence of "personality," "ideals" and other excellent things, they are warring precisely with the *utopian*, unclear, incomplete and therefore worthless doctrine of the "natural course of things." Our sociologists appear never even to have heard what constitutes *the modern scientific conception of the laws underlying the historical development of society*.

Whence arose the utopian lack of clarity in the conception of conformity to law? It arose from the radical defect, which we have already pointed out, in the view of the development of humanity which the Utopians held

—and, as we know already, not they alone. The history of humanity was explained by the nature of man. Once that nature was fixed, there were also fixed the laws of historical development, all history was given *an sich*, as Hegel would have said. Man can just as little interfere in the course of his development as he can cease being man. The *law* of development makes its appearance in the form of Providence.

This is historical fatalism resulting from a doctrine which considers the successes of knowledge—and consequently the conscious activity of man—to be the mainspring of historical progress.

But let us go further.

If the key to the understanding of history is provided by the study of the nature of man, what is important to me is not so much the study of the facts of history as the correct understanding of human nature. Once I have acquired the right view of the latter, I lose almost all interest in social life *as it is*, and concentrate all my attention on social life *as it ought to be in keeping with the nature of man*. Fatalism in history does not in the least interfere with a utopian attitude to reality in practice. On the contrary, it promotes such an attitude, by breaking off the thread of scientific investigation. *Fatalism in general marches frequently hand in hand with the most extreme subjectivism.* Fatalism very commonly proclaims its own state of mind to be an inevitable law of history. It is just of the fatalists that one can say, in the words of the poet:

Was sie den Geist der Geschichte nennen,
Ist nur der Herren eigner Geist.*

---

* "What they call the Spirit of History is only the spirit of these gentlemen themselves." Goethe, *Faust*, Part I.—*Ed.*

The Saint-Simonists asserted that the share of the social product which falls to the exploiters of another's labour, gradually diminishes. Such a diminution was in their eyes the most important law governing the economic development of humanity. As a proof they referred to the gradual decline in the level of *interest and land rent.* If in this case they had kept to the methods of strict scientific investigation, they would have discovered the economic causes of the phenomenon to which they pointed, and for this they would have had attentively to study production, reproduction and distribution of products. Had they done this they would have seen, perhaps, that the decline in the level of interest or even of land rent, if it really takes place, does not by any means prove of itself that there is a decline in the share of the property owners. Then their economic "law" would, of course, have found quite a different formulation. But they were not interested in this. Confidence in the omnipotence of the mysterious laws arising out of the nature of man directed their intellectual activity into quite a different sphere. A tendency which has predominated in history up to now can only grow stronger in the future, said they: the constant diminution in the share of the exploiters will necessarily end in its complete disappearance, i.e., in the disappearance of the class of exploiters itself. Foreseeing this, we must already today invent new forms of social organization in which there will no longer be any place for exploiters. It is evident from other qualities of human nature that these forms must be such and such.... The plan of social reorganization was prepared very rapidly: the extremely important scientific conception of the conformity of social phenomena to law gave birth to a couple of utopian recipes....

Such recipes were considered by the Utopians of that day to be the most important problem with which a thinker was faced. This or that principle of political economy was not important in itself. It acquired importance in view of the practical conclusions which followed from it. J. B. Say argued with Ricardo about what determined the *exchange value* of commodities. Very possibly this is an important question from the point of view of specialists. But even more important is it to know what *ought* to determine value, and the specialists, unfortunately, do not attempt to think about this. Let us think for the specialists. Human nature very clearly tells us so and so. Once we begin to listen to its voice, we see with astonishment that the argument so important in the eyes of the specialists is, in reality, not very important. We can agree with Say, because from his theses there follow conclusions fully in harmony with the requirements of human nature. We can agree with Ricardo too, because his views likewise, being correctly interpreted and supplemented, can only reinforce those requirements. It was in this way that utopian thought unceremoniously interfered in those scientific discussions the meaning of which remained obscure for it. It was in this way that cultivated men, richly gifted by nature, as for example Enfantin, resolved the controversial questions of the political economy of their day.

Enfantin wrote a number of studies in political economy which cannot be considered a serious contribution to science, but which nevertheless cannot be ignored, as is done up to the present day by the historians of political economy and socialism. The economic works of Enfantin have their significance as an interesting phase in the history of the development of socialist thought. But his attitude to the arguments of the economists may be well illustrated by the following example.

It is known that Malthus stubbornly and, by the way, very unsuccessfully contested Ricardo's theory of rent.

Enfantin believed that truth was, in fact, on the side of the first, and not of the second. But he did not even contest Ricardo's theory: he did not consider this necessary. In his opinion all "discussions on the nature of rent and as to the actual relative rise or fall of the part taken by the property-owners from the labourer ought to be reduced to one question: what is the nature of those relations which ought in the interests of society to exist between the producer who has withdrawn from affairs" (that was the name given by Enfantin to the landowners) "and the active producer" (i.e., the farmer)? "When these relations become known, it will be sufficient to ascertain the means which will lead to the establishment of such relations; in doing so it will be necessary to take into account also the present condition of society, but nevertheless any other question" (apart from that set forth above) "would be secondary, and would only impede those combinations which must promote the use of the above-mentioned means."*

The principal task of political economy, which Enfantin would prefer to call *"the philosophical history of industry,"* consists in pointing out both the mutual relations of various strata of producers and the relationships of the whole class of producers with the other classes of society. These indications must be founded on the study of the historical development of the industrial class, and such a study must be founded on "the new conception of the human race," i.e., in other words, of human nature.**

Malthus's challenge to Ricardo's theory of rent was closely bound up with his challenge to the very well-

---

* In his article, "Considérations sur la baisse progressive du loyer des objets mobiliers et immobiliers," *Le Producteur*, Vol. I, p. 564.
** See in particular the article in *Le Producteur*, Vol. IV, "Considérations sur les progrès de l'économie politique."

known—as people now say—labour theory of value. Paying little attention to the substance of the controversy, Enfantin hastened to resolve it by a utopian addition (or, as people in Russia say nowadays, *amendment*) to Ricardo's theory of rent: "If we understand this theory aright," he says, "we ought, it seems to me, to add to it that ... the labourers pay (i.e., pay in the form of rent) some people for the leisure which those enjoy, and for the right to make use of the means of production."

By labourers Enfantin meant here also, and even principally, the capitalist farmers. What he said of their relations with the landowners is quite true. But his "amendment" is nothing more than a sharper expression of a phenomenon with which Ricardo himself was well acquainted. Moreover, this sharp expression (Adam Smith sometimes speaks even more sharply) not only did not solve the question either of value or of rent, but completely removed it from Enfantin's field of view. But for him these questions did not in fact exist. He was interested solely in the future organization of society. It was important for him to convince the reader that private property in the means of production *ought not* to exist. Enfantin says plainly that, but for practical questions of this kind, all the learned disputes concerning value would be simply disputes about words. This, so to speak, is the *subjective method* in political economy.

The Utopians never directly recommended this "method." But that they were very partial to it is shown, among other ways, by the fact that Enfantin reproached Malthus (!) with excessive *objectivity*. Objectivity was, in his opinion, the principal fault of that writer. Whoever knows the works of Malthus is aware that it is precisely objectivity (so characteristic, for example, of Ricardo) that was always foreign to the author of the

Essay on the Principle of Population. We do not know whether Enfantin read Malthus himself (everything obliges us to think that, for example, the views of Ricardo were known to him only from the extracts which the French economists made from his writings); but even if he did read them, he could hardly have assessed them at their true value, he would hardly have been able to show that real life was in contradiction to Malthus. Preoccupied with considerations about what ought to be, Enfantin had neither the time nor the desire attentively to study what really existed. "You are right," he was ready to say to the first sycophant he met. "In present-day social life matters proceed just as you describe them, but you are excessively *objective*; glance at the question from the humane point of view, and you will see that our social life must be rebuilt on new foundations."

Utopian dilettantism was forced to make theoretical concessions to any more or less learned defender of the bourgeois order. In order to allay the consciousness rising within him of his own impotence, the Utopian consoled himself by reproaching his opponents with objectivity: let us admit you are more learned than I, but in return I am kinder. The Utopian did not refute the learned defenders of the bourgeoisie; he only made "footnotes" and "corrections" to their theories. A similar, quite utopian attitude to social science meets the eye of the attentive reader on every page of the works of our "subjective" sociologists. We shall have occasion yet to speak a good deal of such an attitude. Let us meanwhile quote two vivid examples.

In 1871 there appeared the dissertation by the late N. Sieber:[6] "Ricardo's theory of value and capital, in the light of later elucidations." In his foreword the author benevolently, but only in passing, referred to the article of Mr. Y. Zhukovsky:[7] "The school of Adam Smith and positivism in economic science" (this article appeared in the *Sovremennik*[8] of 1864). On the subject of this passing reference, Mr. Mikhailovsky remarks: "It is pleasant for me to recall that in my article 'On the Literary Activity of Y. G. Zhukovsky' I paid a great and just tribute to the services rendered by our economist. I pointed out that Mr. Zhukovsky had long ago expressed the thought that it was necessary to return to the sources of political economy, which provide all the data for a correct solution of the main problems of science, data which have been quite distorted by the modern text-book political economy. But I then indicated also that the honour of priority in this idea, which later on proved so fruitful in the powerful hands of Karl Marx, belonged in Russian literature not to Mr. Zhukovsky, but to another writer, the author of the articles 'Economic Activity and Legislation' (*Sovremennik*, 1859), 'Capital and Labour' (1860), the *Comments on Mill*, etc. In addition to seniority in time, the difference between this writer* and Mr. Zhukovsky can be expressed most vividly in the following way. If, for example, Mr. Zhukovsky circumstantially and in a strictly scientific fashion, even somewhat pedantically, proves that labour is the measure of value and that every value is produced by labour, the author of the above-mentioned articles, without losing sight of the theoretical aspect of the question, lays principal stress on the logical and practical conclusion from it: being produced and measured by labour, every value must belong to labour."** One does not have to be greatly versed in political economy to know that the "author of

---

* The reference is to Nikolai Gavrilovich Chernyshevsky.—*Ed.*
** N. K. Mikhailovsky, *Works*, Vol. II, Second ed., St. Petersburg, 1888, pp. 239-40

the *Comments on Mill*" entirely failed to understand the theory of value which later received such brilliant development "in the powerful hands of Marx." And every person who knows the history of socialism understands *why* that author, in spite of Mr. Mikhailovsky's assurances, did in fact "lose sight of the theoretical aspect of the question" and wandered off into meditations about the basis on which products *ought* to be exchanged in a well-regulated society. The author of the *Comments on Mill* regarded economic questions from the standpoint of a *Utopian*. This was quite natural at the time. But it is very strange that Mr. Mikhailovsky was unable to divest himself of this point of view in the 70s (and did not do so even later, otherwise he would have corrected his mistake in the latest edition of his works) when it was easy to acquire a more correct view of things, even from popular works. Mr. Mikhailovsky did not understand what "the author of the *Comments on Mill*" wrote about value. This took place because he, too, "*lost sight of the theoretical aspect of the question*" *and wandered off into the* "*logical practical conclusion from it,*" i.e., the consideration that "every value ought to belong to labour." We know already that their passion for practical conclusions always had a harmful effect on the theoretical reasoning of the Utopians. And how old is the "conclusion" which turned Mr. Mikhailovsky from the true path is shown by the circumstance that it was being drawn from Ricardo's theory of value by the *English Utopians even of the 1820's*. But, as a Utopian, Mr. Mikhailovsky is not interested even in the history of utopias.

Another example. Mr. V. V., in 1882, explained in the following way the appearance of his book, *The Destinies of Capitalism in Russia*:

"The collection now offered to the reader consists of articles printed earlier in various journals. In publishing them as a separate book, we have brought them only into external unity, disposed the material in a somewhat different fashion and eliminated repetitions" (far from all: very many of them remained in Mr. V. V.'s book—*G.P.*). "Their content has remained the same; few new facts and arguments have been adduced; and if nevertheless we venture for a second time to present our work to the attention of the reader, we do so with one sole aim—by attacking his world-outlook with all the weapons at our command, to force the intelligentsia to turn its attention to the question raised" (an impressive picture: "Using *all the weapons* at his command," Mr. V. V. attacks the world outlook of the reader, and the terrified intelligentsia capitulates, turns its attention, etc.—*G.P.*) "and to challenge our learned and professional publicists of capitalism and Narodism to study the law of the economic development of Russia—the foundation of all the other expressions of the life of the country. Without the knowledge of this law, systematic and successful social activity is impossible, while the conceptions of the immediate future of Russia which prevail amongst us can scarcely be called a law" (*conceptions . . . can be called law?!—G.P.*) "and are hardly capable of providing a firm foundation for a practical world outlook" (Preface, p. 1).

In 1893 the same Mr. V. V., who had by now had time to become a "professional," though, alas! still not a "learned" publicist of Narodism, turned out to be now very remote from the idea that the law of economic development constitutes "the foundation of all the other expressions of the life of the country." Now "using all the weapons" he attacks the "world outlook" of people who hold such a "view"; now he considers that in this "view, the historical process, instead of being the creation of man, is transformed into a creative force, and man into its obedient tool";* now he considers social relations to be "the creation of the spiritual world of man,"** and views with extreme suspicion the theory of the conformity to law of social phenomena, setting up against it "the scientific philosophy of history of Professor of History N. I. Kareyev[9]" (hear, O tongues, and be stilled, since the Professor himself is with us!).[10]***

What a change, with God's help! What brought it about? Why, this. In 1882 Mr. V. V. was looking for the "*law* of the economic development of Russia," imagining that that law would be only the scientific expression of his own "*ideals*." He was even convinced that he had discovered such a "law"—namely, the "law" that Russian capitalism was stillborn. But after this he did not live eleven whole years in vain. He was obliged to admit, even though not aloud, that stillborn capitalism was developing more and more. It turned out that the development of capitalism had become all but the most unquestionable "law of the economic development of Russia." And lo, Mr. V. V. hastened to turn his "philosophy of history" inside out: he who had sought for a "law" began to say that such a search is quite an idle waste of time. The Russian Utopian is not averse to relying on a "law"; but he immediately renounces it, as Peter did Jesus, if only the "law" is at variance with that "ideal" which he has to support, not only for fear, but for conscience's sake. However Mr. V. V. even now has not parted company with the "law" for ever. "The natural striving to systematize its views ought to bring the Russian intelligentsia to the elaboration of an independent scheme of evolution of economic relations, appropriate to the requirements and the conditions of development of this country; and this task

---
* *Our Trends*, St. Petersburg, 1893, p. 138.
** *Op. cit.*, pp. 9, 13, 140, and many others.
*** *Ibid.*, p. 143, *et seq.*

will be undoubtedly performed in the very near future" (*Our Trends*, p. 114). In "elaborating" its "independent scheme," the Russian intelligentsia will evidently devote itself to the same occupation as Mr. V. V. when, in his *Destinies of Capitalism*, he was looking for a "law." When the scheme is discovered—and Mr. V. V. takes his Bible oath that it will be discovered in the immediate future—our author will just as solemnly make his peace with the principle of conformity to law, as the father in the Testament made his peace with his prodigal son. Amusing people! It is obvious that, even at the time when Mr. V. V. was still looking for a "law," he did not clearly realize what meaning this word could have when applied to social phenomena. He regarded "law" as the Utopians of the 20s regarded it. Only this can explain the fact that he was hoping to discover the law of development of *one country*—Russia. But why does he attribute his modes of thought to the Russian Marxists? He is mistaken if he thinks that, in their understanding of the conformity of social phenomena to law, they have gone no further than the Utopians did. And that he does think this, is shown by all his arguments against it. And he is not alone in thinking this: the "Professor of History" Mr. Kareyev himself thinks this; and so do all the opponents of "Marxism." First of all they attribute to Marxists a utopian view of the conformity to law of social phenomena, and then strike down this view with more or less doubtful success. A real case of tilting at windmills!

By the way, about the learned "Professor of History." Here are the expressions in which he recommends the subjective view of the historical development of humanity: "If in the philosophy of history we are interested in the question of progress, this very fact dictates the selection of the essential content of knowledge, its facts and their groupings. But facts cannot be either invented or placed in invented relations" (consequently there must be nothing arbitrary either in the selection or in the grouping? Consequently the grouping must entirely correspond to objective reality? Yes! Just listen!—*G. P.*) "and the presentation of the course of history from a certain point of view will remain objective, in the sense of the truth of the presentation. Here subjectivism of another kind appears on the scene: creative synthesis may bring into existence an entire ideal world of norms, a world of what ought to be, a world of the true and just, with which actual history, i.e., the objective representation of its course, grouped in a certain way from the standpoint of essential changes in the life of humanity, will be compared. On the basis of this comparison there arises an assessment of the historical process which, however, must also not be arbitrary. It must be proved that the grouped facts, as we have them, really do have the significance which we attribute to them, having taken up a definite point of view and adopted a definite criterion for their evaluation."

Shchedrin[11] writes of a "venerable Moscow historian" who, boasting of his objectivity, used to say: "It's all the same to me whether Yaroslav beat Izyaslav or Izyaslav beat Yaroslav." Mr. Kareyev, having created for himself an "entire ideal world of norms, a world of what ought to be, a world of the true and just," has nothing to do with objectivity of that kind. He sympathizes, shall we say, with Yaroslav, and although he will not allow himself to represent his defeat as though it were his victory ("facts cannot be invented"), nevertheless he reserves the precious right of shedding a tear or two about the sad fate of Yaroslav, and cannot refrain from a curse addressed to his conqueror Izyaslav. It is difficult to raise any objection to *that* kind of "subjectivism." But in vain does Mr. Kareyev represent it in such a colourless and therefore harmless plight. To present it in this way means not to understand its true nature, and to drown it in a stream of sentimental phraseology. In reality, the distinguishing feature of "subjective" thinkers consists in the fact that for them the "world of what ought to be, the world of the true and just" stands outside any connection with the objective course of historical development: on one side is *"what ought to be,"* on the other side is *"reality,"* and these two spheres are separated by an entire abyss—that abyss which among the dualists separates the material world from the spiritual world. The task of social science in the nineteenth century has been, among other things, to build a bridge across this evidently bottomless abyss. So long as we do not build this bridge, we shall of necessity close our eyes to *reality* and concentrate all our attention on *"what ought to be"* (as the Saint-Simonists did, for example): which naturally will only have the effect of delaying the translation into life of this *"what ought to be,"* since it renders more difficult the forming of an accurate opinion of it.

We already know that the historians of the Restoration, in contradistinction to the writers of the Enlightenment in the eighteenth century, regarded the political institutions of any country as the result of its civil conditions. This new view became so widespread and developed that in its application to practical questions it reached strange extremes which to us nowadays are almost incomprehensible. Thus, J. B. Say asserted that political questions should not interest an economist, because the national economy can develop equally well even under diametrically opposite political systems. Saint-Simon notes and applauds this idea of Say's, although in fact he does give it a somewhat more profound content. With very few exceptions, all the Utopians of the nineteenth century share this view of "politics."

Theoretically the view is mistaken in two respects. In the first place, the people who held it forgot that in the life of society, as everywhere where it is a case of a *process* and not of some isolated phenomenon, a consequence becomes, in its turn, a cause, and a cause proves to be a consequence. In short, they abandoned here, at quite the wrong moment, that very point of view of *interaction* to which in other cases, also at very much the wrong moment, they limited their analysis. Secondly, if *political* relations are the consequence of *social* relations, it is incomprehensible how consequences which differ to the extreme (political institutions of a diametrically opposite character) can be brought about by one and the same cause—the same state of "wealth." Evidently the very conception of the causal relationship between the political institutions of a country and its economic condition was still extremely vague; and in fact it would not be difficult to show how vague it was with all the Utopians.

In practice this vagueness brought about a double consequence. On the one hand the Utopians, who spoke so much about the *organization of labour*, were ready occasionally to repeat the old watchword of the eighteenth century—"laissez faire, laissez passer." Thus, Saint-Simon, who saw in the organization of industry the greatest task of the nineteenth century, wrote: "l'industrie a besoin d'être gouvernée le moins possible." ("Industry has need of being governed as little as possible.")* On

---

* The writers of the Enlightenment in the eighteenth century contradicted themselves in just the same way, although their contradiction displayed itself otherwise. They stood for non-interference by the state, and yet at times required the most petty regulation by the legislator. The connection of "politics" (which they considered a *cause*) with economy (which they considered a *consequence*) was also unclear to them.

THE UTOPIAN SOCIALISTS

the other hand the Utopians—again with some exceptions falling in the later period—were quite indifferent to current politics, to the political questions of the day.

The political system is a consequence, not a cause. A consequence always remains a consequence, never becoming in its turn a cause. Hence followed the almost direct conclusion that "politics" cannot serve as a means of realizing social and economic "ideals." We can therefore understand the psychology of the Utopian who turned away from politics. But what did they think would help them realize their plans of social transformation? What was it they pinned their practical hopes on? *Everything and nothing. Everything*—in the sense that they awaited help indifferently from the most opposed quarters. *Nothing*—in the sense that all their hopes were quite unfounded.

The Utopians imagined that they were extremely practical people. They hated "doctrinaires," and unhesitatingly sacrificed their most high-sounding principles to their own idées fixes. They were neither Liberals, nor Conservatives, nor Monarchists, nor Republicans. They were quite ready to march indifferently with the Liberals and with the Conservatives, with the Monarchists and with the Republicans, if only they could carry out their *"practical"*—in their view, *extremely practical*—plans. Of the old Utopians Fourier was particularly noteworthy in this respect. Like Gogol's Kostanjoglo,[12] he tried to use every piece of rubbish for the good cause. Now he allured money-lenders with the prospect of the vast interest which their capital would bring them in the future society; now he appealed to the lovers of melons and artichokes, drawing for them a seductive picture of the excellent melons and artichokes of the future; now he assured Louis Philippe that the princesses of the House of Orleans, at whom at the time other princes of the blood were turning up their noses, would have no peace from suitors under the new social order. He snatched at every straw. But, alas! neither the money-lenders, nor the lovers of melons and artichokes, nor the "Citizen King," as they say, pricked up an ear: they did not pay the slightest attention to what, it might have seemed, were the most convincing arguments of Fourier. His practicality turned out to be doomed beforehand to failure, and to be a joyless chase of some *happy accident*.

The chase of the happy accident was the constant occupation of the writers of the Enlightenment in the eighteenth century as well. It was just in hope of such an accident that they sought by every means, fair and foul, to enter into friendly relations with more or less enlightened "legislators" and aristocrats of their age. Usually it is thought that once a man has said to himself that opinion governs the world, he no longer has any reason to despair of the future: la raison finira par avoir raison. But this is not so. When and in what way will reason triumph? The writers of the Enlightenment held that in the life of society everything depends, in the long run, on the "legislator." Therefore they went on their search for legislators. But the same writers knew very well that the character and views of man depend on his upbringing, and that generally speaking their upbringing did not predispose the "legislators" to the absorption of enlightened doctrines. Therefore they could not but realize that there was little hope of the legislators. There remained only to put trust into some happy accident. Imagine that you have an enormous box in which there are very many black balls and two or three white ones. You take out ball after ball. In each individual case you have incomparably fewer chances of taking out a white ball than a black. But, if you repeat the operation a sufficient number of times, you will finally take out a white ball. The same ap-

plies to the "legislators." In each individual case it is incomparably more probable that the legislator will be against the "philosophers": but in the end there must appear, after all, a legislator who would be in agreement with the philosophers. This one will do everything that reason dictates. Thus, *literally thus*, did Helvetius argue.*
The subjective idealist view of history ("opinions govern the world"), *which seems to provide such a wide field for man's freedom of action, in reality represents him as the plaything of accident.* That is why this view *in its essence is very joyless.*

Thus, for example, we know nothing more joyless than the views of the Utopians of the end of the nineteenth century, i.e., the Russian Narodniks and subjective sociologists. Each of them has his ready-made plan for saving the Russian village community, and with it the peasantry generally: each of them has his "formula of progress." But, alas, life moves on, without paying attention to their formulae, which have nothing left but to find their own path, also independently of real life, into the sphere of abstractions, fantasies and logical mischances. Let us, for example, listen to the Achilles of the subjective school, Mr. Mikhailovsky.

"The labour question in Europe is a revolutionary question since it requires the *transfer* of the conditions" (?) "of labour into the hands of the labourer, the expropriation of the present owners. The labour question in Russia is a conservative question, since here all that is needed is *preserving* the conditions of labour in the hands of the labourer, guaranteeing to the present owners the property they possess. Quite close to St. Petersburg itself ... in a district dotted with factories, works,

---
* "Dans un temps plus ou moins long il faut, disent les sages, que toutes les possibilités se réalisent: pourquoi désespérer du bonheur futur de l'humanité?"

parks, country cottages, there are villages the inhabitants of which live on their *own* land, burn their *own* timber, eat their *own* bread, wear coats and sheepskins made by their *own* labour out of the wool of their *own* sheep. Give them a firm guarantee that this property of theirs will remain their own, and the Russian labour question is solved. And for the sake of such a purpose everything else can be given up, if we properly understand the significance of a stable guarantee. It will be said: but we cannot for ever remain with wooden ploughs and three-field economy, with antediluvian methods of making coats and sheepskins. We cannot. There are two ways out of this difficulty. One, approved by the practical point of view, is very simple and convenient: raise the tariffs, dissolve the village community, and that probably will be enough—industry like that of Great Britain will grow up like a mushroom. But it will devour the labourer and expropriate him. There is another way, of course much more difficult: but the simple solution of a question is not necessarily the correct solution. The other way consists in developing those relations between labour and property which already exist, although in an extremely rude and primitive form. Obviously this end cannot be achieved without broad intervention by the state, the first act of which should be the legislative consolidation of the village community."*

> *Through the wide world*
> *For the free heart*
> *There are two paths still.*
> *Weigh your proud strength,*
> *Bend your firm mind,*
> *Choose which you will!***

---

* N. Mikhailovsky, *Works* (Second ed.), Vol. II, pp. 102-03.
** N. Nekrasov's *Who Lives Well in Russia.—Ed.*

We suspect that all the arguments of our author have a strong aroma of melons and artichokes; and our sense of smell hardly deceives us. What was Fourier's mistake in his dealings with melons and artichokes? It was that he fell into "subjective sociology." The objective sociologist would ask himself: is there any probability that the lovers of melons and artichokes will be attracted by the picture I have drawn? He would then ask himself: are the lovers of melons and artichokes in a position to alter existing social relations and the present course of their development? It is most probable that he would have given himself a negative reply to each of these questions, and therefore would not have wasted his time on conversation with the "melon and artichoke lovers." But that is how an *objective* sociologist would have acted, i.e., a man who founded all his calculations upon the given course of social development in conformity to law. The subjective sociologist, on the other hand, discards *conformity to law* in the name of the *"desirable,"* and therefore there remains no other way out for him but to trust in chance. As the old Russian saying has it, in a tight corner you can shoot with a stick too: that is the only consoling reflection upon which a good subjective sociologist can rely.

In a tight corner you can shoot with a stick too. But a stick has two ends, and we do not know which end it shoots from. Our Narodniks and, if I may use the expression, subjectivists have already tried a vast number of sticks (even the argument as to the convenience of collecting arrears of taxes in the village-community system of landholding has sometimes appeared in the role of a magic stick). In the vast majority of cases the sticks proved quite incapable of playing the part of guns, and when by chance they did fire, the bullets hit the Narodniks and subjectivists themselves. Let us recall the Peasant Bank. What hopes were placed upon it, in the sense of reinforcing our social "foundations"![13] How the Narodniks rejoiced when it was opened! And what happened? The stick fired precisely at those who were rejoicing. Now they themselves admit that the Peasant Bank—a very valuable institution in any case—only undermines the "foundations"; and this admission is equivalent to a confession that those who rejoiced were—at least for some time—also engaged in idle chatter.

"But then the Bank undermines the foundations only because its statutes and its practice do not completely correspond to our idea. If our idea had been completely applied, the results would have been quite different...."

"In the first place, they would not have been quite different at all: the Bank in any case would have facilitated the development of money economy, and money economy would inexorably have undermined the 'foundations.' And secondly, when we hear these endless 'ifs', it seems all the time to us, for some reason, that there is a man with a barrow shouting under our windows: 'Here are melons, melons, and good artichokes!'"

It was already in the 20s of the present century that the French Utopians were incessantly pointing out the "conservative" character of the reforms they had invented. Saint-Simon openly tried to frighten both the government and what we nowadays call society with a popular insurrection, which was meant to present itself to the imaginations of the "conservatives" in the shape of the terrible movement of the *sansculottes*, still vividly remembered by all. But of course nothing came of this frightening, and if history really provides us with any *lessons*, one of the most instructive is that which attests the complete unpracticality of all the plans of all the would-be practical Utopians.

When the Utopians, pointing to the conservative character of their plans, tried to incline the government to put them into effect, they usually, to confirm their idea, presented a survey of the historical development of their country over a more or less prolonged epoch—a survey from which it followed that on these or those particular occasions "mistakes" were made, which had given a quite new and extremely undesirable aspect to all social relations. The government had only to realize and correct these "mistakes" immediately to establish on earth something almost resembling paradise.

Thus, Saint-Simon assured the Bourbons that before the revolution the main distinguishing feature of the internal development of France was an alliance between the monarchy and the industrialists. This alliance was equally advantageous for both sides. During the revolution the government, *through a misunderstanding*, came out against the legitimate demands of the industrialists, and the industrialists, *through just as sad a misunderstanding*, revolted against the monarchy. Hence all the evils of the age that followed. But now that the root of the evil had been laid bare things could be put straight very easily, as the industrialists had only to make their peace on certain conditions with the government. It is this that would be the most reasonable, *conservative* way out of the numerous difficulties of both sides. It is unnecessary to add now that neither the Bourbons nor the industrialists followed the sage advice of Saint-Simon.

"Instead of firmly keeping to our age-old traditions; instead of developing the principle of the intimate connection between the means of production and the direct producer, which we inherited; instead of taking advantage of the acquisitions of West European science and applying them for the development of forms of industry, founded on the possession by the peasantry of the implements of production; instead of increasing the productivity of its labour by concentrating the means of production in its hands; instead of taking advantage, not of the form of production, but of its very organization as it appears in Western Europe ... instead of all this, we have taken a quite opposite path. We not only have not prevented the development of the capitalist forms of production, in spite of the fact that they are founded on the expropriation of the peasantry, but on the contrary have tried with all our strength to promote the complete break-up of all our economic life, a break-up which led to the famine of 1891."* Thus laments Mr. N.—on,[14] recommending "society" to correct this mistake, by solving an "extremely difficult" but not "impossible" problem: "to develop the productive forces of the population in such a form that not an insignificant minority, but the entire people could take advantage of them."** Everything depends upon correcting the "mistake."

It is interesting that Mr. N.—on imagines himself to be ever so foreign to any utopias. Every minute he makes references to people to whom we owe the scientific criticism of utopian socialism.[15] Everything depends on the country's economy, he repeats in season and out of season, echoing these people, and all the evil springs from this: "Therefore the means to eliminate the evil, once it has been discovered, must consist likewise in altering the very conditions of production." To explain this he once again quotes one of the critics of utopian socialism: "These means must not be invented by the mind, but discovered by means of the mind in the existing material facts of production."***

---

* Nikolai —on [N. Danielson], *Outlines of Our Social Economy Since the Reform,* St. Petersburg, 1893, pp. 322-23.
** *Ibid.,* p. 343.
*** Engels, *Socialism, Utopian and Scientific,* Ch. III.—*Tr.*

But in what, then, consist those *"material facts of production"* *which will move society to solve, or at least to understand, the problem presented to it by Mr. N.—on?* This remains a mystery not only to the reader but, of course, to the author himself as well. By his "problem" he has very convincingly demonstrated that in his *historical* views he remains a full-blooded Utopian, in spite of his quotations from the works of quite non-utopian writers.*

Can it be said that the plans of Fourier contradicted the "material facts" of production in his times? No, not only did they not contradict them, but they were entirely founded upon those facts, even in their defects. But this did not prevent Fourier from being a Utopian, because, once having founded his plan "by means of the mind" on the material conditions of the production of his age, *he failed to adopt its realization to those same conditions, and therefore with complete futility pestered with his*

---

* Correspondingly, Mr. N.—on's practical plans also represent an almost literal repetition of those "demands" which long ago and, of course, quite fruitlessly were presented by our *utopian Narodniks*, like, for example, Mr. Prugavin. "The ultimate ends and tasks of social and state activity" (you see, neither society nor the state is forgotten) "in the sphere of factory economy must be: on the one hand, the purchase for the state of all implements of labour and the granting of the latter to the people for temporary use, for hire; on the other, the establishment of an organization of the conditions of production" (Mr. Prugavin wants to say simply "production," but as is the custom of all Russian writers, headed by Mr. Mikhailovsky, he uses the expression *"conditions* of production," without understanding what it means) "which would be founded upon the requirements of the people and the state, and not on the interests of the market, of disposal and of competition, which is the case in the commodity-capitalist organization of the economic forces of the country" (V. S. Prugavin, *The Handicraftsman at the Exhibition*, Moscow, 1882, p. 15). Let the reader compare this passage with the above quotation from the book of Mr. N.—on.

"great task" those social strata and classes which, in virtue of those same material conditions, could not have either the inclination to set about its solution or the possibility of solving it. Mr. N.—on sins in this way just as much as Fourier or the Rodbertus whom he loves so little: most of all he reminds one precisely of Rodbertus, because Mr. N.—on's reference to age-old traditions is just in the spirit of that conservative writer.

For the better instruction of "society," Mr. N.—on points to the terrifying example of Western Europe. By such observations our Utopians have long attempted to give themselves the aspect of positive people, who don't get carried away by fantasies but know how to take advantage of the "lessons of history." However this method, too, is *not at all new*. The French Utopians were already attempting to terrify their contemporaries and make them listen to reason by the *example of England*, where "a vast distance separates the employer from the workman" and where there hangs over the latter the yoke of a special kind of despotism. "Other countries which follow England along the path of industrial development," said the *Producteur*, "must understand that they ought to search for the means to prevent such a system arising on their own soil."* The only real obstacle to the appearance of English methods in other countries could be the Saint-Simonists' "organization of labour and labourers."** With the development of the labour movement in France it was Germany that became the principal theatre of day-dreams about avoiding capitalism. *Germany*, in the person of her Utopians, long and stubbornly set herself up against "Western Europe" (den westlichen Ländern). In the Western countries, said the German Utopians, the bear-

---

* *Le Producteur,* Vol. I, p. 140.

** On this organization, see the *Globe* for 1831-32, where it is set forth in detail, with even the preparatory transitional reforms.

THE UTOPIAN SOCIALISTS 79

er of the idea of a new organization of society is the working class, with us it is the educated classes (what is called in Russia the *intelligentsia*). It was precisely the German "intelligentsia" which was thought to be called upon to avert from Germany the cup of capitalism.*

---

* "Unsere Nationalökonomen streben mit allen Kräften, Deutschland auf die Stufe der Industrie zu heben, von welcher herab England jetzt die andern Länder noch beherrscht. England ist ihr Ideal. Gewiss: England sieht sich gern schön an; England hat seine Besitzungen in allen Weltteilen, es weiss seinen Einfluss aller Orten geltend zu machen, es hat die reichste Handels- und Kriegsflotte, es weiss bei allen Handelstraktaten die Gegenkontrahenten immer hinters Licht zu führen, es hat die spekulativsten Kaufleute, die bedeutendsten Kapitalisten, die erfindungsreichsten Köpfe, die prächtigsten Eisenbahnen, die grossartigsten Maschinenanlagen; gewiss, England ist, von dieser Seite betrachtet, ein glückliches Land, aber—es lässt sich auch ein anderer Gesichtspunkt bei der Schätzung Englands gewinnen und unter diesem möchte doch wohl das Glück desselben von seinem *Unglück* bedeutend überwogen werden. England ist auch das Land, in welchem das Elend auf die höchste Spitze getrieben ist, in welchem jährlich Hunderte notorisch Hungers sterben, in welchem die Arbeiter zu Fünfzigtausenden zu arbeiten verweigern, da sie trotz all ihrer Mühe und Leiden nicht so viel verdienen, dass sie notdürftig leben können. England ist das Land, in welchem die Wohltätigkeit durch die Armensteuer zum *äusserlichen* Gesetz gemacht werden musste. Seht doch ihr, Nationalökonomen, in den Fabriken die wankenden, gebückten und verwachsenen Gestalten, seht die bleichen, abgehärmten, schwindsüchtigen Gesichter, seht all das geistige und das leibliche Elend, und ihr wollt Deutschland noch zu einem zweiten England machen? England konnte nur durch Unglück und Jammer zu dem Höhepunkt der Industrie gelangen, auf dem es jetzt steht, und Deutschland könnte nur durch *dieselben* Opfer *ähnliche* Resultate erreichen, d. h. erreichen, dass die Reichen noch reicher und die Armen noch ärmer werden".—"Our national economists strive with all their might to lift Germany on to that stage of industry from which England now still dominates other countries. England is their ideal. Of course, England likes to admire herself: she has her possessions in all parts of the world, she knows how to make her influence count everywhere, she has the richest mercantile marine and navy and knows in all trade agreements how to humbug her

Capitalism was so terrifying to the German Utopians that, for the sake of avoiding it, they were ready in the last resort to put up with complete stagnation. The triumph of a constitutional system, they argued, would lead to the supremacy of the money aristocracy. Therefore let there rather be no constitutional system.* Ger-

---

partner, she has the most speculative merchants, the most important capitalists, the most inventive heads, the most excellent railways, the most magnificent machine equipment. Of course, England when viewed from this aspect is a happy country, but—another point of view might gain the upper hand in assessing England, and from this point of view her happiness might nevertheless be considerably outweighed by her unhappiness. England is also the country in which misery has been brought to its highest point, in which it is notorious that hundreds die of hunger every year, in which the workmen by the fifty thousand refuse to work because, in spite of all their toil and suffering, they do not earn enough to provide themselves with a bare livelihood. England is the country in which philanthropy through the poor rate had to be enacted by *an extreme measure.* Look then, national economists, at the swaying, bowed and deformed figures in the factories, look at the pale, languid, tubercular faces, look at all the spiritual and bodily misery—and you still wish to make Germany into a second England? England was only able through misfortune and misery to reach the high point of industry at which she now stands, and only through the same sacrifices could Germany achieve similar results, i.e., that the rich should become still richer and the poor still poorer." *Trierscher Zeitung,* May 4, 1846, reprinted in Vol. I of the review edited by M. Hess, under the title of *Der Gesellschaftsspiegel. Die Geselschaftlichen Zustände der civilisierten Welt (The Social Mirror, Social Conditions of the Civilized World),* Iserlohn and Elberfeld, 1846.

* "Sollte es den Constitutionellen gelingen," said Büchner "die deutschen Regierungen zu stürzen und eine allgemeine Monarchie oder Republik einzuführen, so bekommen wir hier einen Geldaristokratismus, wie in Frankreich, und lieber soll es bleiben, wie es jetzt ist."

"Should the Constitutionalists succeed," said Büchner, "in overthrowing the German governments and introducing a universal monarchy or republic, we should get here an aristocracy of money as in France; and better it should remain as it now is" (Georg Büchner, *Collected Works,* ed. Franzos, p. 122).

many did not avoid capitalism. Now it is the Russian Utopians who talk about avoiding it. Thus do utopian ideas journey from west to east, everywhere appearing as the heralds of the victory of that same capitalism against which they are revolting and struggling. But the further they penetrate into the east the more their historical significance changes. The French Utopians were in their day bold *innovators* of genius; the Germans proved much lower than they; and the Russians are now capable only of frightening western people by their antediluvian appearance.

It is interesting that even the writers of the French Enlightenment had the idea of avoiding capitalism. Thus, Holbach was very upset by the fact that the triumph of the constitutional order in England led to the complete supremacy of *l'intérêt sordide des marchands.* He was very saddened by the circumstance that the English were tirelessly looking for new markets—this chase of markets distracted them from philosophy. Holbach also condemned the inequality of property existing in England. Like Helvetius, he would have liked to prepare the way for the triumph of reason and equality, and not of mercantile interests.

But neither Holbach nor Helvetius, nor any other of the writers of the Enlightenment could put forward anything against the then course of events except panegyrics of reason and moral instructions addressed to the "people of Albion." In this respect they were just as impotent as our own present-day Russian Utopians.

One more remark, and we shall have finished with the Utopians. The point of view of *"human nature"* brought forth in the first half of the nineteenth century that abuse of *biological* analogies which, even up to the present day, makes itself very strongly felt in Western sociological

—and particularly in Russian quasi-sociological—literature.

If the cause of all historical social progress is to be sought in the nature of man, and if, as Saint-Simon himself justly remarks, society consists of individuals, then the nature of the individual has to provide the key to the explanation of history. The nature of the individual is the subject of *physiology* in the broad sense of the word, i.e., of a science which also covers *psychological* phenomena. That is why physiology, in the eyes of Saint-Simon and his followers, was the basis of *sociology*, which they called *social physics*. In the *Opinions philosophiques, littéraires et industrielles* published during Saint-Simon's lifetime and with his active participation, there was printed an extremely interesting but unfortunately unfinished article of an anonymous *doctor of medicine*, entitled: "De la physiologie appliquée à l'amélioration des institutions sociales."

The author considered *the science of society* to be a component part of *"general physiology"* which, enriched by the observations and experiments of *"special physiology"* of the individual, "devotes itself to considerations of a higher order." Individuals are for it "only organs of the social body," the functions of which it studies *"just as special physiology studies the functions of individuals."* General physiology studies (the author writes: "expresses") the laws of social existence, with which the written laws should be accordingly co-ordinated. Later on the bourgeois sociologists, as for example Spencer, made use of the doctrine of the social organism to draw the most conservative conclusions. But the doctor of medicine whom we quote was first of all a *reformer*. He studied "the social body" with the object of *social reconstruction*, since only *"social physiology"* and the *"hygiene"* closely bound up with it provided "the positive foundations on which it is possible to build the system of social organization required by the present state of the civilized world." But evidently social physiology and hygiene did not provide much food for the reforming fantasy of the author, because in the end he found himself obliged to turn to the *doctors*, i.e., to persons dealing with individual organisms, asking them to give to society, "*in the form of a hygienic prescription*," a "system of social organization."

This view of "social physics" was later on chewed over—or, if you prefer, developed—by Auguste Comte in his various works. Here is what he said about social science still in his youth, when he was writing in the Saint-Simonist *Producteur*: "Social phenomena, being human phenomena, should without doubt be classed among physiological phenomena. But although social physics must find its point of departure in, and be in constant connection with, individual physiology, it nevertheless should be examined and developed as quite a separate science: for various generations of men progressively influence one another. If we maintain the purely physiological point of view, we cannot properly study that influence: yet its evaluation should occupy the *principal* place in social physics."*

Now you can see what hopeless contradictions confront those who regard society from this point of view.

In the first place, since "social physics" has individual physiology as its "point of departure," it is built on a purely *materialist* foundation: in physiology there is no place for an *idealist* view of an object. But the same social physics was principally to concern itself with evaluating the progressive influence of one generation on another. One generation influences the next, passing on to

---

* "Considérations sur les sciences et les savants" in *Le Producteur*, Vol. I, pp. 355-56.

it both the knowledge which it inherited from previous generations, and the knowledge which it acquired itself. "Social physics" therefore examines the development of the human species from the point of view of the development of knowledge and of "enlightenment" (lumières). This is already the purely idealist point of view of the eighteenth century: *opinions govern the world.* Having "closely connected," on Comte's advice, this idealistic point of view with the purely materialist point of view of individual physiology, we turn out to be *dualists* of the purest water, and nothing is easier than to trace the harmful influence of this dualism on the sociological views even of the same Comte. But this is not all. The thinkers of the eighteenth century noticed that in the development of knowledge there is a certain conformity to law. Comte firmly maintained such a conformity, putting into the foreground the notorious law of three stages: theological, metaphysical and positive.

But why does the development of knowledge pass precisely through these stages? Such is the nature of the human mind, replies Comte: "By its nature (par sa nature), the human mind passes wherever it acts through three different theoretical conditions."* Excellent; but to study that "nature" we shall have to turn to individual physiology, and individual physiology does not give us an adequate explanation; and we have again to refer to previous "generations"—and the "generations" again send us back to "nature." This is called a science, but there is no trace of science in it: there is only an endless movement round a vicious circle.

Our own allegedly original, "subjective" sociologists fully share the view-point of the French Utopian of the 20s.

---

* *Ibid.*, Vol. I, p. 304.

"While I was still under the influence of Nozhin,[16]" Mr. Mikhailovsky tells us about himself, "and partly under his guidance, I interested myself in the question of the boundaries between biology and sociology, and the possibility of bringing them together.... I cannot sufficiently highly assess the advantage I gained from communion with the ideas of Nozhin: but nevertheless there was much in them that was accidental, partly because they were still only developing in Nozhin himself, partly because of his limited knowledge in the sphere of the natural sciences. I received from Nozhin really only an impulse in a certain direction, but it was a strong, decisive and beneficent impulse. Without thinking of any special study of biology, I nevertheless read a great deal on Nozhin's suggestion and, as it were, by his testament. This new trend in my reading threw an original and most absorbing light on that considerable—though disorderly, and to some extent simply useless—material, both of facts and ideas, which I had stored up previously."*

Nozhin has been described by Mr. Mikhailovsky in his sketches *In the Intervals*, under the name of Bukhartsev. Bukhartsev "dreamed of reforming the social sciences with the help of natural science, and had already worked out an extensive plan for that purpose." The methods of this reforming activity can be seen from the following. Bukhartsev undertakes to translate into Russian from the Latin an extensive treatise on zoology, and accompanies the translation with his own footnotes, in which he proposes "to include the results of all his independent work," while to these footnotes he adds new footnotes of a "sociological" character. Mr. Mikhailovsky obligingly acquaints the reader with one such second-storey footnote: "Generally speaking, I cannot in my supplements

---

* "Literature and Life," in *Russkaya Mysl*,[17] 1891, Vol. IV, p. 195.

to Van-der-Hoeven proceed too far in theoretical discussions and conclusions regarding the application of all these purely anatomical questions in solving social and economic questions. Therefore I again only draw the attention of the reader to the fact that my whole anatomical and embryological theory has as its main object the discovery of the laws of the physiology of society, and therefore all my later works will, of course, be founded on the scientific data set forth by me in this book."*

Anatomical and embryological theory "has as its main object the discovery of the laws of the physiology of society"! This is very awkwardly put, but nevertheless is very characteristic of the utopian sociologists. He constructs an anatomical theory, with the help of which he intends to write out a number of "hygienic prescriptions" for the society surrounding him. It is to these prescriptions that his social "physiology" is reduced. The social "physiology" of Bukhartsev is, strictly speaking, not "physiology" but the "hygiene" with which we are already acquainted: not a science of what is, but a science of what ought to be, on the basis ... of the "anatomical and embryological theory" of that same Bukhartsev.

Although Bukhartsev has been copied from Nozhin, he, nevertheless, represents to a certain extent the product of the artistic and creative work of Mr. Mikhailovsky (that is, if we can speak of *artistic* work in relation to the sketches quoted). Consequently even his awkward footnote, perhaps, never existed in reality. In that event it is all the more characteristic of Mr. Mikhailovsky, who speaks of it with great respect.

"I chanced nevertheless to come across the direct reflection in literature of the ideas of my unforgettable friend and teacher," says Tyomkin, in whose name the

---

* N. K. Mikhailovsky, *Works*, Vol. IV (Second ed.), pp. 265-66.

story is told. Mr. Mikhailovsky reflected, and still reflects, the ideas of Bukhartsev-Nozhin.

Mr. Mikhailovsky has his own "formula of progress." This formula declares: "Progress is the gradual approach to the integrity of the individual, to the fullest possible and most manifold division of labour between the organs and the least possible division of labour between people. Anything retarding this movement is immoral, unjust, harmful and unreasonable. Only that is moral, just, reasonable and useful which diminishes the heterogeneity of society, thereby increasing the heterogeneity of its individual members."*

What can be the scientific significance of this formula? Does it explain the historical progress of society? Does it tell how that progress took place, and why it took place in one particular way and not in another? Not in the least: and its "main aim" is not that at all. It does not speak of how history advanced, but of how it ought to have advanced to earn the approval of Mr. Mikhailovsky. This is a "hygienic prescription" invented by a Utopian on the basis of "exact investigations of the laws of organic development." It is just what the Saint-Simonist doctor was looking for.

... "We have said that the exclusive use in sociology of the objective method would be equivalent, if it were possible, to adding up arshins and poods:** whence, by the way, it follows, not that the objective method must be completely eliminated from this sphere of research, but that the supreme control must be exercised by the subjective method."***

---

* *Ibid.*, pp. 186-87.
** The first is a measure of length, the second of weight: thus it is like saying that yards should be added to hundredweights.—*Tr.*
*** N. K. Mikhailovsky, *Works*, Vol. IV (Second ed.), p. 185.

"This sphere of research" is precisely the "physiology" of the *desired society*, the sphere of Utopia. Naturally the use of the "subjective method" in it very much facilitates the work of the *"investigator."* But this use is based not at all on any "laws," but on the "enchantment of charming fantasy";[18] whoever once has given way to it, will never revolt even against the use in one and the same "sphere"—true, with different rights—of both methods, subjective and objective, even though such a confusion of methods really does mean "adding up arshins and poods."*

---

* Incidentally, these very expressions—"objective method," "subjective method"—represent a vast confusion, at the very least in terminology.

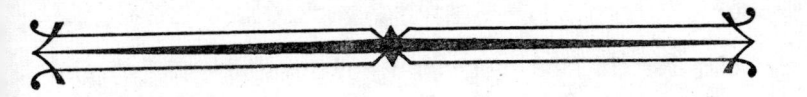

Chapter IV

IDEALIST GERMAN PHILOSOPHY

The materialists of the eighteenth century were firmly convinced that they had succeeded in dealing the death-blow to idealism. They regarded it as an obsolete and completely forsaken theory. But a reaction against materialism began already at the end of that century, and in the first half of the nineteenth century materialism itself fell into the position of a system which all considered obsolete and buried, once for all. Idealism not only came to life again, but underwent an unprecedented and truly brilliant development. There were, of course, appropriate social reasons for this: but we will not touch on them here, and will only consider whether the *idealism* of the nineteenth century had any advantages over the *materialism* of the previous epoch and, if it had, in what these advantages consisted.

French materialism displayed an astonishing and today scarcely credible feebleness every time it came upon questions of evolution in nature or in history. Let us take, for example, *the origin of man*. Although the idea of the *gradual evolution* of this species did not seem "*contradictory*" to the materialists, nevertheless they thought such a "guess" to be most improbable. The authors of the *Système de la Nature* (see Part I, ch. 6) say that if anyone were to revolt against such a piece of conjecture, if anyone were to object "that Nature acts with the help of a certain sum of general and invariable laws," and added in doing so that "man, the quadruped, the fish, the insect, the plant, etc., exist from the beginning of time and remain eternally unaltered" they "would not object to this." They would only remark that such a view also does not contradict the truths they set forth. "Man cannot possibly know everything: he cannot know his origin" —that is all that in the end the authors of the *Système de la Nature* say about this important question.

Helvetius seems to be more inclined to the idea of the gradual evolution of man. "Matter is eternal, but its forms are variable" he remarks, recalling that even now human natures change under the influence of climate.* He even considered that generally speaking all animal species were variable. But this sound idea was formulated by him very strangely. It followed, in his view, that the causes of "dissimilarity" between the different species of animals and vegetables lie *either* in the qualities of their very "embryos," *or* in the differences of their environment, the differences of their "upbringing."**

Thus *heredity* excludes *mutability*, and vice versa. If we adopt the theory of mutability, we must as a consequence presuppose that from any given "embryo" there can arise, in appropriate circumstances, any animal or vegetable: from the embryo of an oak, for example, a bull or a giraffe. Naturally *such* a "conjecture" could not throw any light on the question of the origin of species, and Helvetius himself, having once made it in passing, never returned to it again.

Just as badly were the French materialists able to explain phenomena of *social* evolution. The various systems of "legislation" were represented by them solely as the

---

* *Le vrai sens du système de la nature*, London, 1774, p. 15.
** "De l'homme," *Œuvres complètes de Helvétius*, Paris, 1818, Vol. II, p. 120.

product of the conscious creative activity of "legislators"; the various religious systems as the product of the cunning of priests, etc.

This impotence of French materialism in face of questions of evolution in nature and in history made its philosophical content very poor. In its view of nature, that content was reduced to combating the one-sided conception of matter held by the *dualists*. In its view of man it was confined to an endless repetition of, and some variations upon, Locke's principle that *there are no innate ideas*. However valuable such repetition was in combating out-of-date moral and political theories, it could not have serious scientific value unless the materialists had succeeded in applying their conception to the explanation of the spiritual evolution of mankind. We have already said earlier that some very remarkable attempts were made in this direction by the French materialists (i.e., to be precise, by Helvetius), but that they ended in failure (and if they had succeeded, French materialism would have proved very strong in questions of evolution). The materialists, in their view of history, took up a purely idealistic standpoint—that *opinions govern the world*. Only at times, only very rarely, did materialism break into their historical reflections, in the shape of remarks that some stray atom, finding its way into the head of the "legislator" and causing in it a disturbance of the functions of the brain, might alter the course of history for entire ages. *Such* materialism was essentially *fatalism*, and left no room for the foreseeing of events, i.e., for the conscious historical activity of thinking individuals.

It is not surprising, therefore, that to capable and talented people who had not been drawn into the struggle of social forces in which materialism had been a terrible theoretical weapon of the extreme Left party this doctrine seemed *dry, gloomy, melancholy*. That was, for example, how Goethe[19] spoke of it. In order that this reproach should cease to be deserved, materialism had to leave its dry and abstract mode of thought, and attempt to understand and explain "real life"—the complex and variegated chain of concrete phenomena—from its own point of view. But in its then form it was incapable of solving that great problem, and the latter was taken possession of by *idealist philosophy.*

The main and final link in the development of that philosophy was the system of Hegel: therefore we shall refer principally to that system in our exposition.

Hegel called *metaphysical* the point of view of those thinkers—irrespective of whether they were idealists or materialists—who, failing to understand the process of development of phenomena, willy-nilly represent them to themselves and others as petrified, disconnected, incapable of passing one into another. To this point of view he opposed *dialectics*, which studies phenomena precisely in their development and, consequently, in their interconnection.

According to Hegel, dialectics is *the principle of all life*. Frequently one meets people who, having expressed some abstract proposition, willingly recognize that perhaps they are mistaken, and that perhaps the exactly opposite point of view is correct. These are well-bred people, saturated to their finger tips with *"tolerance"*: live and let live, they say to their intellect. Dialectics has nothing in common with the sceptical tolerance of men of the world, but it, too, knows how to reconcile directly opposite abstract propositions. Man is mortal, we say, regarding death as something rooted in external circumstances and quite alien to the nature of living man. It follows that a man has two qualities: first of being alive, and secondly of also being mortal. But upon closer investigation it turns out that *life* itself bears in itself the germ of *death*, and that in general any phenomenon is *contradictory*, in the sense that it develops out of itself the elements which, sooner or later, will put an end to its existence and will transform it into its own opposite. Everything flows, everything changes; and there is no force capable of holding back this constant flux, or arresting this eternal movement. There is no force capable of resisting the dialectics of phenomena. Goethe personifies dialectics in the shape of a spirit:

> *In Lebensfluthen, im Thatensturm,*
> *Wall'ich, auf und ab,*
> *Webe hin und her!*
> *Geburt und Grab,*
> *Ein ewiges Meer,*
> *Ein wechselnd Weben,*
> *Ein glühend Leben,*
>
> *So schaff'ich am sausenden Webstuhl der Zeit,*
> *Und wirke der Gottheit lebendiges Kleid.**

At a particular moment a moving body is at a particular spot, but at the same time it is outside it as well because, if it were *only* in that spot, it would, at least for that moment, become *motionless*. Every motion is a dialectical process, a living contradiction, and as there is

---

* *In the tides of Life, in Action's storm,*
  A fluctuant wave,
  A shuttle free,
  Birth and the Grave,
  An eternal sea,
  A weaving, flowing,
  Life, all-glowing,
  Thus at Time's humming loom 'tis my hand prepares
  The garment of Life which the Deity wears!

  (*Faust*, Part I, Scene I (Bayard Taylor's translation.)

not a single phenomenon of nature in explaining which we do not have in the long run to appeal to motion, we have to agree with Hegel, who said that *dialectics is the soul of any scientific cognition*. And this applies not only to cognition of nature. What for example is the meaning of the old saw: *summum jus, summa injuria*? Does it mean that we act most justly when, having paid our tribute to law, we at the same time give its due to lawlessness? No, that is the interpretation only of "surface thinking, the mind of fools." The aphorism means that every abstract justice, carried to its logical conclusion, is transformed into injustice, i.e., into its own opposite. Shakespeare's *Merchant of Venice* serves as a brilliant illustration of this. Take a look at economic phenomena. What is the logical conclusion of "free *competition*"? Every capitalist strives to beat his competitors and to remain sole master of the market. And, of course, cases are frequent when some Rothschild or Vanderbilt succeeds in happily fulfilling this ambition. But this shows that free competition leads to monopoly, that is to the negation of competition, i.e., to its own opposite. Or look at the conclusion to which the so-called *labour principle of property*, extolled by our Narodnik literature, leads. Only that belongs to me which has been created by my labour. Nothing can be more just than that. And it is no less just that I use the thing I have created at my own free discretion: I use it myself or I exchange it for something else, which for some reason I need more. It is equally just, then, that I make use of the thing I have secured by exchange—again at my free discretion—as I find pleasant, best and advantageous. Let us now suppose that I have sold the product of my own labour for money, and have used the money to hire a labourer, i.e., I have bought somebody else's labour-power. Having taken advantage of this labour-power of another, I turn out to be the owner of value which is considerably higher than the value I spent on its purchase. This, on the one hand, is very just, because it has already been recognized, after all, that I can use what I have secured by exchange as is best and most advantageous for myself: and, on the other hand, it is very unjust, because I am exploiting the labour of *another* and thereby negating the principle which lay at the foundation of my conception of justice. The property acquired by my personal labour bears me the property created by the labour of another. Summum jus, summa injuria. And such injuria springs up by the very nature of things in the economy of almost any well-to-do handicraftsman, almost every prosperous peasant.*

And so *every phenomenon, by the action of those same forces which condition its existence, sooner or later, but inevitably, is transformed into its own opposite.*

We have said that the idealist German philosophy regarded all phenomena from the point of view of their evolution, and that this is what is meant by regarding them *dialectically*. It must be remarked that the *metaphysicians* know how to distort the very doctrine of evolution itself. They affirm that neither in nature nor in history are there any leaps. When they speak of the *ori-*

---

* Mr. Mikhailovsky thinks this eternal and ubiquitous supremacy of dialectics incomprehensible: everything changes except the laws of dialectical motion, he says with sarcastic scepticism. Yes, that's just it, we reply: and if it surprises you, if you wish to contest this view, remember that you will have to contest the fundamental standpoint of modern science. In order to be convinced of this, it is sufficient for you to recall those words of Playfair which Lyell took as an epigraph to his famous work *Principles of Geology*: "Amid the revolutions of the globe, the economy of Nature has been uniform, and her laws are the only things that have resisted the general movement. The rivers and the rocks, the seas and the continents have been changed in all their parts; but the laws which direct these changes, and the rules to which they are subject, have remained invariably the same."

gin of some phenomenon or social institution, they represent matters as though this phenomenon or institution was once upon a time very tiny, quite unnoticeable, and then gradually grew up. When it is a question of *destroying* this or that phenomenon and institution, they presuppose, on the contrary, its gradual diminution, continuing up to the point when the phenomenon becomes quite unnoticeable on account of its microscopic dimensions. Evolution conceived of in this way explains absolutely nothing; it presupposes the existence of the phenomena which it has to explain, and reckons only with the *quantitative changes* which take place in them. The supremacy of metaphysical thought was once so powerful in natural science that many naturalists could not imagine evolution otherwise than just in the form of such a gradual increase or diminution of the magnitude of the phenomenon being investigated. Although from the time of Harvey it was already recognized that "*everything living develops out of the egg*," no exact conception was linked, evidently, with such development from the egg, and the discovery of spermatozoa immediately served as the occasion for the appearance of a theory according to which in the seminal cell there already existed a ready-made, completely developed but microscopical little animal, so that all its "*development*" amounted to *growth*. Some wise sages, including many famous European evolutionary sociologists, still regard the "evolution," say, of political institutions, precisely in this way: history makes no leaps: *va piano* (go softly)....

German idealist philosophy decisively revolted against such a misshapen conception of evolution. Hegel bitingly ridiculed it, and demonstrated irrefutably that both in nature and in human society *leaps* constituted just as essential a stage of evolution as gradual quantitative changes. "Changes in being," he says, "consist not only in the fact that one quantity passes into another quantity, but also that quality passes into quantity, and vice versa. Each transition of the latter kind represents an *interruption in gradualness* (ein Abbrechen des Allmählichen), and gives the phenomenon a new aspect, qualitatively distinct from the previous one. Thus, water when it is cooled grows hard, not gradually ... but all at once; having already been cooled to freezing-point, it can still remain a liquid only if it preserves a tranquil condition, and then the slightest shock is sufficient for it suddenly to become hard.... In the world of moral phenomena ... there take place the same changes of quantitative into qualitative, and differences in qualities there also are founded upon quantitative differences. Thus, *a little less, a little more* constitutes that limit beyond which frivolity ceases and there appears something quite different, crime.... Thus also, states—other conditions being equal —acquire a different qualitative character merely in consequence of differences in their size. Particular laws and a particular constitution acquire quite a different significance with the extension of the territory of a state and of the numbers of its citizens."*

Modern naturalists know very well how frequently changes of quantity lead to changes of quality. Why does one part of the solar spectrum produce in us the sensation of a red colour, another, of green, etc.? Physics replies that everything is due here to the number of oscillations of the particles of the ether. It is known that this number changes for every colour of the spectrum, rising from red to violet. Nor is this all. The intensity of heat in the spectrum increases in proportion to the approach to the external border of the red band, and reaches its high-

---

* *Wissenschaft der Logik* (Second ed., Leipzig, 1932), Part I, Book I, pp. 383-84.—*Tr.*

est point a little distance from it, on leaving the spectrum. It follows that in the spectrum there are rays of a special kind which do not give light but only heat. Physics says, here too, that the qualities of the rays change in consequence of changes in the number of oscillations of the particles of the ether.

But even this is not all. The sun's rays have a certain chemical effect, as is shown for example by the fading of material in the sun. What distinguishes the violet and the so-called ultra-violet rays, which arouse in us no sensation of light, is their greatest chemical strength. The difference in the chemical action of the various rays is explained once again only by quantitative differences in the oscillations of the particles of the ether: *quantity passes into quality.*

Chemistry confirms the same thing. Ozone has different qualities from ordinary oxygen. Whence comes this difference? In the molecule of ozone there is a different number of atoms from that contained in the molecule of ordinary oxygen. Let us take three hydrocarbon compounds: CH_4 (marsh gas), C_2H_6 (dimethyl) and C_3H_8 (methyl-ethyl). All of these are composed according to the formula: n atoms of carbon and $2n+2$ atoms of hydrogen. If n is equal to 1, you get marsh gas; if n is equal to 2, you get dimethyl; if n is equal to 3, methyl-ethyl appears. In this way entire series are formed, the importance of which any chemist will tell you; and all these series unanimously confirm the principle of the old dialectical idealists that *quantity passes into quality.*

Now we have learned the principal distinguishing features of dialectical thought, but the reader feels himself unsatisfied. But where is the famous triad, he asks, the triad which is, as is well known, the whole essence of Hegelian dialectics? Your pardon, reader, we do not mention the triad for the simple reason that it *does not at all*

IDEALIST GERMAN PHILOSOPHY

play in Hegel's work the part which is attributed to it by people who have not the least idea of the philosophy of that thinker, and who have studied it, for example, from the *"text-book of criminal law"* of Mr. Spasovich.* Filled with sacred simplicity, these light-hearted people are convinced that the whole argumentation of the German idealists was reduced to references to the triad; that whatever theoretical difficulties the old man came up against, he left others to rack their poor "unenlightened" brains over them while he, with a tranquil smile, immediately built up a syllogism: all phenomena occur according to a triad, I am faced with a phenomenon, consequently I shall turn to the triad.** This is simply *lunatic*

---

* "Aspiring to a barrister's career," Mr. Mikhailovsky tells us, "I passionately, though unsystematically, read various legal works. Among them was the text-book of criminal law by Mr. Spasovich. This work contains a brief survey of various philosophical systems in their relation to criminology. I was particularly struck by the famous triad of Hegel, in virtue of which punishment so gracefully becomes the reconciliation of the contradiction between law and crime. The seductive character of the tripartite formula of Hegel in its most varied applications is well known.... And it is not surprising that I was fascinated by it in the text-book of Mr. Spasovich. Nor is it surprising that thereupon it drew me to Hegel and to much else..." (*Russkaya Mysl*, 1891, Vol. III, part II, p. 188). A pity, a very great pity, that Mr. Mikhailovsky does not tell us how far he satisfied his yearning "for Hegel." To all appearances, he did not go very far in this direction.

** Mr. Mikhailovsky assures us that the late N. Sieber, when arguing with him about the inevitability of capitalism in Russia, "used all possible arguments, but at the least danger hid behind the authority of the immutable and unquestionable tripartite dialectical development" (*Russkaya Mysl*, 1892, Vol. VI, part II, p. 196). He assures us also that all of what he calls Marx's prophecies about the outcome of capitalist development repose only on the "triad." We shall discuss Marx later, but of N. Sieber we may remark that we had more than once to converse with the deceased, and not once did we hear from him references to "dialectical development." He himself said more than once that he was quite ig-

nonsense, as one of the characters of Karonin[20] puts it, or *unnaturally idle talk,* if you prefer the expression of Shchedrin. Not once in the eighteen volumes of Hegel's works does the *"triad"* play the part of an *argument,* and anyone in the least familiar with his philosophical doctrine understands that it *could not play such a part.* With Hegel the triad has the same significance as it had previously with Fichte, whose philosophy is essentially different from the Hegelian. Obviously only gross ignorance can consider the principal distinguishing feature of one philosophical system to be that which applies to *at least* two quite different systems.

We are sorry that the "triad" has diverted us from our exposition: but, having mentioned it, we should reach a conclusion. So let us examine what kind of a bird it is.

Every phenomenon, developing to its conclusion, becomes transformed into its opposite; but as the new phenomenon, being opposite to the first, also is transformed in its turn into its own opposite, the third phase of development bears a *formal resemblance to the first.* For the time being, let us leave aside the question of the extent to which such a course of development corresponds to reality: let us admit for the sake of argument that those were wrong who thought that it does so correspond completely. But in any case it is clear that the "triad" only *follows* from one of Hegel's principles: it does not in the least serve him as a main principle itself. This is a very essential difference, because if the triad had figured as a main principle, the people who attribute such an important part to it could really seek protection under its "authority"; but as it plays no such part, the only people who

---

norant of the significance of Hegel in the development of modern economics. Of course, everything can be blamed on the dead, and therefore Mr. Mikhailovsky's evidence is irrefutable.

can hide behind it are maybe those who, as the saying has it, have heard a bell, but where they cannot tell.

Naturally the situation would not change one iota if, without hiding behind the "triad," dialecticians "at the least danger" sought protection "behind the authority" of the principle that every phenomenon is transformed into its own opposite. But they never behaved in that way either, and they did not do so because the principle mentioned does not at all exhaust their views on the evolution of phenomena. They say in addition, for example, that in the process of evolution quantity passes into quality, and quality into quantity. Consequently they have to reckon both with the qualitative and the quantitative sides of the process; and this presupposes an attentive attitude to its *real* course in *actual fact*; and this means in its turn that they do not content themselves with *abstract conclusions from abstract principles*—or, at any rate, must not be satisfied with such conclusions, if they wish to remain true to their outlook upon the world.

"On every page of his works Hegel constantly and tirelessly pointed out that philosophy is identical with the *totality of empirics*, that philosophy requires nothing so insistently as going deeply into the empirical sciences.... Material facts without thought have only a relative importance, thought without material facts is a mere chimera.... Philosophy is that *consciousness* at which the empirical sciences arrive relative to themselves. It cannot be anything else."

That is the view of the task of the thinking investigator which Lassalle drew from the doctrine of Hegelian philosophy:* philosophers must be specialists in those sciences which they wish to help to reach "self-conscious-

---

* See his *System der erworbenen Rechte* (Second ed.), Leipzig, 1880, Preface, pp. xii-xiii.

ness." It seems a very far cry from the special study of a subject to thoughtless chatter in honour of the "triad." And let them not tell us that Lassalle was not a "real" Hegelian, that he belonged to the "Left" and sharply reproached the "Right" with merely engaging in abstract constructions of thought. The man tells you plainly that he borrowed his view directly from Hegel.

But perhaps you will want to rule out the evidence of the author of the *System of Acquired Rights*, just as in court the evidence of relatives is ruled out. We shall not argue and contradict; we shall call as a witness a quite extraneous person, the author of the *Sketches of the Gogol Period*. We ask for attention: the witness will speak long and, as usual, wisely.

"We follow Hegel as little as we follow Descartes or Aristotle. Hegel now belongs to past history; the present has its own philosophy and clearly sees the flaws in the Hegelian system. It must be admitted, however, that the principles advanced by Hegel were indeed very near to the truth, and this thinker brought out some aspects of the truth with truly astonishing power. Of these truths, the discovery of some stands to Hegel's personal credit; others do not belong exclusively to his system, they belong to German philosophy as a whole from the time of Kant and Fichte; but nobody before Hegel had formulated them so clearly and had expressed them with such power as they were in his system.

"First of all we shall point to the most fruitful principle underlying all progress which so sharply and brilliantly distinguishes German philosophy in general, and the Hegelian system in particular, from the hypocritical and craven views that predominated at that time (the beginning of the nineteenth century) among the French and the English: 'Truth is the supreme goal of thought; seek truth, for in truth lies good; whatever truth may be, it is better than falsehood; the first duty of the thinker is not to retreat from any results; he must be prepared to sacrifice his most cherished opinions to truth. Error is the source of all ruin; truth is the supreme good and the source of all other good.' To be able to appraise the extreme importance of this demand, common to German philosophy as a whole since the time of Kant, but expressed with exceptional vigour by Hegel, one must remember what strange and narrow restrictions the thinkers of the other schools of that period imposed upon truth. They began to philosophize, only in order to 'justify their cherished convictions,' i.e., they sought not truth, but support for their prejudices. Each took from truth only what pleased him and rejected every truth that was unpleasant to him, bluntly admitting that a pleasing error suited him much better than impartial truth. The German philosophers (especially Hegel) called this practice of seeking not truth but confirmation of pleasing prejudices 'subjective thinking,'" (Saints above! Is this, perhaps, why our subjective thinkers called Hegel a scholastic?—*Author.*) "philosophizing for personal pleasure, and not for the vital need of truth. Hegel fiercely denounced this idle and pernicious pastime." (Listen well!) "As a necessary precaution against inclinations to digress from truth in order to pander to personal desires and prejudices, Hegel advanced his celebrated 'dialectical method of thinking.' The essence of this method lies in that the thinker must not rest content with any positive deduction, but must find out whether the object he is thinking about contains qualities and forces the opposite of those which the object had presented to him at first sight. Thus, the thinker was obliged to examine the object from all sides, and truth appeared to him only as a consequence of a conflict between all possible opposite opinions. Gradually, as a result of this method, the former one-sided conceptions of an object were supplanted by a full and all-sided investigation, and a living conception was obtained of all the real qualities of an object. To explain reality became the paramount duty of philosophical thought. As a result, extraordinary attention was paid to reality, which had been formerly ignored and unceremoniously distorted in order to pander to personal, one-sided prejudices." (De te fabula narratur!) "Thus, conscientious, tireless search for truth took the place of the former arbitrary interpretations. In reality, however, everything depends upon circumstances, upon the conditions of place and time, and therefore, Hegel found that the former general phrases by which good and evil were judged without an examination of the circumstances and causes that give rise to a given phenomenon, that these general, abstract aphorisms were unsatisfactory. Every object, every phenomenon has its own significance, and it must be judged according to the circumstances, the environment, in which it exists. This rule was expressed by the formula: 'There is no abstract truth; truth is concrete,' i.e., a definite judgement can be pronounced only about a definite fact, after examining all the circumstances on which it depends."*

---

* Chernyshevsky, *Sketches of the Gogol Period of Russian Literature*, St. Petersburg, 1892, pp. 258-59. In a special footnote the author of the *Sketches* magnificently demonstrates what is the precise meaning of this examination of all the circumstances on which the particular phenomenon depends. We shall quote this footnote too. "For example: 'Is rain good or bad?' This is an abstract question; a definite answer cannot be given to it. Sometimes rain is beneficial, sometimes, although more rarely, it is harmful. One must inquire specifically: 'After the grain was sown it rained heavily for five hours—was the rain useful for the crop?'—only here is the answer: 'that rain was very useful' clear and sensible. 'But in that very same summer, just when harvest time arrived, it rained in torrents for a whole week—was that good for the crop?' The answer: 'No. That rain was harmful,' is equally clear and correct. That is how all questions are decided by Hegelian philosophy.

And so, on the one hand, we are told that the distinguishing feature of Hegel's philosophy was its most careful investigation of reality, the most conscientious attitude to any particular subject, the study of the latter in its living environment, with all those circumstances of time and place which condition or accompany its existence. The evidence of N. G. Chernyshevsky is identical in this case with the evidence of F. Lassalle. And on the other hand we are assured that this philosophy was empty scholasticism, the whole secret of which consisted in the sophistical use of the "triad." In this case the evidence of Mr. Mikhailovsky is in complete agreement with the evidence of Mr. V. V., and of a whole legion of other modern Russian writers. How is this divergence of witnesses to be explained? Explain it any way you please: but remember that Lassalle and the author of the *Sketches of the Gogol Period* did know the philosophy they were talking about, while Messrs. Mikhailovsky, V. V., and their brethren have quite certainly not given themselves the trouble of studying even a single work of Hegel.

And notice that in characterizing dialectical thought the author of the *Sketches* did not say one word about the

'Is war disastrous or beneficial?' This cannot be answered definitely in general; one must know what kind of war is meant, everything depends upon circumstances, time and place. For savage peoples, the harmfulness of war is less palpable, the benefits of it are more tangible. For civilized peoples, war usually does more harm than good. But the war of 1812, for example, was a war of salvation for the Russian people. The battle of Marathon was a most beneficial event in the history of mankind. Such is the meaning of the axiom: 'There is no abstract truth; truth is concrete'—a conception of an object is concrete when it presents itself with all the qualities and specific features and in the circumstances, environment, in which the object exists, and not abstracted from these circumstances and its living specific features (as it is presented by abstract thinking, the judgement of which has, therefore, no meaning for real life)."

triad. How is it that he did not notice that same elephant, which Mr. Mikhailovsky and company so stubbornly and so ceremoniously bring out on view to every loafer? Once again please remember that the author of the *Sketches of the Gogol Period* knew the philosophy of Hegel, while Mr. Mikhailovsky and Co. have not the least conception of it.

Perhaps the reader may be pleased to recall certain other judgements on Hegel passed by the author of the *Sketches of the Gogol Period*. Perhaps he will point out to us the famous article: "Criticism of Philosophical Prejudices Against Communal Ownership of Land"? This article does speak about the triad and, to all appearances, the latter is put forward as the main hobby-horse of the German idealist. *But it is only in appearance.* Discussing the history of property, the writer asserts that in the third and highest phase of its development it will return to its point of departure, i.e., that private property in the land and the means of production will yield place to social property. Such a return, he says, is a general law which manifests itself in every process of development. The author's argument is in this case, in fact, nothing else than a reference to the triad. And in this lies its essential defect. *It is abstract*: the development of property is examined without relating it to concrete historical conditions—and therefore the author's arguments are ingenious, brilliant, but not convincing. They only astound, surprise, but do not convince. But is Hegel responsible for this defect in the argument of the author of the "Criticism of Philosophical Prejudices"? Do you really think his argument would have been abstract had he considered the subject just in the way in which, according to his own words, Hegel advised all subjects to be considered, i.e., keeping to the ground of reality, weighing all concrete conditions, all circumstances of time and place? It would seem that that would not be the case; it would seem that then there would not have been just that defect we have mentioned in the article. But what, in that event, gave rise to the defect? The fact that the author of the article "Criticism of Philosophical Prejudices Against Communal Ownership of Land," in controverting the abstract arguments of his opponents, forgot the good advice of Hegel, and *proved unfaithful to the method* of that very thinker to whom he referred. We are sorry that in his polemical excitement he made such a mistake. But, once again, is Hegel to blame because in this particular case the author of "Criticism of Philosophical Prejudices" proved unable to make use of his method? Since when is it that philosophical systems are judged, not by their internal content, but by the mistakes which people referring to them may happen to make?

And once again, however insistently the author of the article I have mentioned refers to the triad, even there he does not put it forward as the main hobby-horse of the dialectical method. Even there he makes it, not the foundation but, at most, an unquestionable consequence. The foundation and the main distinguishing feature of dialectics is brought out by him in the following words: *"Eternal change of forms, eternal rejection of a form brought into being by a particular content or striving, in consequence of an intensification of that striving, the higher development of that same content...*—whoever has understood this great, eternal, ubiquitous law, whoever has learnt how to apply it to every phenomenon—ah, how calmly he calls into play the chance which affrights others," etc.

"Eternal change of forms, eternal rejection of a form brought into being by a particular content" ... dialectical thinkers really do look on such a change, such a "rejection of forms" as a great, eternal, ubiquitous law. At the present time this conviction is not shared only by the representatives of some branches of social science who have not the courage to look truth straight in the eyes, and attempt to defend, albeit with the help of error, the prejudices they hold dear. All the more highly must we value the services of the great German idealists who, from the very beginning of the present century, constantly spoke of the eternal change of forms, of their eternal rejection in consequence of the intensification of the content which brought those forms into being.

Earlier we left unexamined *"for the time being"* the question of whether it is a fact that every phenomenon is transformed, as the German dialectical idealists thought, into its own opposite. Now, we hope, the reader will agree with us that, strictly speaking, this question *need not be examined at all.* When you apply the dialectical method to the study of phenomena, you need to remember that *forms change eternally in consequence of the "higher development of their content."* You will have to trace this process of rejection of forms in all its fullness, if you wish to exhaust the subject. But whether the new form is the opposite of the old you will find from experience, and it is not at all important to know this beforehand. True, it is just on the basis of the historical experience of mankind that every lawyer knowing his business will tell you that every legal institution sooner or later is transformed into its own opposite. Today it promotes the satisfaction of certain social needs; today it is valuable and necessary precisely in view of these needs. Then it begins to satisfy those needs worse and worse. Finally it is transformed into an *obstacle* to their satisfaction. From something *necessary* it becomes something *harmful*—and then it is destroyed. Take whatever you like—the history of literature or the history of species—wherever there is development, you will see similar dialectics. But nevertheless, if someone wanted to penetrate the essence of the dialectical process and were to begin, of all things, with testing the idea of the *oppositeness* of the phenomena which constitute a series in each particular process of development, he would be approaching the problem from the wrong end.

In selecting the view-point for such a test, there would always turn out to be very much that was *arbitrary*. The question must be regarded from its objective side, or in other words one must make clear to oneself what is the inevitable change of forms involved in the development of the particular content? This is the same idea, only expressed in other words. But in testing it in practice there is no place for arbitrary choice, because the point of view of the investigator is determined by *the very character of the forms and content themselves*.

In the words of Engels, Hegel's merit consists in the fact that he was the first to regard all phenomena from the point of view of their *development*, from the point of view of their origin and destruction. "Whether he was the first to do it is debatable," says Mr. Mikhailovsky, "but at all events he was not the last, and the present-day theories of development—the evolutionism of Spencer, Darwinism, the ideas of development in psychology, physics, geology, etc.—have nothing in common with Hegelianism."*

If modern natural science confirms at every step the idea expressed with such genius by Hegel, that quantity passes into quality, can we say that it had nothing in common with Hegelianism? True, Hegel was not the *"last"* of those who spoke of such a transition, but this was just for the very same reason that Darwin was not the "last" of those who spoke of the variability of species and Newton was not the "last" of the Newtonists. What would you have? Such is the course of development of

---

* *Russkoye Bogatstvo*, 1894, Vol. II, Part II, p. 150.

the human intellect! *Express a correct idea*, and you will certainly not be the "last" of those who defend it; talk some *nonsense*, and although people have a great failing for it, you still risk finding yourself to be its "last" defender and champion. Thus, in our modest opinion, Mr. Mikhailovsky runs a considerable risk of proving to be the "last" supporter of the "subjective method in sociology." Speaking frankly, we see no reason to regret such a course of development of the intellect.

We suggest that Mr. Mikhailovsky—who finds "debatable" everything in the world, and much else—should refute our following proposition: that wherever the idea of evolution appears "in psychology, physics, geology, etc." it always has very much "in common with Hegelianism," i.e., in every up-to-date study of evolution there are invariably repeated some of the general propositions of Hegel. We say *some*, and not *all*, because many modern evolutionists, lacking the adequate philosophical education, understand "evolution" *abstractly* and *one-sidedly*. An example are the gentry, already mentioned earlier, who assure us that neither nature nor history makes any leaps. Such people would gain a very great deal from acquaintance with Hegel's *logic*. Let Mr. Mikhailovsky refute us: but only let him not forget that we cannot be refuted by knowing Hegel only from the "text-book of criminal law" by Mr. Spasovich and from Lewes's *Biographical History of Philosophy*. He must take the trouble to study Hegel himself.

In saying that the present-day teachings of the evolutionists always have very much "in common with Hegelianism," we are not asserting that the present evolutionists have borrowed their views from Hegel. Quite the reverse. Very often they have just as mistaken a view of him as Mr. Mikhailovsky has. And if nevertheless their theories, even partially and just at those points where they turn out to be correct, become a new illustration of "Hegelianism," this circumstance only brings out in higher relief the astonishing power of thought of the German idealist: people who never read him, by the sheer force of facts and the evident sense of "reality," are obliged to speak as he spoke. One could not think of a greater triumph for a philosopher: *readers* ignore him, but *life* confirms his views.

Up to this day it is still difficult to say to what extent the views of the German idealists directly influenced German natural science in the direction mentioned, although it is unquestionable that in the first half of the present century even the naturalists in Germany studied philosophy during their university course, and although *such* men learned in the biological sciences as Haeckel speak with respect nowadays of the evolutionary theories of some nature-philosophers. But the philosophy of nature was the weak point of German idealism. Its strength lay in *its theories dealing with the various sides of historical development*. As for those theories, let Mr. Mikhailovsky remember—if he ever knew—that it was just from the school of Hegel that there emerged all that brilliant constellation of thinkers and investigators who gave quite a new aspect to the study of religion, aesthetics, law, political economy, history, philosophy and so forth. In all these "disciplines," during a certain most fruitful period, there was not a single outstanding worker who was not indebted to Hegel for his development and for his fresh views on his own branch of knowledge. Does Mr. Mikhailovsky think that this, too, is "debatable"? If he does, let him just try.

Speaking of Hegel, Mr. Mikhailovsky tries "to do it in such a way as to be understood by people uninitiated in the mysteries of the 'philosophical nightcap of Yegor Fyodorovich' as Belinsky disrespectfully put it when he raised the banner of revolt against Hegel."[21] He takes "for this purpose" two examples from Engels's book *Anti-Dühring* (but why not from Hegel himself? That would be much more becoming to a writer "initiated into the mysteries," etc.).

"A grain of oats falls in favourable conditions: it strikes root and thereby, *as such*, as a grain, *is negated*. In its place there arises a stalk, which is the *negation* of the grain; the plant develops and bears fruit, i.e., new grains of oats, and when these grains ripen, the stalk perishes: it was the *negation* of the grain, and now it is *negated* itself. And thereafter the same process of 'negation' and 'negation of negation' is repeated an endless number" (*sic!*) "of times. At the basis of this process lies *contradiction*: the grain of oats is a grain and at the same time *not* a grain, as it is always in a state of actual or potential development." Mr. Mikhailovsky naturally finds this "debatable." And this is how this attractive *possibility* passes with him into *reality*.

"The first stage, the stage of the grain, is the thesis, or proposition; the second, up to the formation of new grains, is the antithesis, or contradiction; the third is the synthesis or reconciliation" (Mr. Mikhailovsky has decided to write in a popular style, and therefore leaves no Greek words without explanation or translation) "and all together they constitute a triad or trichotomy. And such is the fate of all that is alive: it arises, it develops and provides the origin of its repetition, after which it dies. A vast number of individual expressions of this process immediately rise up in the memory of the reader, of course, and Hegel's law proves justified in the whole organic world (for the present we go no further). If however we regard our example a little more closely, we shall see the extreme superficiality and arbitrariness of our generalization. We took a grain, a stalk and once more a grain or, more

exactly, a group of grains. But before bearing fruit, a plant flowers. When we speak of oats or some other grain of economic importance, we can have in view a grain that has been sown, the straw and a grain that has been harvested: but to consider that the life of the plant has been exhausted by these three stages is quite unfounded. In the life of a plant the point of flowering is accompanied by an extreme and peculiar straining of forces, and as the flower does not arise direct from the grain, we arrive, even keeping to Hegel's terminology, not at a trichotomy but at least at a tetrachotomy, a division into four: the stalk negates the grain, the flower negates the stalk, the fruit negates the flower. The omission of the moment of flowering is of considerable importance also in the following respect. In the days of Hegel, perhaps, it was permissible to take the grain for the point of departure in the life of the plant, and from the business point of view it may be permissible to do so even today: the business year does begin with the sowing of the grain. But the life of the plant does not begin with the grain. We now know very well that the grain is something very complex in its structure, and itself represents the product of development of the cell, and that the cells requisite for reproduction are formed precisely at the moment of flowering. Thus in the example taken from vegetable life not only has the point of departure been taken arbitrarily and incorrectly, but the whole process has been artificially and once again arbitrarily squeezed into the framework of a trichotomy."*
And the conclusion is: "*It is about time we ceased to believe that oats grow according to Hegel.*"

Everything flows, everything changes! In our day, i.e., when the writer of these lines, as a student, studied the natural sciences, oats grew "according to Hegel," while

Ibid., pp. 154-57.

now "*we know very well*" that all that is nonsense: now "nous avons changé tout cela." But really, do we quite "know" what "we" are talking about?

Mr. Mikhailovsky sets forth the example of a grain of oats, which he has borrowed from Engels, quite otherwise than as it is set forth by Engels himself. Engels says: "The grain as such ceases to exist, it is *negated*, and in its place appears the plant which has arisen from it, the negation of the grain. But what is the normal life-process of this plant? It grows, flowers, is fertilized and finally once more produces grains of oats,* and as soon as these have ripened the stalk dies, is in its turn negated. As a result of this negation of the negation we have once again the original grain of oats, but not as a single unit, but ten-, twenty-, or thirty-fold."** For Engels the negation of the grain was the *entire plant*, in the cycle of life of which are included, incidentally, both *flowering* and *fertilization*. Mr. Mikhailovsky "negates" the word plant by putting in its place the word *stalk*. The stalk, as is known, constitutes *only part* of a plant, and naturally is *negated* by its other parts: *omnis determinatio est negatio*. But that is the very reason why Mr. Mikhailovsky "negates" the expression used by Engels, replacing it by his own: the stalk negates the grain, he shouts, the flower negates the stalk, the fruit negates the flower: there's a tetrachotomy at least! Quite so, Mr. Mikhailovsky: but all that only goes to prove that in your argument with Engels you do not stop even at ... how shall I put it more mildly ... at the "*moment*" ... of *altering the words of your opponent*. This method is somewhat ... "subjective."

---

* Engels writes, strictly speaking, of barley, not oats: but this is immaterial, of course.
** *Anti-Dühring*, Moscow, 1954, p. 188.—*Ed.*

Once the "moment" of substitution has done its work, the hateful triad falls apart like a house of cards. You have left out the moment of flowering—the Russian "sociologist" reproaches the German Socialist—and "the omission of the moment of flowering is of considerable importance." The reader has seen that the "moment of flowering" has been omitted not by Engels, but by Mr. Mikhailovsky in setting forth the views of Engels; he knows also that "omissions" of that kind in literature are given considerable, though quite negative, importance. Mr. Mikhailovsky here, too, had recourse to a somewhat unattractive "moment." But what could he do? The "triad" is so hateful, victory is so pleasant, and "people quite uninitiated in the mysteries" of a certain "nightcap" are so gullible!

> *We all are innocent from birth,*
> *To virtue a great price we pin:*
> *But meet such people on this earth*
> *That truly, we can't help but sin...**

The flower is an organ of the plant and, as such, as little negates the plant as the head of Mr. Mikhailovsky negates Mr. Mikhailovsky. But the "fruit" or, to be more exact, the fertilized ovum, is really the negation of the given organism being the point of departure of the development of a new life. Engels accordingly considers the cycle of life of a plant from the beginning of its development out of the fertilized ovum to its *reproduction* of a fertilized ovum. Mr. Mikhailovsky with the learned air of a connoisseur remarks: "The life of a plant does not begin with the grain. We now know very well, etc.": briefly, we now know that the seed is fertilized during the flowering. Engels, of course, knows this just as well as Mr. Mikhailovsky. But what does this prove? If Mr. Mi-

---
* From Offenbach "La Belle Hélène."—*Ed.*

khailovsky prefers, we shall replace *the grain* by *the fertilized seed*, but it will not alter the sense of the life-cycle of the plant, and will not refute the "triad." The oats will still be growing "according to Hegel."

By the way, supposing we admit for a moment that the "moment of flowering" overthrows all the arguments of the Hegelians. How will Mr. Mikhailovsky have us deal with non-flowering plants? Is he really going to leave them in the grip of the triad? That would be wrong, because the triad would in that event have a vast number of subjects.

But we put this question really only in order to make clearer Mr. Mikhailovsky's idea. We ourselves still remain convinced that you can't save yourself from the triad even with "the flower." And are we alone in thinking so? Here is what, for example, the botanical specialist Ph. Van Tieghem says: "Whatever be the form of the plant, and to whatever group it may belong thanks to that form, its body always originates in another body which existed before it and from which it separated. In its turn, at a given moment, it separates from its mass particular parts, which become the point of departure, the germs, of as many new bodies, and so forth. In a word it reproduces itself in the same way as it is born: by dissociation."* Just look at that! A scholar of repute, a member of the Institute, a professor at the Museum of Natural History, and talks like a veritable Hegelian: it begins, he says, with dissociation and finishes up with it again. And not a word about the "moment of flowering"! We ourselves understand how very vexing this must be for Mr. Mikhailovsky; but there's nothing to be done—truth, as we know, is dearer than Plato.

Let us once again suppose that "the moment of flower-

---

* *Traité de Botanique* (2nd ed.), Paris, 1891, Part I, p. 24.

ing" overthrows the triad. In that case, "keeping to Hegel's terminology, we arrive not at a trichotomy but at least at a tetrachotomy, a division into four." "Hegel's terminology" reminds us of his *Encyclopaedia*. We open its first part, and learn from it that there are many cases when *trichotomy* passes into *tetrachotomy*, and that generally speaking trichotomy, as a matter of fact, is supreme only in the sphere of the spirit.* So it turns out that oats grow "according to Hegel," as Van Tieghem assures us, and Hegel thinks about oats *according to Mr. Mikhailovsky*, as is evidenced by the *Enzyklopädie der philosophischen Wissenschaften im Grundrisse*. Marvel upon marvel! "She to him, and he to me, and I to the barman Peter...."[22]

Another example borrowed by Mr. Mikhailovsky from Engels, to enlighten the "uninitiated," deals with the teachings of Rousseau.

"According to Rousseau, people in their natural state and savagery were equal with the equality of animals. But man is distinguished by his perfectibility, and this process of perfection began with the appearance of inequality: thereafter every further step of civilization was contradictory: they were 'steps seemingly towards the perfection of the individual man, but in reality towards the decay of the race.... Metallurgy and agriculture were the two arts the discovery of which produced this great revolution. For the poet it is gold and silver, but for the philosopher iron and corn, which have civilized men and ruined the human race.' Inequality continues to develop and, reaching its apogee, turns, in the eastern despotisms, once again into the universal equality of universal insignificance, i.e., returns to its point of departure: and thereafter the further process in the same way brings one to the equality of the social contract."

---
* *Enzyklopädie*, Erster Teil, § 230, Zusatz.

That is how Mr. Mikhailovsky sets out the example given by Engels. As is quite obvious, he finds this, too, "debatable."

"One could make some remark about Engels's exposition; but it is important for us only to know what precisely Engels values in Rousseau's work (*Discours sur l'origine et les fondements de l'inégalité parmi les hommes*). He does not touch upon the question of whether Rousseau rightly or wrongly understands the course of history, he is interested only in the fact that Rousseau 'thinks dialectically': he sees contradiction in the very content of progress, and disposes his exposition in such a way as to make it adaptable to the Hegelian formula of *negation* and *negation of the negation*. And in reality this can be done, even though Rousseau did not know the Hegelian dialectical formula."

This is only the first outpost attack on "Hegelianism" in the person of Engels. Then follows the attack sur toute la ligne.

"Rousseau, without knowing Hegel, thought dialectically according to Hegel. Why Rousseau and not Voltaire, or not the first man in the street? Because all people, by their very nature, think dialectically. Yet it is precisely Rousseau who is selected, a man who stands out among his contemporaries not only by his gifts—in this respect many were not inferior to him—but in his very mental make-up and in the character of his outlook on the world. Such an exceptional phenomenon, you might think, ought not to be taken as a test for a general rule. But we pick as we choose. Rousseau is interesting and important, first of all, because he was the first to demonstrate sufficiently sharply *the contradictory character* of civilization, and contradiction is the essential condition of the dialectical process. We must however remark that the contradiction discerned by Rousseau has nothing in common with contradiction in the Hegelian sense of the word. The contradiction of Hegel lies in the fact that everything, being in a constant process of motion and change (and precisely by the consistent triple path), is at every given unit of time 'it' and at the same time '*not-it.*' If we leave on one side the obligatory three stages of development, contradiction is here simply, as it were, the lining of changes, motion, development. Rousseau also speaks of the process of change. But it is by no means in the very fact of change that he sees contradiction. A considerable part of his argument, both in the *Discours* and in his other works, can be summarized in the following way: intellectual progress has been accompanied by moral retrogression. Evidently dialectical thinking has absolutely nothing to do with it: there is no 'negation of the negation' here, but only an indication of the simultaneous existence of good and evil in the particular group of phenomena. All the resemblance to the dialectical process is reduced to the *single word* 'contradiction.' This, however, is only one side of the case. In addition, Engels sees an obvious trichotomy in Rousseau's argument: after primitive equality follows its negation—inequality, then follows the negation of the negation—the equality of all in the eastern despotisms, in face of the power of the khan, sultan, shah. 'Here we have the extreme measure of inequality, the final point which completes the circle and meets the point from which we set out.' But history does not stop at this, it develops new inequalities, and so forth. The words we have quoted are the actual words of Rousseau, and it is they which are particularly dear to Engels, as obvious evidence that Rousseau thinks according to Hegel."*

Rousseau "stood out among his contemporaries." That is true. What made him stand out? The fact that he

---

* All these extracts have been taken from the volume of *Russkoye Bogatstvo* already quoted.

thought *dialectically*, whereas his contemporaries were almost without exception *metaphysicians*. His view of the origin of inequality is *precisely a dialectical view*, although Mr. Mikhailovsky denies it.

In the words of Mr. Mikhailovsky, Rousseau only pointed out that intellectual progress was accompanied in the history of civilization by moral retrogression. No, Rousseau did not only point this out. According to him, intellectual progress was the *cause* of moral retrogression. It would be possible to realize this even without reading the works of Rousseau: it would be sufficient to recall, on the basis of the previous extract, what part was played in his work by the working of metals and agriculture, which produced the great revolution that destroyed primitive equality. But whoever has read Rousseau himself has not, of course, forgotten the following passage in his *Discours sur l'origine de l'inégalité*: "Il me reste à considérer et à rapprocher les différents hasards qui ont pu perfectionner la raison humaine en détériorant l'espèce, rendre un être méchant en le rendant sociable...." ("It remains for me to consider and to bring together the different hazards which have been able to perfect human reason by worsening the human species, making this animal wicked by making him sociable...."—*Ed.*)

This passage is particularly remarkable because it illustrates very well Rousseau's view on the capacity of the human race for progress. This peculiarity was spoken of a great deal by his "contemporaries" as well. But with them it was a mysterious force which, out of its own inner essence, brought about the successes of reason. According to Rousseau, this capacity *"never could develop of its own accord."* For its development it required constant impulses from outside. This is one of the most important specific features of the *dialectical* view of intellectual *progress*, compared with the *metaphysical* view.

We shall have to refer to it again later. At present what is important is that the passage just quoted expresses with utmost clarity the opinion of Rousseau as to the causal connection between moral *retrogression* and intellectual *progress*.* And this is very important for ascertaining the view of this writer on the course of civilization. Mr. Mikhailovsky makes it appear that Rousseau simply pointed out a "contradiction," and maybe shed some generous tears about it. In reality Rousseau considered this contradiction to be the mainspring of the historical development of civilization. The founder of civil society, and consequently the grave-digger of primitive equality, was the man who first fenced off a piece of land and said: "It belongs to me." In other words, the foundation of civil society is property, which arouses so many disputes among men, evokes in them so much greed, so spoils their morality. But the origin of property presupposed a certain development of *"technique and knowledge"* (de l'industrie et des lumières). Thus primitive relations perished precisely thanks to this development; but at the time when this development led to the triumph of private property, primitive relations between men, on their part, were already in such a state that their further existence had become *impossible*.** If we judge of Rousseau by the way in which Mr. Mikhailovsky depicts the *"contradiction"* he pointed out, we might think that the famous Genevese was nothing more than a lachrymose

---

* For doubters there is another extract: "J'ai assigné ce premier degré de la décadence des mœurs au premier moment de la culture des lettres dans tous les pays du monde." Lettre à M. l'abbé Raynal, *Œuvres de Rousseau*, Paris, 1820, Vol. IV, p. 43. ("I have assigned this first degree of the decadence of morals to the first moment of the art of letters in all countries of the world." Letter to the Abbé Raynal, in Rousseau's *Works*, Paris, 1820, Vol. IV, p. 43.—*Ed*.)

** See the beginning of Part II of *Discours sur l'inégalité*.

"subjective sociologist," who at best was capable of inventing a highly moral "formula of progress" for the curing of human ills. In reality Rousseau most of all hated just that kind of "formula," and stamped it underfoot whenever he had the opportunity.

Civil society arose on the ruins of primitive relations, which had proved incapable of further existence. These relations contained within themselves the embryo of their own negation. In demonstrating this proposition, Rousseau as it were was illustrating in anticipation the thought of Hegel, that every phenomenon destroys itself, becomes transformed into its own opposite. Rousseau's reflection on despotism may be considered a further illustration of this idea.

Now judge for yourself how much understanding of Hegel and Rousseau Mr. Mikhailovsky displays when he says: "Evidently dialectical thinking has absolutely nothing to do with it"—and when he naïvely imagines that Engels arbitrarily registered Rousseau in the dialectical department only on the grounds that Rousseau used the expressions "contradiction," "cycle," "return to the point from which we set out," etc.

But why did Engels quote Rousseau, and not anyone else? "Why Rousseau and not Voltaire, or not the first man in the street? Because all people, by their very nature, think dialectically...."

You're mistaken, Mr. Mikhailovsky: far from all. You for one would never be taken by Engels for a dialectician. It would be sufficient for him to read your article: "Karl Marx Before the Judgement of Mr. Y. Zhukovsky," for him to put you down without hesitation among the incorrigible metaphysicians.

On dialectical thinking Engels says: "Men thought dialectically long before they knew what dialectics was, just as they spoke prose long before the term prose existed. The law of negation of the negation, which is unconsciously operative in nature and history, and, until it has been recognized, also in our heads, was only first clearly formulated by Hegel."* As the reader sees, this refers to unconscious dialectical thinking, from which it is still a very long way to its conscious form. When we say that *"extremes meet,"* we without noticing it express a dialectical view of things; when we move we, again without suspecting it, are engaged in applied dialectics (we already said earlier that motion is the application of contradiction). But neither motion nor dialectical aphorisms are sufficient to save us *from metaphysics in the sphere of systematical thought.* On the contrary. The history of thought shows that for a long time metaphysics grew more and more strong—and necessarily had to grow strong—at the expense of primitive and naïve dialectics: "The analysis of nature into its individual parts, the grouping of the different natural processes and objects in definite classes, the study of the internal anatomy of organic bodies in their manifold forms—these were the fundamental conditions of the gigantic strides in our knowledge of nature that have been made during the last four hundred years. But this method of work has also left us as legacy the habit of observing natural objects and processes in isolation, apart from their connection with the vast whole; of observing them in repose, not in motion; as constants, not as essentially variables; in their death, not in their life. And when this way of looking at things was transferred by Bacon and Locke from natural science to philosophy, it begot the narrow, metaphysical mode of thought peculiar to the last century."**

Thus writes Engels, from whom we also learn that "the newer philosophy, on the other hand, although in it also

---
* F. Engels, *Anti-Dühring*, Moscow, 1954, p. 197.—*Ed.*
** *Ibid.*, p. 34.

dialectics had brilliant exponents (e.g., Descartes and Spinoza), had, especially through English influence, become more and more rigidly fixed in the so-called metaphysical mode of reasoning, by which also the French of the eighteenth century were almost wholly dominated, at all events in their special philosophical work. Outside philosophy in the restricted sense, the French nevertheless produced masterpieces of dialectic. We need only call to mind Diderot's *Le Neveu de Rameau* and Rousseau's *Discours sur l'origine et les fondements de l'inégalité parmi les hommes*."*

It would seem clear why Engels speaks of Rousseau, and not of Voltaire and not of the first man in the street. We dare not think that Mr. Mikhailovsky has not read that same book of Engels which he quotes, and from which he draws the "examples" which he examines. And if Mr. Mikhailovsky still pesters Engels with his "first man in the street," it remains to suppose merely that our author, here too, has recourse to the "moment" of substitution with which we are already familiar, the "moment" ... of purposeful distortion of the words of his opponent. The exploitation of such a "moment" might seem to him all the more convenient because Engels's book has not been translated into Russian, and does not exist for readers who don't know German. Here "we pick as we choose." Here again there is a new temptation, and once again *"we can't help but sin."*

Oh is it true, each god some pleasure feels
*When 'tis our honour tumbles, head over heels?***

---

* *Ibid.*, pp. 32-33.

** Let the reader not blame us for these quotations from "La Belle Helène." We recently read again Mr. Mikhailovsky's article, "Darwinism and the Operettas of Offenbach," and are still under its potent influence.

But let us take a rest from Mr. Mikhailovsky, and return to the German idealists, *an und für sich*.

We have said that the *philosophy of nature* was the weak point of these thinkers, whose main services are to be sought *in various branches of the philosophy of history*. Now we shall add that it could not be otherwise at that time. Philosophy, which called itself the science of sciences, always had in it much "*worldly content*," i.e., it always occupied itself with many purely scientific questions. But at different times its "worldly content" was different.

Thus to confine ourselves here to examples from the history of modern philosophy, in the seventeenth century the philosophers mainly occupied themselves with questions of mathematics and the natural sciences. The philosophy of the eighteenth century utilized for its purposes the scientific discoveries and theories of the preceding epoch, but itself, if it studied the natural sciences, did so perhaps only in the person of Kant. In France it was *social questions* which then came to the foreground. The same questions continued mainly to preoccupy, although from a different aspect, the philosophers of the nineteenth century. Schelling, for example, said flatly that he thought *the solution of a certain historical problem to be the most important task of transcendental philosophy*. What this problem was, we shall soon see.

If everything flows and everything changes: if every phenomenon negates itself: if there is no such useful institution as will not ultimately become harmful, changing in this way into its own opposite, it follows that it is stupid to seek for "perfect legislation" and that it is impossible to invent a structure of society which would be the *best* for all ages and peoples: everything is good in its right place and at the right time. Dialectical thinking excluded *all Utopias*.

It was all the more bound to exclude them because *"human nature,"* that allegedly constant criterion which, as we have seen, was invariably used both by the writers of the Enlightenment of the eighteenth century and the Utopian Socialists of the first half of the nineteenth century, experienced the common fate of all phenomena: it was itself recognized to be *variable*.

With this there disappeared that naïvely idealist view of history which was also maintained in equal measure both by the writers of the Enlightenment and the Utopians, and which is expressed in the words: *reason, opinions govern the world*. Of course, said Hegel, reason governs history, but in the same sense as it governs the motion of the celestial bodies, i.e., in the sense of *conformity to law*. The motion of the celestial bodies conforms to law, but they naturally have no conception of that conformity. The same applies to the historical progress of humanity. In it, without any doubt, there are particular laws at work; but this does not mean that men are conscious of them, and that therefore human reason, our knowledge, our "philosophy" are the principal factors in historical progress. The owl of Minerva begins to fly only at night. When philosophy begins tracing its grey patterns on a grey background, when men begin to study their own social order, you may say with certainty that that order has outlived its day and is preparing to yield place to a new order, the true character of which will again become clear to mankind only after it has played its historical part: Minerva's owl will once again fly out only at night.[23] It is hardly necessary to say that the periodical aerial travels of the bird of wisdom are very useful, and are even quite essential. But they explain absolutely nothing; they themselves require explanation and, probably, can be explained, because they too *conform to law*.

The recognition of conformity to law in the flights of Minerva's owl was the foundation of quite a new view of the history of mankind's intellectual development. The metaphysicians of all ages, all peoples and all tendencies, once they had acquired a certain philosophical system, considered it to be the truth and all other systems to be unquestionably false. They knew only the *abstract oppositeness* of abstract conceptions—*truth and error*. Therefore the history of thought was for them only a chaotic tangle of partly sad, partly ridiculous mistakes, whose wild dance continued right up to that blessed moment when, at last, the true system of philosophy was invented. That was how J. B. Say, that most confirmed metaphysician of all metaphysicians, regarded the *history* of his branch of knowledge. He recommended not to study it, because there was nothing in it except errors. The *dialectical* idealists looked otherwise at things. *Philosophy is the intellectual expression of its own age*, they said: every philosophy is true for its own age, and mistaken for any other.

But if reason governs the world only in the sense of *the conformity of phenomena to law*: if it is not ideas, not knowledge, not "enlightenment" that direct men in their, so to speak, social housekeeping and in their historical progress, where then is human freedom? Where is the sphere in which man "judges and chooses" without amusing himself, like a child, with some empty toy, without serving as a plaything in the hands of some external force, even though maybe it is not blind?

The old but eternally new question of *freedom and necessity* rose up before the idealists of the nineteenth century, just as it had arisen before the metaphysicians of the preceding century, and as it arose before absolutely all the philosophers who had concerned themselves with questions of *the relationship of being and thought*. Like a sphinx it said to each such thinker: *unravel me, or I shall devour your system!*

The question of freedom and necessity was precisely that problem, the solution of which *in its application to history* Schelling considered to be the greatest task of transcendental philosophy. Did the latter solve it? How did that philosophy decide it?

And note: for Schelling, as for Hegel, this question presented difficulties in its application precisely to history. From the purely *anthropological* point of view it could already be considered solved.

An explanation is necessary here, and in giving it we shall ask the reader to pay it particular attention, in view of the tremendous importance of the subject.

The magnetic needle turns to the north. This arises from the action of a particular form of matter, which itself is subordinated to certain laws: the laws of *the material world*. But for the needle the motions of that matter are unnoticed: it has not the least conception of them. It imagines that it is turning to the north quite independently of any external cause, simply because it finds it pleasant so to turn. Material *necessity presents itself* to the needle in the shape of its own *free spiritual activity*.

By this example Leibniz tried to explain his view of freedom of will. By a similar example Spinoza explains his own quite identical view.

A certain external cause has communicated to a stone a certain quantity of motion. The motion continues, of course, for a certain time even after the cause has ceased to act. This, its continuation, is *necessary according to the laws of the material world.* But imagine that the stone can think, that it is conscious of its own motion which gives it pleasure, but does not know its causes, and does not even know that there was any external reason at all for that motion. How in that event will the stone conceive of its own motion? Inevitably as the result of its own desire, its own free choice. It will say to itself: I am moving because I want to move. "The same is true of that human freedom, of which all men are so proud. Its essence amounts to the fact that men are conscious of their inclinations but do not know the external causes which give rise to those inclinations. Thus a child imagines that it is free to desire that milk which constitutes its sustenance...."

Many even present-day readers will find such an explanation "*crudely materialistic*," and they will be surprised that Leibniz, an idealist of the purest water, could give it. They will say in addition that in any case comparison is not proof, and that even less of a proof is the fantastic comparison of man with a magnetic needle or a stone. To this we shall observe that the comparison will cease to be fantastic as soon as we recall the phenomena which take place every day in *the human head*. The materialists of the eighteenth century were already pointing out the circumstance that to every willed movement in the brain there corresponds a certain motion of the brain fibres. What is a fantasy in respect of the magnetic needle or the stone becomes an unquestionable fact in relation to the brain: a movement of matter, taking place according to the fatal laws of necessity, is in fact accompanied in the brain by what is called the free operation of thought. And as for the surprise, quite natural at first sight, on account of the materialist argument of the idealist Leibniz, we must remember that, as has already been pointed out, all the consistent idealists were *monists*, i.e., in their outlook upon the world there was no place at all for that impassable abyss which separates matter from spirit in the view of the *dualists*. In the opinion of the dualists, a given aggregation of matter can prove capable of thought only in the event of a particle of spirit entering into it:

matter and spirit, in the eyes of the dualists, are two quite independent substances which have nothing in common between them. The comparison made by Leibniz will seem wild to him, for the simple reason that the magnetic needle has no soul. But imagine that you are dealing with a man who argues in this way: the needle is really something quite material. But what is matter itself? I believe it owes its existence to the spirit, and not in the sense that it *has been created by the spirit*, but in the sense that it itself is *the spirit*, only existing in another shape. That shape does not correspond to the true nature of the spirit: it is even directly opposed to that nature; but this does not prevent it from being a form of existence of the spirit—because, by its very nature, the spirit must change into its own opposite. You may be surprised by this argument as well, but you will agree at all events that the man who finds it convincing, the man who sees in matter only the "*other existence of the spirit*," will not be repelled by explanations which attribute to matter the functions of the spirit, or which make those functions intimately dependent upon the laws of matter. Such a man may accept a *materialist explanation* of spiritual phenomena and at the same time give it (whether by far-fetched reasoning or otherwise, is a different question) a strictly *idealist sense*. And that was how the German idealists acted.

The spiritual activity of man is subjected to the laws of material necessity. But this in no way destroys human freedom. The laws of material necessity themselves are nothing else than the laws of action of the spirit. *Freedom presupposes necessity, necessity passes entirely into freedom*, and therefore man's freedom in reality is incomparably wider than the dualists suppose when, trying to delimit *free* activity and *necessary* activity, they thereby tear away from the *realm of freedom* all that region (even in their opinion, a very wide region) which they set apart for *necessity*.

That was how the dialectical idealists argued. As the reader sees, they held firmly to the "magnetic needle" of Leibniz: only that needle was completely transformed, or so to speak spiritualized, in their hands.

But the transformation of the needle did not yet solve all the difficulties involved in the question of the relationship between freedom and necessity. Let us suppose that the individual is quite free in spite of his subordination to the laws of necessity, or moreover just *because* of that subordination. But in society, and consequently in history too, we are dealing not with a single individual but with a whole mass of individuals. The question arises, is not the freedom of *each* infringed by the freedom of *the rest*? I have the intention of doing this and that—for example, of realizing truth and justice in social relations. This intention has been *freely* adopted by myself, and no less *free* will be those actions of mine with the help of which I shall try to put it into effect. But my neighbours hinder me in pursuing my aim. They have revolted against my intention, just as *freely* as I adopted it. And *just as free* are their actions directed against me. How shall I overcome the obstacles which they create? Naturally, I shall argue with them, try to persuade them, and maybe even appeal to them or frighten them. But how can I know whether this will lead to anything? The French writers of the Enlightenment used to say: *la raison finira par avoir raison*. But in order that my reason should triumph, I require that my neighbours should recognize it to be *their* reason as well. And what grounds have I for hoping that this will take place? To the extent that their activity is free—and it is quite free—to the extent that, by paths unknown to me, material *necessity* has passed into *freedom*—and, by supposition, it has *completely passed into free-*

dom—to that extent the acts of my fellow-citizens evade any foretelling. I might hope to foresee them only on the condition that I could examine them as I examine all other phenomena of the world surrounding me, i.e., as the *necessary* consequences of *definite causes* which are already known, or may become known, to me. In other words, my freedom would not be an empty phrase only if *consciousness* of it could be accompanied by *understanding the reasons* which give rise to the *free* acts of my neighbours, i.e., if I could examine them from the aspect of their *necessity*. Exactly the same can my neighbours say about *my own* acts. But what does this mean? This means *that the possibility of the free (conscious) historical activity of any particular person is reduced to zero, if at the very foundation of free human actions there does not lie necessity which is accessible to the understanding of the doer*.

We saw earlier that metaphysical French materialism led, in point of fact, to *fatalism*. For in effect, if the fate of an entire people depends on one stray atom, then all we can do is to sit back, because we are absolutely incapable and never will be capable, either of foreseeing such tricks on the part of individual atoms or of preventing them.

Now we see that *idealism can lead to exactly the same fatalism*. If there is nothing of necessity in the acts of my fellow-citizens, or if they are inaccessible to my understanding from the angle of their necessity, then all I can do is to rely on beneficent Providence: my wisest plans, my most generous desires, will be broken against the quite unforeseen actions of millions of other men. In that event, as Lucretius has it, *out of everything anything may come*.

And it is interesting that the more idealism attempted to underline the aspect of freedom in *theory*, the more it would be obliged to reduce it to nothingness in the sphere of *practical activity*, where idealism would not have the strength to grapple with *chance, armed with all the powers of freedom*.

The dialectical idealists understood it perfectly well. In *their* practical philosophy *necessity was the truest and only reliable guarantee of freedom*. Even moral duty cannot reassure me as to the results of my actions, Schelling said, if the results depend only on freedom. "*In freedom there must be necessity.*"

But of what necessity, then, can there be any question in this case? I am hardly likely to derive much satisfaction from constant repetition of the thought that certain willed movements necessarily correspond to certain movements of the substance of the brain. No practical calculations can be founded on such an abstract proposition, and there is no further prospect of progress in this direction, because the head of my neighbour is not a glass beehive, and his cerebral fibres are not bees; and I could not observe their motions even if I knew with certainty—and we are still a long way from that situation—that after such and such a movement of such and such a nervous fibre there will follow such and such an intention in the soul of my fellow-citizen. Consequently we have to approach the study of the necessity of human actions from some other angle.

This is all the more necessary because the owl of Minerva flies out, as we know, only in the evening, i.e., the social relations between men do not *represent the fruit of their conscious activity*. Men consciously follow their private and personal ends. Each of them consciously strives, let us suppose, to round off his own property; yet out of the sum-total of their individual actions there arise certain social results which perhaps they did not at all desire, and certainly did not foresee. Wealthy Roman citizens bought up the lands of poor farmers. Each of them knew, of course, that thanks to his efforts such and such Tullies and Juliuses were becoming landless proletarians. But who among them foresaw that the great estates would destroy the republic, and with it Italy itself? Who among them realized, or *could* realize, the historical consequences of his acquisitiveness? None of them could, and none of them did. Yet these were the consequences—thanks to the great estates, both the republic and Italy perished.

Out of the conscious and free acts of individual men there necessarily follow consequences, unexpected for them and unforeseen by them, which affect the whole of society, i.e., which influence the sum-total of mutual relationships of the same men. *From the realm of freedom we thus pass into the realm of necessity.*

If the social consequences of the individual acts of men, arrived at unconsciously for themselves, lead to the alteration of the social system—which takes place always, though far from with equal speed—then new individual aims arise before men. Their free conscious activity necessarily takes a new form. *From the realm of necessity we again pass into the realm of freedom.*

Every necessary process is a process taking place in conformity to law. Changes in social relations which are unforeseen by men, but which of necessity appear as a result of their actions, evidently take place according to definite laws. Theoretical philosophy *has to discover them.*

The same evidently applies to changes introduced into the aims of life, into the free activity of men, by the changed social relations. In other words, *the passing of necessity into freedom also takes place according to definite laws, which can and must be discovered by theoretical philosophy.*

And once theoretical philosophy has performed this

task, it will provide quite new and unshakable foundation for *practical* philosophy. Once I know the laws of social and historical progress, I can influence the latter according to my aims, without being concerned either by the tricks of stray atoms or by the consideration that my fellow-countrymen, as beings gifted with free will, are every moment getting ready for me whole piles of the most astonishing surprises. Naturally, I shall not be in a condition to go bail for every individual fellow-countryman, especially if he belongs to the "intellectual class"; but in broad outline I shall know the direction of the forces of society, and it will remain for me only to rely on their resultant to achieve my ends.

And so if I could arrive, for example, at the blissful conviction that in Russia, unlike other countries, it is the "foundations of society" that will triumph, this will only be to the extent that I succeed in understanding the actions of the glorious "Russ" as actions which are in conformity to law, and in examining them from the standpoint of necessity and not from the standpoint of freedom. *World history is progress in the consciousness of freedom*, says Hegel, *progress which we must understand in its necessity*.

Further, however well we may have studied "the nature of man," we shall still be very far from understanding those social results which follow from the actions of individual men. Let us suppose that we have admitted, just as the economists of the old school did, that striving for profit is the chief distinguishing feature of human nature. Shall we be in a position to anticipate the forms which that striving will take? Given definite social relations, known to us—yes; but these given, definite, known social relations will themselves change under the pressure of "human nature," under the influence of the acquisitive activity of our fellow-citizens. In what direction will they change? This will be just as little known to us as that new direction which the striving for profit itself will take, in the new and changed social relations. We shall find ourselves in quite the same situation if, together with the German "Katheder Sozialisten," we begin asserting that the nature of man is not exhausted by the mere striving for profit, but that he also has a "social sense" (Gemeinsinn). This will be a new song to an old tune. In order to emerge from ignorance, covered up by more or less learned terminology, we have to pass on from the study of the *nature of man* to the study of the *nature of social relations*; we have to understand those relations as essential process conforming to law. And this brings us back to the question: *what underlies, what determines, the nature of social relations?*

We saw that neither the materialists of last century nor the Utopian Socialists gave a satisfactory reply to this question. Did the dialectical idealists succeed in answering it?

No, they too did not succeed, and they did not succeed precisely because they were *idealists*. In order to grasp their view, let us recall the argument referred to earlier about what depends on what—the constitution on manners, or manners on the constitution. Hegel rightly remarked on this discussion that the question had been put here quite wrongly, as in reality, although the manners of a particular people undoubtedly influence its constitution, and its constitution its manners, nevertheless both of them represent the result of some *"third"* or special force, which creates both the manners influencing the constitution and the constitution influencing manners. But what, according to Hegel, is this special force, this ultimate foundation on which stand both the nature of men and the nature of social relations? This force is "Notion" or, what is the same thing, the "Idea," the realization of which is the whole history of the particular people concerned. *Every people puts into effect its own particular idea*, and every particular idea of each individual people represents a stage in the development of the *Absolute Idea*. History thus turns out to be, as it were, applied logic: to explain a particular historical epoch means showing to what stage of the logical development of the Absolute Idea it corresponds. But what, then, is this "Absolute Idea"? Nothing else than the personification of our own logical process. Here is what a man says of it who himself passed through a thorough grounding in the school of idealism, and himself was passionately devoted to it, but noticed very soon wherein lies the radical defect of this tendency in philosophy:

"If from real apples, pears, strawberries and almonds, I form the general idea '*Fruit*'; if I go further and imagine that my abstract idea 'Fruit,' derived from real fruit, is an entity existing outside me, is indeed the true essence of the pear, apple, etc.; then, in the language of speculative philosophy, I am declaring that 'Fruit' is the *substance* of the pear, the apple, the almond, etc. I am saying, therefore, that to be a pear is not essential to the pear, that to be an apple is not essential to the apple; that what is essential to these things is ... the essence that I have abstracted from them and then foisted on to them, the essence of my idea—'Fruit.' I therefore declare apples, pears, almonds, etc., to be mere forms of existence, *modi*, of 'Fruit.' My finite understanding, supported by my senses, does, of course, distinguish an apple from a pear and a pear from an almond; but my speculative reason declares these sensuous differences to be unessential, indifferent. It sees in the apple the same as in the pear, and in the pear the same as in the almond, namely 'Fruit.' Particular real fruits are no more than *semblances* whose true essence is 'the Substance'—'Fruit.'

"By this method one attains to no particular wealth of definition. The mineralogist whose whole science consisted in the statement that all minerals are really 'Mineral' would be a mineralogist only in his imagination...

"Having reduced the different real fruits to the one fruit of abstraction—'Fruit,' speculative philosophy must, in order to attain some appearance of real content, try somehow to find its way back from 'Fruit,' from 'Substance,' to the different profane real fruits, the pear, the apple, the almond, etc. It is as hard to produce real fruits from the abstract idea 'Fruit' as it is easy to produce this abstract idea from real fruits. Indeed, it is impossible to arrive at the opposite of an abstraction without relinquishing the abstraction.

"The speculative philosopher therefore relinquishes the abstraction 'Fruit,' but in a speculative, mystical fashion.... Thus he rises above his abstraction only in appearance. He argues like this:

" 'If apples, pears, almonds and strawberries are really nothing but *Substance*, *Fruit*, the question arises: Why does *Fruit* manifest itself to me sometimes as an apple, sometimes as a pear, sometimes as an almond? Whence this *appearance of diversity* which so strikingly contradicts my speculative conception of *Unity*, *Substance*, *Fruit*?

" 'This,' answers the speculative philosopher, 'is because *Fruit* is not dead, undifferentiated, motionless, but living, self-differentiating, moving. The diversity of profane fruits is significant not only to my sensuous understanding, but also to *Fruit* itself and to speculative reason. The different profane fruits are different manifestations of the life of the one *Fruit*.... In the apple, *Fruit* gives itself an apple-like existence, in the pear, a pear-like existence.... *Fruit* presents itself as a pear, *Fruit* presents itself as an apple, *Fruit* presents itself as an almond, and the differences which distinguish apples, pears and almonds from one another are the self-differentiations of *Fruit* making the particular fruits subordinate members of the life-process of *Fruit.*' "*

All this is very biting, but at the same time undoubtedly just. By personifying our own process of thought in the shape of an Absolute Idea, and by seeking in this Idea the explanation of all phenomena, idealism thereby led itself into a blind alley, out of which it could emerge only by abandoning the "Idea," i.e., *by saying good-bye to idealism.* Here, for example: do the following words of Schelling explain to you to any extent the nature of magnetism? "Magnetism is a general act of animation, the embedding of Unity into Multitude, Concept into Diversity? That same invasion of the subjective into the objective, which in the ideal ... is self-consciousness, is here expressed in being." These words don't explain anything at all, do they? Just as unsatisfactory are similar explanations in the sphere of *history*. Why did Greece fall? Because the idea which constituted the principle of Greek life, the centre of the Greek spirit (*the Idea of the Beautiful*) could be only a very short-lived phase in the development of the world spirit. Replies of this kind only repeat the question in a positive and, moreover, a pompous form, as it were on stilts. Hegel, who gave the explanation of the fall of Greece which has just been quoted, seems himself to have felt this, and hastens to supplement his idealist explanation by a reference to the economic reality of ancient Greece. He says: "*Lacedaemon fell mainly on account of inequality of property.*" And he acts in this way not only where Greece is concerned. This, one may say, is his invariable approach in the

---

* The quotation is from Marx, *The Holy Family* (*Gesamtausgabe*, Abt. I, Bd. 3, S. 228-29).—*Tr.*

philosophy of history: first a few vague references to the qualities of the Absolute Idea, and then much more extensive and, of course, much more convincing indications of the character and development of the property relations of the people to whom he is referring. Strictly speaking, in explanations of this latter kind there's really nothing at all idealist left and, in having recourse to them, Hegel—who used to say that *"idealism proves to be the truth of materialism"*—was signing a certificate about the poverty of idealism, tacitly admitting as it were that in essence matters stand in exactly the opposite way, and that *materialism proves to be the truth of idealism*.

However, the *materialism* which Hegel here approached was a quite undeveloped, embryonic materialism, and immediately passed once more into *idealism* as soon as he found it necessary to explain whence came these or those particular property relations. True, here also it would happen that Hegel frequently expressed quite materialist views. But as a rule he regarded property relations as the realization of conceptions of Right which developed by their own internal force.

And so what have we learned about the dialectical idealists?

They abandoned the standpoint of human nature and, thanks to this, got rid of the utopian view of social phenomena: they began to examine social life as a necessary process, with its own laws. But in a roundabout fashion, by personifying the process of our logical reason (i.e., one of the sides of *human nature*), they returned to the same unsatisfactory point of view, and *therefore the true nature of social relations remained incomprehensible for them.*

Now once again a little digression into the sphere of our own domestic, Russian philosophy.

Mr. Mikhailovsky has heard from Mr. Filippov, who

in his turn has heard from the American writer Frazer, that all the philosophy of Hegel amounts to "*galvanic mysticism.*" What we have said already of the aims which the idealist German philosophy set before itself will be enough to show the reader how nonsensical is Frazer's opinion. Messrs. Filippov and Mikhailovsky themselves feel that their American has gone too far: "It is sufficient to recall the successive course and influence (on Hegel) of preceding metaphysics, beginning with the ancients, with Heraclitus..." says Mr. Mikhailovsky, adding immediately, however: "Nevertheless the remarks of Frazer are in the highest degree interesting, and undoubtedly contain a certain element of truth." We must admit, although we cannot but recognize.... Shchedrin long ago held up this "formula" to ridicule. But what would you have his former assistant, Mr. Mikhailovsky,[24] do, when he has undertaken to interpret to the "uninitiated" a philosopher whom he knows only by hearsay? Willy-nilly you will go on repeating, with the learned air of a scholar, phrases which say nothing....

Let us however recall the "successive course" of development of German idealism. "The experiments in galvanism produce an impression on all the thinking people of Europe, including the then young German philosopher Hegel," says Mr. Mikhailovsky. "Hegel creates a colossal metaphysical system, thundering throughout the world, so that there's no getting away from it even on the banks of the River Moskva." ... The case is represented here as though Hegel had become infected with "galvanic mysticism" direct from the physicists. But Hegel's system represents only the further development of the views of Schelling: clearly the infection must have previously influenced the latter. So it did, reassuringly replies Mr. Mikhailovsky, or Mr. Filippov, or Frazer: "Schelling, and particularly some doctors who had been his pupils, carried the teaching of polarity to the last extreme." Very good. But the predecessor of Schelling was, as is known, Fichte. How did the galvanic infection affect him? Mr. Mikhailovsky says nothing about this: probably he thinks that it had no influence at all. And he is quite right if he really does think so; in order to be convinced of this, it is sufficient to read one of the first philosophical works of Fichte, *Grundlage der gesammten Wissenschaftslehre*, Leipzig, 1794. In this work no microscope will discover the influence of "galvanism"; yet there, too, appears that same notorious "triad" which, in the opinion of Mr. Mikhailovsky, constitutes the main distinguishing feature of the Hegelian philosophy, and the genealogy of which Frazer, allegedly with "a certain element of truth," traces from the "experiments of Galvani and Volta." ... We must admit that all this is very strange, although we cannot but recognize that nevertheless Hegel, etc., etc.

The reader knows already what were Schelling's views on magnetism. The defect of German idealism lay not at all in its being founded allegedly on an excessive and unjustified captivation (in a mystical form) by the scientific discoveries of its age, but, on the contrary, in its attempt to explain all the phenomena of nature and history with the help of the process of thought which it had personified.

In conclusion, one comforting piece of news. Mr. Mikhailovsky has discovered that "metaphysics and capitalism are most intimately connected; that, to use the language of economic materialism, metaphysics is an essential component part of the 'super-structure' over the capitalist form of production, although at the same time capital swallows up and adapts to itself all the technical advances of science, founded on experiment and observation, which is hostile to metaphysics." Mr. Mikhailovsky promises to discuss "this curious contradiction" some other time. Mr. Mikhailovsky's examination will be "curious" indeed! Just think: what he calls metaphysics underwent a brilliant development both in ancient Greece and in Germany of the eighteenth and the first half of the nineteenth centuries. Up to now it was thought that ancient Greece was not a capitalist country at all, and in Germany, at the time indicated, capitalism had only just begun to develop. Mr. Mikhailovsky's research will demonstrate that from the point of view of *"subjective sociology"* this is quite untrue, and that precisely ancient Greece and Germany in the days of Fichte and Hegel were classical countries of capitalism. You see now why this is important. Let our author, then, hasten to publish his remarkable discovery. Sing, my dear, don't be shy!

Chapter V

MODERN MATERIALISM

The bankruptcy of the idealist point of view in explaining the phenomena of nature and of social development was bound to force, and really did force, *thinking* people (i.e., *not* eclectics, *not* dualists) to return to the materialist view of the world. But the new materialism could no longer be a simple repetition of the teachings of the French materialist of the end of the eighteenth century. Materialism rose again enriched by all the acquisitions of idealism. The most important of these acquisitions was the *dialectical method,* the examination of phenomena in their development, in their origin and destruction. The genius who represented this new direction of thought was Karl Marx.

Marx was not the first to revolt against idealism. The banner of revolt was raised by Ludwig Feuerbach. Then, a little later than Feuerbach, the Bauer brothers appeared on the literary scene: their views merit particular attention on the part of the present-day Russian reader.

The views of the Bauers were a reaction against Hegel's idealism. Nevertheless, they themselves were saturated through and through with a very superficial, one-sided and eclectic idealism.

We have seen that the great German idealists did not succeed in understanding the real nature or discovering the real basis of social relations. They saw in social development a necessary process, conforming to law, and in this respect they were quite right. But when it was a question of the prime mover of historical development, they turned to the Absolute Idea, the qualities of which were to give the ultimate and most profound explanation of that process. This constituted the weak side of idealism, against which accordingly a philosophical revolution first broke out. The extreme Left-wing of the Hegelian school revolted with determination against the "Absolute Idea."

The Absolute Idea exists (if it exists at all) outside time and space and, in any case, outside the head of each individual man. Reproducing in its historical development the course of the logical development of the Absolute Idea, mankind obeys a force alien to itself, standing outside itself. In revolting against the Absolute Idea, the young Hegelians revolted first of all in the name of the independent activity of man, in the name of ultimate human reason.

"Speculative philosophy," wrote Edgar Bauer, "is very mistaken when it speaks of reason as some abstract, absolute force.... Reason is not an objective abstract force, in relation to which man represents only something subjective, accidental, passing; no, the dominating force is man himself, his consciousness of self, and reason is only the strength of that consciousness. Consequently there is no Absolute Reason, but there is only reason which changes eternally with the development of consciousness of self: it does not exist at all in its final form, it is eternally changing."*

And so there is no Absolute Idea, there is no abstract

---

* Edgar Bauer, *Der Streit der Kritik mit Kirche und Staat*, Berne, 1844, p. 184.

Reason, but there is only man's consciousness, the ultimate and eternally changing human reason. This is quite true; against this even Mr. Mikhailovsky would not argue, although as we already know he can find anything "debatable" ... with more or less doubtful success. But, strangely enough, the more we underline this correct thought, the more difficult becomes our position. The old German idealists adapted the conformity to law of every process in nature and in history to the Absolute Idea. The question arises, to what will we adapt this conformity to law when we have destroyed its carrier, the Absolute Idea? Let us suppose that in relation to nature a satisfactory reply can be given in a few words: we adapt it to the qualities of matter. But in relation to history things are far from being as simple: the dominating force in history turns out to be man's consciousness of self, eternally changing ultimate human reason. Is there any conformity to law in the development of this reason? Edgar Bauer would naturally have replied in the affirmative, because for him man, and consequently his reason, were not at all something accidental, as we have seen. But if you had asked the same Bauer to explain to you his conception of conformity to law in the development of human reason: if you had asked him, for example, why in a particular historical epoch reason developed in this way, and in another epoch in that way, practically speaking you would have received no reply from him. He would have told you that "eternally developing human reason creates social forms," that "historical reason is the motive force of world history" and that consequently every particular social order proves to be obsolete as soon as reason makes a new step in its development.* But all these and similar assurances would not be a reply to the question,

---

* *Loc. cit.*, p. 185.

but rather a wandering around the question of why human reason takes new steps in its development, and why it takes them in this direction and not in that. Obliged by you to deal precisely with this question, E. Bauer would have hastily put it aside with some meaningless reference to the qualities of the ultimate, eternally changing human reason, just as the old idealists confined themselves to a reference to the qualities of the Absolute Idea.

To treat reason as the motive force of world history, and to explain its development by some kind of special, immanent, internal qualities meant to transform it into something unconditional—or, in other words, to resurrect in a new form that same Absolute Idea which they had just proclaimed to be buried for ever. The most important defect of this resurrected Absolute Idea was the circumstance that it peacefully co-existed with the most absolute dualism or, to be more precise, even unquestionably presupposed it. As the processes of nature were not conditioned by ultimate, eternally changing human reason, two forces turned out to be in existence: in nature—matter, in history—human reason. And there was no bridge connecting the motion of matter with the development of reason, the realm of necessity with the realm of freedom. That was why we said that the views of Bauer were saturated through and through with a very superficial, one-sided and eclectical idealism.

"Opinion governs the world"—thus declared the writers of the French Enlightenment. Thus also spoke, as we see, the Bauer brothers when they revolted against Hegelian idealism. But if opinion governs the world, then the prime movers of history are those men whose thought criticizes the old and creates the new opinions. The Bauer brothers did in fact think so. The essence of the historical process reduced itself, in their view, to the refashioning by the "critical spirit" of the existing store of opinions, and of the forms of life in society conditioned by that store. These views of the Bauers were imported in their entirety into Russian literature by the author of the *Historical Letters*[25]—who, by the way, spoke not of the critical "spirit" but of critical "thought," because to speak of the spirit was prohibited by *Sovremennik*.

Once having imagined himself to be the main architect, the Demiurge of history, the "critically thinking" man thereby separates off himself and those like him into a special, higher variety of the human race. This higher variety is contrasted to the *mass*, foreign to critical thought, and capable only of playing the part of clay in the creative hands of "critically thinking" personalities. "*Heroes*" are contrasted to the "*crowd*." However much the hero loves the crowd, however filled he may be with sympathy for its age-long needs and its continuous sufferings, he cannot but look down on it from above, he cannot but realize that everything depends upon him, the hero, while the crowd is a mass alien to every creative element, something in the nature of a vast quantity of ciphers, which acquire some positive significance only in the event of a kind, "critically thinking" entity condescendingly taking its place at their head. The eclectic idealism of the Bauer brothers was the basis of the terrible, and one may say repulsive, self-conceit of the "critically thinking" German "intellectuals" of the 1840s; today, through its Russian supporters, it is breeding the same defect in the intelligentsia of Russia. The merciless enemy and accuser of this self-conceit was Marx, to whom we shall now proceed.

Marx said that the contrasting of "critically thinking" personalities with the "mass" was nothing more than a caricature of the Hegelian view of history: a view which in its turn was only the speculative consequence of the old doctrine of the oppositeness of Spirit and Matter. "Already in Hegel the Absolute Spirit of history* treats the mass as material and finds its true expression only in *philosophy*. But with Hegel the philosopher is only the organ through which the creator of history, the Absolute Spirit, arrives at self-consciousness by retrospection after the movement *has ended*. The participation of the philosopher in history is reduced to this retrospective consciousness, for the real movement is accomplished by the Absolute Spirit unconsciously,** so that the philosopher appears post festum.

"Hegel is doubly inconsistent: first because while declaring that philosophy constitutes the Absolute Spirit's existence he refuses to recognize the real philosophical individual as the Absolute Spirit; secondly because according to him the Absolute Spirit makes history only *in appearance*. For as the Absolute Spirit becomes conscious of itself as the creative World Spirit only in the philosopher and post festum, its manufacture of history exists only in the opinion and conception of the philosopher, i.e., only in the speculative imagination. Mr. Bruno Bauer*** eliminates Hegel's inconsistency.

"First, he proclaims Criticism to be the Absolute Spirit and himself to be Criticism. Just as the element of criticism is banished from the mass, so the element of the mass is banished from Criticism. Therefore Criticism sees itself embodied not in a *mass*, but in a small *handful* of chosen men, exclusively in Mr. Bauer and his followers.

---

* The same as the Absolute Idea.—*G.P.*

** The reader will not have forgotten the expression of Hegel quoted earlier: the owl of Minerva begins to fly only in the evening. —*G.P.*

*** Bruno Bauer was the elder brother of Edgar, mentioned earlier, and the author of a book famous in its day, *Kritik der evangelischen Geschichte der Synoptiker*.

"Mr. Bauer further does away with Hegel's other inconsistency. No longer, like the Hegelian spirit, does he make history post festum and in imagination. He *consciously* plays the part of the World Spirit in opposition to the mass of the rest of mankind; he enters in the present into a *dramatic* relation with that mass; he invents and carries out history with a purpose and after mature meditation.

"On one side stands the Mass, that *material*, passive, dull and unhistorical element of history. On the other side stand The Spirit, Criticism, Mr. Bruno and Co., as the active element from which arises all *historical* action. The act of social transformation is reduced to the *brain work* of Critical Criticism."*

These lines produce a strange illusion: it seems as though they were written, not fifty years ago, but some month or so ago, and are directed, not against the German Left Hegelians, but against the Russian "subjective" sociologists. The illusion becomes still stronger when we read the following extract from an article of Engels:

"Self-sufficient Criticism, complete and perfect in itself, naturally must not recognize history as it really took place, for that would mean recognizing the base mass in all its mass massiness, whereas the problem is to redeem the mass from massiness. History is therefore liberated from its massiness, and Criticism, which has a

---

* F. Engels und K. Marx, *Die heilige Familie, oder Kritik der Kritischen Kritik. Gegen Bruno Bauer und Consorten.* Frankfurt am Main, 1845, pp. 126-28. This book is a collection of articles by Engels and Marx directed against various opinions expressed in the "Critical Criticism." The passage quoted is taken from an article by Marx against an article by Bruno Bauer. It was also from Marx that the passage quoted in the preceding chapter (see pp. 137-39.—*Ed.*) was taken.

[The passage is in chapter 6—by Marx—of *The Holy Family* (*Gesamtausgabe*, Abt. I, Bd. 3, SS. 257-58).—*Tr.*]

free attitude to its object, calls to history, saying: 'You ought to have happened in such and such a way!' All the laws of criticism have retrospective force: history behaved quite differently before the decrees of Criticism than it did after them. Hence mass history, the so-called *real* history, deviates considerably from *critical* history...."*

Who is referred to in this passage? Is it the German writers of the 40s, or some of our contemporary "sociologists," who gravely discourse on the theme that the Catholic sees the course of historical events in one way, the Protestant in another, the monarchist in a third, the republican in a fourth: and that therefore a good subjective person not only can, but must, invent for himself, for his own spiritual use, such a history as would fully correspond to the best of ideals? Did Engels really foresee our Russian stupidities? Not at all! Naturally, he did not even dream of them, and if his irony, half a century later, fits our subjective thinkers like a glove, this is to be explained by the simple fact that our subjective nonsense has absolutely nothing original in it: it represents nothing more than a cheap Suzdal[26] print from a caricature of that same "Hegelianism" against which it wars so unsuccessfully....

From the point of view of "Critical Criticism," all great historical conflicts amounted to the conflict of *ideas*. Marx observes that *ideas* "were worsted" every time they did not coincide with the real economic interests of that social stratum which at the particular time was the bearer of historical progress. It is only the understanding of those interests that can give the key to understanding the true course of historical development.

We already know that the French writers of the Enlightenment themselves did not close their eyes to interests,

---

* *Ibid.*, S. 183.

and that they too were not averse to turning to them for an explanation of the given condition of a given society. But their view of the decisive importance of *interests* was merely a variation of the "formula" that opinions govern the world: according to them, the interests themselves depend on men's opinions, and change with changes in the latter. *Such* an interpretation of the significance of interests represents the triumph of idealism in its application to history. It leaves far behind even German dialectical idealism, according to the sense of which men discover new material interests every time the Absolute Idea finds it necessary to take a new step in its logical development. Marx understands the significance of material interests quite otherwise.

To the ordinary Russian reader the historical theory of Marx seems some kind of disgraceful libel on the human race. G. I. Uspensky,[27] if we are not mistaken, in his *Ruin*, has an old woman, the wife of some official who even in her death-bed delirium obstinately goes on repeating the shameful rule by which she was guided all her life: "Aim at the pocket, the pocket!" The Russian intelligentsia naïvely imagines that Marx attributes this base rule to all mankind: that he asserts that, whatever the sons of man have busied themselves with, they have always, exclusively and consciously "*aimed at the pocket.*" The selfless Russian "intellectual" naturally finds such a view just as "disagreeable" as the theory of Darwin is "disagreeable" for some official dame who imagines that the whole sense of this theory amounts to the outrageous proposition that she, forsooth, a most respectable official's lady, is nothing more than a monkey dressed up in a bonnet. In reality Marx slanders the "intellectuals" just as little as Darwin does official dames.

In order to understand the historical views of Marx, we must recall the conclusions at which philosophy and social and historical science had arrived in the period immediately preceding his appearance. The French historians of the Restoration came as we know to the conclusion that "civil conditions," "property relations," constitute the basic foundation of the entire social order. We know also that the same conclusion was reached, in the person of Hegel, by idealist German philosophy—against its will, against its spirit, simply on account of the inadequacy and bankruptcy of the idealist explanation of history. Marx, who took over all the results of the scientific knowledge and philosophic thought of his age, completely agrees with the French historians and Hegel about the conclusion just mentioned. I became convinced, he said, that "legal relations as well as forms of state are to be grasped neither from themselves nor from the so-called general development of the human mind, but rather have their roots in the material conditions of life, the sum-total of which Hegel, following the example of the Englishmen and Frenchmen of the eighteenth century, combines under the name of 'civil society,' that, however, the anatomy of civil society is to be sought in political economy."*

But on what does the economy of the given society depend? Neither the French historians, nor the Utopian Socialists, nor Hegel have been able to reply to this at all satisfactorily. All of them, directly or indirectly, referred to human nature. The great scientific service rendered by Marx lies in this, that he approached the question from the diametrically opposite side, and that he regarded man's nature itself as the eternally changing result of historical progress, the cause of which lies *outside* man. In order to exist, man must support his organism, borrowing the substances he requires from the *external na-*

───────────
* K. Marx and F. Engels, *Selected Works*, Vol. I, Moscow, 1955, p. 362.—*Ed.*

ture surrounding him. This borrowing presupposes a certain action of man on *that* external nature. But, "acting on the external world, he changes his own nature." In these few words is contained the essence of the whole historical theory of Marx, although naturally, taken by themselves, they do not provide an adequate understanding of it, and require explanations.

Franklin called man "a tool-making animal." The use and production of tools in fact does constitute the distinguishing feature of man. Darwin contests the opinion that only man is capable of the use of tools, and gives many examples which show that in an embryonic form their use is characteristic for many mammals. And he naturally is quite right from his point of view, i.e., in the sense that in that notorious "human nature" there is not a single feature which is not to be found in some other variety of animal, and that therefore there is absolutely no foundation for considering man to be some special being and separating him off into a special "kingdom." But it must not be forgotten that *quantitative differences pass into qualitative.* What exists as an *embryo* in one species of animal can become the *distinguishing feature* of another species of animal. This particularly applies to the use of tools. An elephant breaks off branches and uses them to brush away flies. This is interesting and instructive. But in the history of the evolution of the species *"elephant"* the use of branches in the fight against flies probably played no essential part; elephants did not become elephants because their more or less elephant-like ancestors brushed off flies with branches. It is quite otherwise with man.*

---

* "So thoroughly is the use of tools the exclusive attribute of man that the discovery of a single artificially-shaped flint in the drift or cave-breccia is deemed proof enough that man has been there." Daniel Wilson, *Prehistoric Man*, Vol. I, pp. 151-52, London, 1876.

The whole existence of the Australian savage depends on his boomerang, just as the whole existence of modern Britain depends on her machines. Take away from the Australian his boomerang, make him a tiller of the soil, and he of necessity will change all his mode of life, all his habits, all his manner of thinking, all his "nature."

We have said: make him *a tiller of the soil*. From the example of agriculture it can clearly be seen that the process of the productive action of man on nature presupposes not only the implements of labour. The implements of labour constitute only part of the means necessary for production. Therefore it will be more exact to speak, not of the development of the *implements of labour*, but more generally of the development of the *means of production*, the *productive forces*—although it is quite certain that the most important part in this development belongs, or at least belonged up to the present day (until important *chemical* industries appeared) precisely to the *implements of labour*.

In the implements of labour man acquires new organs, as it were, which change his anatomical structure. From the time that he rose to the level of using them, he has given quite a new aspect to the history of his development. Previously, as with all the other animals, it amounted to changes in his natural organs. Since that time it has become first of all *the history of the perfecting of his artificial organs, the growth of his productive forces.*

Man—*the tool-making animal*—is at the same time a *social animal*, originating in ancestors who for many generations lived in more or less large herds. For us it is not important at this point why our ancestors began to live in herds—the *zoologists* have to ascertain, and are ascertaining, this—but from the point of view of the philosophy of history it is extremely important to note that from the time the artificial organs of man began to play a decisive part in his existence, his social life itself began to change, in accordance with the course of development of his productive forces.

"In production, men not only act on nature but also on one another. They produce only by co-operating in a certain way and mutually exchanging their activities. In order to produce, they enter into definite connections and relations with one another and only within these social connections and relations does their action on nature, does production, take place."*

The artificial organs, the implements of labour, thus turn out to be organs not so much of individual as of *social man*. That is why every essential change in them brings about changes in the social structure.

"These social relations into which the producers enter with one another, the conditions under which they exchange their activities and participate in the whole act of production, will naturally vary according to the character of the means of production. With the invention of a new instrument of warfare, fire-arms, the whole internal organization of the army necessarily changed; the relationships within which individuals can constitute an army and act as an army were transformed and the relations of different armies to one another also changed. Thus the social relations within which individuals produce, the social relations of production, change, are transformed, with the change and development of the material means of production, the productive forces. The relations of production in their totality constitute what are called the social relations, society, and, specifically, a society at

---

* K. Marx and F. Engels, *Selected Works*, Vol. I, Moscow, 1955, p. 89.—*Ed*.

a definite stage of historical development, a society with a peculiar, distinctive character. Ancient society, feudal society, bourgeois society are such totalities of production relations, each of which at the same time denotes a special stage of development, in the history of mankind."*

It is hardly necessary to add that the earlier stages of human development represent also no less distinct totalities of production relations. It is equally unnecessary to repeat that, at these earlier stages too, the state of the productive forces had a decisive influence on the social relations of men.

At this point we must pause in order to examine some, at first sight fairly convincing, objections.

The first is as follows.

No one contests the great importance of the implements of labour, the vast role of the forces of production in the historical progress of mankind—the Marxists are often told—but it was man who invented the implements of labour and made use of them in his work. You yourselves recognize that their use presupposes a comparatively very high degree of intellectual development. Every new step forward in the perfecting of the implements of labour requires new efforts of the human intellect. Efforts of the intellect are the *cause*, and the development of the productive forces the *consequence*. Therefore the intellect is the prime mover of historical progress, which means that those men were right who asserted that opinions govern the world, i.e., that human reason is the governing element.

Nothing is more natural than such an observation, but this does not prevent it from being groundless.

Undoubtedly the use of the implements of labour presupposes a high development of the intellect in the animal

---
* *Ibid.*, pp. 89-90.—*Ed.*

man. But see the reasons which modern natural science gives as an explanation for this development.

"Man could not have attained his present dominant position in the world without the use of his hands, which are so admirably adapted to act in obedience to his will," says Darwin.* This is not a new idea: it was previously expressed by Helvetius. But Helvetius, who was never able to take his stand firmly on the view-point of evolution, was not able to clothe his own thought in a more or less convincing form. Darwin put forward in its defence an entire arsenal of arguments, and although they all naturally have a purely hypothetical character, still in their sum-total they are sufficiently convincing. What does Darwin say, then? Whence did quasi-man get his present, quite human hands, which have exercised such a remarkable influence in promoting the successes of his "intellect"? Probably they were formed in virtue of certain peculiarities of the *geographical environment* which made useful a physiological division of labour between the front and rear limbs. The successes of "intellect" appeared as the *remote consequence* of this division and—again in favourable external circumstances—became in their turn the *immediate reason* for the appearance of man's artificial organs, the use of tools. These new artificial organs rendered new services to his intellectual development, and the successes of "intellect" again reflected themselves upon the organs. We have before us a long process in which cause and consequence are constantly alternating. But it would be a mistake to examine this process from the standpoint of *simple interaction*. In order that man should take advantage of the successes already achieved by his "intellect" to perfect his artificial implements, i.e., *to increase his power over nature*, he had to be in a *certain*

---

* *The Descent of Man*, London, 1875, p. 51.—*Tr.*

geographical environment, capable of providing him with (1) materials necessary for that perfecting, (2) the object the working up of which would presuppose perfected implements. Where there were no metals, the intellect of social man alone could not in any circumstances lead him beyond the boundaries of the "polished stone period"; and in just the same way in order to pass on to the pastoral and agricultural life he required certain fauna and flora, without which "intellect would have remained motionless." But even this is not all. The intellectual development of primitive societies was bound to proceed the more quickly, the greater were the mutual connections between them, and these connections were, of course, the more frequent, the more varied were the geographical conditions of the localities which they inhabited, i.e., the less similar, consequently, were the products of one locality and those of another.* Lastly, all know how important in this respect are the natural means of communication. It was already Hegel who said that mountains divide men, while seas and rivers bring them together.**

---

* In the well-known book of von Martius, on the primitive inhabitants of Brazil, several interesting examples can be found which show how important are what seem to be the most insignificant peculiarities of various localities, in developing mutual relations between their inhabitants.

** However, it must be observed about the sea that it does not always bring men together. Ratzel (*Anthropo-Geographie*, Stuttgart, 1882, p. 92) justly remarks that at a certain low stage of development the sea is an *absolute* frontier, i.e., it renders impossible any relations whatsoever between the peoples it divides. For their part, relations which are made possible originally only by the characteristics of geographical environment leave their impression on the physiognomy of primitive tribes. Islanders are markedly distinguished from those dwelling on continents.

"Die Bevölkerungen der Inseln sind in einigen Fällen völlig andere als die des nächst gelegenen Festlandes oder der nächsten

Geographical environment exercises no less decisive an influence on the fate also of larger societies, the fate of states arising on the ruins of the primitive clan organizations. "It is not the mere fertility of the soil, but the differentiation of the soil, the variety of its natural products, the changes of the seasons, which form the physical basis for the social division of labour, and which, by changes in the natural surroundings, spur man on to the multiplication of his wants, his capabilities, his means and modes of labour. It is the necessity of bringing a natural force under the control of society, of economizing, of appropriating or subduing it on a large scale by the work of man's hand, that first plays the decisive part in the history of industry. Examples are, the irrigation works in Egypt, Lombardy, Holland, or in India and Persia where irrigation, by means of artificial canals, not only supplies the soil with the water indispensable to it, but also carries down to it, in the shape of sediment from the hills, mineral fertilizers. The secret of the flourishing state of industry in Spain and Sicily under the dominion of the Arabs lay in their irrigation works."*

---

grösseren Insel; aber auch wo sie ursprünglich derselben Rasse oder Völkergruppe angehören, sind sie immer weit von der selben verschieden; und zwar, kann man hinzusetzen, in der Regel weiter als die entsprechenden festländischen Abzweigungen dieser Rasse oder Gruppe untereinander" (Ratzel, *loc. cit.*, S. 96). ("The inhabitants of islands are in some cases totally different from those of the nearest mainland or the nearest larger island; but even where they originally belonged to the same race or group of peoples, they are always widely different from the latter; and indeed one can add, as a rule, that they differ more widely than do the corresponding branches of this race or group on the mainland among themselves.") (P. 96.—*Ed.*) Here is repeated the same law as in the formation of the species and varieties of animals.

* Marx, Das Kapital. 3. Aufl. S. 524-526. In a footnote Marx adds: "One of the material bases of the power of the State over the small disconnected producing organisms in India, was the

Thus *only thanks to certain particular qualities of the geographical environment could our anthropomorphic ancestors rise to that height of intellectual development which was necessary to transform them into tool-making animals. And in just the same way only certain peculiarities of the same environment could provide the scope for using in practice and constantly perfecting this new capacity of "tool-making."** In the historical process of the

---

regulation of the water supply. The Mohammedan rulers of India understood this better than their English successors." We may compare with the opinion of Marx, quoted above, the opinion of a most recent investigator: "Unter dem, was die lebende Natur dem Menschen an Gaben bietet, ist nicht der Reichtum an Stoffen, sondern der an Kräften oder, besser gesagt, Kräfteanregungen am höchsten zu schätzen" (Ratzel, *loc. cit.*, S. 343).

["Among the gifts which living Nature offers to men, that to be prized most highly is not material wealth, but energy, or rather the means of producing energy" (Ratzel, *loc. cit.*, p. 343).]

* *Editor's Note*: Plekhanov's arguments about the significance of the geographical environment in social progress (see pp. 162-63, 270-71 of this edition) cannot be regarded as absolutely correct. In his later works Plekhanov even speaks of the determining influence of the geographical environment on the entire course of social progress.

While pointing out quite rightly that the geographical environment influences man through social relations, that the latter, once they have arisen, develop in conformity with their inner laws, Plekhanov is mistaken when he says that social structure "is determined in the long run by the characteristics of the geographical environment" (p. 271) and that "the capacity of man for tool-making must be regarded first of all as a *constant magnitude*, while the surrounding external conditions for the use of this capacity in practice have to be regarded as a *constantly varying magnitude*" (p. 162).

Geographical environment is unquestionably one of the constant and indispensable conditions of development of society and, of course, influences the development of society, accelerates or retards its development. But its influence is not the *determining* influence, inasmuch as the changes and development of society proceed at an incomparably faster rate than the changes and development of

development of productive forces, the capacity of man for "tool-making" must be regarded first of all as a *constant magnitude*, while the surrounding external conditions for the use of this capacity in practice have to be regarded as a *constantly varying magnitude*.*

---

geographical environment. In the space of three thousand years three different social systems have been successively superseded in Europe: the primitive communal system, the slave system and the feudal system. In the eastern part of Europe, in the U.S.S.R., even four social systems have been superseded. Yet during this period geographical conditions in Europe have either not changed at all, or have changed so slightly that geography takes no note of them. And that is quite natural. Changes in geographical environment of any importance require millions of years, whereas a few hundred or a couple of thousand years are enough for even very important changes in the system of human society.

It follows from this that geographical environment cannot be the chief cause, the *determining* cause of social development, for that which remains almost unchanged in the course of tens of thousands of years cannot be the chief cause of development of that which undergoes fundamental changes in the course of a few hundred years.

* "We must beware," says L. Geiger, "of ascribing to premeditation too great a part in the origin of implements. The discovery of the first implements of the highest importance took place, of course, by accident, like many great discoveries of modern times. They were of course rather discovered than invented. I arrived at this view in particular on account of the circumstance that the names of implements never arise from their manufacture, that those names never have a genetic character, but arise from the use which is made of the implement. Thus, in the German language Scheere (scissors), Säge (saw), Hacke (pick-axe) are objects which shear (scheeren), saw (sägen), hack (hacken). This law of language must all the more attract our attention because the names of devices which do not represent tools are formed by a genetic or passive method, from the material or from the work of which or thanks to which they arise. Thus, a skin as a receptacle for wine in many languages originally means the skin torn off an animal: to the German Schlauch corresponds the English slough (snakeskin): the Greek ascós is simultaneously a skin in the sense of receptacle, and

The difference in results (*the stages of cultural development*) achieved by various human societies is explained precisely by the fact that environment did not permit the various human tribes to make practical use to an equal extent of their capacity to "invent." There is a school of anthropologists who trace the origin of the difference in results mentioned in the different qualities of *the races of man*. But the view of this school does not hold water: it is merely a new variation of the old method of explaining historical phenomena by references to "human nature" (or here, references to *racial nature*), and in its scientific profundity it has not gone very much farther than the views of Molière's doctor, who sagely proclaimed that opium sends one to sleep because it has the quality of sending to sleep (a race is backward because it has the quality of backwardness).

Acting on external nature, man changes his own nature. He develops all his capacities, among them also the capacity of "tool-making." *But at any given time the measure of that capacity is determined by the measure of the development of productive forces already achieved.*

Once an implement of labour has become an object of production, the very possibility—as well as the greater or lesser degree—of perfecting its manufacture entirely depends on the implements of labour with the help of which it is manufactured. This is comprehensible to any

---

the skin of a beast. Here, consequently, language shows us quite evidently how and out of what was manufactured the device called a skin. It is otherwise in relation to implements; and they at first— if we base ourselves on language—were not manufactured at all. Thus the first knife could be found by accident, and I would say made use of in play, in the shape of a sharpened stone." L. Geiger, *Die Urgeschichte der Menschheit im Lichte der Sprache, mit besonderer Beziehung auf die Entstehung des Werkzeugs*, pp. 36-37 (in the collection *Zur Entwicklungsgeschichte der Menschheit*, Stuttgart, 1878).

one even without explanation. But this is what, for example, may seem quite incomprehensible at first glance. Plutarch, when mentioning the inventions made by Archimedes during the siege of Syracuse by the Romans, finds it necessary to *apologize* for the inventor. It is, of course, indecent for a philosopher to occupy himself with things of this kind, he reflects, but Archimedes was justified by the extremity in which his country found itself. We ask, who would now think of seeking for circumstances which extenuate the guilt of Edison? We nowadays do not consider shameful—quite the opposite—the use by man in practice of his capacity for mechanical inventions, while the Greeks (or if you prefer the Romans), as you see, took quite a different view of this. Hence the course of mechanical discovery and invention among them was bound to proceed—and actually did proceed—incomparably more slowly than amongst ourselves. Here once again it might seem that *opinions govern the world*. But whence did the Greeks derive such a strange "opinion"? Its origin cannot be explained by the qualities of the human "intellect." It remains only to recall their social relations. The societies of Greece and Rome were, as we know, societies of *slave-owners*. In such societies all physical labour, all the work of production, fell to the lot of the slaves. The free man was *ashamed* of such labour, and therefore naturally there was established a contemptuous attitude even to the most important inventions which bore on the processes of production—and among them to the mechanical inventions. That is why Plutarch looked on Archimedes in a very different way from that in which we now regard Edison.* But why was slavery

---

* "For the art of mechanics... was first originated by Eudoxus and Archytas, who embellished geometry with its subtleties, and gave to problems incapable of proof by word and diagram a support derived from mechanical illustrations that were patent to the

established in Greece? Was it not because the Greeks, on account of some errors of their "intellect," considered the slave-owning order to be the best? No, it was not because of that. There was a time when the Greeks also had no slavery, and at that time they did not at all consider the slave-owning social order to be natural and inevitable. Later on, slavery arose among the Greeks, and gradually began to play a more and more important part in their life. Then the view of the citizens of Greece also changed: they began to defend slavery as a quite natural and unquestionably essential institution. But why, then, did slavery arise and develop among the Greeks? Evidently, for the same reason that it arose and developed in other countries as well, at a certain stage of their social development. And this reason is well known: it consists in the state of the productive forces. For, in fact, in order that it should be more profitable for me to make my conquered enemy into a slave, rather than into roast meat, it is necessary that the product of his unfree labour should be able to maintain not only his own existence but, at least in part, mine too: in other words, a certain stage of development of the productive forces at my disposal is essential. And it is precisely through this door that slavery enters history. Slave labour is not very favourable to the development of the productive forces;

---

senses.... But Plato was incensed at this, and inveighed against them as corrupters and destroyers of the pure excellence of geometry, which thus turned her back upon the incorporeal things of abstract thought and descended to the things of sense, making use, moreover, of objects which required much mean and manual labour. For this reason mechanics was made entirely distinct from geometry, and being for a long time ignored by philosophers came to be regarded as one of the military arts" (*Plutarchi*, Vita Marcelli, edit. Teubneriana, C. Sintenis, Lipsiae 1883, Ch. XIV, pp. 135-36). As the reader will see, Plutarch's view was far from new at that time.

in conditions of slavery it advances extremely slowly, but still it does advance. Finally there arrives a moment at which the exploitation of slave labour proves to be less advantageous than the exploitation of free labour. Then slavery is *abolished*, or gradually *dies out*. It is shown to the door by that same development of the productive forces which introduced it into history.* Thus we, returning to Plutarch, see that his view of Archimedes's inventions was conditioned by the state of the productive forces of his age. And as views of this kind undoubtedly have a vast influence on the further course of discovery and invention, we can say all the more that *for every given people, at every given period of its history, the further development of its productive forces is determined by their condition in the period under examination.*

Naturally, wherever we have to deal with inventions and discoveries, we deal also with "reason." Without reason discoveries and inventions would have been just as impossible as they were before man appeared on the earth. The teaching we are setting forth does not at all leave out of account the role of reason; it only tries to explain why reason at every given time *acted in this way, and*

---

* It is known that for a long time the Russian peasants themselves could have, and not infrequently did have, their own serfs. The condition of a serf could not be attractive to a peasant. But in the then state of the productive forces of Russia not a single peasant could find that condition abnormal. A "muzhik" who had made some money just as naturally began to think about buying serfs as a Roman freeman strove to acquire slaves. The slaves who revolted under the leadership of Spartacus waged war with their lords, but not with slavery; if they had succeeded in winning their freedom, they would themselves, in favourable circumstances, and with the most tranquil conscience, have become slave-owners. Willy-nilly one recalls at this point the words of Schelling, which acquire a new meaning, that *freedom must be necessary.* History shows that any of the forms of freedom makes its appearance only where it becomes an economic necessity.

not otherwise; it does not despise the successes of reason, but only seeks to find a sufficient cause for them.

Lately another objection has begun to be made to the same teaching, and we shall leave Mr. Kareyev to set it forth:

"In course of time," says this writer, having more or less successfully expounded the historical philosophy of Engels, "Engels supplemented his view by new considerations which introduced an essential alteration. If previously he had recognized as the foundation of the material conception of history only the investigation of the economic structure of society, later on he recognized as equally important the study of family structure. This took place under the influence of new conceptions of the primitive forms of marriage and family relations, which forced him to take into account not only the process of the production of products but also the process of the reproduction of human generations. In this respect the influence came in part from Morgan's '*Ancient Society*,'" etc.*

And so, if earlier Engels "recognized as the foundation of the material" (?) "conception of history the investigation of the economic structure of society," later on, "having recognized as equally important," etc., he, practically speaking, ceased to be an "economic" materialist. Mr. Kareyev sets forth this event in the tone of a dispassionate historian, while Mr. Mikhailovsky "skips and jumps" on the same subject; but both of them say essentially one and the same thing, and both repeat what before them was said by the extremely superficial German writer Weisengrün in his book, *Entwicklungsgesetze der Menschheit*.

---

* See *Economic Materialism in History*, in *Vestnik Yevropy*,[28] August 1894, p. 601.

It is quite natural that such a remarkable man as Engels, who during whole decades followed attentively the advance of science of his time, should very substantially "supplement" his basic view of the history of humanity. But there are supplements and supplements, as there are "fagot et fagot." In this case the whole question is, did Engels *change his views* as a result of the "supplements" which were introduced in them? Was he really obliged to recognize, side by side with the development of "production," the action of another factor, allegedly "equally important" with the first? It is easy for anyone to reply to this question who has even the least willingness to make an attentive and serious approach to it.

Elephants sometimes beat off flies with branches, says Darwin. We have remarked in this connection that nevertheless these branches play no essential part in the life of elephants, and that the elephant did not become an elephant because he used branches. But the elephant multiplies. The male elephant has a certain relationship with the female. The male and the female have a certain relationship with their young. It is clear that these relations have not been created by "branches": they have been created by the general conditions of life of this species, conditions in which the role of a "branch" is so infinitely small that it can without error be equated to *zero*. But imagine that in the life of the elephant the branch begins to play a more and more important part, in the sense that it begins more and more to influence the structure of those general conditions on which depend all the habits of elephants, and in the long run their very existence. Imagine that the branch has acquired at length a *decisive* influence in creating these conditions. Then we shall have to recognize that it determines in the long run also the relations of the male elephant with the female and with his young. Then we shall have to recognize that there was a time when the "family" relations of elephants developed independently (in the sense of their relation with the branch), but that later on there came a time when those relations began to be determined by the "branch." Will there be anything strange in such an admission? Absolutely nothing, except the strangeness of the very hypothesis that a branch might suddenly acquire a decisive importance in the life of the elephant. And we know ourselves that in relation to the elephant this hypothesis cannot but seem strange; but in application to the history of *man* things are different.

Man only gradually separated off from the animal world. There was a time when in the life of our anthropoid ancestors tools played just as insignificant a part as branches play in the life of the elephant. During this very long period, the relations between the anthropoid males and the anthropoid females, just as the relations between each and their anthropoid young, were determined by the general conditions of life of this species, which bore no relation whatsoever to the *implements of labour*. On what did then depend the "family" relations of our ancestors? It is the naturalists who must explain this: the historian has as yet nothing to do in this sphere. But now the implements of labour begin to play a more and more important part in the life of man, the productive forces develop more and more, and there comes at length a moment when they acquire a decisive influence on the whole structure of social, and among them of family, relations. It is at this point that *the work of the historian begins*: he has to show how and why the family relations of our ancestors changed in connection with the development of their productive forces, how the family developed in accordance with economic relations. But obviously, once he sets about such an explanation, he has in studying the primitive family to reckon not only with economics: for people multiplied even before the implements of labour acquired their decisive significance in human life: even before this time there existed some kind of family relations which were determined by the general conditions of existence of the species homo sapiens. What then has the historian to do here? He will have, first of all, to ask for a service record of this species from the naturalist, who is passing over to him the further study of the development of man; and he will have secondly to supplement this record "out of his own resources." In other words he will have to take the "family," as it came into existence, shall we say, in the zoological period of the development of humanity, and then show what changes were introduced into it during the *historical* period, under the influence of the development of the productive forces, in consequence of changes in economic relations. That is all Engels says. And we ask: when he says this, is he in the least changing his "original" view of the significance of the productive forces in the history of humanity? Is he accepting, side by side with the working of this factor, the working of some other, "of equal importance"? It would seem that he is changing nothing, it would seem that he is accepting no such factor. Well, but if he is not, then why do Messrs. Weisengrün and Kareyev talk about a change in his views, why does Mr. Mikhailovsky skip and jump? Most probably because of their own thoughtlessness.

"But after all, it is really strange to reduce the history of the family to the history of economic relations, even during what you call the historical period," shout our opponents in chorus. It may be strange, and maybe it is not strange: this is debatable, we shall say in the words of Mr. Mikhailovsky. And we don't mind debating it with you, gentlemen, but only on one condition: during the debate behave seriously, study attentively the meaning of our words, don't attribute to us your own inventions, and don't hasten to discover in us contradictions which neither we nor our teachers have, or ever had. Are you agreed? Very well, let's debate.

One cannot explain the history of the family by the history of economic relations, you say: it is narrow, one-sided, unscientific. We assert the contrary, and turn to the mediation of specialist investigators.

Of course you know the book of Giraud-Teulon: *Les origines de la famille*? We open this book which you know, and we find in it for example the following passage:

"The reasons which brought about the formation within the primitive tribe" (Giraud-Teulon says, in point of fact, "within the horde"—de la horde) "of separate family groups are evidently connected with the growth in wealth of this tribe. The introduction into use, or the discovery, of some grain, the domestication of new species of animals, could be a sufficient reason for radical transformations in savage society: all great successes of civilization always coincided with profound changes in the economic life of the population" (p. 138).*

A few pages further on we read:

"Apparently the transition from the system of female kinship to the system of male kinship was particularly heralded by conflicts of a juridical character on the basis of property right" (p. 141).

And further on: "The organization of the family in which male right predominates was everywhere aroused, it seems to me, by the action of a force as simple as elemental: *the right of property*" (p. 146).

You know, of course, what significance in the history of the primitive family McLennan attributes to the killing of children of the female sex? Engels, as we know,

---

* We quote from the French edition of 1874.

has a very negative attitude to McLennan's researches; but all the more interesting is it for us in the present case to learn the views of McLennan on the reason which gave rise to the appearance of infanticide, which allegedly exercised such a decisive influence on the history of the family.

"To tribes surrounded by enemies, and, unaided by art, contending with the difficulties of subsistence, sons were a source of strength, both for defence and in the quest for food, daughters a source of weakness."*

What was it, then, that brought about, in McLennan's opinion, the killing of children of the female sex by the primitive tribes? The insufficiency of the means of existence, the weakness of the productive forces: if these tribes had enough food, probably they would not have killed their little girls merely out of fear that one day an enemy might come and possibly kill them, or take them away into captivity.

We repeat that Engels does not share McLennan's view of the history of the family, and we too find it very unsatisfying; but what is important at this stage is that McLennan, too, shares in the sin with which Engels is reproached. He, too, seeks in the state of the productive forces the answer to the riddle of the history of family relations.

Need we continue our extracts, and quote from Lippert or Morgan? We see no need of this, for whoever has read them knows that in this respect they are just as great sinners as McLennan and Engels. Not without sin on this occasion, as is well known, is Herbert Spencer himself, although his sociological views have absolutely nothing in common with "economic materialism."

---

* J. F. McLennan, *Studies in Ancient History: Primitive Marriage*, 1876, p. 111.

Of course it is possible to take advantage of this last circumstance for polemical purposes, and to say: there you are! So one can agree with Marx and Engels on this or that individual question, and not share their general historical theory! Of course one can. The only question is, on whose side will logic be.

Let us go further.

The development of the family is determined by the development of property right, says Giraud-Teulon, adding that all successes of civilization in general coincide with changes in the economic life of humanity. The reader probably has noticed himself that Giraud-Teulon is not quite precise in his terminology: his conception of "property right" is covered, as it were, by the conception of "economic life." But after all, right is right, and economy is economy, and the two conceptions should not be mixed up. Where has this property right come from? Perhaps it arose under the influence of the economy of the given society (civil law always serves merely as the expression of economic relations, says Lassalle), or perhaps it owes its origin to some quite different reason. Here we must continue the analysis, and not interrupt it precisely at the moment when it is becoming of particularly profound and most vital interest.

We have seen already that the French historians of the Restoration did not find a satisfactory reply to the question of the origin of property right. Mr. Kareyev, in his article "Economic Materialism in History," deals with the German historical school of law. It will not be a bad thing for us also to recall the views of this school.

Here is what our professor says about it. "When at the beginning of the present century there arose in Germany the so-called 'historical school of law,' which began to examine law not as a motionless system of juridical norms, as it was conceived of by previous jurists, but as something moving, changing, developing, there appeared in this school a strong tendency to contrast the historical view of law, as the sole and exclusively correct view, with all other possible views in this sphere. The historical view never tolerated the existence of scientific truths applicable to all ages, i.e., what in the language of modern science are called general laws, and even directly denied these laws, and together with them any general theory of law, in favour of the idea that law depends on local conditions—a dependence which has always and everywhere existed, but does not exclude principles which are common to all nations."*

In these few lines there are very many ... how shall we put it? ... shall we say, inexactitudes, against which the representatives and supporters of the historical school of law would have raised a protest. Thus, for example, they would have said that, when Mr. Kareyev ascribes to them the denial of "what in the language of science are called general laws," he either deliberately distorts their view, or else is confusing conceptions in a way most unbefitting a "historiosophist," mixing up those "laws" which fall within the scope of the history of law, and those which determine the historical development of nations. The historical school of law never dreamed of denying the existence of the second kind of law, and always tried to discover them, although its efforts were not crowned with success. But the very cause of its failure is extremely instructive, and if Mr. Kareyev were to give himself the trouble of thinking about it, perhaps—who knows —he too would make clear for himself, at last, the *"substance of the historical process."*

In the eighteenth century people were inclined to explain the history of law by the action of the "legislator."

---

* *Vestnik Yevropy*, July 1894, p. 12.

The historical school strongly revolted against this inclination. As early as 1814, Savigny formulated the new view in this way: "The sum-total of this view consists of the following: every law arises from what in common usage, but not quite exactly, is called *customary law*, i.e., it is brought into being first of all by the custom and faith of the people, and only afterwards by jurisprudence. Thus it is everywhere created by internal forces, which act unnoticed, and not by the personal will of the legislator."*

This view was later developed by Savigny in his famous work *System des heutigen römischen Rechts*. "Positive law," he says in this work, "lives in the general consciousness of a people, and therefore we have to call it *popular law*.... But this must not in any event be understood as meaning that law has been created by individual members of the people arbitrarily.... Positive law is created by the spirit of a people, living and acting in its individual members, and therefore positive law, not by accident but of necessity, is one and the same law in the consciousness of individual persons."**

Savigny continues: "If we consider the question of the origin of the State, we shall have in the same way to locate it in supreme necessity, in the action of a force building outward from within, as was shown earlier in the case of law in general; and this applies not only to the existence of the State in general, but also to that particular form which the State assumes in every individual nation."***

Law arises in exactly the same "invisible way" as lan-

---

* Friedrich Karl von Savigny, *Vom Beruf unserer Zeit für Gesetzgebung und Rechtswissenschaft*, 3d ed., Heidelberg, 1840, p. 14. The first edition appeared in 1814.
** Berlin edition, 1840, Vol. I, p. 14.
*** *Ibid.*, p. 22.

guage, and it lives in the general consciousness of a people, not in the shape "of abstract rules, but in the shape of a living conception of institutions of law and in their organic connection, so that, when necessity arises, the abstract rule has to be formed in its logical shape from this general conception, by means of a certain artificial process (durch einen künstlichen Prozess)."*

We are not interested here in the practical aspirations of the historical school of law; but as far as its *theory* is concerned, we can already say, on the basis of the words of Savigny here quoted, that it represents:

1. A reaction against the view held widely in the eighteenth century that law is created by the arbitrary will of individual persons ("Legislators"); and an attempt to furnish a scientific explanation of the history of law, to understand that history as a process which is necessary, and which, therefore, conforms to law.

2. An attempt to explain that process, starting from a completely *idealist point of view*: "the spirit of a people," the "consciousness of a people," is the final authority to which the historical school of law appealed.

Puchta expressed the idealist character of the views of this school even more sharply.

Primitive law, with Puchta, just as with Savigny, is customary law. But how does customary law arise? The opinion is often expressed that this law is created by everyday practice (Uebung), but this is only a particular case of the materialist view of the origin of popular conceptions. "Exactly the opposite view is the right one: everyday practice is only the last moment, it only expresses and embodies the law which has arisen, and which lives in the conviction of the individuals belonging to the particular people. Custom influences convic-

---

* *Ibid.*, p. 16.

tion only in the sense that the latter, thanks to custom, becomes more conscious and more stable."*

And so the conviction of a people concerning this or that legal institution arises independently of everyday practice, and earlier than "custom." Whence does this conviction come from, then? It arises from the depth of the spirit of the people. The particular form this conviction takes with a particular people is to be explained by the particular features of the spirit of the people concerned. This is very obscure—so obscure that it does not contain any symptom of a scientific explanation. Puchta himself feels that things here are not quite satisfactory, and tries to put them right with an observation of this kind: "Law arises by an imperceptible path. Who could take upon himself to trace those paths which lead to the origin of the given conviction, to its conception, its growth, its flourishing, its manifestation? Those who tried to do so, for the most part started from mistaken ideas."**

"For the most part." ... That means that there also existed investigators whose initial ideas were correct. To what conclusions, then, about the genesis of popular views on law did these persons arrive? We must suppose that this remained a secret for Puchta, because he does not go one step further than meaningless references to the qualities of the spirit of the people.

---

* *Cursus der Institutionen*, Leipzig, 1841, Vol. I, p 31. In a footnote Puchta speaks sharply of the eclectics who strive to reconcile contradictory views of the origin of law, and uses such expressions that willy-nilly the question arises: can he possibly have anticipated the appearance of Mr. Kareyev? But on the other hand it must be said that in Germany at the time of Puchta they had quite enough eclectics of their own. Whatever else there may be a shortage of, there are always and everywhere inexhaustible reserves of that type of mind.

** *Ibid.*, p. 28.

Nor is any explanation provided by the above-quoted remark of Savigny that law lives in the general consciousness of a people, not in the shape of abstract rules, but "in the shape of a living conception of legal institutions in their organic connection." And it is not difficult to understand what it was that impelled Savigny to give us this somewhat muddled information. If we had presumed that law exists in the consciousness of a people "in the shape of abstract rules," we should thereby in the first place have come up against the "general consciousness" of the jurists, who know very well with what difficulty a people grasps these abstract rules, and secondly, our theory of the origin of law would have assumed a too incredible form. It would have appeared that before entering into any practical relations one with another, before acquiring any practical experience whatsoever, the men constituting the given people work out definite legal conceptions for themselves, and having laid in a store of these, as a tramp does of crusts, they set forth into the sphere of everyday practice, enter upon their historical path. Nobody, of course, would believe this, and so Savigny eliminates the "abstract rules": law exists in the consciousness of the people not in the shape of definite conceptions, it represents, not a collection of already fully-shaped crystals, but a more or less saturated solution out of which, "when necessity for this arises," i.e., when coming up against everyday practice, the required juridical crystals are precipitated. Such an approach is not without its ingenuity, but naturally it does not in the least bring us nearer to a scientific understanding of phenomena.

Let us take an example:

The Eskimos, Rink tells us, scarcely have any regular property; but in so far as it can be spoken of, he enumerates three forms which it takes:

"1. Property owned by an association of generally more than one family—e.g., the winter-house....

"2. Property, the common possession of one, or at most of three families of kindred—viz., a tent and everything belonging to the household, such as lamps, tubs, dishes of wood, soapstone pots; a boat, or *umiak*, which can carry all these articles along with the tent; one or two sledges with the dogs attached to them;... the stock of winter provisions....

"3. As regards personal property—i.e., owned by every individual ... his clothes ... weapons, and tools or whatever was specially used by himself. These things were even regarded as having a kind of supernatural relation to the owner, reminding us of that between the body and the soul. Lending them to others was not customary."*

Let us try and conceive of the origin of these three views of property from the standpoint of the old historical school of law.

As, in the words of Puchta, convictions precede everyday practice, and do not arise on the basis of custom, one must suppose that matters proceeded in the following way. Before living in winter houses, even before they began to build them, the Eskimos came to the conviction that once winter houses appeared among them, they must belong to a union of several families. In the same way, our savages convinced themselves that, once there appeared among them summer tents, barrels, wooden plates, boats, pots, sledges and dogs, all these would have to be the property of a single family or, at most, of three kindred families. Finally, they formed no less firm a conviction that clothes, arms and tools must constitute personal property, and that it would be wrong even

---

* H. J. Rink, *Tales and Traditions of the Eskimo*, 1875, pp. 9-10, 30.

to lend these articles. Let us add to this that probably all these "convictions" existed, not in the shape of abstract rules, but "in the shape of a living conception of legal institutions in their organic connection," and that out of this solution of legal conceptions there were precipitated—"when necessity for this arose," i.e., as they encountered winter dwellings, summer tents, barrels, stone pots, wooden plates, boats, sledges and dogs—the norms of customary Eskimo law in their more or less "logical form." And the qualities of the above-mentioned legal solution were determined by the mysterious qualities of the Eskimo spirit.

This is not a scientific explanation at all, but a mere "way of talking"—Redensarten, as the Germans say.

That variety of idealism which was maintained by the supporters of the historical school of law proved in its explanation of social phenomena to be even more fallacious than the much more profound idealism of Schelling and Hegel.

How did science emerge from that blind alley in which idealism found itself? Let us hear what Mr. M. Kovalevsky, one of the most distinguished representatives of modern comparative law, has to say.

Pointing out that the social life of primitive tribes bears on itself the stamp of communism, Mr. Kovalevsky (listen, Mr. V. V.: he also is a "professor") says:

"If we enquire as to the real foundations for such an order of things, if we try and discover the reasons which forced our primitive forefathers, and still oblige modern savages, to maintain a more or less sharply expressed communism, we shall have in particular to learn the primitive modes of production. For the distribution and consumption of wealth must be determined by the methods of its creation. And as to this, ethnography states the following: hunting and fishing peoples secure their food as a rule in hordes.... In Australia the kangaroo is hunted by armed detachments of several tens, and even hundreds, of natives. The same takes place in northern countries when hunting the reindeer. ... It is beyond doubt that man is incapable of maintaining his existence alone; he needs help and support, and his forces are multiplied ten-fold by association.... Thus we see social production at the beginning of social development and, as the necessary natural consequence of this, social consumption. Ethnography abounds in facts which prove this."*

Having quoted the idealist theory of Lermina, according to which private property arises from the self-consciousness of the individual, Mr. Kovalevsky continues:

"No, this is not so. It is not for this reason that primitive man arrives at the idea of the personal appropriation of the chipped stone which serves him as a weapon, or of the skin which covers his body. He arrives at this idea in consequence of the application of his individual forces to the production of the object concerned. The flint which serves him as an axe has been chipped by his own hands. At the hunt in which he engaged together with many comrades, he struck the final blow at the animal, and therefore the skin of that animal becomes his personal property. The customary law of savages is distinguished by great exactness on this question. It carefully provides beforehand, for example, for the case in which the hunted animal fell under the joint blows of two hunters: in that event the animal's skin becomes the property of the hunter whose arrow penetrated nearest to the

---

* M. Kovalevsky, *Tableau des origines et de l'évolution de la famille et de la propriété*, Stockholm, 1890, pp. 52-53. The late N. Sieber's *Outlines of Primitive Economic Culture* contains numerous facts demonstrating with the utmost clarity that modes of appropriation are determined by modes of production.

heart. It also provides for the case in which an already wounded animal was given the finishing blow by a hunter who turned up accidentally. The application of individual labour logically gives rise, consequently, to individual appropriation. We can trace this phenomenon through all history. He who planted a fruit tree becomes its owner.... Later a warrior who won a certain booty becomes its exclusive owner, so that his family no longer has any right to it. In just the same way a priest's family has no right to the sacrifices which are made by the faithful, and which become his personal property. All this is equally well confirmed by the Indian laws and by the customary law of the South Slavs, Don Cossacks or ancient Irish. And it is important not to make any mistake as to the true principle of such appropriation, which is the result of the application of personal effort to the procuring of a definite object. For when the personal efforts of a man are supplemented by the help of his kin ... the objects secured no longer become private property."*

After all that has been said, it will be comprehensible why it is arms, clothes, food, adornments, etc., that first become objects of personal appropriation. "Already from the first steps taken, the domestication of animals—dogs, horses, cats, working cattle—constitutes the most important fund of personal and family appropriation...."** But to what extent the organization of production continues to influence the modes of appropriation is shown, for example, by such a fact: among the Eskimos the hunting of whales takes place in big boats and big detachments, and the boats which serve for this purpose represent social property. But the little boats which serve for transporting the objects of family property themselves

---

* *Ibid.*, p. 95.
** *Ibid.*, p. 57.

belong to separate families, or "at most to three kindred families."

With the appearance of agriculture, the land also becomes an object of appropriation. The subjects of property in land become more or less large unions of kindred. This, naturally, is one of the forms of *social* appropriation. How is its origin to be explained? "It seems to us," says Mr. Kovalevsky, "that its reasons lie in that same social production which once upon a time involved the appropriation of the greater part of movable objects."*

Naturally, once it has arisen, *private* property enters into contradiction to the more ancient mode of *social* appropriation. Wherever the rapid development of productive forces opens a wider and wider field for "individual efforts," social production fairly rapidly disappears, or continues to exist in the shape, so to speak, of a *rudimentary* institution. We shall see later on that this process of the disintegration of primitive social property at various times and in various places through the most natural, *material* necessity, was bound to be marked by great variety. At present we will only stress the general conclusion of the modern science of law that *legal conceptions*—or convictions, as Puchta would have said —are everywhere *determined by the modes of production.*

Schelling said on one occasion that the phenomenon of magnetism must be understood as the embedding of the "subjective" in the "objective." All attempts to discover an idealist explanation for the history of law represent no more than a supplement, a "Seitenstück," to idealist natural philosophy. It amounts always to the same, sometimes brilliant and ingenious, but always arbitrary and

---
* *Ibid.*, p. 93.

always groundless meditations on the theme of the self-sufficing, *self-developing* spirit.

Legal conviction could not *precede* everyday practice for this one reason alone that, if it had not *grown out of that practice*, it would have *no reason* for existence whatsoever. The Eskimo stands for the personal appropriation of clothes, arms and implements of labour for the simple reason that such appropriation is much more convenient, and is suggested by *the very qualities of the things involved*. In order to learn the proper use of his weapon, his bow or his boomerang, the primitive hunter must *adapt himself to it*, study all its individual peculiarities, and if possible *adapt it* to his own individual peculiarities.* Private property here is in the nature of things, much more than any other form of appropriation, and therefore the savage is "convinced" of its advantages: as we know, he even attributes to the implements of individual labour and to arms some kind of mysterious

---

* It is known that the intimate connection between the hunter and his weapon exists in all primitive tribes. "Der Jäger darf sich keiner fremden Waffen bedienen," ("The hunter must not make use of a stranger's weapons."—*Ed.*) says Martius of the primitive inhabitants of Brazil, explaining at the same time whence these savages derived such a "conviction": "Besonders behaupten diejenigen Wilden, die mit dem Blasrohr schiessen, dass dieses Geschoss durch den Gebrauch eines Fremden verdorben werde, und geben es nicht aus ihren Händen" ("Von dem Rechtszustande unter den Ureinwohnern Brasiliens," München, 1832, S. 50). ("In particular these savages who shoot with a blowpipe insist that this weapon is spoiled when used by a stranger, and don't allow it out of their hands.") "Die Führung dieser Waffen (bows and arrows) erfordert eine grosse Geschicklichkeit und beständige Uebung Wo sie bei wilden Völkern im Gebrauche sind, berichten uns die Reisenden, dass schon die Knaben sich mit Kindergeräten im Schiessen üben." (Oskar Peschel, *Völkerkunde*, Leipzig, 1875, S. 190.) ("The use of these weapons (bows and arrows) requires great skill and constant practice. Where they are in use among savage peoples, we are told by travellers, the boys already practise shooting with toy weapons.")

connection with their owner. But his conviction grew up on the basis of everyday practice, and did not precede it: and it owes its origin, not to the qualities of his "spirit," but to the qualities of the articles which he is using, and to the character of those modes of production which are inevitable for him in the existing state of his productive forces.

To what extent everyday practice precedes legal "conviction" is shown by the numerous symbolic acts existing in primitive law. The modes of production have changed, with them have likewise changed the mutual relations of men in the process of production, everyday practice has changed, yet "conviction" has retained its old shape. It contradicts the new practice, and so fictions appear, symbolic signs and actions, the sole purpose of which is formally to eliminate this contradiction. In the course of time the contradiction is at last eliminated in an essential way: on the basis of the new economic practice a new legal conviction takes shape.

It is not sufficient to register the appearance, in a given society, of private property in this or that object, to be able thereby to determine the character of that institution. Private property always has limits which depend entirely on the economy of society. "In the savage state man appropriates only the things which are directly useful to him. The surplus, even though it is acquired by the labour of his hands, he usually gives up gratuitously to others: to members of his family, or of his clan, or of his tribe," says Mr. Kovalevsky. Rink says exactly the same about the Eskimos. But whence did such ways arise among the savage peoples? In the words of Mr. Kovalevsky, they owe their origin to the fact that savages are not acquainted with *saving*.* This is not a very clear ex-

---
* *Loc. cit.,* p. 56.

pression, and is particularly unsatisfactory because it was very much abused by the vulgar economists. Nevertheless, it can be understood in what sense our author uses the expression. "Saving" is really unknown to primitive peoples, for the simple reason that it is inconvenient and, one may say, impossible for them to practise it. The flesh of an animal that has been killed can be "saved" only to an inconsiderable extent: it goes bad, and then becomes quite unsuitable for use. Of course, if it could be sold, it would be very easy to "save" the money got for it. But money does not yet exist at this stage of economic development. Consequently, the economy of primitive society itself fixes narrow limits within which the spirit of "thrift" can develop. Moreover, today I was lucky enough to kill a big animal, and I shared its meat with others, but tomorrow (hunting is an uncertain business) I will return with empty hands, and others of my kin will share their booty with me. The custom of sharing thus appears as something in the nature of mutual insurance, without which the existence of hunting tribes would be quite impossible.

Finally, one must not forget that private property among such tribes exists only in an embryo form, while the prevailing property is *social*. The habits and customs which have grown up on this basis, in their turn, set limits to the arbitrary will of the owner of private property. Conviction, here too, follows economy.

The connection of the legal conceptions of men with their economic life is well illustrated by the example which Rodbertus readily and frequently used in his works. It is well known that the ancient Roman writers energetically protested against *usury*. Cato the Censor considered that a usurer was twice as bad as a thief (that was just what the old man said: exactly twice). In this respect the Fathers of the Christian Church were completely at one with the heathen writers. But—a remarkable fact—both revolted only against interest produced by *money* capital. But to loans in kind, and *to the surplus which they brought*, there was an incomparably milder attitude. Why this difference? Because it was precisely money or usurers' capital that was effecting terrible devastations in society at that time: because it was precisely this that was *"ruining Italy."* Legal "conviction," here too, went hand-in-hand with economy.

"Law is the pure product of necessity or, more exactly, of need," says Post. "In vain should we seek in it any ideal basis whatsoever."* We should say that this was quite in the spirit of the most modern science of law, if our scholar did not display a fairly considerable confusion of conceptions, very harmful in its consequences.

Speaking generally, every social union strives to work out such a system of law as would best satisfy its needs and would be most useful for it at the given time. The circumstance that the particular sum-total of legal institutions is useful or harmful for society cannot in any way depend on the qualities of any "idea" whatsoever, from whomsoever the idea might come; *it depends*, as we have seen, *on the modes of production and on those mutual relations between people which are created by those modes*. In this sense law has not and cannot have any *ideal* foundations, as its foundations are always *real*. But the *real foundations* of every given system of law do not exclude *an ideal attitude* towards that system on the part of the members of the given society. Taken as a whole, society only gains from such an attitude of its members towards that system. On the contrary, in its transitional epochs, when the system of law existing

---

* Dr. Albert Hermann Post, *Der Ursprung des Rechts. Prolegomena zu einer allgemeinen vergleichenden Rechtswissenschaft*, Oldenburg, 1876, S. 25.

in society no longer satisfies its needs, which have grown in consequence of the further development of productive forces, the advanced part of the population can and must idealize *a new system of institutions*, more in keeping with the "spirit of the time." French literature is full of examples of such an idealization of the new advancing order of things.

The origin of law in *"need"* excludes an *"ideal"* basis of law only in the conception of those people who are accustomed to relegate *need* to the sphere of *crude matter*, and to contrast this sphere to the "pure spirit," foreign to need of every kind. In reality, only that is "ideal" which is useful to men, and every society in working out its *ideals* is guided only by its needs. The seeming exceptions from this incontestably general rule are explained by the fact that, *in consequence of the development of society*, its *ideals* frequently lag behind its *new needs.**

The realization of the dependence of social relations on the state of productive forces is penetrating more and more into modern social science, in spite of the inevitable eclecticism of many scientists and in spite of their idealist prejudices. "Just as comparative anatomy has raised to the level of a scientific truth the Latin proverb that

---

* Post belongs to the category of these people who have far from parted with idealism yet. Thus, for example, he shows that the union of kindred corresponds to hunting and nomad society, and that with the appearance of agriculture and the stable settlement bound up with it, the union of kindred yields place to "Gaugenossenschaft" (we should call it the neighbour-community). It would seem clear that the man is seeking the key to the explanation of the history of social relations in nothing else than the development of productive forces. In individual cases Post is almost always true to such a principle. But this does not prevent him regarding "im Menschen schaffend ewigen Geist" ("the Eternal Spirit creating in Man"—*Ed.*) as the fundamental cause of the history of law. This man has been, as it were, specially created in order to delight Mr. Kareyev.

'from the claws I recognize the lion,' so the study of peoples can from the armament of a particular people form an exact conclusion as to the degree of its civilization," says Oscar Peschel, whom we have already quoted.*
... "With the mode of procuring food is bound up most intimately the dissection of society. Wherever man joins with man a certain authority appears. Weakest of all are the social ties among the wandering hunter hordes of Brazil. "But they have to defend their areas and need at least a military chief. The pastoral tribes are for the most part under the authority of patriarchal sovereigns, as the herds belong as a rule to a single master, who is served by his fellow-tribesmen or by previously independent but later impoverished possessors of herds. The pastoral form of life is mostly, though not exclusively, characterized by great migrations of peoples, both in the north of the Old World and in South Africa; on the other hand, the history of America knows only of individual attacks by wild hunter tribes on the fields of civilized peoples which attract them. Entire peoples which leave their previous places of habitation could make great and prolonged journeys only when accompanied by their herds, which provided them with the necessary food on their way. Furthermore, prairie cattle-breeding itself impels a change of pastures. But with the settled mode of life and agriculture there immediately appears the striving to make use of the labour of slaves.... Slavery leads sooner or later to tyranny, since he who has the largest number of slaves

---

* *Loc. cit.*, p. 139. When we were making this extract, we imagined Mr. Mikhailovsky quickly rising in his seat, crying: "I find this debatable: the Chinese may be armed with English rifles. Can one on the basis of these rifles judge of the degree of their civilization?" Very well asked, Mr. Mikhailovsky: from English rifles it is not logical to draw conclusions about Chinese civilization. It is of English civilization that one must judge from them.

can with their help subject the weakest to his will.... The division into free men and slaves is the beginning of the division of society into estates."*

Peschel has many considerations of this kind. Some of them are quite just and very instructive; others are "debatable" for more than Mr. Mikhailovsky. But what we are concerned with here are not particular details but the general direction of Peschel's thought. And that general direction completely coincides with what we have already seen in the work of Mr. Kovalevsky: *it is in the modes of production, in the state of the productive forces, that he seeks the explanation of the history of law and even of the whole organization of society.*

And this is precisely what Marx long ago and insistently advised writers on social science to do. And in this lies to a considerable extent, though not completely (the reader will see later why we say: not completely), the sense of that remarkable preface to *A Critique of Political Economy* which had such bad luck here in Russia, which was so terribly and so strangely misunderstood by the majority of Russian writers who read it in the original or in extracts.

"In the social production of their life, men enter into definite relations that are indispensable and independent of their will, *relations of production* which correspond to a definite stage of development of their material productive forces. The sum-total of these relations of production constitutes the *economic structure* of society, the real foundation, on which rises a legal and political superstructure...."**

Hegel says of Schelling that the fundamental principles of the system of that philosopher remain undeveloped,

---
* *Loc. cit.*, pp. 252-53.
** K. Marx and F. Engels, *Selected Works*, Vol. I, Moscow, 1955, pp. 362-63.—*Ed.*

and his absolute spirit appears unexpectedly, *like a pistol-shot* (wie aus der Pistole geschossen). When the average Russian intellectual hears that in Marx "everything is reduced to the economic foundation" (others say simply: "to the economic"), he loses his head, as though someone had suddenly fired a pistol by his ear. "But why to the economic?" he asks dejectedly and uncomprehendingly. "Of course the economic is also important (especially for the poor peasants and workmen). But after all, no less important is the intellectual (particularly for us intellectuals)." What has just been set forth has, we hope, shown the reader that the perplexity of the average Russian intellectual occurs in this case only because he, that intellectual, was always a little careless about what was *"particularly important intellectually"* for himself. When Marx said that *"the anatomy of civil society is to be sought in political economy,"* he did not at all intend to upset the world of learning by sudden pistol-shots: he was only giving a direct and exact reply to the "damned questions" which had tormented thinking heads *for a whole century.*

The French materialists, consistently developing their sensationalist views, came to the conclusion that man, with all his thoughts, feelings and aspirations, is the product of his social environment. In order to go further in applying the materialist view to the study of man, it was necessary to solve the problem of what conditions the structure of the social environment, and what are the laws of its development. The French materialists were unable to reply to this question, and thereby were forced to be false to themselves and return to the old *idealist* point of view which they had so strongly condemned: they said that environment is created by the *"opinion"* of men. Dissatisfied with this superficial reply, the French historians of the Restoration set themselves the task of analyzing social environment. The result of their analysis was the conclusion, extremely important for science, that *political constitutions* are rooted *in social relations*, while social relations are determined by the *state of property*. With this conclusion there arose before science a new problem, without solving which it could not proceed: *what then determines the state of property*? The solution of this problem proved to be beyond the powers of the French historians of the Restoration, and they were obliged to dismiss it with remarks on the qualities of human nature which explained absolutely nothing at all. The great idealists of Germany—Schelling and Hegel—who were their contemporaries in life and work, already well understood how unsatisfactory was the point of view of human nature: Hegel made caustic fun of it. They understood that the key to the explanation of the historical advance of humanity must be sought *outside* human nature. This was a great service which they rendered: but in order that that service should prove completely fruitful for science, it was necessary to show *where precisely that key should be sought*. They looked for it in the *qualities of the spirit*, in the logical *laws of development of the absolute idea*. This was a radical error of the great idealists, which returned them by roundabout ways to the *point of view of human nature*, since the absolute idea, as we have already seen, is nothing else than the personification of our logical process of thought. The discovery of the genius of Marx corrects this radical error of idealism, thereby inflicting on it a deadly blow: the state of property, and with it all the qualities of the social environment (we saw in the chapter of idealist philosophy that Hegel, too, was forced to recognize the decisive importance of the "state of property") are determined, not by the qualities of the absolute spirit and not by the character of human nature, but by those mutual relations into which men of necessity enter one with another "in the social production of their life," i.e., in their struggle for existence. Marx has often been compared with Darwin—a comparison which arouses Messrs. Mikhailovsky, Kareyev and their fraternity to laughter. Later we shall say in what sense that comparison should be understood, although probably many readers already see it without our help. Here we shall permit ourselves, with all due respect to our subjective thinkers, another comparison.

Before Copernicus, astronomy taught that the earth is a motionless centre, around which revolve the sun and the other celestial bodies. This view made it impossible to explain very many phenomena of celestial mechanics. The Polish genius approached their explanation from quite the opposite point of view: he presupposed that it was not the sun that revolves around the earth, but on the contrary the earth around the sun. The correct viewpoint had been discovered, and much became clear that had been unclear before Copernicus.

Before Marx, writers on social science had taken human nature as their point of departure, and thanks to this, the most important questions of human development had remained unanswered. Marx's teaching gave affairs quite a different turn: *while man, to maintain his existence, acts on the external world, he changes his own nature*, said Marx. Consequently the scientific explanation of historical development should be begun at the opposite end: it is necessary to ascertain in what way does this process of the productive action of man on external nature take place. In its great importance for science, this discovery can be boldly placed on a par with the discovery of Copernicus, and on a par with the greatest and most fruitful discoveries of science in general.

Strictly speaking, previous to Marx social science had

much less in the way of a firm foundation than astronomy before Copernicus. The French used to call, and still call, all the sciences bearing on human society, "sciences morales et politiques" as distinct from "science" in the strict sense of the word, under which name were understood, and are still understood, only the exact sciences. And it must be admitted that, before Marx, social science was not and could not be exact. So long as learned men appealed to human nature as to the highest authority, of necessity they had to explain the social relations of men by their views, their *conscious activity*; but the conscious activity of man necessarily has to present itself to him as *free* activity. But free activity excludes the *conception of necessity*, i.e., of conformity to law: and conformity to law is the necessary foundation of any scientific explanation of phenomena. *The idea of freedom obscured the conception of necessity, and thereby hindered the development of science.* This aberration can up to the present day be observed with amazing clarity in the "sociological" works of "subjective" Russian writers.

But we already know that *freedom must be necessary*. By obscuring the conception of necessity, the idea of freedom itself became extremely dim and a very poor comfort. Driven out at the door, necessity flew in at the window; starting from their idea of freedom, investigators every moment came up against necessity, and in the long run arrived at the melancholy recognition of its fatal, irresistible and utterly invincible action. To their horror, freedom proved to be an eternally helpless and hopeless tributary, an impotent plaything in the hands of blind necessity. And truly pathetic was the despair which at times seized upon the clearest and most generous idealistic minds. "For several days now I have been taking up my pen every minute," says Georg Büchner, "but cannot write a word. I have been studying the history of the revolution. I have felt myself crushed, as it were, by the frightful fatalism of history. I see in human nature the most repulsive dullness, but in human relations an invincible force, which belongs to all in general and to no one in particular. The individual personality is only foam on the crest of the wave, greatness is only an accident, the power of genius is only a puppet-show, a ridiculous attempt to fight against iron law, which at best can only be discovered, but which it is impossible to subject to one's will."* It may be said that, to avoid such bursts of what naturally was quite legitimate despair, it was worth while even for a time abandoning one's old point of view, and attempting to *liberate freedom*, by appealing to that same *necessity* which made a mock of her. It was necessary once again to review the question which had already been put by the *dialectical* idealists, as to whether freedom does not follow from necessity, and whether the latter does not constitute the only firm foundation, the only stable guarantee and inevitable condition of human freedom?

We shall see to what such an attempt led Marx. But as a preliminary let us try and clear up for ourselves his historical views, so that no misunderstandings should remain in our minds on that subject.

On the basis of a particular state of the productive forces there come into existence certain relations of production, which receive their ideal expression in the legal notions of men and in more or less "abstract rules," in unwritten customs and written laws. We no longer require to demonstrate this: as we have seen, the present-

---

* In a letter to his betrothed, written in 1833. *Footnote for Mr. Mikhailovsky*: This is not the Büchner who preached materialism in the "general philosophical sense": it is his brother, who died young, the author of a famous tragedy, *The Death of Danton*.

day science of law demonstrates it for us (let the reader remember what Mr. Kovalevsky says on this subject). But it will do no harm if we examine the question from the following different point of view. Once we have ascertained in what way the legal *notions* of men are created by their *relations in production,* we shall not be surprised by the following words of Marx: "It is not the consciousness of men that determines their being" (i.e., the form of their social existence—*G.P.*), "but, on the contrary, their social being that determines their consciousness."* Now we know already that at least in relation to one sphere of consciousness this is really so, and why it is so. We have only to decide whether it is always so, and, if the answer is in the affirmative, why it is always so? Let us keep for the time being to the same legal notions.

"At a certain stage of their development, the *material productive forces* of society come in conflict with the existing *relations of production*, or—what is but a legal expression for the same thing—with the property relations within which they have been at work hitherto. From forms of *development* of the productive forces these relations turn into their fetters. Then begins an epoch of social revolution."**

Social ownership of movable and immovable property arises because it is convenient and moreover necessary for the process of primitive production. It maintains the existence of primitive society, it facilitates the further development of its productive forces, and men cling to it, they consider it natural and necessary. But now, *thanks to those property relations and within them*, the productive forces have developed to such an extent that a wider

---
* K. Marx and F. Engels, *Selected Works*, Vol. I, Moscow, 1955, p. 363.—*Ed.*
** *Ibid.*, p. 368.

field has opened for the application of individual efforts. Now social property becomes in some cases *harmful* for society, it impedes the further development of its productive forces, and therefore it yields place to *personal appropriation*: a more or less rapid revolution takes place in the legal institutions of society. This revolution necessarily is accompanied by a revolution in the legal conceptions of men: people who thought previously that only social property was good, now began to think that in some cases individual appropriation was better. But no, we are expressing it inaccurately, we are representing as two separate processes what is completely inseparable, what represents only two sides of one and the same process: *in consequence of the development of the productive forces, the actual relations of men in the process of production were bound to change, and these new de facto relations expressed themselves in new legal notions.*

Mr. Kareyev assures us that materialism is just as one-sided in its application to history as idealism. Each represents, in his opinion, only a "moment" in the development of complete scientific truth. "After the first and second moments must come a third moment: the one-sidedness of the thesis and that of the antithesis will find their application in the synthesis, as the expression of the complete truth."* It will be a most interesting synthesis. "In what that synthesis will consist, I shall not for the time being say," the Professor adds. A pity! Fortunately, our "historiosophist" does not very strictly observe this vow of silence which he has imposed upon himself. He immediately gives us to understand in what will consist and whence will arise that complete scientific truth which will, in time, be understood by all enlightened humanity, but for the time being is known only to Mr. Ka-

---

* *Vestnik Yevropy*, July 1894, p. 6.

reyev. It will grow out of the following considerations: "Every human personality, consisting of body and soul, leads a two-fold life—physical and psychical—appearing before us neither exclusively as flesh with its material requirements, nor exclusively as spirit with its intellectual and moral requirements. Both the body and the soul of man have their requirements, which seek satisfaction and which place the individual personality in different relationships to the external world, i.e., to nature and to other men, i.e., to society, and these relationships are of a two-fold character."*

That man consists of soul and body is a just "synthesis," though hardly what one would call a very new discovery. If Mr. Professor is acquainted with the history of modern philosophy, he must know that it has been breaking its teeth on this same synthesis for whole centuries, and has not been able to cope with it properly. And if he imagines that this "synthesis" will reveal to him "the essence of the historical process," Mr. V. V. himself will have to agree that something is going wrong with his "professor," and that it is not Mr. Kareyev who is destined to become the Spinoza of "historiosophy."

With the development of the productive forces, which lead to changes in the mutual relationships of men in the social process of production, there change all property relations. But it was already Guizot who told us that political constitutions are rooted in property relations. This is fully confirmed by modern knowledge. The union of kindred yields place to the territorial union precisely on account of the changes which arise in property relations. More or less important territorial unions amalgamate in organisms called states, again in consequence of changes which have taken place in property relations,

---

* *Ibid.*, p. 7.

or in consequence of new requirements of the social process of production. This has been excellently demonstrated, for example, in relation to the large states of the East.* Equally well this has been explained in relation to the states of the ancient world.** And, speaking generally, it is not difficult to demonstrate the truth of this for any particular state on whose origin we have sufficient information. In doing so we only need not to narrow, consciously or unconsciously, Marx's view. What we mean is this.

The particular state of productive forces conditions the *internal* relations of the given society. But the same state of the productive forces also conditions *its external relations* with other societies. On the basis of these external relations, society forms *new requirements*, to satisfy which *new organs* arise. At a superficial glance, the mutual relations of individual societies present themselves as a series of "political" acts, having no direct bearing on economics. In reality, what underlies relations between societies is precisely *economics*, which determines both the real (not only external) causes of inter-tribal and international relations, and their results. To each stage in the development of the productive forces corresponds its own particular system of armament, its military tactics, its diplomacy, its international law. Of course many

---

* See the book of the late L. Mechnikov[29] on the *Great Historical Rivers*. In this book the author in essence only summarized the conclusions arrived at by the most authoritative specialist historians, such as Lenormant. Elisee Reclus says in his introduction to the book that Mechnikov's view will mark an epoch in the history of science. This is untrue, in the sense that the view is not a new one: Hegel expressed it in the most definite way. But undoubtedly science will gain a great deal if it consistently adheres to that view.

** See Morgan's *Ancient Society* and Engels's book, *Origin of the Family, Private Property and the State*.

cases may be pointed out in which international conflicts have no direct relationship with economics. And none of the followers of Marx will dream of disputing the existence of such cases. All they say is: don't stop at the surface of phenomena, go down deeper, ask yourself on what basis did this international law grow up? What created the possibility of international conflicts of this kind? And what you will arrive at in the long run is economics. True, the examination of individual cases is made more difficult by the fact that not infrequently the conflicting societies are going through *dissimilar phases of economic development.*

But at this point we are interrupted by a chorus of acute opponents. "Very well," they cry. "Let us admit that political relations are rooted in economic relations. But once political relations have been given, then, wherever they came from, they, in turn, influence economics. Consequently, there is interaction here, and nothing but interaction."

This objection has not been invented by us. The high value placed upon it by opponents of "economic materialism" is shown by the following fact.

Marx in his *Capital* cites facts which show that the English aristocracy used the political power to achieve its own ends in the sphere of landownership. Dr. Paul Barth, who wrote a critical essay entitled *Die Geschichtsphilosophie Hegel's und der Hegelianer*, has seized on this to reproach Marx with contradicting himself: you yourself, he says, admit that there is interaction here: and to prove that interaction really exists, our doctor refers to the book of Sternegg, a writer who has done much for the study of the economic history of Germany. Mr. Kareyev thinks that "the pages devoted in Barth's book to the criticism of economic materialism may be recommended as a model of how the problem of the role of the economic factor in history should be solved." Naturally, he has not failed to point out to his readers the objections raised by Barth and the authoritative statement of Inama-Sternegg, "who even formulates the general proposition that interaction between politics and economy is the fundamental characteristic of the development of all states and peoples." We must bring at least a little light into this muddle.

First of all, what does Inama-Sternegg actually say? On the subject of the Carolingian period in the economic history of Germany he makes the following remark: "The interaction between politics and economics which constitutes the main feature of development of all states and all peoples can be traced here in the most exact fashion. As always the political role which falls to the lot of a given people exercises a decisive influence on the further development of its forces, on the structure and elaboration of its social institutions; on the other hand, the internal strength innate in a people and the natural laws of its development determine the measure and the nature of its political activity. In precisely this way the political system of the Carolings no less influenced the changing of the social order and the development of the economic relations in which the people lived at that time than the elemental forces of the people—its economic life—influenced the direction of that political system, leaving on the latter its own peculiar imprint."* And that's all. It's not very much; but this is thought sufficient to refute Marx.

Now let us recall, in the second place, what Marx says about the relations between economies on the one hand, and law and politics on the other.

"Legal and political institutions are formed on the

* *Deutsche Wirtschaftsgeschichte bis zum Schluss der Karolingenperiode*, Leipzig, 1889, Band I, S. 233-34.

basis of the actual relations of men in the social process of production. For a time these institutions *facilitate* the further development of the productive forces of a people, the prosperity of its economic life." These are the exact words of Marx; and we ask the first conscientious man we meet, do these words contain any denial of the importance of political relations in economic development, and is Marx refuted by those who remind him of that importance? Is it not true that there is not a trace of any such denial in Marx, and the people just mentioned are refuting nothing at all? To such an extent is it true that one has to consider the question, not of whether Marx has been refuted, but of why he was so badly understood? And to this question we can reply only with the French proverb: la plus belle fille du monde ne peut donner que ce qu'elle a (the most beautiful girl in the world can only give what she has got—*Ed.*). The critics of Marx cannot surpass that measure of understanding with which a bountiful Nature has endowed them.*

---

* Marx says that *"every class struggle is a political struggle."* *Consequently, concludes Barth, politics in your opinion does not influence economics at all, yet you yourself quote facts proving... etc.* Bravo, exclaims Mr. Kareyev, that's what I call a model of how one ought to argue with Marx! The "model" of Mr. Kareyev displays a remarkable power of thought altogether. "Rousseau," says the model, "lived in a society where class distinctions and privileges were carried to the extreme, where all were subjected to an all-powerful despotism; and yet the method of the rational structure of the state borrowed from antiquity—the method which was also used by Hobbes and Locke—led Rousseau to create an ideal of society based on universal equality and popular self-government. This ideal completely contradicted the order existing in France. Rousseau's theory was carried out in practice by the Convention; consequently, philosophy influenced politics, and through it economics" (*loc. cit.*, p. 58). How do you like this brilliant argument, to serve which Rousseau, the son of a poor Genevese Republican, turns out to be the product of aristocratical society? To refute Mr. Barth means to repeat oneself. But what are we to say

Interaction between politics and economics exists: that is just as unquestionable as the fact that Mr. Kareyev does not understand Marx. But does the existence of interaction prohibit us from going further in our analysis of the life of society? No, to think that would mean almost the same as to imagine that the lack of understanding displayed by Mr. Kareyev can prevent *us* from attaining correct "historiosophical" conceptions.

Political institutions influence economic life. They *either facilitate* its development *or impede* it. The first case is in no way surprising from the point of view of Marx, because the given political system has been created for the very purpose of *promoting the further development of the productive forces* (whether it is consciously or unconsciously created is in this case all one to us). The second case does not in any way contradict Marx's point of view, because historical experience shows that once a given political system ceases to correspond to the state of the productive forces, once it is transformed into an obstacle to their further development, it begins to decline and finally is eliminated. Far from contradicting the teachings of Marx, this case confirms them in the best possible way, because it is this case that shows in what sense economics dominates politics, in what way the development of productive forces outdistances the political development of a people.

Economic evolution brings in its wake legal revolutions. It is not easy for a *metaphysician* to understand this because, although he does shout about interaction, he is accustomed to examine phenomena one after another, and one independently of another. But it will be understood without difficulty by anyone who is in the least

---

of Mr. Kareyev, who applauds Barth? Ah, Mr. V. V., your "professor of history" is poor stuff, really he is! We advise you quite disinterestedly: find yourself a new "professor."

capable of *dialectical* thinking. He knows that *quantitative changes*, accumulating gradually, *lead* in the end to *changes of quality*, and that these changes of qualities represent *leaps, interruptions in gradualness.*

At this point our opponents can stand it no longer, and pronounce their "word and deed";[30] why, that's how Hegel used to talk, they shout. That's *how all Nature acts,* we reply.

A tale is soon told, but work goes more slowly. In its application to history, this proverb may be altered in this way: a tale is told very simply, but work is complex in the extreme. Yes, it's easy to say that the development of productive forces brings in its train revolutions in legal institutions! These revolutions represent complex processes, in the course of which the interests of individual members of society group themselves in the most whimsical fashion. For some it is profitable to support the old order, and they defend it with every resource at their command. For others the old order has become already harmful and hateful, and they attack it with all the strength at their disposal. And this is not all. The interests of the innovators are also far from similar in all cases: for some one set of reforms are more important, for others another set. Disputes arise in the camp of the reformers itself, and the struggle becomes more complicated. And although, as Mr. Kareyev so justly remarks, man consists of soul and body, the struggle for the most indisputably material interests necessarily rises before the disputing sides the most undoubtedly spiritual problem of *justice.* To what extent does old order contradict justice? To what extent are the new demands in keeping with justice? These questions inevitably arise in the minds of those who are contesting, although they will not always call it simply justice, but may personify it in the shape of some goddess in human, or even in animal shape. Thus, notwithstanding the injunction pronounced by Mr. Kareyev, the "body" gives birth to the "soul": the *economic* struggle arouses *moral* questions —and the "soul" at closer examination proves to be the "body." *The "justice" of the old believers* not infrequently turns out to be *the interests of the exploiters.*

Those very same people who, with such astounding inventiveness, attribute to Marx the denial of the significance of politics assert that he attached no significance whatsoever to the moral, philosophical, religious or aesthetic conceptions of men, everywhere and anywhere seeing only "the economic." This once again is unnatural chatter, as Shchedrin put it. Marx did not deny the "*significance*" of all these conceptions, but only ascertained whence they came.

"What is electricity? A particular form of motion. What is heat? A particular form of motion. What is light? A particular form of motion. Oh, so that's it! So you don't attach any meaning either to light, or to heat, or to electricity! It's all one motion for you; what one-sidedness, what narrowness of conception!" Just so, gentlemen, narrowness is the word. You have understood perfectly the meaning of the doctrine of the transformation of energy.

Every given stage of development of the productive forces necessarily involves *definite grouping of men* in the social process of production, i.e., *definite relations of production,* i.e., *a definite structure of the whole of society.* But once the structure of society has been given, it is not difficult to understand that the character of that structure will be reflected generally in the entire *psychology* of men, in all their habits, manners, feelings, views, aspirations and ideals. Habits, manners, views, aspirations and ideals will necessarily have to adapt themselves to men's way of life, to their *mode of procuring their subsistence* (to use Peschel's expression). *The psychology of society is always expedient in relation to its economy, always corresponds to it, is always determined by it.* The same phenomenon is repeated here which the Greek philosophers themselves noticed in nature: expediency triumphs, for the reason that that which is inexpedient is by its very character doomed to perish. Is it advantageous for society, in its struggle for existence, that there should be this adaptation of its psychology to its economy, to the conditions of life? Very advantageous, because habits and views which did not correspond to its economy and which contradicted the conditions of existence would interfere with the maintenance of that existence. An expedient psychology is just as useful for society as organs which are well fitted for their task are useful for the organism. But to say that the organs of animals must be appropriate to the conditions of their existence—does that mean the same as saying that the organs have no significance for the animal? Quite the contrary. It means recognizing their colossal and *essential* significance. Only very weak heads could understand matters otherwise. Now the same, the very same, gentlemen, is the case with psychology. Recognizing that it adapts itself to the economy of society, Marx thereby was recognizing its vast and irreplaceable significance.

The difference between Marx and, for example, Mr. Kareyev reduces itself in this case to the fact that the latter, in spite of his inclination to "synthesis," remains a dualist of the purest water. In his view, economics are here and psychology is there: the soul is in one pocket and the body in another. Between these two substances there is interaction, but each of them maintains its independent existence, the origin of which is wrapped in the darkest mystery.* The point of view of Marx eliminates this dualism. With him *the economy of society* and its *psychology* represent two sides of one and the same phenomenon of the "production of life" of men, their struggle for existence, in which they are grouped in a particular way thanks to the particular state of the productive forces. The struggle for existence creates their *economy*, and on the same basis arises their *psychology* as well. Economy itself is something derivative, just like psychology. And that is the very reason why the economy of every progressing society *changes*: the new state of productive forces brings with it a new economic structure just as it does a new psychology, a new "spirit of the age." From this it can be seen that only in a popular speech could one talk about economy as the *prime cause* of all social phenomena. Far from being a prime cause, it is itself a consequence, a "function" of the productive forces.

And now follow the points promised in the footnote. "Both the body and the soul of man have their requirements, which seek satisfaction and which place the individual personality in different relationships to the external world, i.e., to nature and to other men.... The relation of man to nature, according to the physical and spiritual needs of the personality, therefore creates, on the one hand, various kinds of arts aiming at ensuring the material existence of the personality and, on the other hand, all intellectual and moral culture...." The

---

* Don't imagine that we are slandering the worthy professor. He quotes with great praise the opinion of Barth, according to which "law carries on a separate, though not independent existence." Now, it's just this "separateness though not independence" that prevents Mr. Kareyev from mastering "the essence of the historical process." How precisely it prevents him will be immediately shown by points *in the text*.

materialist attitude of man to nature rests upon the requirements of the body, the qualities of matter. It is in the requirements of the body that one must discover "the causes of hunting, cattle-breeding, agriculture, manufacturing industry, trade and monetary operations."

From a commonsense point of view this is so, of course: for if we have no body, why should we need cattle and beasts, land and machines, trade and gold? But on the other hand, we must also say: what is body without soul? No more than matter, and matter after all is dead. Matter of itself can create nothing if in its turn it does not consist of soul and body. Consequently matter traps wild beasts, domesticates cattle, works the land, trades and presides over the banks not of its own intelligence, but by direction of the soul. Consequently it is in the soul that one must seek the ultimate cause for the origin of the materialist attitude of man to nature. Consequently the soul also has dual requirements; consequently it also consists of soul and body—and that somehow sounds not quite right. Nor is that all. Willy-nilly "opinion" arises about the following subject as well. According to Mr. Kareyev it appears that the materialist relation of man to nature arises on the basis of his bodily requirements. But is that exact? Is it only to nature that such relations arise? Mr. Kareyev, perhaps, remembers how the abbé Guibert condemned the municipal communes who were striving for their liberation from the feudal yoke as "base" institutions, the sole purpose of existence of which was, he said, to avoid the proper fulfilment of feudal obligations. What was then speaking in the abbé Guibert—"body" or "soul"? If it was the "body" then, we say again, that body also consisted of "body" and "soul"; and if it was the "soul" then it consisted of "soul" and "body," for it displayed in this case under examination very little of that unselfish attitude to phenomena which, in the words of Mr. Kareyev, represents the distinctive feature of the "soul." Try and make head or tail of that! Mr. Kareyev will say, perhaps, that in the abbé Guibert it was the soul that was speaking, to be exact, but that it was speaking under dictation from the body, and that the same takes place when man is occupied with hunting, with banks, etc. But first of all, in order to dictate, the body again must consist both of body and of soul. And secondly, a crude materialist may remark: well, there's the soul talking under the dictation of the body, consequently the fact that man consists of soul and body does not in itself mean anything at all. Perhaps throughout history all the soul has been doing is to talk under dictation from the body? Mr. Kareyev, of course, will be indignant at such a supposition, and will begin refuting the "crude materialist." We are firmly convinced that victory will remain on the side of the worthy professor; but will he be greatly helped in the fray by that unquestionable circumstance that man consists of soul and body?

And even this is not all. We have read in Mr. Kareyev's writings that on the basis of the spiritual requirements of personality there grow up "mythology and religion... literature and arts" and in general "the theoretical attitude to the external world" (and to oneself also), "to questions of being and cognition," and likewise "the unselfish creative reproduction of external phenomena" (and of one's own intentions). We believed Mr. Kareyev. But... we have an acquaintance, a technological student, who is passionately devoted to the study of the technique of manufacturing industry, but has displayed no "theoretical" attitude to all that has been listed by the professor. And so we find ourselves asking, can our friend be composed only of a body? We beg Mr. Kareyev to resolve as quickly as he can this doubt, so tormenting for ourselves and so humiliating for a young, extremely gifted technologist, who maybe is even a genius!

If Mr. Kareyev's argument has any sense, it is only the following: man has requirements of a higher and lower order, he has egotistical strivings and altruistic feelings. This is the most incontestable truth, but quite incapable of becoming the foundation of "historiosophy." You will never get any further with it than hollow and long-since hackneyed reflections on the theme of human nature: it is no more than such a reflection itself.

While we have been chatting with Mr. Kareyev, our perspicacious critics have had time to catch us contradicting ourselves, and above all Marx. We have said that economy is not the prime cause of all social phenomena, yet at the same time we assert that the psychology of society adapts itself to its economy: the first contradiction. We say that the economy and the psychology of society represent two sides of one and the same phenomenon, whereas Marx himself says that economy is the real foundation on which arise the ideological superstructures: a second contradiction, all the more lamentable for us because in it we are diverging from the views of the man whom we undertook to expound. Let us explain.

That the principal cause of the social historical process is the development of the productive forces, we say word for word with Marx: so that here there is no contradiction. Consequently, if it does exist anywhere, it can only be in the question of the relationship between the economy of society and its psychology. Let us see whether it exists.

The reader will be good enough to remember how private property arises. The development of the productive forces places men in such relations of production that the personal appropriation of certain objects proves to be more convenient for the process of production. In keeping with this the legal conceptions of primitive man change. The *psychology* of society adapts itself to its *economy*. On the given *economic foundation* there rises up fatally the *ideological superstructure* appropriate to it. But on the other hand each new step in the development of the productive forces places men, in their daily life, in new mutual relations which do not correspond to the relations of production now becoming outdated. These new and unprecedented situations reflect themselves in the psychology of men, and very strongly change it. In what direction? Some members of society defend the old order: these are the people of stagnation. Others—to whom the old order is not advantageous—stand for progress; their psychology changes in the direction of *those relations of production which in time will replace the old economic relations, now becoming outdated*. The adaptation of psychology to economy, as you see, continues, but slow psychological evolution *precedes* economic revolution.*

Once this revolution has taken place, a complete harmony is established between the psychology of society and its economy. Then on the basis of the new economy there takes place the full flowering of the new psychology. For a certain time this harmony remains unbroken, and even becomes stronger and stronger. But little by little the first shoots of a new discord make their appearance; the psychology of the foremost class, for the reason mentioned above, again outlives old relations of production: without for a moment ceasing to adapt itself to economy, it again adapts itself to the *new* relations

---

* In essence this is the very psychological process which the proletariat of Europe is now going through: its psychology is already adapting itself to the new, future relations of production.

of production, constituting the germ of the future economy. Well, are not these two sides of one and the same process?

Up to now we have been illustrating the idea of Marx mainly by examples from the sphere of the law of property. This law is undoubtedly the same ideology we have been concerned with, but ideology of the first or, so to speak, lower sort. How are we to understand the view of Marx regarding ideology of the higher sort—science, philosophy, the arts, etc.?

In the development of these ideologies, economy is the foundation in this sense, that society must achieve a certain degree of prosperity in order to produce out of itself a certain stratum of people who could devote their energies exclusively to scientific and other similar occupations. Furthermore, the views of Plato and Plutarch* which we quoted earlier show that the very *direction* of intellectual work in society is determined by the *production relations of the latter.* It was already Vico who said of the sciences that they grow out of social needs. In respect of such a science as political economy, this is clear for everyone who has the least knowledge of its history. Count Pecchio justly remarked that political economy particularly confirms the rule that practice always and everywhere precedes science.** Of course, this

---

* See pages 163-66 of this edition.—*Tr.*

** "Quand'essa cominciava appena a nascere nel diciassettesimo secolo, alcune nazioni avevano già da più secoli fiorito colla loro sola esperienza, da cui poscia la scienza ricavò i suoi dettami." *Storia della Economia pubblica in Italia, ecc.*, Lugano, 1829, p. 11.

[Even before it (political economy) began to take shape in the seventeenth century, some nations had been flourishing for several centuries relying solely on their practical experience. That experience was later used by this science for its propositions.—*Ed.*]

John Stuart Mill repeats: "In every department of human affairs,

too can be interpreted in a very abstract sense; one may say: "Well, naturally science needs experience, and the more the experience the fuller the science." But this is not the point here. Compare the economic views of Aristotle or Xenophon with the views of Adam Smith or Ricardo, and you will see that between the economic science of ancient Greece, on the one hand, and the economic science of bourgeois society, on the other, there exists not only a *quantitative* but also a *qualitative* difference—the point of view is quite different, the attitude to the subject is quite different. How is this difference to be explained? Simply by the fact that *the very phenomena have changed*: relations of production in bourgeois society don't resemble production relations in ancient society. Different relations in production create different views in science. Furthermore, compare the views of Ricardo with the views of some Bastiat, and you will see that these men have different views of production relations which were the same in their *general character*, being *bourgeois* production relations. Why is this? Because at the time of Ricardo these relations were still only flowering and becoming stronger, while in the time of Bastiat they had already begun to decline. Different conditions of the same production relations necessarily had to reflect themselves in the views of the persons who were defending them.

Or let us take the science of public law. How and why did its theory develop? "The scientific elaboration of public law," says Professor Gumplowicz, "begins only where the dominating classes come into conflict among

---

Practice long precedes Science.... The conception, accordingly, of Political Economy as a branch of Science is extremely modern; but the subject with which its enquiries are conversant has in all ages necessarily constituted one of the chief practical interests of mankind." *Principles of Political Economy*, London, 1843, Vol. I, p. 1

themselves regarding the sphere of authority belonging to each of them. Thus, the first big political struggle which we encounter in the second half of the European middle ages, the struggle between the secular and the ecclesiastic authority, the struggle between the Emperor and the Pope, gives the first impetus to the development of the German science of public law. The second disputed political question which brought division into the midst of the dominating classes, and gave an impulse to the elaboration by publicists of the appropriate part of public law was the question of the election of the Emperor,"* and so on.

What are the mutual relations of classes? They are, in the first place, just those relations which people adopt to one another in the social process of production—*production relations*. These relations find their expression in the political organization of society and in the political struggle of various classes, and that struggle serves as an impetus for the appearance and development of various *political theories*: on the economic foundation there necessarily arises its appropriate ideological superstructure.

Still, all these ideologies, too, may be of the first quality, but are certainly not of the highest order. How do matters stand, for example, with philosophy or art? Before replying to this question, we must make a certain digression.

Helvetius started from the principle that l'homme n'est que sensibilité. From this point of view it is obvious that man will avoid unpleasant sensations and will strive to acquire only those which are pleasant. This is the inevitable, natural egotism of sentient matter. But if this is so, in what way do there arise in man quite

---

* *Rechtsstaat und Sozialismus*, Innsbruck, 1881, S. 124-25.

unselfish strivings, like love of truth or heroism? Such was the problem which Helvetius had to solve. He did not prove capable of solving it, and in order to get out of his difficulty he simply crossed out that same X, that same unknown quantity, which he had undertaken to define. He began to say that there is not a single learned man who loves truth unselfishly, that every man sees in it only the path to glory, and in glory the path to money, and in money the means of procuring for himself pleasant physical sensations, as for example, by purchasing savoury food or beautiful slaves. One need hardly say how futile are such explanations. They only demonstrated what we noted earlier—the incapacity of French *metaphysical* materialism to grapple with *questions of development.*

The father of modern *dialectical* materialism is made responsible for a view of the history of human thought which would be nothing else than a repetition of the metaphysical reflections of Helvetius. Marx's view of the history of, say, philosophy is often understood approximately as follows: if Kant occupied himself with questions of transcendental aesthetics, if he talked of the categories of mind or of the antinomies of reason, these were only empty phrases. In reality he wasn't at all interested in either aesthetics, or antinomies, or categories. All he wanted was one thing: to provide the class to which he belonged, i.e., the German petty bourgeoisie, with as many savoury dishes and "beautiful slaves" as possible. Categories and antinomies seemed to him an excellent means of securing this, and so he began to "breed" them.

Need I assure the reader that such an impression is absolute nonsense? When Marx says that a given theory corresponds to such and such a period of the economic development of society, he does not in the least intend to say thereby that the thinking representatives of the class which ruled during this period deliberately adapted their views to the interests of their more or less wealthy, more or less generous benefactors.

There have always and everywhere been sycophants, of course, but it is not they who have advanced the human intellect. And those who really moved it forward were concerned for the truth, and not for the interests of the great ones in this world.*

"Upon the different forms of property," says Marx, "upon the social conditions of existence, rises an entire superstructure of distinct and peculiarly formed sentiments, illusions, modes of thought and views of life. The entire class creates and forms them out of its material foundations and out of the corresponding social relations."** The process by which the ideological superstructure arises takes place *unnoticed by man*. They regard that superstructure, not as the temporary product of temporary relations, but as something natural and essentially obligatory. Individuals whose views and feelings have been formed under the influence of education and environment may be filled with the most sincere, most *devoted* attitude to the views and forms of social existence which arose historically on the basis of more or less *narrow class interests*. The same applies to whole parties. The French democrats of 1848 expressed the aspirations of the petty bourgeoisie. The petty bourgeoisie naturally strove to defend its class interests. But "one must not form the narrow-minded notion that the petty bourgeoisie, on principle, wishes to enforce an egoistic

---

* This did not prevent them from sometimes fearing the strong. Thus, for example, Kant said of himself: "No one will force me to say that which is against my beliefs; but I will not venture to say *all* I believe."

** K. Marx and F. Engels, *Selected Works*, Vol. I, Moscow, 1955, p. 272.—*Ed.*

class interest. Rather, it believes that the *special* conditions of its emancipation are the *general* conditions within the frame of which alone modern society can be saved and the class struggle avoided. Just as little must one imagine that the democratic representatives are indeed all shopkeepers or enthusiastic champions of shopkeepers. According to their education and their individual position they may be as far apart as heaven from earth. What makes them representatives of the petty bourgeoisie is the fact that in their minds they do not get beyond the limits which the latter do not get beyond in life, that they are consequently driven, theoretically, to the same problems and solutions to which material interest and social position drive the latter practically. This is, in general, the relationship between the political and literary representatives of a class and the class they represent."*

---

* Proving that the conditions of life (les circonstances) influence the organization of animals, Lamarck makes an observation which it will be useful to recall here in order to avoid misunderstandings. "It is true, if this statement were to be taken literally, I should be convicted of an error; for whatever the environment may do, it does not work any direct modification whatever in the shape and organization of animals." Thanks to considerable changes in that environment, however, new requirements, different from those previously existing, make their appearance. If these new requirements last a long time, they lead to the appearance of new *habits*. "Now, if a new environment ... induces new *habits* in these animals, that is to say, leads them to new activities which have become habitual, the result will be the use of some one part in preference to some other part, and in some cases the total disuse of some part no longer necessary." The increasing of use or its absence will not remain without influence on the *structure* of organs, and consequently of the whole organism. (Lamarck, *Zoological Philosophy*, Vol. I, ch. VII, in Elliot's translation, London, 1914, pp. 107-08.—*Tr.*)

In the same way must also be understood the influence of economic requirements, and of others following from them, on the

Marx says this in his book on the coup d'état of Napoleon III. In another of his works he perhaps still better elucidates for us the psychological dialectics of *classes*. He is speaking of the emancipatory role which sometimes individual classes have to play.

"No class in civil society can play this part unless it calls forth a phase of enthusiasm in its own ranks and those of the masses: a phase when it fraternizes and intermingles with society in general, is identified with society, is felt and recognized to be the *universal representative* of society, and when its own demands and rights are really the demands and rights of society itself, and it is in truth the social head and the social heart. Only in the name of society and its rights in general can a particular class vindicate its general domination. The position of liberator cannot be taken by storm, simply through revolutionary energy and intellectual self-confidence. If the emancipation of a particular class is to be identified with the revolution of a people, if one social class is to be treated as the whole social order, then, on the other hand, all the deficiencies of society must be concentrated in another class; a definite class must be the universal stumbling-block, the embodiment of universal fetters.... If one class is to be the liberating class par excellence, then another class must contra-

---

psychology of a people. Here there takes place a slow process of adaptation by exercise or non-exercise; while our opponents of "economic" materialism imagine that, in Marx's opinion, people when they experience new requirements immediately and deliberately change their views. Naturally this seems to them a piece of stupidity. But it is they themselves who invented this stupidity: Marx says nothing of the kind. Generally speaking, the objections of these thinkers remind us of the following triumphant refutation of Darwin by a certain clergyman: "Darwin says, throw a hen into the water and she will grow webbed feet. I assert that the hen will simply drown."

riwise be the obvious subjugator. The general negative significance of the French aristocracy and clergy determined the general positive significance of the bourgeoisie, the class immediately confronting and opposing them."*

After this preliminary explanation, it will no longer be difficult to clear up for oneself Marx's view on ideology of the highest order, as for example philosophy and art. But to make it still clearer, we shall compare it with the view of H. Taine:

"In order to understand a work of art, an artist, a group of artists," says this writer, "one must picture to oneself exactly the general condition of minds and manners of their age. There lies the ultimate explanation, there is to be found the first cause which determines all the rest. This truth is confirmed by experience. In fact, if we trace the main epochs of the history of art, we shall find that the arts appear and disappear together with certain conditions of minds and manners with which they are connected. Thus, Greek tragedy—the tragedy of Aeschylus, Sophocles and Euripides—appears together with the victory of the Greeks over the Persians, in the heroic epoch of the little city republics, at the moment of that great effort thanks to which they won their independence and established their hegemony in the civilized world. That tragedy disappears, together with that independence and that energy, when the degeneration of characters and the Macedonian conquest hand over Greece to the power of foreigners.

"In exactly the same way Gothic architecture develops together with the final establishment of the feudal order,

---

* *Contribution to the Critique of the Hegelian Philosophy of Law (Deutsch-Französische Jahrbücher, 1844).*

in the semi-renaissance of the eleventh century, at a time when society, freed from Northmen and robbers, begins to settle down. It disappears at the time when this military regime of small independent barons is disintegrating, towards the end of the fifteenth century, together with all the manners which followed from it, in consequence of the coming into existence of the new monarchies.

"Similarly Dutch art flourishes at that glorious moment when, thanks to its stubbornness and its valour, Holland finally throws off the Spanish yoke, fights successfully against England, and becomes the wealthiest, freest, most industrious, most prosperous state in Europe. It declines at the beginning of the eighteenth century, when Holland falls to a secondary role, yielding the first to England, and becomes simply a bank, a commercial house, maintained in the greatest order, peaceful and well-kept, in which man may live at his ease like a sagacious bourgeois, with no great ambitions or great emotions. Finally, just in the same way does French tragedy appear at the time when, under Louis XIV, the firmly established monarchy brings with it the rule of decorum, court life, the brilliance and elegance of the domestic aristocracy; and disappears when noble society and court manners are abolished by the Revolution.... Just as naturalists study the physical temperature in order to understand the appearance of this or that plant, maize or oats, aloes or pine, in exactly the same way must one study the moral temperature in order to explain the appearance of this or that form of art: pagan sculpture or realistic painting, mystic architecture or classical literature, voluptuous music or idealistic poetry. The works of the human spirit, like the works of living Nature, are explained only by their environment."*

Any follower of Marx will unquestionably agree with all this: yes, any work of art, like any philosophical system, can be explained by the state of minds and manners of the particular age. But what explains this general state of minds and manners? The followers of Marx think that it is explained by the social order, the qualities of the social environment. "When a great change takes place in the condition of humanity, it brings by degrees a corresponding change in human conceptions," says the same Taine.** That, too, is correct. The only question is, what is it that causes changes in the position of social man, i.e., in the social order? It is only on this question that "economic materialists" differ from Taine.

For Taine the task of history, as of science, is in the last resort a *"psychological task."* According to him, the general state of minds and manners creates not only the different forms of art, literature and philosophy but also the *industry of the given people* and all its social institutions. And this means that social environment has its ultimate cause in "the state of minds and manners."

Thus it turns out that the *psychology* of social man is determined by his *position*, and his *position* by his *psychology*. This is once again the antinomy we know so well, with which the writers of the Enlightenment of the eighteenth century failed to grapple. Taine did not resolve this antinomy. He only gave, in a number of remarkable works, numerous brilliant illustrations of its first proposition—the thesis that *the state of minds*

---

* *Philosophie de l'art* (12me édition), Paris, 1872, pp. 13-17.
** *Philosophie de l'art dans les Pays-Bas*, Paris, 1869, p. 96.

and manners is determined by the social environment.

Taine's contemporaries in France, who contested his aesthetic theory, put forward the *antithesis* that *the qualities of the social environment are determined by the state of minds and manners.** This kind of discussion could be carried on until the second advent, not only without resolving the fateful antinomy, but even without noticing its existence.

It is only the historical theory of Marx that resolves the antinomy and thereby brings the argument to a satisfactory conclusion or, at any rate, provides the *possibility* of concluding it satisfactorily, if people have ears to hear and a brain wherewith to think.

The qualities of the social environment are determined by the state of the productive forces in every given age. Once the state of the productive forces is determined,

---

* "Nous subissons l'influence du milieu politique ou historique, nous subissons l'influence du milieu social, nous subissons aussi l'influence du milieu physique. Mais il ne faut pas oublier que si nous la subissons, nous pouvons pourtant aussi lui resister et vous savez sans doute qu'il y en a de mémorables exemples.... Si nous subissons l'influence du milieu, un pouvoir que nous avons aussi, c'est de ne pas nous laisser faire, ou pour dire encore quelque chose de plus, c'est de conformer, c'est d'adapter le milieu lui-même, à nos propres convenances." (F. Brunetière, *L'évolution de la critique depuis la renaissance jusqu'à nos jours*, Paris, 1890, p. 260-61.)

("We experience the influence of the political or historical environment, we experience the influence of the social environment, we also experience the influence of the physical environment. But it must not be forgotten that, if we experience it, we can however also resist it, and you know doubtless that there are memorable examples of this.... If we experience the influence of environment, a power which we also have is not to let ourselves be swayed, or to say more, it is the power of making the environment conform, of adapting it to our own convenience."—*Ed.*)

the qualities of the social environment are also determined, and so is the psychology corresponding to it, and the interaction between the environment on the one side and minds and manners on the other. Brunetière is quite right when he says that we not only adapt ourselves to our environment, but also adapt it to our needs. You will ask, but whence come the needs which do *not* correspond with the qualities of the environment around us? They arise in us—and, in saying this, we have in view not only the material but also all the so-called spiritual needs of men—thanks to that same historical movement, that same development of the productive forces, owing to which every particular social order sooner or later proves to be unsatisfactory, out of date, requiring radical reconstruction, and maybe fit only for the scrapheap. We have already pointed earlier to the example of legal institutions to show how the psychology of men may outdistance the particular forms of their social life.

We are sure that, on reading these lines, many readers —even those favourably inclined towards us—have remembered a mass of examples and of historical phenomena which apparently cannot in any way be explained from our point of view. And the readers are already prepared to tell us: "You are right, but not entirely; equally right, but also not entirely, are the people who hold views opposite to yours; both you and they see only half the truth." But wait, reader, don't seek salvation in *eclecticism* without grasping all that the *modern monist*, i.e., *materialist*, view of history can give you.

Up to this point our propositions, of necessity, were very abstract. But we already know that *there is no abstract truth, truth is always concrete*. We must give our propositions a more concrete shape.

As almost every society is subjected to the influence of its neighbours, it may be said that *for every society there exists, in its turn, a certain social historical environment which influences its development.* The sum of influences experienced by every given society at the hands of its neighbours can never be equal to the sum of the influences experienced at the same time by another society. Therefore *every society lives in its own particular historical environment, which may be, and very often is, in reality very similar to the historical environment surrounding other nations and peoples, but can never be, and never is, identical with it.* This introduces an extremely powerful element of diversity into that process of social development which, from our previous abstract point of view, seemed most schematic.

For example, the clan is a form of community characteristic of all human societies at a particular stage of their development. But the influence of the historical environment very greatly varies the destinies of the clan in different tribes. It attaches to the clan itself a particular, so to speak individual, character, it retards or accelerates its disintegration, and in particular it diversifies the process of that disintegration. But diversity in the process of the disintegration of the clan determines the diversity of those forms of community which succeed clan life. Up to now we have been saying that the development of the productive forces leads to the appearance of private property and to the disappearance of primitive communism. Now we must say that the character of the private property which arises on the ruins of primitive communism is diversified by the influence of the historical environment which surrounds each particular society. "The careful study of the Asiatic, particularly Indian, forms of communal property would show how from different forms of primitive communal property there follow different forms of its disintegration. Thus, for example, different original types of Roman and German private property could be traced back to different forms of the Indian communal property."*

The influence of the historical environment of a given society tells, of course, on the development of its ideologies as well. Do foreign influences weaken, and if so to what extent do they weaken, the dependence of this development on the economic structure of society?

Compare the Aeneid with the Odyssey, or the French classical tragedy with the classical tragedy of the Greeks. Compare the Russian tragedy of the eighteenth century with classical French tragedy. What will you see? The Aeneid is only an imitation of the Odyssey, the classical tragedy of the French is only an imitation of Greek tragedy; the Russian tragedy of the eighteenth century has been composed, although by unskilful hands, after the image and likeness of the French. Everywhere there has been imitation; but the imitator is separated from his model by all that distance which exists between the society which gave him, the *imitator*, birth and the society in which the *model* lived. And note that we are speaking, not of the greater or lesser perfection of *finish*, but of what constitutes the *soul* of the work of art in question. Whom does the Achilles of Racine resemble —a Greek who has just emerged from a state of barbarism, or a marquis—talon rouge—of the seventeenth century? The personages of the Aeneid, it has been observed, were Romans of the time of Augustus. True, the characters of the Russian so-called tragedies of the eighteenth century can hardly be described as giving us a picture of the Russian people of the time, but their very

---

* Marx, *Zur Kritik der politischen Oekonomie*, Anmerkung, S. 10.

worthlessness bears witness to the state of Russian society: they bring out before us *its immaturity*.

Another example. Locke undoubtedly was the teacher of the vast majority of the French philosophers of the eighteenth century (Helvetius called him the greatest metaphysician of all ages and peoples). Yet, between Locke and his French pupils there is precisely that same distance which separated English society at the time of the "Glorious Revolution" from French society as it was several decades before the "Great Rebellion" of the French people.

A third example. The "true Socialists" of Germany in the 40s imported their ideas direct from France. Yet nevertheless these ideas, one may say, had already at the frontier stamped on them the mark of the society in which they were destined to spread.

Thus *the influence of the literature of one country on the literature of another is directly proportional to the similarity of the social relations of these countries*. It does not exist at all when that similarity is equal to zero. As an example, the African Negroes up to the present time have not experienced the least influence of the European literatures. *This influence is one-sided when one people through its backwardness can give nothing to another, either in the sense of form or in the sense of content.* As an example, the French literature of last century, influencing Russian literature, did not itself experience the least Russian influence. Finally, *this influence is reciprocal when, in consequence of the similarity of social life, and consequently of cultural development, each of the two peoples making the exchange can borrow something from the other.* As an example, French literature, influencing English, experienced the influence of the latter in its turn.

The pseudo-classical French literature was very much

to the liking, at one time, of the English aristocracy. But the English imitators could never equal their French models. This was because all the efforts of the English aristocrats could not transport into England those relations of society in which the French pseudo-classical literature flourished.

The French philosophers were filled with admiration for the philosophy of Locke; but they went much further than their teacher. This was because the class which they represented had gone in France, fighting against the old regime, much further than the class of English society whose aspirations were expressed in the philosophical works of Locke.

When, as in modern Europe, we have an entire system of societies, which influenced one another extremely powerfully, *the development of ideology* in each of these societies becomes just as increasingly complex as its *economic development* becomes more and more complex, under the influence of constant trade with other countries.

We have in these conditions one literature, as it were, common to all civilized mankind. But just as a zoological genus is subdivided into species, so this world literature is subdivided into the literatures of the individual nations. Every literary movement, every philosophical idea assumes its own distinctive features, sometimes quite a new significance with every particular civilized nation.* When Hume visited France, the French "philosophers" greeted him as their fellow-thinker. But on one occasion, when dining with Holbach, this undoubted fellow-thinker of the French philosophers began talking about "natural religion." "As regards atheists," he said, "I do not admit their existence: I have never met a single

---

* This sentence is to be found only in the first Russian edition.—*Ed.*

one." "You have not had much luck up to now," retorted the author of the *System of Nature*. "Here, for a start, you can see seventeen atheists seated at table." The same Hume had a decisive influence on Kant, whom he, as the latter himself admitted, awakened from his *dogmatic drowsiness*. But the philosophy of Kant differs considerably from the philosophy of Hume. The very same fund of ideas led to the militant atheism of the French materialists, to the religious indifferentism of Hume and to the "practical" religion of Kant. The reason was that the religious question in England at that time did not play the same part as it was playing in France, and in France not the same as in Germany. And this difference in the significance of the religious question was caused by the fact that in each of these three countries the social forces were not in the same mutual relationship as in each of the others. Similar in their *nature*, but dissimilar in their degree of development, the elements of society combined differently in the different European countries, with the result that in each of them there was a very particular "*state of minds and manners*," which expressed itself in the national literature, philosophy, art, etc. In consequence of this, one and the same question might excite Frenchmen to passion and leave the English cold; one and the same argument might be treated by a progressive German with respect, while a progressive Frenchman would regard it with bitter hatred. To what did German philosophy owe its colossal successes? To German realities, answers Hegel: the French have no time to occupy themselves with philosophy, life pushes them into the practical sphere (zum Praktischen), while German realities are more reasonable, and the Germans may perfect theory in peace and quiet (beim Theoretischen stehen bleiben). As a matter of fact, this imaginary reasonableness of German realities reduced itself to the poverty of German social and political life, which left educated Germans at that time no other choice than to serve as officials of unattractive "realities" (to adapt themselves to the "Practical") or to seek consolation in *theory*, and to concentrate in this sphere all the strength of their passion, all the energy of their thought. But if the more advanced countries, going away into the "Practical," had not pushed forward the theoretical reasoning of the Germans, if they had not awakened the latter from their "dogmatic drowsiness," never would that negative quality—the poverty of social and political life—have given birth to such a colossal positive result as the brilliant flowering of German philosophy.

Goethe makes Mephistopheles say: "Vernunft wird Unsinn, Wohltat—Plage." ("Reason has become unreason and right wrong."—*Ed.*) In its application to the history of German philosophy, one may almost venture such a paradox: nonsense gave birth to reason, poverty proved a benefaction.

But I think we may finish this part of our exposition. Let us recapitulate what has been said in it.

Interaction exists in international life just as it does in the internal life of peoples; it is quite natural and unquestionably inevitable; nevertheless *by itself* it explains nothing. In order to understand interaction, one must ascertain the attributes of the interacting forces, and these attributes cannot find their ultimate explanation in the fact of interaction, however much they may change thanks to that fact. In the case we have taken, the qualities of the interacting forces, the attributes of the social organisms influencing one another, are explained in the long run by the cause we already know: *the economic structure of these organisms, which is determined by the state of their productive forces.*

Now the historical philosophy we are setting forth has assumed, we hope, a somewhat more concrete shape. But it is still abstract, it is still far from "real life." We have to make yet a further step towards the latter.

At first we spoke of "society": then we went on to the interaction of societies. But societies, after all, are not homogeneous in their composition: we already know that the break-up of primitive communism leads to inequality, to the origin of classes which have different and often quite opposed interests. We already know that classes carry on between themselves an almost uninterrupted, now hidden, now open, now chronic, now acute struggle. And this struggle exercises a vast and in the highest degree important influence on the development of ideology. It may be said without exaggeration that we shall understand nothing of this development *without taking into account the class struggle.*

"Do you wish to discover, if one may put it that way, the true cause of the tragedy of Voltaire?" asks Brunetière. "Look for it, first, in the personality of Voltaire, and particularly in the necessity which hung over him of doing something different from what Racine and Quinault had already done, yet at the same time of following in their footsteps. Of the romantic drama, the drama of Hugo and Dumas, I will permit myself to say that its definition is fully comprised in the definition of the drama of Voltaire. If romanticism did not want to do this or that on the stage, it was because it wanted to do the opposite of classicism.... In literature as in art, after the influence of the individual, the most important influence is that of some works on others. Sometimes we strive to compete with our predecessors in their own field, and in that way certain methods become stable, schools are established, traditions formed. Or sometimes we try to act otherwise than they did, and then development proceeds in contradiction to tradition, new schools appear, methods are transformed."*

Leaving aside for the time being the question of the role of the individual, we shall remark that it has long been time to ponder over "the influence of some works on others." In absolutely all ideologies development takes place in the way indicated by Brunetière. The ideologists of one epoch *either* move in the tracks of their predecessors, developing *their* thoughts, applying *their* methods and only allowing themselves to "compete" with their forerunners, *or else* they revolt against the old ideas and methods, *enter into contradiction to them. Organic* epochs, Saint-Simon would have said, are replaced by *critical* epochs. The latter are particularly noteworthy.

Take any question, like for example that of money. For the Mercantilists money was wealth par excellence: they attributed to money an exaggerated, almost exceptional importance. The people who revolted against the Mercantilists, entering into *"contradiction"* to them, not only corrected their exceptionalism but themselves, at least the most headstrong among them, fell into exceptionalism, and precisely into the opposite extreme: they said that money is simply a symbol, which in itself has absolutely no value. That was the view of money held, for example, by Hume. If the view of the Mercantilists can be explained by the immaturity of commodity production and circulation in their day, it would be strange to explain the views of their opponents simply by the fact that commodity production and circulation had developed very strongly. For that subsequent development did not for a moment actually transform money into a mere symbol, deprived of internal value. Whence did the excep-

---

* *Loc. cit.*, pp. 262-63.

tionalism of Hume's view, then, originate? It originated in the fact of struggle, in *"contradiction"* to the Mercantilists. He wanted to "do the opposite" to the Mercantilists, just as the Romantics "wanted to do the opposite" to the classics. Therefore one may say, just as Brunetière says of the romantic drama, that Hume's view of money is completely included in the view of the Mercantilists, being *its opposite*.

Another example. The philosophers of the eighteenth century resolutely and sharply struggle against any kind of mysticism. The French Utopians are all more or less imbued with religious feeling. What brought about this return of mysticism? Did such men as the author of *The New Christianity** have less "lumières" than the Encyclopaedists? No, they had no less lumières, and, generally speaking, their views were very closely linked with the views of the Encyclopaedists: they were descended from the latter in the direct line. But they entered into "contradiction" to the Encyclopaedists on some questions—particularly, that is, on the question of the organization of society—and there appeared in them the striving to "do the opposite" to the Encyclopaedists. Their attitude to religion was simply the opposite of the attitude to it taken up by the "philosophers"; their view of religion was already included in the view of the latter.

Take, finally, the history of philosophy. *Materialism* triumphed in France during the second half of the eighteenth century; under its banner marched the extreme section of the French tiers état (Third Estate.—*Ed.*). In England in the seventeenth century materialism was the passion of the defenders of the old regime, the aristocrats, the supporters of absolutism. The reason, here too, is clear. Those to whom the English aristocrats of the

---
* Saint-Simon.—*Ed.*

Restoration were "in contradiction" were extreme religious fanatics; in order "to do the opposite" to what they were doing, the *reactionaries* had to go as far as *materialism*. In France of the eighteenth century things were exactly opposite: the defenders of the *old* order stood for religion, and it was the extreme revolutionaries who arrived at *materialism*. The history of human thought is full of such examples, and all of them confirm one and the same thing: *in order to understand the "state of minds" of each particular critical epoch, in order to explain why during this epoch precisely these, and not those, teachings gain the upper hand, we must as a preliminary study the "state of minds" in the preceding epoch, and discover what teachings and tendencies were then dominant*. Without this we shall not understand at all the intellectual condition of the epoch concerned, however well we get to know its economy.

But even this must not be understood in abstract fashion, as the Russian "intelligentsia" is accustomed to understand everything. The ideologists of one epoch never wage against their predecessors a struggle sur toute la ligne, on all questions of human knowledge and social relations. The French Utopians of the nineteenth century were completely at one with the Encyclopaedists on a number of anthropological views; the English aristocrats of the Restoration were quite at one with the Puritans, whom they so hated, on a number of questions, such as civil law, etc. The territory of psychology is subdivided into provinces, the provinces into counties, the counties into rural districts and communities, and the communities represent unions of individuals (i.e., of individual questions). When a "contradiction" arises, when struggle blazes up, its passion seizes, as a rule, only upon individual provinces—if not individual counties—and only its reflection falls upon the neighbouring areas.

First of all that province to which *hegemony belonged* in the preceding epoch is subjected to attack. It is only gradually that the "miseries of war" spread to its nearest neighbours and most faithful allies of the province which has been attacked. Therefore we must add that, in ascertaining the character of any particular critical epoch, it is necessary to discover not only the general features of the psychology of the previous organic period, but also the individual peculiarities of that psychology. During one period of history hegemony belongs to religion, during another to politics, and so forth. This circumstance inevitably reflects itself in the character of the corresponding critical epochs, each of which, according to circumstances, either continues formally to recognize the old hegemony, introducing a new, *opposite* content into the dominating conceptions (as, for example, the first English Revolution), or else completely rejects them, and hegemony passes to new provinces of thought (as, for example, the French literature of the Enlightenment). If we remember that these disputes over the hegemony of individual psychological provinces also extend to their neighbours, and moreover extend to a different degree and in a different direction in each individual case, we shall understand to what an extent here, as everywhere, one cannot confine oneself to abstract proposition.

"All that may be so," retort our opponents. "But we don't see what the class struggle has got to do with all this, and we strongly suspect that, having begun with a toast to its health, you're now finishing with one for rest to its soul. You yourself now recognize that the movements of human thought are subjected to certain specific laws, which have nothing in common with the laws of economics or with that development of the productive forces which you have talked about till we are sick of hearing it." We hasten to reply.

That in the development of human thought, or, to speak more exactly, *in the co-ordination of human conceptions and notions there are specific laws*—this, so far as we know, not a single one of the "economic" materialists has ever denied. None of them has ever identified, for example, the laws of logic with the laws of the circulation of commodities. But nevertheless not one of this variety of materialists has found it possible to seek in the laws of thought the ultimate cause, the *prime mover* of the intellectual development of humanity. And it is precisely this which distinguishes, and *advantageously distinguishes*, "economic materialists" from idealists, and particularly from eclectics.

Once the stomach has been supplied with a certain quantity of food, it sets about its work in accordance with the general laws of stomachic digestion. But can one, with the help of these laws, reply to the question of why savoury and nourishing food descends every day into your stomach, while in mine it is a rare visitor? Do these laws explain why some eat too much, while others starve? It would seem that the explanation must be sought in some other sphere, in the working of some other kind of laws. The same is the case with the mind of man. Once it has been placed in a definite situation, once its environment supplies it with certain impressions, it co-ordinates them according to certain general laws (moreover here, too, the results are varied in the extreme by the variety of impressions received). But what places it in that situation? What determines the influx and the character of new impressions? That is the question which cannot be answered by any laws of thought.

Furthermore, imagine that a resilient ball falls from a high tower. Its movement takes place according to a universally known and very simple *law of mechanics*. But suddenly the ball strikes an inclined plane. Its movement is changed in accordance with another, also very simple and universally known *mechanical law*. As a result, we have a broken line of movement, of which one can and must say that it owes its origin to the joint action of the two laws which have been mentioned. But where did the inclined plane which the ball struck come from? This is not explained either by the first or the second law, or yet by their joint action. Exactly the same is the case with human thought. Whence came the circumstances thanks to which its movements were subjected to the combined action of such and such laws? This is not explained either by its individual laws or by their combined action.

The circumstances which condition the movement of thought must be looked for where the writers of the French Enlightenment sought for them. But nowadays we no longer halt at that "limit" which they could not cross. We not only say that man with all his thoughts and feelings is the product of his social environment; we try *to understand the genesis of that environment*. We say that its qualities are determined by such and such reasons, lying outside man and hitherto independent of his will. The multiform changes in the *actual mutual relations of men* necessarily bring in their train changes in the "state of minds," *in the mutual relations of ideas, feelings, beliefs*. Ideas, feelings and beliefs are co-ordinated according to their own particular laws. But these laws are brought into play by external circumstances which have nothing in common with these laws. Where Brunetière sees only the influence of some literary works on others, we see in addition the mutual influences of social groups, strata and classes, influences that lie more deeply. Where he simply says: contradiction appeared, men wanted to do the opposite of what their predecessors had been doing, we add: and the reason why they wanted it was because a new contradiction had appeared in their *actual relations*, because a new social stratum or class had come forward, which could no longer live as the people had lived in former days.

While Brunetière only knows that the Romantics wished to contradict the classics, Brandes tries to explain their propensity to "contradiction" by the position of the class in society to which they belonged. Remember, for example, what he says of the reason for the romantic mood of the French youth during the period of the Restoration and under Louis Philippe.

When Marx says: "If one class is to be the liberating class par excellence, then another class must contrariwise be the obvious subjugator," he also is pointing to a particular, and moreover very important, law of development of social thought. But this law operates, and can operate, only in societies which are divided into classes; it does not operate, and cannot operate, in primitive societies where there are neither classes nor their struggle.

Let us consider the operation of this law. When a certain class is the enslaver of all in the eyes of the rest of the population, then the ideas which prevail in the ranks of that class naturally present themselves to the population also as ideas worthy only of slave-owners. The social consciousness enters into "contradiction" to them: it is attracted by *opposite* ideas. But we have already said that this kind of struggle is never carried on all along the line: there always remain a certain number of ideas which are equally recognized both by the revolutionaries and by the defenders of the old order. The strongest attack, however, is made on the ideas which serve to express the most injurious sides of the dying order at the given time. It is on *those* sides of ideology that the revolutionaries experience an irrepressible desire to *"contradict"* their predecessors. But in relation to other ideas, even though they did grow up on the basis of old social relations, they often remain quite indifferent, and sometimes by tradition continue to cling to them. Thus the French materialists, while waging war on the philosophical and political ideas of the old regime (i.e., against the clergy and the aristocratic monarchy), left almost untouched the old traditions in *literature.* True, here also the aesthetic theories of Diderot were the expression of the new social relations. But the struggle in this sphere was very weak, because the main forces had been concentrated on another field.* Here the standard of revolt was raised only later and, moreover, by people who, warmly sympathizing with the old regime overthrown by the revolution, ought, it would seem, to have sympathized with the literary views which were formed in the golden age of that regime. But even this seeming peculiarity is explained by the principle of "contradiction." How can you expect, for example, that Chateaubriand should sympathize with the old aesthetic theory, when Voltaire—the hateful and harmful Voltaire—was one of its representatives?

"Der Widerspruch ist das Fortleitende" ("Contradiction leads the way forward."—*Ed.*), says Hegel. The history of ideologies seems once more to demonstrate that the old "metaphysician" was not mistaken. It also demonstrates apparently the passing of quantitative changes into qualitative. But we ask the reader not to be upset by this, and to hear us out to the end.

Up to now we have been saying that once the productive forces of society have been determined, its structure also has been determined and, consequently, its psychol-

---

* In Germany the struggle between literary views, as is known, went on with much greater energy, but here the attention of the innovators was not distracted by political struggle.

ogy as well. On this foundation the idea might be attributed to us that from the economic state of a given society one can with precision form a conclusion as to the make-up of its ideas. But this is not the case, because the ideologies of every particular age are always most closely connected—whether positively or negatively—with the ideologies of the preceding age. The "state of minds" of any given age can be understood only in connection with the state of the minds of the previous epoch. Of course, not a single class will find itself captivated by ideas which contradict its aspirations. Every class excellently, even though unconsciously, always adapts its "ideals" to its economic needs. But this adaptation can take place in various ways, and why it takes place in this way, not in that, is explained not by the situation of the given class taken in isolation, but by all the particular features of the relations between this class and its antagonist (or antagonists). With the appearance of classes, *contradiction* becomes not only *a motive force*, but also *a formative* principle.*

But what then is the role of the individual in the history of ideology? Brunetière attributes to the individual a vast importance, *independent* of his environment. Guyau asserts that a genius always creates something new.**

We shall say that in the sphere of social ideas a genius outdistances his contemporaries, in the sense that *he grasps earlier than they do the meaning of new social*

---

* One might ask, what relation to the class struggle has the history of such an art as, shall we say, architecture? Yet it too is closely connected with that struggle. See E. Corroyer, *L'architecture gothique* (Paris, 1891), particularly Part IV: "L'architecture civile."

** "Il introduit dans le monde des idées et des sentiments, des types nouveaux." ("He introduces into the world new ideas, sentiments, types.—*Ed.*) *L'art au point de vue sociologique*, Paris, 1889, p. 31.

relations which are coming into existence. Consequently it is impossible in this case even to speak of the genius being independent of his environment. In the sphere of natural science a genius discovers laws the operation of which does not, of course, depend upon social relations. But the role of the social environment in the history of any great discovery is manifested, first of all, in the accumulation of that store of knowledge without which not a single genius will do anything at all and, secondly, in turning the attention of the genius in this or that direction.* In the sphere of art the genius gives the best possible expression of the prevailing aesthetic tendencies of the given society, or given class in society.** Lastly,

---

* However, it is only in the formal sense that this influence is of a dual nature. Every given store of knowledge has been accumulated just because social needs impelled people to its accumulation, turned their attention in the appropriate direction.

** And to what extent the aesthetic inclinations and judgements of any given class depend on its economic situation was well known to the author of *Aesthetic Relations of Art and Reality.* (Chernyshevsky.—*Ed.*) The beautiful is life, he said, and explained his thought by such considerations as the following. "Among the common people, the 'good life,' 'life as it should be,' means having enough to eat, living in a good house, having enough sleep; but at the same time, the peasant's conception of life always contains the concept—work: it is impossible to live without work; indeed, life would be dull without it. As a consequence of a life of sufficiency, accompanied by hard but not exhausting work, the peasant lad or maiden will have a very fresh complexion—and rosy cheeks—the first attribute of beauty according to the conceptions of the common people. Working hard, and therefore being sturdily built, the peasant girl, if she gets enough to eat, will be buxom—this too is an essential attribute of the village beauty: rural people regard the 'ethereal' society beauty as decidedly 'plain,' and are even disgusted by her, because they are accustomed to regard 'skinniness' as the result of illness or of a 'sad lot.' Work, however, does not allow one to get fat: if a peasant girl is fat, it is regarded as a kind of malady, they say she is 'flabby,' and the people regard obesity, as a

in all these three spheres the influence of social environment shows itself in the affording of a lesser or greater possibility of development for the genius and capacities of individual persons.

Of course we shall never be able to explain the entire *individuality* of a genius by the influence of his environment; but this does not prove anything by itself.

---

defect. The village beauty cannot have small hands and feet, because she works hard—and these attributes of beauty are not mentioned in our songs In short, in the descriptions of feminine beauty in our folk songs you will not find a single attribute of beauty that does not express robust health and a balanced constitution, which are always the result of a life of sufficiency, and constant real hard, but not exhausting, work. The society beauty is entirely different. For a number of generations her ancestors have lived without performing physical work; with a life of idleness, little blood flows to the limbs; with every new generation the muscles of the arms and legs grow feebler, the bones become thinner. An inevitable consequence of all this are small hands and feet—they are the symptoms of the only kind of life the upper classes of society think is possible—life without physical work. If a society lady has big hands and feet, it is either regarded as a defect, or as a sign that she does not come from a good, ancient family.... True, good health can never lose its value for a man, for even in a life of sufficiency and luxury, bad health is a drawback; hence, rosy cheeks and the freshness of good health are still attractive also for society people; but sickliness, frailty, lassitude and languor also have the virtue of beauty in their eyes as long as it seems to be the consequence of a life of idleness and luxury. Pallid cheeks, languor and sickliness have still another significance for society people: peasants seek rest and tranquillity, but those who belong to educated society, who do not suffer from material want and physical fatigue, but often suffer from ennui resulting from idleness and the absence of material cares, seek the 'thrills, excitement and passions,' which lend colour, diversity and attraction to an otherwise dull and colourless society life. But thrills and ardent passions soon wear a person out; how can one fail to be charmed by a beauty's languor and paleness when they are a sign that she has lived a 'fast life.'"
(N. G. Chernyshevsky, *Selected Philosophical Essays*, Moscow, 1953, pp. 287-88.)

Ballistics can explain the movement of a shell fired from a gun. It can foresee its motion. But it will never be able to tell you exactly into how many pieces the given shell will burst, and where precisely each separate fragment will fly. However this does not in any way weaken the authenticity of the conclusions at which ballistics arrives. We do not need to take up an idealist (or eclectic) point of view in ballistics: mechanical explanations are quite enough for us, although who can deny that these explanations do leave in obscurity for us the "individual" destinies, size and form of the particular fragments?

A strange irony of fate! That same principle of contradiction against which our subjectivists go to war with such fire, as an empty invention of the "metaphysician" Hegel, seems to be bringing us closer to nos chers amis les ennemis. If Hume denies the inner value of money for the sake of contradicting the Mercantilists; if the Romantics created their drama only in order "to do the opposite" to what the classics did; then there is no objective truth, there is only that which is true for me, for Mr. Mikhailovsky, for Prince Meshchersky[31] and so forth. Truth is subjective, all is true that satisfies our need of cognition.

No, that is not so! The principle of contradiction does not destroy objective truth, but only leads us to it. Of course, the path along which it forces mankind to move is *not at all a straight line*. But in mechanics, too, cases are known when what is lost in distance is gained in speed: a body moving along a *cycloid* sometimes moves more quickly from one point to another, lying below it, than if it had moved along a *straight* line. "Contradiction" appears where, and only where, there is struggle, where there is movement; and where there is movement, thought goes *forward*, even though by roundabout ways.

Contradiction to the Mercantilists brought Hume to a mistaken view of money. But the movement of social life, and consequently of human thought too, did not stop at the point which it reached at the time of Hume. It placed us in a state of "contradiction" to Hume, and this contradiction resulted in a correct view of money. And this correct view, being the result of the examination of reality from all sides, is now *objective truth*, which no further contradictions will eliminate. It was the author of the *Comments on Mill** who said with enthusiasm:

> *What Life once has taken*
> *Fate cannot snatch from us....***

In the case of knowledge, this is unquestionably true. No fate is now strong enough to take from us the discoveries of Copernicus, or the discovery of the transformation of energy, or the discovery of the mutability of species, or the discoveries of the genius Marx.

Social relations change, and with them change scientific theories. As a result of these changes there appears, finally, the examination of reality from all sides, and consequently objective truth. Xenophon had economic views which were different from those of Jean Baptiste Say. The views of Say would certainly have seemed rubbish to Xenophon; Say proclaimed the views of Xenophon to be rubbish. But we know now whence came the views of Xenophon, whence came the views of Say, whence came their one-sidedness. And this knowledge is now objective truth, and no "fate" will move us any more from this correct point of view, discovered at last.

"But human thought, surely, is not going to stop at what you call the discovery or the discoveries of Marx?"

---

* N. G. Chernyshevsky.—*Ed.*
** Quoted from Nekrasov's poem *New Year.*—*Ed.*

Of course not, gentlemen! It will make new discoveries, which will supplement and confirm this theory of Marx, just as new discoveries in astronomy have supplemented and confirmed the discovery of Copernicus.

The "subjective method" in sociology is the greatest nonsense. But every nonsense has its sufficient cause, and we, the modest followers of a great man, can say—not without pride—that we know the sufficient cause of that nonsense. Here it is:

The "subjective method" was first discovered not by Mr. Mikhailovsky and not even by the "angel of the school," i.e., not by the author of the *Historical Letters*.[32] It was held by Bruno Bauer and his followers—that same Bruno Bauer who gave birth to the author of the *Historical Letters*, that same author who gave birth to Mr. Mikhailovsky and his brethren.

"The objectivity of the historian is, like every objectivity, nothing more than mere chatter. And not at all in the sense that objectivity is an unattainable ideal. To objectivity, i.e., to the view characteristic of the majority, to the world outlook of the mass, the historian can only *lower himself*. And once he does this, he ceases to be a creator, he is working for piece-rate, he is becoming the hireling of his time."*

These lines belong to Szeliga, who was a fanatical follower of Bruno Bauer, and whom Marx and Engels held up to such biting ridicule in their book *The Holy Family*. Substitute "sociologist" for "historian" in these lines, substitute for the "artistic creation" of history the creation of social "ideals," and you will get the "subjective method in sociology."

Try and imagine the psychology of the idealist. For

---

* *Die Organisation der Arbeit der Menschheit und die Kunst der Geschichtschreibung Schlosser's, Gervinus's, Dahlmann's und Bruno Bauer's*, Scharlottenburg, 1846, S. 6.

him the "opinions" of men are the fundamental, ultimate cause of social phenomena. It seems to him that, according to the evidence of history, very frequently the most stupid opinions were put into effect in social relations. "Why then," he meditates, "should not my opinion too be realized, since, thank God, it is far from being stupid. Once a definite ideal exists, there exists, at all events, the possibility of social transformations which are desirable from the standpoint of that ideal. As for testing that ideal by means of some objective standard, it is impossible, because such a standard does not exist: after all, the opinions of the majority cannot serve as a measure of the truth."

And so there is a possibility of certain transformations because my ideals call for them, because I consider these transformations useful. And I consider them useful because I want to do so. Once I exclude the objective standard, I have no other criterion than my own desires. Don't interfere with my will!—that is the ultimate argument of subjectivism. The subjective method is the reductio ad absurdum of idealism, and certainly of eclecticism too, as all the mistakes of the "respectable gentlemen" of philosophy, eaten out of hearth and home by that parasite, fall on the latter's head.

From the point of view of Marx it is impossible to counterpose the *"subjective"* views of the individual to the views of "the mob," "the majority," etc., as to something *objective*. The mob consists of men, and the views of men are always *"subjective,"* since views of one kind or another are one of the qualities of the *subject*. What are objective are not the views of the "mob" but the *relations*, in nature or in society, *which are expressed in those views*. The criterion of truth lies not in me, but in the relations which exist outside me. Those views are *true* which correctly present those relations; those views are *mistaken* which distort them. That theory of natural science is *true* which correctly grasps the mutual relations between the phenomena of nature; that historical description is *true* which correctly depicts the social relations existing in the epoch described. Where the historian has to describe the struggle of opposite social forces, he will inevitably sympathize with one or another, if only he himself has not become a dry pedant. In this respect he will be *subjective*, independently of whether he sympathizes with *the minority* or *the majority*. But such subjectivism will not prevent him from being a perfectly objective historian if he does not only begin *distorting those real economic relations on the basis of which there grew up the struggling social forces*. The follower of the "subjective" method, however, forgets these *real relations*, and therefore he can produce nothing but his precious sympathy or his terrible antipathy, and therefore he makes a big noise, reproaching his opponents for insulting morality, every time he is told that that's not enough. He feels that he cannot penetrate into the secret of real social relations, and therefore every allusion to their objective force seems to him an insult, a taunt at his own impotence. He strives to drown these relations in the waters of his own moral indignation.

From the point of view of Marx it turns out, consequently, that ideals are of all kinds: base and lofty, true and false. *That ideal is true which corresponds to economic reality*. The subjectivists who hear this will say that if I begin adapting my ideals to reality, I shall become a miserable lickspittle of "the jubilant idlers." But they will say this only because, in their capacity of metaphysicians, they don't understand the dual, *antagonistic* character of all reality. *"The jubilant crowd of idlers" are relying on reality which is already passing away*, under which *a new* reality is being born, the reality of the future, to serve which means to promote the triumph of *"the great cause of love."*[33]

The reader now sees whether that conception of the Marxists, according to which they *attribute no importance to ideals*, corresponds to *"reality."* This picture of them proves to be *the exact opposite of "reality."* If one is to speak in the sense of "ideals," one must say that the theory of Marx is the *most idealistic theory which has ever existed in the history of human thought.* And this is equally true in respect both of its purely *scientific* tasks and of its *practical* aims.

"What would you have us do, if Mr. Marx does not understand the significance of consciousness of self and its strength? What would you have us do, if he values so low the recognized truth of self-consciousness?"

These words were written as long ago as 1847 by one of the followers of Bruno Bauer;[*] and although nowadays they do not speak in the language of the 40s, the gentry who reproach Marx with ignoring the element of thought and feeling in history have even now not gone any further than Opitz. All of them are still convinced that Marx values very low the force of human self-consciousness; all of them in various ways assert one and the same thing.[**] In reality Marx considered the explanation of human *"self-consciousness"* to be the most important task of social science.

---

[*] Theodor Opitz, *Die Helden der Masse. Charakteristiken*, Grünberg, 1848, pp. 6-7. We very much advise Mr. Mikhailovsky to read this work. He will find in it many of his own *original* ideas.

[**] But no, not all: no one has yet conceived of beating Marx by pointing out that "man consists of soul and body." Mr. Kareyev is doubly original, (1) no one before him has argued with Marx in this way, (2) no one after him, probably, will argue with Marx thus. From this footnote Mr. V. V. will see that we, too, can pay our tribute of respect to his "professor."

He said: "The chief defect of all hitherto existing materialism—that of Feuerbach included—is that the thing (Gegenstand), reality, sensuousness, is conceived only in the form of the *object* (Objekt) or of *contemplation* (Anschauung), but not as *human sensuous activity, practice,* not subjectively. Hence it happened that the *active* side, in contradistinction to materialism, was developed by idealism—but only abstractly, since, of course, idealism does not know real, sensuous activity as such." Have you tried to understand, gentlemen, the meaning of these words of Marx? We shall tell you what they mean.

Holbach, Helvetius and their followers bent all their efforts on proving the possibility of a materialist explanation of nature. Even the denial of innate ideas did not lead these materialists further than the examination of man as a member of the animal kingdom, as matière sensible. They did not attempt to explain the *history of man* from their point of view, and if they did (Helvetius) their attempts ended in failure. But man becomes a *"subject" only in history*, because only in the latter is his *self-consciousness* developed. To confine oneself to examining man as a member of the animal kingdom means to confine oneself to examining him as an *"object,"* to leave out of account his historical development, his social "practice," concrete human activity. But to leave all this out of account means to make materialism *"dry, gloomy, melancholy"* (Goethe).[34] More than that, it means making materialism—as we have already shown earlier—*fatalistic*, condemning man to complete subordination to blind matter. Marx noticed this failing of French materialism, and even of Feuerbach's, and set himself the task of *correcting* it. His "economic" materialism is the reply to the question of how the *"concrete activity"* of man develops, how in virtue of it there develops his *self-consciousness*, how the *subjective side of history* comes about. When this question is answered even in part, materialism will cease to be dry, gloomy, melancholy, and it will cease to yield idealism first place in explaining the active side of human existence. Then it will free itself of its characteristic fatalism.

Sensitive but weak-headed people are indignant with the theory of Marx because they take its *first* word to be its *last*. Marx says: in explaining the *subject,* let us see into what mutual relations people enter under the influence of *objective* necessity. Once these relations are known, it will be possible to ascertain how human self-consciousness develops under their influence. *Objective reality* will help us to clarify the *subjective side* of history. And this is the point at which the sensitive but weak-headed people usually interrupt Marx. It is here that is usually repeated something astonishingly like the conversation between Chatsky and Famusov.[35] "In the social production of their life, men enter into definite relations that are indispensable and independent of their will, relations of production...." "Oh, good heavens, he's a fatalist!..." "On the economic foundation rise ideological superstructures...." "What is he saying? And he talks as he writes! He simply does not recognize the role of the individual in history!..." "But hear me out, if only for once; from what I said earlier, it follows that...." "I won't listen, send him for trial! Send him for moral trial by actively progressive personalities, under open observation by subjective sociology!"

Chatsky was rescued, as you know, by the appearance of Skalozub.[36] In the arguments between the Russian followers of Marx and their strict subjective judges, matters have hitherto taken another turn. Skalozub gagged the mouth of Chatskys, and then the Famusovs of subjective sociology took the fingers out of their ears and said, with a full consciousness of their superiority: "There you are, they've only said two words. Their views have remained completely unclarified."

It was Hegel who said that any philosophy may be reduced to *empty formalism*, if one confines oneself to the simple repetition of its fundamental principles. But Marx is not guilty of that sin either. He did not confine himself to repeating that the development of the productive forces lies at the basis of the entire historical progress of mankind. You will hardly find another thinker who has done so much as he to develop his fundamental propositions.

"But where precisely, where did he develop his views?" the subjectivist gentry sing, howl, appeal and thunder in various voices. "Look at Darwin, now: he's got a *book*. But Marx hasn't even got a book, and one has to *reconstruct* his views."

Undoubtedly, "reconstruction" is an unpleasant and difficult business, particularly for those who have no "*subjective*" gifts of correctly understanding, and therefore of "reconstructing" other people's ideas. But there's no need for reconstruction, and the book whose absence the subjectivists lament has long ago been in existence. There are even several books, one explaining better than another the historical theory of Marx.

The first book is the history of philosophy and social science, beginning with the end of the eighteenth century. Study that interesting book (of course, it won't be enough to read *Lewes*): it will show you why there appeared, why *there had to appear*, the theory of Marx, to what previously unanswered and unanswerable questions it provided the replies, and consequently what is its *real significance*.

The second book is *Capital*, that same *Capital* which

you have all "read," with which you are all "at one," but which not one of you, dear sirs, has understood.

The third book is the history of European events beginning with 1848, i.e., with the appearance of a certain "manifesto."[37] Give yourselves the trouble of penetrating into the contents of that vast and instructive book and tell us, in all fairness—if only there is impartiality in your "subjective" fairness—did not the theory of Marx provide him with an astounding, previously unknown, capacity to foresee events? What has now become of the Utopians of reaction, stagnation, or progress who were his contemporaries? Into what putty has gone the dust into which their *"ideals"* were transformed at their first contact with *reality*? Not a trace has been left even of the dust, while what Marx said comes into effect—naturally, in broad outlines—every day, and will invariably come into effect until, at last, *his* ideals are fully realized.

Is not the evidence of these three books sufficient? And it seems to us that you cannot deny the existence of any of them? You will say, of course, that we are reading from them what is not written in them? Very well, say it and prove it; we await your proofs with impatience, and in order that you should not be too muddled in them, we shall for a beginning explain to you the meaning of the second book.

You recognize the *economic* views of Marx while denying his historical theory, you say. One must admit that this says a very great deal—namely, *that you understand neither his historical theory nor his economic views.*

What does the first volume of *Capital* discuss? It speaks, for example, of value. It says that value is a *social relation of production.* Do you agree to this? If not, then you are denying your own words about agreement with the economic theory of Marx. If you do, then you are admitting his *historical theory*, although evidently you don't understand it.

Once you recognize that men's own relations in production, existing independently of their will, acting behind their back, are reflected in their heads in the shape of various categories of political economy: *in the shape of value, in the shape of money, in the shape of capital*, and so forth, you thereby admit that on a certain economic basis there invariably arise certain ideological superstructures which correspond to its character. In that event the cause of your conversion is already three parts won, for all you have to do is to apply your "own" view (i.e., borrowed from Marx) to the analysis of ideological categories of the higher order: law, justice, morality, equality and so forth.

Or perhaps you are in agreement with Marx only in regard to the second volume of his *Capital*? For there are people who "recognize Marx" only to the extent that he wrote the so-called letter to Mr. Mikhailovsky.[38]

You don't recognize the historical theory of Marx? Consequently, in your opinion, he was mistaken in his assessment, for example, of the events of French history from 1848 to 1851 in his newspaper, *Neue Rheinische Zeitung* and in the other periodicals of that time, and also in his book *The Eighteenth Brumaire of Louis Bonaparte*? What a pity that you have not taken the pains to show where he was mistaken; what a pity that your views remained *undeveloped*, and that *it is impossible even to "reconstruct" them for insufficiency of data.*

You don't recognize Marx's historical theory? Therefore in your opinion he was mistaken in his view, for example, of the importance of the philosophical teachings of the French materialists of the eighteenth century? It is a pity that you have not refuted Marx in this case either. Or perhaps you don't even know where he discussed that subject? Well, in that event, we don't want to help you out of your difficulty; after all, you must know the "literature of the subject" on which you undertook to argue; after all, many of you—to use the language of Mr. Mikhailovsky—bear the title of ordinary and extraordinary bellmen of science. True, that title did not prevent you from concerning yourselves mainly with "private" sciences: subjective sociology, subjective historiosophy, etc.

"But why did not Marx write a book which would have set forth his point of view of the entire history of mankind from ancient times to our day, and which would have examined all spheres of development: economic, juridical, religious, philosophical and so forth?"

The first characteristic of any cultivated mind consists in the ability to formulate questions, and in knowing what replies can and what cannot be required of modern science. But among the opponents of Marx this characteristic seems to be conspicuous by its absence, in spite of their *extraordinary,* and sometimes even *ordinary* quality—or maybe, by the way, just because of it. Do you really suppose that in biological literature there exists a book which has fully set forth the entire history of the animal and vegetable kingdom from the point of view of Darwin? Have a talk about this with any botanist or zoologist, and he, after first having a hearty laugh at your childish simplicity, will let you know that the presentation of all the long history of species from the point of view of Darwin is the *ideal* of modern science, and we do not know when it will attain that ideal. What we have discovered is the *point of view* which alone can give us the key to the understanding of the history of species.*

---

* "Alle diese verschiedenen Zweige der Entwickelungsgeschichte, die jetzt noch teilweise weit auseinanderliegen und die

Matters stand in exactly the same way in modern historical science.

"What is essentially the work of Darwin?" asks Mr. Mikhailovsky. "A few generalizing ideas, most intimately interconnected, which crown a whole Mont Blanc of factual material. Where is the corresponding work of Marx? It does not exist.... And not only is there no such work of Marx, but there is no such work in all Marxist literature, in spite of all its extensiveness and wide distribution.... The very foundations of economic materialism, repeated as axioms innumerable times, still remain unconnected among themselves and untested by facts, which particularly deserves attention in a theory which in principle relies upon material and tangible facts, and which arrogates to itself the title of being particularly 'scientific.' "*

That the very foundations of the theory of economic materialism remain unconnected among themselves is *sheer untruth*. One need only read the preface to the *Critique of Political Economy*, to see how intimately and

---

von den verschiedensten empirischen Erkenntnissquellen ausgegangen sind, werden von jetzt an mit dem steigenden Bewusstsein ihres einheitlichen Zusammenhanges sich höher entwickeln. Auf den verschiedensten empirischen Wegen wandelnd und mit den mannigfaltigsten Methoden arbeitend werden sie doch alle auf ein und dasselbe Ziel hinstreben, auf das grosse Endziel einer universalen monistischen *Entwickelungsgeschichte*" (E. Haeckel, *Ziele und Wege der heutigen Entwickelungsgeschichte*, Jena, 1875, S. 96). ("All these different branches of the history of evolution, which now to some extent lie widely scattered, and which have proceeded from the most varied empirical sources of knowledge, will from now onward develop with the growing consciousness of their interdependence. Walking along different empirical paths, and working with manifold methods, they will nevertheless all strive towards the same goal, that great final goal of a universal monist history of evolution."—*Ed.*)

* *Russkoye Bogatstvo*, January 1894, Part II, pp. 105-06.

harmoniously they are interconnected. That these propositions have not been tested is also untrue: they have been tested with the help of an analysis of social phenomena, both in *The Eighteenth Brumaire* and in *Capital*, and moreover not at all "particularly" in the chapter on primitive accumulation, as Mr. Mikhailovsky thinks, but *absolutely in all the chapters, from the first to the last.* If nevertheless this theory has not once been set forth in connection with "a whole Mont Blanc" of factual material, which in Mr. Mikhailovsky's opinion distinguishes it to its disadvantage from Darwin's theory, there's again a misunderstanding here. With the help of the factual material making up, for example, *The Origin of Species*, it is chiefly the *mutability* of species that is demonstrated; *when Darwin touches on the history of a few separate species, he does it only in passing, and only hypothetically*; history might have gone this way or other, but one thing was certain—that *there had been a history, and that species had varied.* Now we shall ask Mr. Mikhailovsky: was it necessary for Marx to prove that mankind doesn't stand still, that social forms change, that the views of men replace one another—in a word, was it necessary to prove the *variability* of this kind of phenomena? Of course it was not, although in order to prove it, it would have been easy to pile up a dozen "Mont Blancs of factual material." What did Marx have to do? The preceding history of social science and philosophy had piled up a "whole Mont Blanc" of *contradictions*, which urgently demanded solution. *Marx did precisely solve them with the help of a theory which, like Darwin's theory, consists of a "few generalizing ideas, most intimately connected among themselves."* When these ideas appeared, it turned out that, with their help, all the contradictions which threw previous thinkers into confusion could be resolved. Marx required, not to accumulate mountains of factual material—which had been collected by his predecessors—but to take advantage of this material, among other matter, and to begin the study of the real history of mankind from the new point of view. And this is what Marx did, turning to the study of the history of the capitalist epoch, as a result of which there appeared *Capital* (not to speak of monographs such as *The Eighteenth Brumaire*).

But in *Capital*, Mr. Mikhailovsky remarks, "only one historical period is discussed, and even within those limits the subject, of course, is not even approximately exhausted." That is true. But we shall again remind Mr. Mikhailovsky that the first sign of a cultivated mind is knowledge of what demands can be made of men of learning. Marx simply could not in his research cover all historical periods, just as Darwin could not write the history of *all* animal and vegetable species.

"Even in respect of one historical period the subject is not exhausted, even approximately." No, Mr. Mikhailovsky, it is not exhausted even approximately. But, in the first place, tell us what subject has been exhausted in Darwin, even "approximately." And secondly, we shall explain to you now, how it is and why it is that the subject is not exhausted in *Capital*.

According to the new theory, the historical progress of humanity is determined by the development of the productive forces, leading to changes in economic relations. Therefore any historical research has to begin with studying the condition of the productive forces and the economic relations of the given country. But naturally research must not stop at this point: it has to show how the dry skeleton of economy is covered with the living flesh of social and political forms, and then—and this is the most interesting and most fascinating side of the problem—of human ideas, feelings, aspirations and

MODERN MATERIALISM

ideals. The investigator receives into his hands, one may say, *dead matter* (here the reader will see that we have even begun to use partly the style of Mr. Kareyev), but *an organism full of life* has to emerge from his hands. Marx succeeded in exhausting—and that, of course, only approximately—solely questions which referred in the main to the material conditions of the period he had selected. Marx died not a very old man. But if he had lived another twenty years, he would probably still have continued (apart again from, perhaps, individual monographs) to exhaust the questions of the *material conditions of the same period*. And this is what makes Mr. Mikhailovsky angry. With his arms akimbo, he begins lecturing the famous thinker: "How now, brother?... only one period... and that not fully.... No, I can't approve of it, I simply can't.... Why didn't you follow Darwin's example?" To all this subjective harangue the poor author of *Capital* only replies with a deep sigh and a sad admission: "Die Kunst ist lang und kurz ist unser Leben." ("Art is long and time is fleeting!"—*Ed.*)

Mr. Mikhailovsky rapidly and sternly turns to the "*crowd*" of followers of Marx: "In that case, what have *you* been doing, why didn't you support the old man, why haven't you exhausted all the periods?"—"We hadn't the time, Mr. Subjective Hero," reply the followers, bowing from the waist, and cap in hand: "We had other things to think about, we were fighting against those conditions of production which lie like a crushing yoke on modern humanity. Don't be hard on us! But, by the way, we have done something, all the same, and if you only give us time we will do still more."

Mr. Mikhailovsky is a little mollified: "So you yourselves now see that it wasn't fully exhausted?" "Of course, how couldn't we but see! And it's not fully exhausted even among the Darwinists,* and not even in subjective sociology—and that's a different story."

Mention of the Darwinists arouses a new attack of irritation in our author. "What do you come pestering me with Darwin for?" he shouts. "Darwin was the passion of decent people, many professors approved of him: but who are the followers of Marx? Only workmen, and a few private bellmen of science, without diplomas from anybody."

The dressing-down is assuming such an interesting character that willy-nilly we continue to take notice of it.

"In his book on *The Origin of the Family*, Engels says in passing that Marx's *Capital* was 'hushed up' by the professional German economists, and in his book *Ludwig Feuerbach* remarks that the theoreticians of economic materialism 'from the outset addressed themselves by preference to the working class, and here found the response which they neither sought nor expected from officially recognized science.' To what extent are these facts correct, and what is their significance? First of all, to 'hush up' anything valuable for a long time is hardly possible even here in Russia, with all the weakness and pettiness of our scientific and literary life. All the more is it impossible in Germany with its numerous universities, its general literacy, its innumerable newspapers and sheets of every possible tendency, with the importance of the part played there not only by the printed but also the spoken word. And if a certain number of the official high

---

* It is interesting that the opponents of Darwin long asserted, and even up to the present day have not stopped asserting, that what's lacking in his theory is precisely a "Mont Blanc" of factual proofs. As is well known, Virchow spoke in this sense at the Congress of German Naturalists and Doctors at Munich in September 1877. Replying to him, Haeckel justly remarked that, if Darwin's theory has not been proved by the facts which we know already, no new facts will say anything in its favour.

priests of science in Germany did meet *Capital* at first in silence, this can hardly be explained by the desire to 'hush up' the work of Marx. It would be more true to suppose that the motive for the silence was failure to understand it, by the side of which there rapidly grew up both warm opposition and complete respect; as a result of which the theoretical part of *Capital* very rapidly took an unquestionably high place in generally recognized science. Quite different has been the fate of economic materialism as a historical theory, including also those prospects in the direction of the future which are contained in *Capital*. Economic materialism, in spite of its half-century of existence, has not exercised up to the present any noticeable influence in the sphere of learning, but is really spreading very rapidly in the working class."*

Thus, after a short silence, an opposition rapidly grew up. That is so. To such an extent is it a warm opposition, that not a single lecturer will receive the title of professor if he declares that even the "economic" theory of Marx is correct. To such an extent is it a warm opposition that any crammer, even the least talented, can reckon on rapid promotion if he only succeeds in inventing even a couple of objections to *Capital* which will be forgotten by everybody the next day. Yes, it must be admitted—a very warm opposition.

And complete respect.... That's true also, Mr. Mikhailovsky, it is really respect. Exactly the same kind of respect with which the Chinese must now be looking at the Japanese army: they fight well, and it's most unpleasant to come under their blows. With such respect for the author of *Capital* the German professors were and still remain filled, up to the present day. And the cleverer the professor, the more knowledge he has, the more re-

---

* *Russkoye Bogatstvo*, January 1894, Part II, pp. 115-16.

spect he has—because all the more clearly does he realize that he stands no chance of refuting *Capital*. That is why not a single one of the leading lights of official science ventures to attack *Capital*. The leading lights prefer to send into battle the young, inexperienced "private bellmen" who want promotion.

> *No use to waste a clever lad,*
> *You just send along Réad*
> *And I'll wait and see.*[39]

Well, what can you say: great is respect of that kind. But we haven't heard of any other kind of respect, and there can be none in any professor—because they don't make a man a professor in Germany who is filled with it.

But what does this respect show? It shows the following. The field of research covered by *Capital* is precisely that which *has already been worked over* from the new point of view, from the point of view of the *historical theory of Marx*. That's why adversaries don't dare to attack that field: they "respect it." And that, of course, is very sensible of the adversaries. But one needs to have all the simplicity of a "subjective" sociologist to ask with surprise why these adversaries don't up to this day set about cultivating the neighbouring fields with their own forces, in the spirit of Marx. "That's a tall order, my dear hero! Even the one field worked over in this spirit gives us no rest! Even with that we don't know where to turn for trouble—and you want us to cultivate the neighbouring fields as well in the same system?!" Mr. Mikhailovsky is a bad judge of the inner essence of things, and therefore he doesn't understand "the destinies of economic materialism as a historical theory," or the attitude of the German professors to "prospects of the future" either. They haven't time to think about the *future*, sir, when the *present* is slipping from under their feet.

But after all, surely not all the professors in Germany are to such an extent saturated with the spirit of class struggle and "scientific" discipline? Surely there must be specialists who think of nothing else but science? Of course there must be, and there are naturally such men, and not only in Germany. But these specialists—precisely because they are specialists—are entirely *absorbed in their subject*; they are cultivating their own little plot in the scientific field, and take no interest in any general philosophical and historical theories. Such specialists have rarely any idea of Marx, and if they have, it's usually of some unpleasant person who worried someone, somewhere. How do you expect them to write in the spirit of Marx? Their monographs usually contain *absolutely no spirit of philosophy*. But here there takes place something similar to those cases when stones cry out, if men are silent. The specialist research workers themselves know nothing about the theory of Marx; but the results they have secured shout loudly in its favour. And there is not a single serious specialist piece of research in the history of political relations, or in the history of culture, which does not confirm that theory in one way or another. There are a number of astonishing examples which demonstrate to what great extent the whole spirit of modern social science obliges the specialist unconsciously to adopt the point of view of the historical theory of Marx (precisely the *historical* theory, Mr. Mikhailovsky). The reader saw earlier two examples of this kind—Oscar Peschel and Giraud-Teulon. Now let us give a third. In his work: *La Cité Antique*, the famous Fustel de Coulanges expressed the idea that religious views lay at the bottom of all the social institutions of antiquity. It would seem that he ought to have stuck to this idea in studying individual questions of the history of Greece and Rome. But Fustel de Coulanges had to touch on the question of *the fall of Sparta*; and it turned out that, according to him, the reason for the fall was purely economic.* He had occasion to touch on the question of the fall of the Roman Republic: and once again he turned to economics.** What conclusion can we draw? In particular cases the man confirmed the theory of Marx: but if you were to call him a Marxist, he would probably begin waving both his arms in protest, which would have given untold pleasure to Mr. Kareyev. But what would you have, if not everybody is consistent to the bitter end?

But, interrupts Mr. Mikhailovsky, allow me also to quote some examples. "Turning ... to ... the work of Blos, we see that this is a very worthy work which, however, bears no special signs of a radical revolution in historical science. From what Blos says about the class struggle and economic conditions (comparatively very little) it does not yet follow that he builds his history on the self-development of the forms of production and exchange: it would be even difficult to avoid mentioning economic conditions in telling the story of the events of 1848. Strike out of the book of Blos his panegyrics of Marx, as the creator of a revolution in historical science, and a few hackneyed phrases in Marxist terminology, and you would not even imagine that you were dealing

---

* See his book, *Du droit de propriété à Sparte*. We are not at all concerned here with the view of the history of primitive property which it contains.

** "Il est assez visible pour quiconque a observé le détail (precisely le détail, Mr. Mikhailovsky) et les textes, que ce sont les intérêts materiels du plus grand nombre qui en ont été le vrai mobile," etc. ("Histoire des institutions politiques de l'ancienne France. Les origines du système féodal." Paris, 1890, p. 94.) ["It is sufficiently visible for anyone who has observed the details" (precisely "the details," Mr. Mikhailovsky) "and the texts, that it is the material interests of the greatest number which were its true motive force," etc.—*Ed.*]

with a follower of economic materialism. Individual good pages of historical content in the works of Engels, Kautsky and some others could also do without the label of economic materialism, as in practice they take into account the whole totality of social life, even though the economic string may prevail in this chord."*

Mr. Mikhailovsky evidently keeps firmly before him the proverb: "You called yourself a mushroom, now get into the basket." He argues in this way: if you are an economic materialist, that means that you must keep your eyes fixed on *the economic*, and not deal with "the whole totality of social life, even though the economic string may prevail in this chord." But we have already reported to Mr. Mikhailovsky that the scientific task of the Marxist lies precisely in this: having begun with the "string," he must explain the whole totality of social life. How can he expect them, in that case, to renounce this task and to remain Marxists at one and the same time? Of course, Mr. Mikhailovsky has never wanted to think seriously about the meaning of the task in question: but naturally that is not the fault of the historical theory of Marx.

We quite understand that, so long as we don't renounce that task, Mr. Mikhailovsky will often fall into a very difficult position: often, when reading "a good page of historical content" he will be very far from thinking ("you wouldn't even imagine") that it has been written by an "economic" materialist. That's what they call "landing in a mess"! But is it Marx who is to blame that Mr. Mikhailovsky will find himself so placed?

The Achilles of the subjective school imagines that "economic" materialists must only talk about "the self-

---

* *Russkoye Bogatstvo*, January 1894, Part II, p. 117. (The reference is to W. Blos, *History of the German Revolution of 1848* (1891).—*Tr.*)

development of the forms of production and exchange." What sort of a thing is that "self-development," oh profound Mr. Mikhailovsky? If you imagine that, in the opinion of Marx, the forms of production can develop "of themselves," you are cruelly mistaken. What are *the social relations of production*? They are relations between men. How can they develop, then, without men? If there were no men, surely there would be no relations of production! The chemist says: matter consists of atoms which are grouped in molecules, and the molecules are grouped in more complex combinations. All chemical processes take place according to definite laws. From this you unexpectedly conclude that, in the chemist's opinion, it's all a question of laws, that matter—atoms and molecules—needn't move at all, and that this wouldn't in the least prevent the "self-development" of chemical combinations. Everyone would see the stupidity of such a conclusion. Unfortunately, not everyone yet sees the stupidity of an exactly similar (so far as its internal value is concerned) contrasting of *individuals* to *the laws of social life*, and of the activity of men to the internal logic of the forms in which they live together.

We repeat, Mr. Mikhailovsky, that the task of the new historical theory consists in explaining "*the whole totality of social life*" by what you call the economic string, i.e., in reality *the development of productive forces*. The "string" is in a certain sense the basis (we have already explained in what particular sense): but in vain does Mr. Mikhailovsky think that the Marxist "breathes only with the string," like one of the characters in G. I. Uspensky's "Budka."[40]

It's a difficult job to explain the entire historical process, keeping consistently to one principle. But what would you have? Science generally is not an easy job, providing only it's not "subjective" science: in that, all questions are explained with amazing ease. And since we have mentioned it, we shall tell Mr. Mikhailovsky that it is possible that in questions affecting the development of ideology, even those best acquainted with the "string" will sometimes prove powerless if they don't possess a certain particular gift, namely *artistic feeling*. Psychology adapts itself to economy. But this adaptation is a complex process, and in order to understand its whole course and vividly to represent it to oneself and to others as it actually takes place, more than once the talent of the artist will be needed. For example, Balzac has already done a great deal to explain the psychology of various classes in the society in which he lived. We can learn a lot from Ibsen too, and from not a few more. Let's hope that in time there will appear many such artists, who will understand on the one hand the "iron laws" of movement of the "string," and on the other will be able to understand and to show how, on the "string" and precisely thanks to its movement, there grows up the *"garment of Life" of ideology*. You will say that where poetical fantasy has crept in there cannot but occur the whim of the artist, the guesswork of fantasy. Of course, that is so: that will happen too. And Marx knew it very well: that is just why he says that we have strictly to distinguish between *the economic condition* of a given epoch, *which can be determined with the exactness of natural science*, and *the condition of its ideas*. Much, very much is still obscure for us in this sphere. But there is even more that is obscure for the idealists, and yet more for eclectics, who have never understood the significance of the difficulties they encounter, imagining that they will always be able to settle any question with the help of their notorious *"interaction."* In reality, they never settle anything, but only hide behind the back of the difficulties they encounter. Hitherto, in the words of

Marx, concrete human activity has been explained solely from the idealist point of view. Well, and what happened? Did they find many satisfactory explanations? Our judgements on the activity of the human "spirit" lack firm foundation and remind one of the judgements on nature pronounced by the ancient Greek philosophers: at best we have hypotheses of genius, sometimes merely ingenious suppositions, which, however, it is impossible to confirm or prove, for lack of any fulcrum of scientific proof. Something was achieved only in those cases where they were forced to connect social psychology with the "string." And yet, when Marx noticed this, and recommended that the attempts which had begun should not be abandoned, and said that we must always be guided by the "string," he was accused of one-sidedness and narrow-mindedness! If there is any justice in this, it is only the subjective sociologist, possibly, who knows where it is.

Yes, you can talk, Mr. Mikhailovsky sarcastically continues: your new discovery "was made fifty years ago." Yes, Mr. Mikhailovsky, about that time! And all the more regrettable that you have still failed to understand it. Are there not many such "discoveries" in science, made tens and hundreds of years ago, but still remaining unknown to millions of *"personalities"* carefree in respect of science? Imagine that you have met a Hottentot and are trying to convince him that the earth revolves around the sun. The Hottentot has his own "original" theory, both about the sun and about the earth. It is difficult for him to part with his theory. And so he begins to be sarcastic: you come to me with your new discoveries, and yet you yourself say that it's several hundred years old! What will the Hottentot's sarcasm prove? Only that the Hottentot is a Hottentot. But then that did not need to be proved.

However, Mr. Mikhailovsky's sarcasm proves a great deal more than would be proved by the sarcasm of a Hottentot. It proves that our "sociologist" belongs to the category of people who forget their *kinship*. His subjective point of view has been inherited from Bruno Bauer, Szeliga and other *predecessors* of Marx in the *chronological sense*. Consequently, Mr. Mikhailovsky's "discovery" is in any case a bit older than ours, even chronologically, while in its internal content it is much older, because the historical idealism of Bruno Bauer was a return to the views of the materialists of last century.*

Mr. Mikhailovsky is very worried because the book of the American Morgan on "ancient society" appeared many years after Marx and Engels had advanced the fundamental principles of economic materialism, and quite "independently of it." To this we shall observe:

In the first place, Morgan's book is not "independent" of so-called economic materialism for the simple reason that Morgan himself adopts that view-point, as Mr. Mikhailovsky will easily see for himself if he reads the book to which he refers. True, Morgan arrived at the viewpoint of economic materialism independently of *Marx and Engels*, but that's all the better for their theory.

Secondly, what's wrong if the theory of Marx and Engels was "many years later" confirmed by the discoveries of Morgan? We are convinced that there will yet be very many discoveries confirming that theory. As to Mr. Mikhailovsky, on the other hand, we are convinced

---

* As for the application of biology to the solution of social problems, Mr. Mikhailovsky's "discoveries" date, as we have seen, in their "nature" from the 20s of the present century. Very respectable ancients are the "discoveries" of Mr. Mikhailovsky! In them the *"Russian mind and Russian soul"* truly *"repeats old stuff and lies for two."*[41]

of the contrary: not a single discovery will justify the "subjective" point of view, either in five years or in five thousand.

From one of Engels's prefaces Mr. Mikhailovsky has learned that the knowledge of the author of the *Condition of the Working Class in England*, and of his friend Marx, in the sphere of economic history was in the 40s "inadequate" (the expression of Engels himself). Mr. Mikhailovsky skips and jumps on this subject: so you see, the entire theory of "economic materialism," which arose precisely in the 40s, was built on an inadequate foundation. This is a conclusion worthy of a witty fourth form schoolboy. A grown-up person would understand that, in their application to scientific knowledge as to everything else, the expressions "adequate," "inadequate," "little," "big" must be taken in their relative sense. After the fundamental principles of the new historical theory had been proclaimed Marx and Engels went on living for several decades. They zealously studied economic history, and achieved vast successes in that sphere, which is particularly easy to understand in view of their unusual capacity. Thanks to these successes, their former information must have seemed to them *"inadequate"*; but this does not yet prove that their theory was *unfounded*. Darwin's book on the origin of species appeared in 1859. One can say with certainty that, ten years later, Darwin already thought inadequate the knowledge which he possessed when his book was published. But what does that matter?

Mr. Mikhailovsky displays not a little irony also on the theme that "for the theory which claimed to throw light on world history, forty years after it had been enunciated" (i.e., allegedly up to the appearance of Morgan's book) "ancient Greek and German history remained an unsolved problem."* This irony is only founded on a "misunderstanding."

That *the class struggle underlay Greek and Roman history* could not but be known to Marx and Engels at the end of the 40s, if only for the simple reason that it had already been known to the Greek and Roman writers. Read Thucydides, Xenophon, Aristotle, read the Roman historians, even though it be Livy, who in his description of events too often passes, by the way, to a "subjective" point of view—and in each of them you will find the firm conviction that economic relations, and the struggle of classes which they aroused, were the foundation of the internal history of the societies of that day. This conviction took in them the direct form of the simple recording of a simple, well-known everyday fact: although in Polybius there is already something in the nature of a philosophy of history, based on recognition of this fact. However that may be, the fact was recognized by all, and does Mr. Mikhailovsky really think that Marx and Engels "had not read the ancients"? What remained unsolved problems for Marx and Engels, as for all men of learning, were questions concerning the forms of *prehistoric life* in Greece and Rome and among the German tribes (as Mr. Mikhailovsky himself says elsewhere). *These* were the questions answered by Morgan's book. But does our author by any chance imagine that no unsolved questions in biology existed for Darwin at the time he wrote his famous book?

"The category of necessity," continues Mr. Mikhailovsky, "is so universal and unchallengeable that it embraces even the most fantastic hopes and the most senseless apprehensions, with which it apparently has been called upon to fight. From its point of view, the hope

---
* *Russkoye Bogatstvo*, January 1894, Part II, p. 108.

of breaking through a wall by striking it with one's forehead is not stupidity but necessity, just as Quasimodo was not a hunch-back but necessity, Cain and Judas were not evil-doers but necessity. In brief, if we are guided in practical life only by necessity, we come into some fantastic, boundless expanse where there are no ideas and things, no phenomena, but only inconspicuous shadows of ideas and things."* Just so, Mr. Mikhailovsky: even deformities of all kinds represent just as much a product of necessity as the most normal phenomena, although it does not at all follow from this that Judas was not a criminal, since it is absurd to contrast the conception of "criminal" with the conception of "necessity." But if, my dear sir, you are aspiring to the rank of hero (and every subjective thinker is a hero, so to speak, by profession), then try and prove that you are not a "mad" hero, that your "hopes" are not "fantastic," that your "apprehensions" are not "senseless," that you are not a "Quasimodo" in thought, that you are not inviting the *crowd* to "break through a wall with its forehead." In order to prove all this, you should have to turn to the category of necessity: but you don't know how to operate with it, your subjective point of view excludes the very possibility of such operations. Thanks to this "category," reality for you becomes the kingdom of shadows. Now that's just where you get into your blind alley, it's at this point you sign the "testimonium paupertatis" for your "sociology," it's just here that you begin asserting that the "category of necessity" proves nothing, because allegedly it proves too much. A certificate of theoretical poverty is the only document with which you supply your followers, searching for higher things. It's not very much, Mr. Mikhailovsky!

---

* *Ibid.*, pp. 113-14.

A tom-tit asserts that it is a heroic bird and, in that capacity, it would think nothing of setting fire to the sea.[42] When it is invited to explain on what physical or chemical *laws* is founded its plan for setting fire to the sea, it finds itself in difficulties and, in order to get out of them somehow, begins muttering in a melancholy and scarcely audible whisper that "laws" is only a manner of speaking, but in reality laws explain nothing, and one can't found any plans on them; that one must hope for a lucky accident, since it has long been known that at a pinch you can shoot with a stick too; but that generally speaking *la raison finit toujours par avoir raison.* What a thoughtless and unpleasant bird!

Let us compare with this indistinct muttering of the tom-tit the courageous, astonishingly harmonious, historical philosophy of Marx.

Our anthropoid ancestors, like all other animals, were in complete subjection to *nature*. All their development was that completely unconscious development which was conditioned by adaptation to their environment, by means of natural selection in the struggle for existence. This was the dark kingdom of *physical necessity*. At that time even the *dawn of consciousness*, and therefore of *freedom*, was not breaking. But physical necessity brought man to a stage of development at which he began, little by little, to separate himself from the remaining animal world. He became a *tool-making animal*. The tool is an organ with the help of which man acts on nature to achieve his ends. It is an organ which subjects *necessity* to the human *consciousness*, although at first only to a very weak degree, by fits and starts, if one can put it that way. *The degree of development of the productive forces determines the measure of the authority of man over nature.*

The development of the productive forces is itself determined by the qualities of the geographical environment surrounding man. In this way nature itself gives man the means for its own subjection.

But man is not struggling with nature individually: the struggle with her is carried on, in the expression of Marx, by social man (der Gesellschaftsmensch), i.e., a more or less considerable social union. The characteristics of *social* man are determined at every given time by the degree of development of the productive forces, because on the degree of the development of those forces depends the entire structure of the social union. Thus, this structure is determined in the long run by the characteristics of the geographical environment, which affords men a greater or lesser possibility of developing their productive forces.* But once definite social relations have arisen, their further development takes place according to *its own inner laws*, the operation of which accelerates or retards the development of the productive forces which conditions the historical progress of man. The dependence of man on his geographical environment is transformed from *direct* to *indirect*. The *geographical* environment influences man through the *social* environment. But *thanks to this*, the relationship of man with his geographical environment becomes extremely changeable. At every new stage of development of the productive forces it proves to be different from what it was before. The geographical environment influenced the Britons of Caesar's time quite otherwise than it influences the present inhabitants of Great Britain. That is how modern *dialectical materialism* resolves the contradictions with which the writers of the Enlightenment of the eighteenth century could not cope.**

---

* See Editor's note on pp. 161-62.
** Montesquieu said: once the geographical environment is given,

The development of the social environment is subjected to its own laws. This means that its characteristics depend just as little on the will and consciousness of men as the characteristics of the geographical environment. The productive action of man on nature gives rise to a new form of dependence of man, a new variety of his slavery: *economic necessity.* And the greater grows man's authority over nature, the more his productive forces develop, the more stable becomes this new slavery: *with the development of the productive forces the mutual relations of men in the social process of production become more complex*; the course of that process completely slips from under their control, *the producer proves to be the slave of his own creation* (as an example, the capitalist anarchy of production).

But just as the nature surrounding man itself gave him the first opportunity to develop his productive forces and, consequently, gradually to emancipate himself from nature's yoke—so the relations of production, social relations, by the very logic of their development bring man to realization of the causes of his enslavement by *economic* necessity. This provides the opportu-

---

the characteristics of the social union are also given. In one geographical environment only despotism can exist, in another—only small independent republican societies, etc. No, replied Voltaire: in one and the same geographical environment there appear in the course of time various social relations, and consequently geographical environment has no influence on the historical fate of mankind. It is all a question of the opinions of men. Montesquieu saw one side of the antinomy, Voltaire and his supporters another: the antinomy was usually resolved only with the help of *interaction.* *Dialectical materialism* recognizes, as we see, the existence of interaction, but explains it by pointing to the development of the productive forces. The antinomy which the writers of the Enlightenment could at best only hide away in their pockets, is resolved very simply. *Dialectical reason*, here too, proves infinitely stronger than the *common sense* ("reason") of the writers of the Enlightenment.

nity for a new and final triumph of *consciousness* over *necessity*, of *reason* over blind *law*.

Having realized that the cause of his enslavement by his own creation lies in the anarchy of production, the producer ("social man") organizes that production and thereby subjects it to his will. Then terminates the kingdom of *necessity*, and there begins the reign of *freedom*, which itself proves to be *necessity*. The prologue of human history has been played out, history begins.*

---

* After all that has been said it will be clear, we hope, what is the relation between the teaching of Marx and the teaching of Darwin. Darwin succeeded in solving the problem of how there originate vegetable and animal species in the struggle for existence. Marx succeeded in solving the problem of how there arise different types of social organization in the struggle of men for their existence. Logically, the investigation of Marx begins precisely where the investigation of Darwin ends. Animals and vegetables are under the influence of their *physical* environment. The physical environment acts on social man through those social relations which arise on the basis of the productive forces, which at first develop more or less quickly according to the characteristics of the physical environment. Darwin explains the origin of species not by an allegedly *innate* tendency to develop in the animal organism, as Lamarck did, but by the adaptation of the organism to the conditions existing outside it: not by the *nature of the organism* but by the influence of *external nature*. Marx explains the historical development of man not by the *nature of man*, but by the characteristics of those social *relations* between men which arise when social man is acting on *external nature*. The spirit of their research is absolutely the same in both thinkers. That is why one can say that Marxism is Darwinism in its application to social science (we know that *chronologically* this is not so, but that is unimportant). And that is its only *scientific* application; because the conclusions which were drawn from Darwinism by some bourgeois writers were not its scientific application to the study of the development of social man, but a mere bourgeois utopia, a moral sermon with a very ugly content, just as the subjectivists engage in sermons with a beautiful content. The bourgeois writers, when referring to Darwin, were in reality recommending to their readers *not the scientific method of Darwin, but only the bestial instincts*

Thus dialectical materialism not only does not strive, as its opponents attribute to it, to convince man that it is absurd to revolt against economic necessity, but it is the first to point out *how to overcome* the latter. Thus is eliminated the *inevitably fatalist* character inherent in *metaphysical materialism*. And in exactly the same way is eliminated every foundation for that pessimism to which, as we saw, consistent *idealist* thinking leads of necessity. The individual personality is only foam on the crest of the wave, men are subjected to an iron law which can only be discovered, but which cannot be subjected to the human will, said Georg Büchner. No, replies Marx: once we have *discovered* that iron law, it depends on us to overthrow its yoke, it depends on us to make *necessity* the obedient slave of *reason*.

I am a worm, says the idealist. I am a worm while I am ignorant, retorts the dialectical materialist: but I am a god when I *know*. Tantum possumus, quantum scimus (we can do as much as we know)!

And it is against this theory, which for the first time established the rights of human reason on firm foundations, which was the first that began examining reason, not as the impotent plaything of accident but as a great and invincible force, that they revolt—in the name of the rights of that same reason which it is alleged to be treading underfoot, in the name of ideals which it is alleged to despise! And this theory they dare to accuse of quietism, of striving to reconcile itself with its environment and almost of ingratiating itself with the environment, as Molchalin[43] ingratiated himself with all who were superior to him in rank! Truly one may say that here is a case of laying one's own fault at another man's door.

---

of those animals about whom Darwin wrote. Marx forgathers with *Darwin*: the bourgeois writers forgather *with the beasts and cattle which Darwin studied*.

Dialectical materialism* says that human reason could not be the demiurge of history, because it is itself the *product* of history. But once that product has appeared, it *must* not—and in its nature it *cannot*—be obedient to the reality handed down as a heritage by previous history; of necessity it strives to transform that reality after its own likeness and image, *to make it reasonable.*

Dialectical materialism says, like Goethe's Faust:

> *Im Anfang war die Tat!*
> (*In the Beginning was the Deed!—Ed.*)

Action (the activity of men in conformity to law in the social process of production) explains to the dialectical materialist the historical development of the reason of social man.** It is to action also that is reduced all his *practical philosophy. Dialectical materialism is the philosophy of action.*

When the subjective thinker says "*my ideal,*" he thereby says: *the triumph of blind necessity.* The subjective thinker is unable to found his ideal upon the process of development of reality; and therefore immediately beyond the walls of the tiny little garden of his ideal there begins the boundless field of chance—and consequently, of blind necessity. Dialectical materialism points out the methods with the help of which all that boundless field

---

* We use the term "dialectical materialism" because it alone can give an accurate description of the philosophy of Marx. Holbach and Helvetius were *metaphysical* materialists. They fought against *metaphysical* idealism. Their materialism gave way to *dialectical idealism*, which in its turn was overcome by *dialectical materialism*. The expression "economic materialism" is extremely inappropriate. Marx never called himself an economic materialist.

** "Social life is essentially practical. All mysteries which mislead theory to mysticism find their rational solution in human practice and in the comprehension of this practice." (K. Marx and F. Engels, *Selected Works*, Vol. II, Moscow, 1955, p. 404.—*Ed.*)

can be transformed into the flourishing *garden of the ideal*. It only adds that the means for this transformation are buried *in the heart of that same field, that one only must discover them and be able to use them.*

Unlike subjectivism, dialectical materialism does not limit the rights of human reason. It knows that the rights of reason are as boundless and unlimited as its powers. It says that all that is reasonable in the human head, i.e., all that represents not an illusion but the true knowledge of reality, will unquestionably pass into that reality, and will unquestionably bring into it its own share of reason.

From this one can see what constitutes, in the opinion of dialectical materialists, the role of the individual in history. Far from reducing the role to zero, they put before the individual a task which—to make use of the customary though incorrect term—one must recognize as *completely and exceptionally idealistic.* As human reason can triumph over blind necessity only by becoming aware of the latter's peculiar inner laws, only by beating it with its own strength, the development of knowledge, the development of human consciousness, is the greatest and most noble task of the thinking personality. "Licht, mehr Licht!"*—that is what is most of all needed.

It has long ago been said that no one kindles a torch in order to leave it under a bushel. So that the dialectical materialist adds that one should not leave the torch in the narrow study of the "intellectual." So long as there exist "heroes" who imagine that it is sufficient for them to enlighten their own heads to be able to lead the crowd wherever they please, and to mould it, like clay, into anything that comes into their heads, the kingdom of reason remains a pretty phrase or a noble dream. It be-

---

* Goethe's last words.—*Ed.*

gins to approach us with seven-league strides only when the "crowd" itself becomes the hero of historical action, and when in it, in that colourless "crowd," there develops the appropriate consciousness of self. Develop human consciousness, we said. Develop the self-consciousness of the producers, we now add. Subjective philosophy seems to us harmful just because it prevents the intelligentsia from helping in the development of that self-consciousness, opposing heroes to the crowd, and imagining that the crowd is no more than a totality of ciphers, the significance of which depends only on the ideals of the hero who gives them the lead.

If there's only a marsh, there'll be devils enough, says the popular proverb in its coarse way. If there are only heroes, there'll be a crowd for them, say the subjectivists; and these heroes are we ourselves, the subjective intelligentsia. To this we reply: your contrasting of heroes to the crowd is mere conceit and therefore self-deception. And you will remain mere... talkers, until you understand that for the triumph of your own ideals you must eliminate the very possibility of such contrasting, you must awaken in the crowd the heroic consciousness of self.*

Opinions govern the world, said the French materialists, we are the representatives of opinion, therefore we are the demiurges of history: we are the heroes, and for the crowd it remains only to follow us.

This narrowness of views corresponded to the exceptional position of the French writers of the Enlightenment. They were representatives of the *bourgeoisie.*

---

* "Mit der Gründlichkeit der geschichtlichen Action wird der Umfang der Masse zunehmen, deren Action sie ist." Marx, *Die heilige Familie*, S. 120. ("Together with the thoroughness of the historical action will grow the volume of the mass whose action it is.") (—*Ed.*)

Modern dialectical materialism strives for the elimination of classes. It appeared, in fact, when that elimination became an historical necessity. Therefore it turns to the producers, who are to become the heroes of the historical period lying immediately ahead. Therefore, for the first time since our world has existed and the earth has been revolving around the sun, there is taking place the coming together of science and workers: science hastens to the aid of the toiling mass, and the toiling mass relies on the conclusions of science in its conscious movement.

If all this is no more than metaphysics, we really don't know what our opponents call metaphysics.

"But all you say refers only to the realm of prophecy. It's all mere guesswork, which assumes a somewhat systematic form only because of the tricks of Hegelian dialectics. That's why we call you metaphysicians," reply the subjectivists.

We have already shown that to drag the "triad" into our dispute is possible only when one has not the least idea of it. We have already shown that with Hegel himself it never played the part of an *argument*, and that it was not at all a distinguishing feature of his philosophy. We have also shown, we make bold to think, that it is not references to the triad but scientific investigation of the historical process that constitutes the strength of historical materialism. Therefore we might now pay no attention to this retort. But we think it will not be useless for the reader to recall the following interesting fact in the history of Russian literature in the 70s.

When examining *Capital*, Mr. Y. Zhukovsky remarked that the author in his guesses, as people now say, relies only on *"formal"* considerations, and that his line of argument represents only an unconscious play upon notions. This is what the late N. Sieber replied to this charge:

"We remain convinced that the investigation of the material problem everywhere in Marx precedes the formal side of his work. We believe that, if Mr. Zhukovsky had read Marx's book more attentively and more dispassionately, he would himself have agreed with us in this. He would then undoubtedly have seen that it is precisely by investigating the material conditions of the period of capitalist development in which we are living that the author of *Capital* proves that mankind sets itself only such tasks as it can solve. Marx step by step leads his readers through the labyrinth of capitalist production and, analyzing all its component elements, makes us understand its provisional character."*

"Let us take... factory industry," continues N. Sieber, "with its uninterrupted changing from hand to hand at every operation, with its feverish motion which throws workmen almost every day from one factory to another. Do not its material conditions represent a preparatory environment for new forms of social order, of social co-operation? Does not the operation of periodically repeated economic crises move in the same direction? Is it not to the same end that the narrowing of markets, the reduction of the working day, the rivalry of various countries in the general market, and the victory of large-scale capital over capital of insignificant dimensions tend?..." Pointing out also the incredibly rapid growth of the productive forces in the process of development of capitalism, N. Sieber again asks: "Or are all these not material, but purely formal transformations?... Is not a real contradiction of capitalist production, for example, the circumstance that periodically it floods the world market with goods, and forces millions to starve at a time when there

___

* N. Sieber, "Some Remarks on the Article of Mr. Y. Zhukovsky 'Karl Marx and His Book on Capital'" (*Otechestvenniye Zapiski*, November 1877, p. 6).

are too many articles of consumption?.... Is it not a real contradiction of capitalism, furthermore—one which, be it said in passing, the owners of capital themselves willingly admit—that it sets free a great number from work and at the same time complains of lack of working hands? Is it not a real contradiction that the means for reducing physical labour, such as mechanical and other improvements and betterments, are transformed by it into means for lengthening the working day? Is it not a real contradiction that, while proclaiming the inviolability of property, capitalism deprives the majority of the peasants of land, and keeps the vast majority of the population on a mere pittance? Is all this, and much else, mere metaphysics, non-existent in reality? But it is sufficient to take up any issue of the English *Economist* to become immediately convinced of the contrary. And so the investigator of present social and economic conditions does not have artificially to adapt capitalist production to preconceived formal and dialectical contradictions: he has more than enough real contradictions to last him his lifetime."

Sieber's reply, convincing in its content, was mild in its form. Very different was the character of the reply to the same Mr. Zhukovsky which followed from Mr. Mikhailovsky.

Our worthy subjectivist even up to the present day understands the work, which he then defended, extremely *"narrowly,"* not to say one-sidedly, and even tries to convince others that his one-sided understanding is the proper assessment of the book. Naturally, such a person could not be a reliable defender of *Capital*; and his reply was therefore filled with the most childish curiosities. Here, for example, is one of them. The charge against Marx of formalism and of abusing Hegelian dialectics was supported by Mr. Zhukovsky with a quotation, among other things, from a passage in the preface to *The Crit-*

ique of Political Economy. Mr. Mikhailovsky found that Marx's opponent "rightly saw a reflection of Hegelian philosophy" in this preface, and that *"if Marx had only written this preface to the 'Critique,' Mr. Zhukovsky would have been quite right,"** i.e., it would have been proved that Marx was only a formalist and Hegelian. Here Mr. Mikhailovsky so successfully missed the mark, and to such a degree "exhausted" the act of missing the mark, that willy-nilly one asks oneself, had our then hopeful young author read the preface he was quoting?** One might refer to several other similar curiosities (one of them will be mentioned later on): but they are not the question at issue here. However badly Mr. Mikhailovsky understood Marx, he nevertheless saw immediately that Mr. Zhukovsky had *"talked nonsense"* about *"formalism"*; and had nevertheless realized that such nonsense is the simple product of *unceremoniousness*.

"If Marx had said," Mr. Mikhailovsky justly observed, "that the law of development of modern society is such that itself it spontaneously negates its previous condition, and then negates this negation, reconciling the contradictions of the stages gone through in the unity of individual and communal property: if he had said this and *only* this (albeit in many pages), he would have been a pure Hegelian, building laws out of the depths of his spirit, and resting on principles that were purely formal, i.e., independent of content. But everyone who has read *Capital* knows that he said more than this." In the words of Mr. Mikhailovsky, the Hegelian formula can just as easily be removed from the economic content allegedly forced into it by Marx as a glove from the hand or a hat from the head. "Regarding the stages of economic

---
* N. K. Mikhailovsky, *Works*, Vol. II, p. 356

** In this passage Marx sets forth his materialist conception of history.

development passed through there can be hardly any doubts.... Just as indubitable is the further course of the process: the concentration of the means of production more and more in a smaller number of hands. As regards the future there can, of course, be doubts. Marx considers that as the concentration of capital is accompanied by the socialization of labour, the latter is what will constitute the economic and moral basis" (how can socialization of labour "constitute" the *moral* basis? And what about the "self-development of forms"?—*G.P.*) "on which the new legal and political order will grow up. Mr. Zhukovsky was fully entitled to call this guesswork, but had no right (moral right, of course—*G.P.*) to pass by in complete silence the significance which Marx attributes to the process of socialization."*

"The whole of *Capital*," Mr. Mikhailovsky rightly remarks, "is devoted to the study of how a social form, once it has arisen, constantly develops, intensifies its typical features, subordinating to itself and assimilating" (?) "discoveries, inventions, improvements in the means of production, new markets, science itself, forcing them to work for it, and how finally the given form becomes incapable of withstanding further changes of the material conditions."**

With Marx "it is precisely the analysis of the relations between the social form" (i.e., of capitalism, Mr. Mikhailovsky, isn't that so?—*G.P.*) "and the material conditions of its existence" (i.e., the productive forces which make the existence of the capitalist form of production more and more unstable, isn't that so, Mr. Mikhailovsky?—*G.P.*) "that will always remain a monument of the logical system and vast erudition of the author. Mr. Zhukovsky has the moral courage to assert that this

---
* *Russkoye Bogatstvo*, pp. 353-54.
** *Ibid.*, p. 357.

is the question which Marx evades. There's nothing more one can do here. It remains only to watch with amazement the further puzzling exercises of the critic, performing his somersaults for the amusement of the public, part of which undoubtedly will understand at once that a courageous acrobat is performing before it, while another part may perchance attribute quite a different meaning to this amazing spectacle."*

Summa summarum: if Mr. Zhukovsky accused Marx of formalism, this charge, in the words of Mr. Mikhailovsky, represented "one big lie composed of a number of little lies."

Severe is the sentence, but absolutely just. And if it was just in respect of Zhukovsky, it is just also in relation to all those who now repeat that the "guesses" of Marx are based only on the Hegelian triad. And if that sentence is just in respect of all such people, then... have the goodness to read the following extract:

"He [Marx] to such an extent filled the empty dialectical scheme with a content of fact that it could be removed from that content, as a cover from a cup, without changing anything, without damaging anything except for one point—true, of vast importance. Namely, regarding the future, the 'immanent' laws of society are formulated only dialectically. For the orthodox Hegelian it is sufficient to say that 'negation' must be followed by the 'negation of the negation'; but those who are not privy to the Hegelian wisdom cannot be satisfied with that, for them a dialectical deduction is not a proof, and a *non*-Hegelian who has believed it must know that he has only believed it, not been convinced by it."**

Mr. Mikhailovsky has pronounced his own sentence.

Mr. Mikhailovsky knows himself that he is now repeat-

---
* *Ibid.*, pp. 357-58.
** *Russkoye Bogatstvo*, February 1894, Part II, pp. 150-51.

ing the words of Mr. Y. Zhukovsky regarding the "formal character" of Marx's arguments in favour of his "guesses." He has not forgotten his article "Karl Marx Before the Judgement of Mr. Y. Zhukovsky," and even fears lest his reader might recall it at some untimely moment. Therefore he begins by making it appear that he is saying the same now as he said in the 70s. With this object he repeats that the "dialectical scheme" may be removed "like a cover," etc. Then there follows "*only one point*" in relation to which Mr. Mikhailovsky, unbeknown to his reader, is completely at one with Mr. Y. Zhukovsky. But this "one point" is that same point of "*vast importance*" which served as a pretext for exposing Mr. Zhukovsky as an "acrobat."

In 1877 Mr. Mikhailovsky said that Marx in relation to the future also, i.e., precisely in relation to "one point of vast importance," did not confine himself to a reference to Hegel. Now it appears from Mr. Mikhailovsky that he *did* so confine himself. In 1877 Mr. Mikhailovsky said that Marx with astonishing "logical force," with "vast erudition," demonstrated how the "given form" (i.e., capitalism) "becomes incapable of withstanding" further changes in the "*material conditions*" of its existence. That referred precisely to "one point of vast importance." Now Mr. Mikhailovsky has forgotten how much that was convincing Marx had said about this point, and how much logical strength and vast erudition he had displayed in doing so. In 1877 Mr. Mikhailovsky wondered at the "moral courage" with which Mr. Zhukovsky had passed over in silence the fact that Marx, in confirmation of his guesses, had referred to the socialization of labour which was already taking place in capitalist society. This also had reference to "one point of vast importance." At the present day Mr. Mikhailovsky assures his readers that Marx on this point is guessing "purely dialectically." In

1877 "everyone who has read *Capital*" knew that Marx "said *more than this*." Now it turns out that he said "only this," and that the conviction of his followers as to the future "holds exclusively by the end of a Hegelian three-tailed chain."* What a turn, with God's help!

Mr. Mikhailovsky has pronounced his own sentence, and knows that he has pronounced it.

But what made Mr. Mikhailovsky bring himself under the operation of the ruthless sentence he himself had pronounced? Did this man who so passionately, once upon a time, exposed literary "acrobats," in his old age himself feel an inclination to "the acrobatic art"? Are such transformations really possible? All transformations are possible, oh reader! And people with whom such transformations occur are worthy of every condemnation. It is not we who will justify them. But even they should be treated as human creatures, as people say. Remember the profoundly humane words of the author of the *Comments on Mill*: when a man behaves badly, it is often not so much his fault as his misfortune. Remember what the same author said about the literary activity of N. A. Polevoi:[44]

"N. A. Polevoi was a follower of Cousin, whom he considered to be the solver of all riddles and the greatest philosopher in the world.... The follower of Cousin could not reconcile himself to the Hegelian philosophy, and when the Hegelian philosophy penetrated into Russian literature, the pupils of Cousin turned out to be backward people; and there was nothing morally criminal on their part in the fact that they defended their convictions, and called stupid that which was said by people who had outdistanced them in intellectual progress. One cannot accuse a man because others, gifted with fresher forces and greater resolution, have outpaced him. They are right

---
* *Ibid.*, p. 166.

because they are nearer to the truth, but it is not his fault: he is only mistaken."*

Mr. Mikhailovsky all his life has been an *eclectic*. He could not reconcile himself to the historical philosophy of Marx by the very make-up of his mind, by the whole character of his previous philosophical education—if one can use such an expression in connection with Mr. Mikhailovsky. When the ideas of Marx began to penetrate into Russia, he tried at first to defend them, and even then did not do so, naturally, without numerous reservations and very considerable "failures to understand." He thought then that he would be able to grind down these ideas, too, in his eclectical mill, and thereby introduce still greater variety into his intellectual diet. Then he saw that the ideas of Marx are not at all suitable as decorations for those mosaics which are called world outlook in the case of eclectics, and that their diffusion threatens to destroy the mosaics he loves so well. So he declared war against these ideas. Of course he immediately turned out to be lagging behind intellectual progress: but really it seems to us that it is not his fault, that he is only making a mistake.

"But then all that does not justify 'acrobatics'!"

And we are not attempting to justify them: we are only pointing out extenuating circumstances. Quite without noticing it, Mr. Mikhailovsky, owing to the development of Russian social thought, has fallen into a state from which one can only get out by means of "acrobatics." There is, true, another way out, but only a man filled with *genuine* heroism would choose it. That way out is to *lay down the arms of eclecticism*.

---

* *Sketches of the Gogol Period in Russian Literature*, St. Petersburg, 1892, pp. 24-25. (The author in question is N. G. Chernyshevsky.—*Ed.*)

CONCLUSION

Up to this point, in setting forth the ideas of Marx, we have been principally examining those objections which are put forward against him from the theoretical point of view. Now it is useful for us to become acquainted also with the *"practical reason"* of at any rate a certain part of his opponents. In doing so we shall use the method of *comparative history*. In other words we shall first see how the "practical reason" of the *German Utopians* met the ideas of Marx, and will thereafter turn to the reason of our dear and respected fellow countrymen.

At the end of the 40s Marx and Engels had an interesting dispute with the well-known Karl Heinzen. The dispute at once assumed a very warm character. Karl Heinzen tried to laugh out of court, as they call it, the ideas of his opponents, and displayed a skill in this occupation which in no way was inferior to the skill of Mr. Mikhailovsky. Marx and Engels, naturally, paid back in kind. The affair did not pass off without some sharp speaking. Heinzen called Engels "a thoughtless and insolent urchin"; Marx called Heinzen a representative of "der grobianischen Literatur," and Engels called him "the most ignorant man of the century." But what did the argument turn about? What views did Heinzen attribute to Marx and Engels? They were these. Heinzen assured his readers that from the point of view of Marx *there was* *nothing to be done in Germany of that day* by anyone filled with any generous intentions. According to Marx, said Heinzen, "there must first arrive the supremacy of the bourgeoisie, which must manufacture the factory proletariat," which only then will begin acting on its own.*

Marx and Engels "did not take into account *that* proletariat which has been created by the thirty-four German Vampires," i.e., the whole German people, with the exception of the factory workers (the word "proletariat" means on the lips of Heinzen only the miserable condition of that people). This numerous proletariat had not in Marx's opinion, he alleged, any right to demand a better future, because it bore on itself "*only the brand of oppression, and not the stamp of the factory*; it must patiently starve and die of hunger (hungern und verhungern) until Germany has become England. The factory is the school which the people must go through beforehand in order to have the right of setting about improving its position."**

Anyone who knows even a little of the history of Germany knows nowadays how absurd were these charges by Heinzen. Everyone knows whether Marx and Engels closed their eyes to the miserable condition of the German people. Everyone understands whether it was right to attribute to them the idea that there was nothing for a man of generous character to do in Germany so long as it had not become England: it would seem that these men did something even without waiting for such a transformation of their country. But why did Heinzen attribute to them all this nonsense? Was it really because of his bad faith? No, we shall say again that this was not so much his fault as his misfortune. He simply did not understand

---

* *Die Helden des deutschen Kommunismus*, Bern, 1848, S. 12.
** *Ibid.*, p. 22.

the views of Marx and Engels, and therefore they seemed to him harmful; and as he passionately loved his country, he went to war against these views which were seemingly harmful to his country. But lack of comprehension is a bad adviser, and a very unreliable assistant in an argument. That was why Heinzen landed in the most absurd situation. He was a very witty person, but wit alone without understanding will not take one very far: and now the last laugh *is not on his side.*

The reader will agree that Heinzen must be seen in the same light as our quite similar argument, for example, with Mr. Mikhailovsky. And is it only Mr. Mikhailovsky? Do not all those who attribute to the "disciples"* the aspiration to enter the service of the Kolupayevs and Razuvayevs[45]—and their name is legion—do not they all repeat the mistake of Heinzen? Not one of them has invented a single argument against the "economic" materialists which did not already figure, *nearly fifty years ago*, in the arguments of Heinzen. If they have anything original, it is only this—their naïve ignorance of how *unoriginal* they really are. They are constantly trying to find "new paths" for Russia, and owing to their ignorance "poor Russian thought" only stumbles across tracks of European thought, full of ruts and long ago abandoned. It is strange, but quite comprehensible if we apply to the explanation of this seemingly strange phenomenon "the category of necessity." *At a certain stage of the economic development of a country, certain well-meaning stupidities "necessarily" arise in the heads of its intellectuals.*

How comical was the position of Heinzen in his argument with Marx will be shown by the following example. He pestered his opponents with a demand for a detailed

---

* "Disciples" was the "Aesopian" word for Marxists.—*Ed.*

"ideal" of the future. Tell us, he said to them, how property relations ought to be organized according to your views? What should be the limits of private property, on the one hand, and social property on the other? They replied to him that at every given moment the property relations of society are determined by the state of its productive forces, and that therefore one can only point out the general direction of social development, but not work out beforehand any exactly formulated draft legislation. We can already say that the socialization of labour created by modern industry must lead to the nationalization of the means of production. But one cannot say to what extent this nationalization could be carried out, say, in the next ten years: this would depend on the nature of the mutual relations between small- and large-scale industry at that time, large land-owning and peasant landed property, and so forth. Well, then you have no ideal, Heinzen concluded: a fine ideal which will be *manufactured only later, by machines*!

Heinzen adopted the *utopian* standpoint. The Utopian in working out his "ideal" always starts, as we know, from some abstract *notion*—for example, the notion of human nature—or from some abstract *principle*—for example, the principle of such and such rights of personality, or the principle of "individuality," etc., etc. Once such a principle has been adopted, it is not difficult, starting from it, to define with the most perfect exactness and to the last detail what *ought to be* (naturally, we do not know at what time and in what circumstances) the property relations between men, for example. And it is comprehensible that the Utopian should look with astonishment at those who tell him that there cannot be property relations which are good in themselves, without any regard for the circumstances of their time and place. It seems to him that such people have absolutely no "ideals."

If the reader has followed our exposition not without attention, he knows that in that event the Utopian is often wrong. Marx and Engels had an ideal, and a very definite *ideal*: the subordination of *necessity* to *freedom*, of blind *economic forces* to the *power of human reason*. Proceeding from this ideal, they directed their practical activity accordingly—and it consisted, of course, not in serving the bourgeoisie but in developing the self-consciousness of those same producers who must, in time, become masters of their products.

Marx and Engels had no reason to "worry" about transforming Germany into England or, as people say in Russia nowadays, serving the bourgeoisie: the bourgeoisie developed without their assistance, and it was impossible to arrest that development, i.e., there were no social forces capable of doing that. And it would have been needless to do so, because the old economic order was in the last analysis no better than the bourgeois order, and in the 40s had to such an extent grown out of date that it had become *harmful for all*. But the impossibility of arresting the development of capitalist production was not enough to deprive the thinking people of Germany of the possibility of *serving the welfare of its people*. The bourgeoisie has its inevitable fellow-travellers: all those who really serve its purse *on account of economic necessity*. The more developed the consciousness of these unwilling servants, the easier their position, the stronger their resistance to the Kolupayevs and Razuvayevs of all lands and all peoples. Marx and Engels accordingly set themselves this particular task of developing that self-consciousness: in keeping with the spirit of dialectical materialism, from the very beginning they set themselves a *completely and exclusively idealistic task.*

The criterion of the ideal is economic reality. That was what Marx and Engels said, and on this foundation they were suspected of some kind of economic Molchalinism,[46] readiness to tread down into the mud those who were economically weak and to serve the interests of the economically strong. The source of such suspicion was a *metaphysical conception of what* Marx and Engels meant by the words *"economic reality."* When the metaphysician hears that one who serves society must take his stand on reality, he imagines that he is being advised to make his peace with that reality. He is unaware that in every economic reality there exist *contradictory elements*, and that to make his peace with reality would mean making his peace with only one of its elements, namely that which *dominates* for the moment. The dialectical materialists pointed, and point, to another element of reality, hostile to the first, and *one in which the future is maturing*. We ask: if one takes one's stand on *that* element, if one takes *it* as the criterion of one's "ideals," does this mean entering the service of the Kolupayevs and Razuvayevs?

But if it is economic reality that must be the criterion of the ideal, then it is comprehensible that a *moral* criterion for the ideal is *unsatisfactory*, not because the moral feelings of men deserve indifference or contempt, but because these feelings are not enough to show us the right way of serving the interests of our neighbour. It is not enough for the doctor to sympathize with the condition of his patient: he has to reckon with the *physical reality* of the organism, to start from it in fighting it. If the doctor were to think of confining himself to moral indignation against the disease, he would deserve the most malicious ridicule. It was in this sense that Marx ridiculed the *"moralizing criticism"* and *"critical morality"* of his opponents. But his opponents thought that he was laughing at *"morality."* "Human morality and will have no value in the eyes of men who themselves have neither morality nor will," exclaimed Heinzen.*

One must, however, remark that if our Russian opponents of the "economic" materialists in general only repeat—without knowing it—the arguments of their German predecessors, nevertheless they do diversify their arguments to some extent in minor detail. Thus, for example, the German Utopians did not engage in long dissertations about the "law of economic development" of Germany. With us, however, dissertations of that kind have assumed truly terrifying dimensions. The reader will remember that Mr. V. V., even at the very beginning of the 80s, promised that he would reveal the law of economic development of Russia. True, Mr. V. V. began later on to be frightened of that law, but himself showed at the same time that he was afraid of it only temporarily, only until the time that the Russian intellectuals discovered a very good and kind law. Generally speaking, Mr. V. V., too, willingly takes part in the endless discussions of whether Russia must or must not go through the phase of capitalism. As early as the 70s the teaching of Marx was dragged into these discussions.

How such discussions are carried on amongst us is shown by the latest and most up-to-date work of Mr. S. Krivenko.[47] This author, replying to Mr. P. Struve,[48] advises his opponent to think harder about the question of the "necessity and good consequences of capitalism."

"If the capitalist regime represents a fatal and inevitable stage of development, through which any human society must pass, if it only remains to bow one's head before that historical necessity, should one have recourse to measures which can only delay the coming of the capitalist order and, on the contrary, should not one try to facil-

---

* *Die Helden des deutschen Kommunismus*, Bern, 1848, S. 22.

itate the transition to it and use all one's efforts to promote its most rapid advent, i.e., strive to develop capitalist industry and capitalization of handicrafts, the development of kulakdom ... the destruction of the village community, the expropriation of the people from the land, generally speaking, the smoking-out of the surplus peasantry from the villages into the factories."*

Mr. S. Krivenko really puts two questions here, (1) does capitalism represent a fatal and inevitable stage, (2) if so, what practical tasks follow from it? Let us begin with the first.

Mr. S. Krivenko formulates it correctly in this sense that one, and moreover the overwhelming, part of our intellectuals did precisely concern itself with the question in that form: does capitalism represent a fatal and inevitable stage through which every human society must pass? At one time they thought that Marx replied in the affirmative to this question, and were very upset thereby. When there was published the well-known letter of Marx, allegedly to Mr. Mikhailovsky,** they saw with surprise that Marx did not recognize the "inevitability" of this stage, and then they decided with malignant joy: hasn't he just put to shame his Russian disciples! But those who were rejoicing forgot the French proverb: il bien rira qui rira le dernier (he laughs best who laughs last —*Ed.*).

From beginning to end of this dispute the opponents of the "Russian disciples" of Marx were indulging in the most "unnatural idle chatter."

The fact is that, when they were discussing whether the historical theory of Marx was applicable to Russia, they forgot one trifle: they forgot to ascertain what that

---
* *Russkoye Bogatstvo*, December 1893, Part II, p. 189.
** In this draft unfinished sketch of a letter, Marx writes not to Mr. Mikhailovsky, but to the Editor of *Otechestvenniye Zapiski*. Marx speaks of Mr. Mikhailovsky in the third person.

theory consists of. And truly magnificent was the plight into which, thanks to this, our subjectivists fell, with Mr. Mikhailovsky at their head.

Mr. Mikhailovsky read (*if* he has read) the preface to the *Critique of Political Economy,* in which the philosophical-historical theory of Marx is set forth, and decided it was nothing more than Hegelianism. Without noticing the elephant where the elephant really was,* Mr. Mikhailovsky began looking round, and it seemed to him that he had at last found the elephant he was looking for in the chapter about primitive capitalist accumulation—where Marx is writing about the historical progress of Western capitalism, and not at all of the whole history of humanity.

Every process is unquestionably "inevitable" where it exists. Thus, for example, the burning of a match is inevitable for it, once it has caught fire: the match "inevitably" goes out, once the process of burning has come to an end. *Capital* speaks of the course of capitalist development which was "inevitable" for those countries where that development has taken place. Imagining that in the chapter of *Capital* just mentioned he has before him an entire historical philosophy, Mr. Mikhailovsky decided that, in the opinion of Marx, capitalist production is inevitable for all countries and for all peoples.** Then he

---

* There is a well-known Russian story of the man who went to the zoo and "didn't notice" the elephant.—*Tr.*

** See the article, "Karl Marx before the Judgement of Mr. Y. Zhukovsky," in *Otechestvenniye Zapiski* for October 1877. "In the sixth chapter of *Capital* there is a paragraph headed: 'The so-called primitive accumulation.' Here Marx had in view a historical sketch of the first steps in the capitalist process of production, but he provided something which is much more—an entire philosophical-historical theory." We repeat that all this is absolute nonsense: the historical philosophy of Marx is set forth in the preface to the *Critique of Political Economy*, so incomprehensible for Mr. Mikhai-

began to *whine* about the embarrassing position of those Russian people who, etc.; and—the joker!—having paid the necessary tribute to his subjective necessity to whine, he importantly declared, addressing himself to Mr. Zhukovsky: you see, we too know how to criticize Marx, we too do not blindly follow what "the master has said"! Naturally all this did not advance the question of "inevitability" one inch; but after reading the whining of Mr. Mikhailovsky, Marx had the intention of going to his assistance. He sketched out in the form of a letter to the editor of *Otechestvenniye Zapiski* his remarks on the article by Mr. Mikhailovsky. When, after the death of Marx, this draft appeared in our press, Russian people who, etc., had at least the *opportunity* of finding a correct solution to the question of "inevitability."

What could Marx say about the article of Mr. Mikhailovsky? A man had fallen into misfortune, by taking the philosophical-historical theory of Marx to be that which it was not in the least. It was clear that Marx had first of all to rescue from misfortune a hopeful young Russian writer. In addition, the young Russian writer was complaining that Marx was sentencing Russia to capitalism. He had to show the Russian writer that dialectical materialism doesn't sentence any countries to anything at all,

---

lovsky, in the shape of "a few generalizing ideas, most intimately interconnected." But this in passing. Mr. Mikhailovsky has managed not to understand Marx even in what referred to the "inevitability" of the capitalist process for the West. He has seen in factory legislation a "correction" to the fatal inflexibility of the historical process. Imagining that according to Marx *"the economic"* acts on its own, without any part played by men, he was consistent in seeing a correction in every intervention by men in the course of their process of production. The only thing he did not know was that according to Marx that very intervention, *in every given form*, is the inevitable product of the given economic relations. Just try and argue about Marx with men who don't understand him with such notable consistency!

that it doesn't point out a way which is general and "inevitable" for all nations at all times; that the further development of every given society always depends on the relationships of social forces within it; and that therefore any serious person must, without guessing or whimpering about some fantastic "inevitability," first of all study those relations. Only such a study can show what is "inevitable" and what is not "inevitable" for the given society.

And that's just what Marx did. First of all he revealed the "misunderstanding" of Mr. Mikhailovsky: "The chapter on primitive accumulation does not pretend to do more than trace the path by which, in Western Europe, the capitalist order of economy emerged from the womb of the feudal order of economy. It therefore describes the historic movement which, by divorcing the producers from their means of production, converts them into wage-workers (proletarians in the modern sense of the word) while it converts those who possess the means of production into capitalists. In that history, 'all revolutions are epoch-making that act as levers for the advancement of the capitalist class in course of formation.... But the basis of this whole development is the expropriation of the agricultural producer.' ... At the end of the chapter the historical tendency of production is summed up thus ... that capitalist property ... cannot but transform itself into social property. At this point I have not furnished any proof, for the good reason that this statement is itself nothing else but a general summary of long expositions previously given in the chapters on capitalist production."*

In order better to clear up the circumstance that Mr. Mikhailovsky had taken to be an historical theory what

---
* K. Marx and F. Engels, *Selected Correspondence*, Moscow, 1955, pp. 378-79.--*Ed.*

was not and could not be such a theory, Marx pointed to the example of ancient Rome. A very convincing example! For indeed, if it is "inevitable" for all peoples to go through capitalism, what is to be done with Rome, what is to be done with Sparta, what is to be done with the State of the Incas, what is to be done with the many other peoples who disappeared from the historical scene without fulfilling this imaginary obligation? The fate of these peoples did not remain unknown to Marx: consequently he could not have spoken of the universal "inevitability" of the capitalist process.

"My critic," says Marx, "feels he absolutely must metamorphose my historical sketch of the genesis of capitalism in Western Europe into an historico-philosophic theory of the general path every people is fated to tread, whatever the historical circumstances in which it finds itself.... But I beg his pardon. (He is both honouring and shaming me too much.)"

We should think so! Such an interpretation was transforming Marx into one of those "people with a formula" whom he had already ridiculed in his polemics against Proudhon. Mr. Mikhailovsky attributed to Marx a "formula of progress," and Marx replied: no, thank you very much, I don't need these goods.

We have already seen how the Utopians regarded the laws of historical development (let the reader remember what we said about Saint-Simon). The conformity to law of historical movement assumed in their eyes a *mystical* appearance; the path along which mankind proceeds was in their imagination *marked out beforehand*, as it were, and no historical events could change the direction of that path. An interesting psychological aberration! "Human nature" is for the Utopians the point of departure of their investigation. But the laws of development of that nature, immediately acquiring in their eyes a mysterious character, *are transferred somewhere outside man and outside the actual relationship of men,* into some "*superhistorical*" sphere.

Dialectical materialism, here also, transfers the question to quite another ground, thereby giving it quite another appearance.

The dialectical materialists "reduce everything to economics." We have already explained how this is to be understood. But what are economics? They are the sum-total of the actual relationships of the men who constitute the given society, in their process of production. These relationships do not represent a motionless metaphysical essence. They are eternally changing under the influence of the development of the productive forces, and under the influence of the historical environment surrounding the given society. Once the actual relations of men in the process of production are given, there fatally follow from these relations certain consequences. In this sense social movement conforms to law, and no one ascertained that conformity to law better than Marx. But as the economic movement of every society has a "*peculiar*" form in consequence of the "*peculiarity*" of the conditions in which it takes place, there can be no "formula of progress" covering the past and foretelling the future of the economic movement of *all* societies. The formula of progress is that abstract truth which, in the words of the author of the *Sketches of the Gogol Period of Russian Literature*, was so pleasing to the metaphysicians. But, as he remarks himself, there is no abstract truth: truth is always concrete: everything depends on the circumstances of time and place. And if everything depends on these circumstances, it is the latter that must be studied by people who, etc.

"In order that I might be specially qualified to estimate the economic development in Russia, I learnt Russian and then for many years studied the official publications and others bearing on this subject."

The Russian disciples of Marx are faithful to him in this case also. Of course one of them may have greater and another less extensive economic knowledge, *but what matters here is not the amount of the knowledge of individual persons, but the point of view itself*. The Russian disciples of Marx are not guided by a subjective ideal or by some "formula of progress," but turn to the economic reality of their country.

To what conclusion, then, did Marx come regarding Russia? "If Russia continues to pursue the path she has followed since 1861, she will lose the finest chance ever offered by history to a people and undergo all the fatal vicissitudes of the capitalist regime." A little further on Marx adds that in recent years Russia "has been taking a lot of trouble" in the sense of proceeding along the path mentioned. Since the letter was written (i.e., since 1877), we will add for our part, Russia has been moving along that path still further and ever more quickly.

What then follows from Marx's letter? Three conclusions:

1. He shamed by his letter not his Russian disciples, but the subjectivist gentlemen who, not having the least conception of his scientific point of view, were attempting to refashion Marx himself after their own likeness and image, and to transform him into a *metaphysician and utopian*.

2. The subjectivist gentlemen were not *ashamed* of the letter for the simple reason that—true to their "ideal"—they didn't understand the letter either.

3. If the subjectivist gentlemen want to argue with us on the question of how and where Russia is moving, they must at every given moment start from an *analysis of economic reality*.

The study of that reality in the 70s brought Marx to the *conditional* conclusion: "If Russia continues to pursue the path she has followed since the emancipation of the peasantry ... she will become a perfect capitalist nation ... and after that, once fallen in the bondage of the capitalist regime, she will experience the pitiless laws of capitalism like other profane peoples. That is all."[49]

That is all. But a Russian desiring to work for the welfare of his native land cannot be satisfied with such a conditional conclusion. The question will inevitably arise in his mind, will Russia continue to proceed along this path? Do data by any chance exist which allow one to hope that she will leave this path?

In order to reply to this question, one must once again turn to a study of the actual position of the country, an analysis of its present-day internal life. The Russian disciples of Marx, *on the basis of such an analysis*, assert that *she will continue. There are no data allowing one to hope that Russia will soon leave the path of capitalist development upon which it entered after 1861. That is all!*

The subjectivist gentlemen think that the "disciples" are mistaken. They will have to prove it with the help of data supplied by the same Russian *actuality*. The "disciples" say: Russia will continue to proceed along the path of capitalist development, not because there exists some external force, some mysterious law pushing it along that path, but because there is no effective internal force capable of pushing it from that path. If the subjectivist gentlemen think that there is such a force, let them say what it consists of, and let them prove its presence. We shall be very glad to hear them out. Up to now we have not heard anything definite from them on this score.

"What do you mean: there is no force? And what about our ideals?" exclaim our dear opponents.

Oh gentlemen, gentlemen! Really you are touchingly simple! The very question is, how to realize, even for the sake of argument, your ideals—though they represent something fairly muddled? Put in this way, the question, naturally, sounds very prosaic, but so long as it is unanswered, your "ideals" will have only an "ideal" significance.

Imagine that a young hero has been brought into a prison of stone, put behind iron bars, surrounded by watchful guards. The young hero only smiles. He takes a bit of charcoal he has put away beforehand, draws a little boat on the wall, takes his seat in the boat and ... farewell prison, farewell watchful guards, the young hero is once again at large in the wide world.

A beautiful story! But it is ... *only a story.* In reality, a little boat drawn on the wall has *never carried anyone away anywhere.*

Already since the time of the abolition of serfdom Russia has patently entered the path of capitalist development. The subjectivist gentlemen see this perfectly well, and themselves assert that our old economic relations are breaking up with amazing and constantly increasing speed. But that's nothing, they say to one another: we shall embark Russia in the little boat of our ideals, and she will float away from this path beyond distant lands, into far-off realms.

The subjectivist gentlemen are good story-tellers, but ... *"that is all"*! That is all—and that's terribly little, and never before have stories changed the historical movement of a people, for the same prosaic reason that not a single nightingale has ever been well fed on fables.*

The subjectivist gentlemen have adopted a strange classification of "Russian people who..."—into two catego-

---
* One of the most popular Russian proverbs: "The nightingale is not fed on fables"—"fine words butter no parsnips."—*Tr*

ries. Those who *believe* in the possibility of floating away on the little boat of the subjective ideal are recognized as good people, true well-wishers of the people. But those who say that that faith is *absolutely unfounded* are attributed a kind of unnatural malignancy, the determination to make the Russian muzhik die of hunger. No melodrama has ever had such villains as must be, in the opinion of the subjectivist gentlemen, the consistent Russian "economic" materialists. This amazing opinion is just as well founded as was that of Heinzen, which the readers already know, when he attributed to Marx the intention of leaving the German people "hungern und verhungern."

Mr. Mikhailovsky asks himself why is it that just now gentlemen have appeared who are capable "with a tranquil conscience to condemn millions of people to starvation and poverty?" Mr. S. N. Krivenko thinks that once a consistent person has decided that capitalism is inevitable in Russia it "remains for him only to strive to develop ... capitalization of handicrafts, the development of kulakdom ... the destruction of the village community, the expropriation of the people from the land and, generally speaking, the smoking-out of the surplus peasantry from the villages." Mr. S. N. Krivenko thinks so only because he himself is incapable of *"consistent" thinking*.

Heinzen did at least recognize in Marx a prejudice in favour of toilers who bore the "factory stamp." The subjectivist gentlemen evidently do not recognize even this little weakness in the "Russian disciples of Marx": they, forsooth, consistently hate all the sons of man, without exception. They would like to starve them all to death, with the exception possibly of the representatives of the merchant estate. In reality, if Mr. Krivenko had admitted any good intentions in the "disciples," as regards the factory workers, he would not have written the lines just quoted.

"To strive ... generally speaking, for the smoking-out of the surplus peasantry from the villages." The saints preserve us! Why strive? Surely the influx of new labour into the factory population will lead to a lowering of wages. And even Mr. Krivenko knows that lowering of wages cannot be beneficial and pleasant for the workers. Why should the consistent "disciples," then, try to do harm to the workman and bring him unpleasantness? Obviously these people are consistent only in their hatred of mankind, they don't even love the factory worker! Or perhaps they do love him, but in their own peculiar way —they love him and therefore they try to do him harm: "Spare the rod and spoil the child." Strange people! Remarkable consistency!

"To strive ... for the development of kulakdom, the destruction of the village commune, the expropriation of the people from the land." What horrors! But why strive for all this? Surely the development of kulakdom and the expropriation of the people from the land may reflect themselves in the lowering of their purchasing power, and the lowering of their purchasing power will lead to a reduction of demand for factory goods, will reduce the demand for labour, i.e., will lower wages. No, the consistent "disciples" don't love the working man; and is it only the working man? For surely the reduction in the purchasing power of the people will harmfully affect even the interests of the employers who constitute, the subjectivist gentlemen assure us, the object of the disciples' most tender care. No, you can say what you like, but these disciples are really queer people!

"To strive ... for the capitalization of handicrafts" ... not to "stick at either the buying-up of peasant land, or the opening of shops and public houses, or at any other shady occupation." But why should consistent people do all this? Surely they are convinced of the inevitability of the capitalist process; consequently, if the introduction of public houses were an essential part of that process, there would inevitably appear public houses (which, one must suppose, do not exist at present). It seems to Mr. Krivenko that shady activity must accelerate the capitalist process. But, we shall say again, if capitalism is inevitable, "shadiness" will appear of its own accord. Why should the consistent disciples of Marx so "strive" for it?

"Here their theory grows silent before the demands of moral feeling: they see that shadiness is inevitable, they adore it for that inevitability, and from all sides they hasten to its assistance, or else maybe that poor inevitable shadiness will not get the upper hand soon enough, without our assistance."

Is that so, Mr. Krivenko? If it is not, then all your arguments about the "consistent" disciples are worthless. And if it is, then your personal consistency and your own "capacity of cognition" are worthless.

Take whatever you like, even though it be the capitalization of handicrafts. It represents a two-fold process: there appear first of all people who *accumulate* in their hands the means of production, and secondly people who *make use* of these means of production for a certain payment. Let us suppose that shadiness is the distinguishing feature of persons of the first category; but surely the people who work for them for hire may, it might seem, escape that "phase" of moral development? And if so, what will there be shady in my activity if I devote it to those people, if I develop their self-consciousness and defend their material interests? Mr. Krivenko will say perhaps that such activity will delay the development of capitalism. Not in the least. The example of England, France and Germany will show him that in those countries such activity has not only not delayed the development of capitalism but, on the contrary, has accelerated it, and by the way has thereby brought nearer the practical solution of some of their "accursed" problems.

Or let us take the destruction of the village community. This also is a two-fold process: the peasant holdings are being concentrated in the hands of the kulaks, and an ever-growing number of previously independent peasants are being transformed into proletarians. All this, naturally, is accompanied by a clash of interests, by struggle. The "Russian disciple" appears on the scene, attracted by the noise: he lifts up his voice in a brief but deeply-felt hymn to the "category of necessity" and ... *opens a public house*! That's how the most "consistent" among them will act: the more moderate man will confine himself to opening a *little shop*. That's it, isn't it, Mr. Krivenko? But why shouldn't the "disciple" take the side of the village poor?

"But if he wants to take their side, he will have to try and interfere with their expropriation from the land?" *All right, let's admit it: that's what he must try for.* "But that will delay the development of capitalism." *It won't delay it in the least.* On the contrary, it will even accelerate it. The subjectivist gentlemen are always imagining that the village community "of itself" tends to pass into some "higher form." They are mistaken. The only real tendency of the village community is *the tendency to break up*, and the better the conditions of the peasantry, the sooner would the community break up. Moreover, that break-up can take place in conditions which are *more or less advantageous for the people.* The "disciples" must "strive" to see to it that the break-up takes place in conditions *most advantageous for the people.*

"But why not prevent the break-up itself?"

And why didn't you prevent the famine of 1891? You couldn't? We believe you, and we should consider our cause lost if all we had left were to make *your morality* responsible for such *events* which were independent of your will, instead of refuting your *views* with the help of *logical arguments*. But why then do you pay us back in a different measure? Why, in arguments with us, do you represent the poverty of the people as though we were responsible for it? Because where *logic* cannot help you, sometimes *words* can, particularly *pitiful words*. You could not prevent the famine of 1891? Who then will go bail that you will be able to prevent the break-up of the village community, the expropriation of the peasantry from their land? Let us take the middle path, so dear to eclectics: let's imagine that in some cases you will succeed in preventing all this. Well, but in those cases where your efforts prove unsuccessful, where in spite of them the community nevertheless breaks up, where the peasants nevertheless prove landless—how will you act with these victims of the fateful process? Charon carried across the Styx only those souls who were able to pay him for his work. Will you begin to take into your little boat, for transporting into the realm of the subjective ideal, only genuine members of the village commune? Will you begin using your oars to beat off the village proletarians? Probably you yourselves will agree, gentlemen, that this would be very "*shady*." And once you agree with this, you will have to act in their regard in just the same way as, in your opinion, any decent man will have to act, i.e., not to set up public houses to sell them dope, but to increase their strength of *resistance* to the public house, to the publican and to every other dope which history serves up, or will serve up, to them.

Or perhaps it is *we* now who are beginning to tell fairy-tales? Perhaps the village community is *not* breaking up? Perhaps the expropriation of the people from the land is *not* in fact taking place? Perhaps we invented this with the sole aim of plunging the peasant into poverty, after he had hitherto been enjoying an enviably prosperous existence? Then open any investigation by your own partisans, and it will show you how matters have stood up to now, i.e., before even a single "disciple" has opened a public house or started a little shop. When you argue with us, you represent matters as though the people are already living in the realm of your subjective ideals, while we, through our inherent hatred of mankind, are dragging them down by the feet, into the prose of capitalism. But matters stand in exactly the opposite way. It is the capitalist prose that exists, and we are asking ourselves, how can this prose be fought, how can we put the people in a situation even somewhat approaching the "ideal"? You may find that we are giving the wrong answer to the question: but why distort our intentions? Really, you know, that is "shady": really such *"criticism"* is unworthy even of *"Suzdal folks."*[50]

But how then can one fight the capitalist prose which, we repeat, already exists independently of our and your efforts? You have one reply: to "consolidate the village community," to strengthen the connection of the peasant with the land. And we reply that that is an answer worthy only of Utopians. Why? Because it is an abstract answer. According to your opinion, the village community is good always and everywhere, while in our opinion there is no abstract truth, truth is always concrete, everything depends on the circumstances of time and place. There was a time when the village community could be advantageous for the *whole* people; there are probably even now places where it is of advantage to the agriculturists. It is not we who will begin a revolt against *such* a community. But in a number of cases the village community has been transformed into a means of *exploiting* the peasant. Against such a commune we revolt, just as against everything that is harmful for the people. Remember the peasant whom G. I. Uspensky makes pay *"for nothing."*[51] What should one do with him, in your opinion? Transport him into the realm of the ideal, you reply. Very good, transport him with God's help. But while he has not yet been transported, while he has not yet taken his seat on the little boat of the ideal, while the little boat has not yet sailed up to him and as yet we don't know when it will do so, wouldn't it be better for him to be free from paying "for nothing"? Wouldn't it be better for him to stop being a member of a village community which only means that he will have absolutely unproductive expenses, and perhaps in addition only a periodical flogging at the *Volost* office? We think it *would*, but you charge us for this with intending to starve the people to death. Is that just? Isn't there something "shady" about it? Or perhaps you really are incapable of understanding us? Can that really be so? Chaadayev[52] said once that the Russian doesn't even know the syllogism of the West. Can that really be just your case? We will admit that Mr. S. Krivenko quite sincerely does not understand this; we admit it also in relation to Mr. Kareyev and Mr. Yuzhakov.[53] But Mr. Mikhailovsky always seemed to us a man of a much more "acute" mind.

What have you invented, gentlemen, to improve the lot of the millions of peasants who have in fact lost their land? When it is a question of people who pay "for nothing," you are able only to give one piece of advice: although he does pay "for nothing," nevertheless he mustn't destroy his connection with the village community because, once it has been destroyed, it can never be restored. Of course, this will involve temporary inconvenience for those who pay for nothing, but ... "what the muzhik suffers is no disaster."*

---

* From Nekrasov's poem "Meditations at the Main Entrance." —*Ed.*

And that's just how it turns out that our subjectivist gentlemen are ready to bring the most vital *interests of the people* as a sacrifice to *their ideals*! *And that is just how it turns out that their preaching in reality is becoming more and more hurtful for the people.*

"To be an enthusiast had become her social vocation," says Tolstoi about Anna Pavlovna Sherer.[54] To hate capitalism has become the social vocation of our subjectivists. What good could the enthusiasm of an old maid do Russia? None whatsoever. What good does the "subjective" hatred of capitalism do the Russian producers? Also none whatsoever.

But the enthusiasm of Anna Pavlovna was at least harmless. The utopian hatred of capitalism is beginning to do positive harm to the Russian producer, because it makes our intellectuals extremely unsqueamish about the means of consolidating the village community. Scarcely does anyone mention such consolidation when immediately a darkness falls in which all cats seem grey, and the subjectivist gentlemen are ready warmly to embrace the *Moskovskiye Vedomosti*.[55] And all this "subjective" darkening of the intellect goes precisely to aid that *public house* which the "disciples" are alleged to be ready to cultivate. It's shameful to say it, but sinful to hide, that *the utopian enemies of capitalism prove in reality to be the accomplices of capitalism in its most coarse, shameful and harmful form.*

Up to now we have been speaking of Utopians who have tried, or nowadays try, to invent some argument or other *against Marx*. Let us see now how those Utopians behave, or behaved, who were *inclined to quote from him*.

Heinzen, whom the Russian subjectivists now reproduce with such astonishing accuracy in their arguments with the "Russian disciples," was a Utopian of a democratic-bourgeois tendency. But there were many Utopians of an opposite tendency in Germany in the 40s.

The social and economic position of Germany was then in broad outline as follows.

On the one hand, the bourgeoisie was rapidly developing, and insistently demanding every kind of assistance and support from the German governments. The well-known Zollverein (Customs Union—*Ed.*) was entirely the result of its work, and advocacy in favour of it was carried on not only with the help of "petitions," but also by means of more or less scientific research: let us recall the name of Friedrich List.[56] On the other hand, the destruction of the old economic "foundations" had left the German people defenceless in relation to capitalism. The peasants and handicraftsmen were already sufficiently involved in the process of capitalist advance to experience on themselves all its disadvantageous sides, which make themselves felt with particular force in *transitional periods*. But the working mass was at that time still little capable of resistance. It could not as yet withstand the representatives of capital to any noticeable extent. Way back *in the 60s* Marx said that Germany was suffering simultaneously both *from the development of capitalism and from the insufficiency of its development.* In the 40s her sufferings from the insufficiency of development of capitalism were even greater. Capitalism had destroyed the old foundations of peasant life; the *handicraft* industry, which had previously flourished in Germany, now had to withstand the competition of *machine* production, which was much too strong for it. The handicraftsmen grew poorer, falling every year more and more into helpless dependence on the *middlemen.* And at the same time the peasants had to discharge a long series of such services, in relation to the landlords and the state, as might perhaps have been bearable in previous days, but in the 40s became all the more oppressive because they less and less corresponded to the actual conditions of peasant life. The poverty of the peasantry reached astounding dimensions; the kulak became the complete master of the village; the peasant grain was frequently bought by him while it was still not yet reaped; begging had become a kind of seasonal occupation. Investigators at that time pointed out village communities in which, out of several thousand families, only a few hundred were not engaged in begging. In other places—a thing almost incredible, but placed on record at the time by the German press—*the peasants fed on carrion.* Leaving their villages, they could not find sufficient employment in the industrial centres, and the press pointed out the growing unemployment and the increasing emigration which it was producing.

Here is how one of the most advanced organs of the time describes the position of the working mass: "One hundred thousand spinners in the Ravensberg district, and in other places of the German Fatherland, can no longer live by their own labour, and can no longer find an outlet for their manufacture" (it was a question chiefly of handicraftsmen). "They seek work and bread, without finding one or the other, because it is difficult if not impossible for them to find employment outside spinning. There exists a vast competition among the workers for the most miserable wage."*

The morality of the people was undoubtedly declining. The destruction of old *economic relations* was paralleled by the shattering of old *moral notions*. The newspapers and journals of that time were filled with complaints of drunkenness among the workers, of sexual dissoluteness in their midst, of coxcombry and extravagance which

---
* *Der Gesellschafts-Spiegel*, Band I, S. 78. A letter from Westphalia.

developed among them, side by side with the decrease in their wages. There were no signs as yet in the German workman of a *new* morality, that morality which began rapidly to develop later, on the basis of the new movement of emancipation aroused by the very development of capitalism. The mass movement for emancipation was not even beginning at that time. The dull discontent of the mass made itself felt from time to time only in hopeless strikes and aimless revolts, in the senseless destruction of machines. But the sparks of consciousness were beginning to fall into the heads of the German workmen. Books which had represented an unnecessary luxury under the old order became an article of necessity in the new conditions. A passion for reading began to take possession of the workers.

Such was the state of affairs with which the right-thinking portion of the German intellectuals (der Gebildeten—as they said then) had to reckon. What was to be done, how could the people be helped? *By eliminating capitalism,* replied the intellectuals. The works of Marx and Engels which appeared at that time were joyfully accepted by part of the German intellectuals as constituting a number of new scientific arguments *in favour of the necessity of eliminating capitalism.* "While the liberal politicians have with new strength begun to sound List's trumpet of the protective tariff, trying to assure us ... that they are worrying about an expansion of industry mainly in the interests of the working class, while their opponents, the enthusiasts of free trade, have been trying to prove that England has become the flourishing and classical country of trade and industry not at all in consequence of protection, the excellent book of Engels on the condition of the working class in England has made a most timely appearance, and has destroyed the last illusions. All have recognized that this book constitutes one of the most remarkable works of modern times.... By a number of irrefutable proofs it has shown into what an abyss that society hurries to fall which makes its motive principle personal greed, the free competition of private employers, for whom money is their God."*

And so capitalism must be eliminated, or else Germany will fall into that abyss at the bottom of which England is already lying. This has been proved by Engels. And who will eliminate capitalism? The intellectuals, die Gebildeten. The peculiarity of Germany, in the words of one of these Gebildeten, was precisely that it was the German intellectuals who were called upon to eliminate capitalism in her, while "in the West" (in den westlichen Ländern) "it is more the workmen who are fighting it."** But how will the German intellectuals eliminate capitalism? By organizing production (Organisation der Arbeit). And what must the intellectuals do to organize production? *Allgemeines Volksblatt* which was published at Cologne in 1845 proposed the following measures:

1. Promotion of popular education, organization of popular lectures, concerts, etc.

2. Organization of big workshops in which workmen, artisans and handicraftsmen could work for themselves, not for an employer or a merchant. *Allgemeines Volksblatt* hoped that in time these artisans and handicraftsmen would themselves, on their own initiative, be grouped in an association.

---

* *Ibid.*, S. 86. *Notizen und Nachrichten.* (Notes and News.—*Ed.*)
** See the article by Hess in the same volume of the same review, p. 1 *et seq.* See also *Neue Anekdoten, herausgegeben von Karl Grün*, Darmstadt, 1845, p. 220. In Germany, as opposed to France, it is the educated minority which engages in the struggle with capitalism and *"ensures victory over it."*

3. Establishment of stores for the sale of the goods manufactured by the artisans and handicraftsmen, and also by national workshops.

These measures would save Germany from the evils of capitalism. And it was all the more easy to adopt them, added the sheet we have quoted, because "here and there people have already begun to establish permanent stores, so-called industrial bazaars, in which artisans can put out their goods for sale," and immediately receive a certain advance on account of them.... Then followed an exposition of the advantages which would follow from all this, both for the producer and for the consumer.

The elimination of capitalism seems easiest of all where *it is still poorly developed.* Therefore the German Utopians frequently and willingly underlined the circumstance that Germany was not yet England: Heinzen was even ready flatly to deny the existence of a factory proletariat in Germany. But since, for the Utopians, the chief thing was to prove to "society" the necessity of organizing production, they passed at times, without difficulty and without noticing it, over to the standpoint of people who asserted that *German capitalism could no longer develop any further, in consequence of its inherent contradictions, that the internal market had already been saturated, that the purchasing power of the population was falling, that the conquest of external markets was improbable and that therefore the number of workers engaged in manufacturing industry must inevitably and constantly diminish.* This was the point of view adopted by the journal *Der Gesellschafts-Spiegel,* which we have quoted several times, and which was one of the chief organs of the German Utopians of that day, after the appearance of the interesting pamphlet of L. Buhl: *Andeutungen über die Noth der arbeitenden Klassen und über die Aufgabe der Vereine zum Wohl derselben*

("Suggestions on the needy state of the working class and on the tasks of the unions for the welfare thereof."—*Ed.*), Berlin, 1845. Buhl asked himself, were the unions for promoting the welfare of the working class in a position to cope with their task? In order to reply to this question, he put forward another, namely, whence arose at the present time the poverty of the working class? The poor man and the proletarian are not at all one and the same thing, says Buhl. The poor man won't or can't work; the proletarian seeks work, he is capable of doing it, but it does not exist, and he falls into poverty. Such a phenomenon was quite unknown in previous times, although there always were the poor and there were always the oppressed—for example, the serfs.

Where did the proletarian come from? He was created by *competition*. Competition, which broke the old bonds that fettered production, brought forth an unprecedented industrial prosperity. But it also forces employers to lower the price of their goods. Therefore they try to reduce wages or the number of the employed. The latter object is achieved by the perfecting of machinery, which throws many workers on to the streets. Moreover, artisans cannot stand up to the competition of machine production, and are also transformed into proletarians. Wages fall more and more. Buhl points to the example of the cotton print industry, which was flourishing in Germany as late as the 20s. Wages were then very high. A good workman could earn from 18 to 20 thalers a week. But machines appeared, and with them female and child labour—and wages fell terribly. The principle of free competition acts thus always and everywhere, wherever it achieves predominance. *It leads to overproduction,* and overproduction to unemployment. And the more developed becomes large-scale industry, the more unemployment grows and the smaller becomes the number of workmen engaged in industrial undertakings. That this is really so is shown by the fact that the disasters mentioned occur only in industrial countries. Agricultural countries don't know them. But the state of affairs created by free competition is extremely dangerous for society (für die Gesellschaft), and therefore society cannot remain indifferent to it. What then must society do? Here Buhl turns to the question which holds first place, so to speak, in his work: is any *union* at all able to eradicate the poverty of the working class?

The local Berlin union for assisting the working class has set itself the object "not so much of eliminating existing poverty, as of preventing the appearance of poverty in the future." It is to this union that Buhl now turns. How will you prevent the appearance of poverty in the future, he asks: what will you do for this purpose? The poverty of the modern worker arises from the lack of demand for his labour. The worker needs not charity but work. But where will the union get work from? In order that the demand for labour should increase, it is necessary that the demand for the products of labour should increase. But this demand is diminishing, thanks to the diminution of the earnings of the working mass. Or perhaps the union will discover new markets? Buhl does not think that possible either. He comes to the conclusion that the task which the Berlin union has set itself is merely a *"well-intentioned illusion."*

Buhl advises the Berlin union to meditate more deeply on the causes of the poverty of the working class, before beginning the struggle against it. He considers *palliatives* to be of no importance. "Labour exchanges, savings banks and pension funds, and the like, can of course improve the position of a few individuals: but they will not eradicate the evil." Nor will associations do that:

"Associations also will not escape the harsh necessity (dura necessitas) of competition."

Where Buhl himself discerned the means of eradicating the evil, it is difficult to ascertain exactly from his pamphlet. It seems as though he hints that the interference of the state is necessary to remedy the evil, adding however that the result of such interference would be *doubtful*. At any rate, his pamphlet made a deep impression on the German intellectuals at that time; and not at all in the sense of disillusioning them. On the contrary, they saw in it a new proof of *the necessity of organizing labour*.

Here is what the journal *Der Gesellschafts-Spiegel* wrote of Buhl's pamphlet:

"The well-known Berlin writer L. Buhl has published a work entitled *Andeutungen, etc.* He thinks—and we share his opinion—that the miseries of the working class follow from the excess of productive forces; that that excess is the consequence of free competition and of the latest discoveries and inventions in physics and mechanics; that a return to guilds and corporations would be just as harmful as impeding discoveries and inventions; that therefore *in existing social conditions*" (the italics are those of the writer of the review) "there are no effective means of helping the workmen. Assuming that present-day egotistical private-enterprise relations remain unchanged, one must agree with Buhl that no union will be in a position to abolish the existing poverty. But such an assumption is not at all necessary; on the contrary, there could arise and already do arise unions the aim of which is to eliminate by peaceful means the above-mentioned egotistical basis of our society. All that is necessary is that the government should not handicap the activity of such unions."

It is clear that the reviewer had not understood, or had not wished to understand, Buhl's idea: but this is not important for us. We turned to Germany only in order, with the help of the lessons provided by *her* history, better to understand certain intellectual tendencies in present-day Russia. And in this sense the movement of the German intellectuals of the 40s comprises much that is instructive for us.

In the first place, the line of argument of Buhl reminds us of that of Mr. N. —on. Both one and the other begin by pointing to the development of the productive forces as the reason for the decline in the demand for labour, and consequently for the relative reduction of the number of workers. Both one and the other speak of the saturation of the internal market, and of the necessity arising therefrom of a further diminution in the demand for labour. Buhl did not admit, apparently, the possibility that the Germans might conquer foreign markets; Mr. N. —on resolutely refuses to recognize this possibility as regards the Russian manufacturers. Finally, both one and the other leave this question of foreign markets entirely without investigation: neither brings forward a single serious argument in favour of his opinion.

Buhl makes no obvious conclusion from his investigation, except that one must meditate more deeply on the position of the working class before helping it. Mr. N. —on comes to the conclusion that our society is faced with, true, a difficult but not an insoluble task—that of organizing our national production. But if we supplement the views of Buhl by the considerations set forth in connection with them by the reviewer of *Der Gesellschafts-Spiegel* whom we have quoted, the result is precisely the conclusion of Mr. N. —on. *Mr. N. —on=Buhl+the reviewer.* And this "formula" leads us to the following reflections.

Mr. N.—on in our country is called a Marxist, and even the only "true" Marxist. But can it be said that the sum of the views of Buhl and his reviewer on the position of Germany in the 40s was equivalent to the views of Marx on the same position? In other words, was Buhl supplemented by his reviewer, a Marxist—and withal the only true Marxist, the Marxist par excellence? Of course not. From the fact that Buhl pointed out the contradiction into which capitalist society falls, thanks to the development of the productive forces, it does not yet follow that he adopted the point of view of Marx. He examined these contradictions from a very abstract point of view, and already thanks to this alone his investigation had not, *in its spirit*, anything in common with the views of Marx. After hearing Buhl one might have thought that German capitalism, *today or tomorrow*, would be suffocated under the weight of its own development, that it had nowhere any longer to go, that handicrafts had been finally capitalized, and that the number of German workers would rapidly decline. Such views Marx never expressed. On the contrary, when he had occasion to speak of the immediate future of German capitalism, at the end of the 40s and particularly at the beginning of the 50s, he said something quite different. Only people who did not in the least understand his views could have considered the German N.—ons to be true Marxists.*

---

* There were many N.—ons in Germany at that time, and of the most varying tendencies. The most remarkable, perhaps, were the *conservatives*. Thus for example, Dr. Karl Vollgraf, ordentlicher Professor der Rechte, in a pamphlet bearing an extremely long title ("Von der über und unter ihr naturnothwendiges Mass erweiterten und herabgedrückten Concurrenz in allen Nahrungs- und Erwerbszweigen des bürgerlichen Lebens, als der nächsten Ursache des allgemeinen, alle Klassen mehr oder weniger drückenden Nothstandes in Deutschland, insonderheit des Getreidewuchers, sowie von den Mitteln zu ihrer Abstellung," Darmstadt 1848) (*On the*

The German N. —ons argued just as abstractly as our present Buhls and Vollgrafs. To argue abstractly means to make mistakes, even in those cases when you start from an absolutely correct principle. Do you know, reader, what were the *antiphysics* of D'Alembert? D'Alembert said that, on the basis of the most unquestionable physical laws, he would prove the inevitability of phenomena which were quite impossible in reality. One must

Competition Extended Over and Depressed Below Its Natural Level in All Branches of Trade and Industry in Civil Life, as the Immediate Cause of the Depression Affecting More or Less All Classes in Germany, Particularly of the Usurious Trade in Corn; and on the Measures for Ending the Same.—Ed.) represented the economic situation of the "German Fatherland" amazingly like the way the Russian economic situation is represented in the book *Sketches of Our Social Economy since the Reform.*[57] Vollgraf also presented matters as though the development of productive forces had *already* led, "under the influence of free competition," to the relative diminution of the number of workers engaged in industry. He described in greater detail than Buhl the influence of unemployment on the state of the internal market. Producers in one branch of industry are at the same time consumers for products of other branches, but an unemployment deprives the producers of purchasing power, demand diminishes, in consequence of it unemployment becomes general and there arises complete pauperism (völliger Pauperismus). *"And as the peasantry is also ruined owing to excessive competition, a complete stagnation of business arises. The social organism decomposes, its physiological processes lead to the appearance of a savage mass, and hunger produces in this mass a ferment against which public penalties and even arms are impotent."* Free competition leads in the villages to reduction of peasant holdings to tiny dimensions. *In no peasant household do the working hands find sufficient employment all the year round.* "Thus in thousands of villages, particularly those in areas of poor fertility, almost exactly as in Ireland, the poor peasants stand without work or employment before the doors of their houses. None of them can help one another, for they all have too little, all need wages, all seek work and do not find it." Vollgraf for his part invented a number of "measures" for combating the destructive operation of "free competition," though not in the spirit of the socialist journal *Der Gesellschafts-Spiegel.*

CONCLUSION

only, in following the operation of every given law, forget for the time being that there exist other laws altering its operation. The result would certainly be quite nonsensical. To prove this D'Alembert gave several really brilliant examples, and even intended to write a complete *antiphysics* in his leisure moments. The Messrs. Vollgrafs and N. —ons are already writing an *anti-economics*, not as a joke but quite seriously. Their method is as follows. They take a certain indisputable economic law, and correctly indicate its *tendency*; then they forget that the realization of this law is in life an *entire historical process*, and represent matters as though the tendency of the law in question had already been *completely put into effect* by the time they began writing their work. If at the same time the Vollgraf, Buhl or N. —on in question accumulates a pile of ill-digested statistical material, and sets about relevantly and irrelevantly quoting Marx, his "sketch" acquires the appearance of a scientific and convincing piece of research, in the spirit of the author of *Capital*. But this is an optical illusion, no more.

That, for example, Vollgraf left out a great deal in analyzing the economic life of the Germany of his day is shown by an indubitable fact: his prophecy about "*the decomposition of the social organism*" of that country completely failed to materialize. And that Mr. N. —on quite in vain makes use of the name of Marx, just as Mr. Y. Zhukovsky in vain used to have recourse to the integral calculus, even the most worthy S. N. Krivenko will understand without difficulty.

In spite of the opinion of those gentlemen who reproach Marx with one-sidedness, that writer never examined the economic progress of a particular country *apart from its connection with those social forces which, growing up on its basis, themselves influenced its further development.* (This is not yet quite clear to you, Mr.

S. N. Krivenko: but patience!) Once a certain economic condition is known, certain social forces become known, and their action will necessarily affect the further development of that condition (is patience deserting you, Mr. Krivenko? Here is a practical example for you). We know the economy of England in the epoch of primitive capitalist accumulation. Thereby we know the social forces which, by the way, sat in the English parliament of that day. The action of those social forces was the necessary condition for the further development of the known economic situation, while the direction of their action was conditioned by the characteristics of that situation.

Once we know the economic situation of modern England, we know thereby her modern social forces, the action of which will tell in her future economic development. When Marx was engaged in what some please to call his guesswork, he took into account these social forces, and did not imagine that their action could be stopped at will by this or that group of persons, strong only in their excellent intentions ("Mit der Gründlichkeit der geschichtlichen Action wird der Umfang der Masse zunehmen, deren Action sie ist") ("Together with the thoroughness of the historical action will also grow the volume of the mass whose action it is."—*Ed.*).

The German Utopians of the 40s argued otherwise. When they set themselves certain tasks, they had in mind only the adverse sides of the economic situation of their country, forgetting to investigate the social forces which had grown up from that situation. The economic situation of our people is distressful, argued the above-mentioned reviewer: consequently we are faced with the difficult but not insoluble problem of organizing production. But will not that organization be prevented by those same social forces which have grown up on the basis of the distressful economic situation? The well-meaning reviewer did not ask himself this question. The Utopian never reckons sufficiently with the social forces of his age, for the simple reason that, to use the expression of Marx, he always *places himself above society*. And for the same reason, again to use the expression of Marx, all the calculations of the Utopian prove to be made "ohne Wirth gemacht" ("without reckoning with his host"—*Ed.*), and all his "criticism" is no more than complete absence of criticism, incapacity critically to look at the reality around him.

The organization of production in a particular country could arise only as a result of the operation of those social forces which existed in that country. What is necessary for the organization of production? The conscious attitude of the producers to the process of production, *taken in all its complexity and totality*. Where there is no such conscious attitude as yet, only those people can put forward the idea of organizing production as the immediate task of society, who remain incorrigible Utopians all their lives, even though they should repeat the name of Marx five milliard times with the greatest respect. What does Mr. N.—on say about the consciousness of the producers in his notorious book? Absolutely nothing: he pins his hope on the consciousness of "society." If after this he can and must be recognized as a true Marxist, we see no reason why one should not recognize Mr. Krivenko as being the only true Hegelian of our age, the Hegelian par excellence.

But it is time to conclude. What results have we achieved by our use of the comparative historical method? If we are not mistaken, they are the following:

1. The conviction of Heinzen and his adherents that Marx was condemned by his own views to inaction in Germany proved to be nonsense. Equally nonsense will also prove the conviction of Mr. Mikhailovsky that the

persons who nowadays, in Russia, hold the views of Marx cannot bring any benefit to the Russian people, but on the contrary must injure it.

2. The views of the Buhls and Vollgrafs on the economic situation of Germany at that time proved to be narrow, one-sided and mistaken because of their abstract character. There is ground for fear that the further economic history of Russia will disclose the same defects in the views of Mr. N. —on.

3. The people who in Germany of the 40s made their immediate task the organization of production were Utopians. Similar Utopians are the people who talk about organizing production in present-day Russia.

4. History has swept away the illusions of the German Utopians of the 40s. There is every justification for thinking that the same fate will overtake the illusions of our Russian Utopians. Capitalism laughed at the first; with pain in our heart, we foresee that it will laugh at the second as well.

But did these illusions really bring no benefit to the German people? In the economic sense, absolutely none —or, if you require a more exact expression, *almost* none. All these bazaars for selling handicraft goods, and all these attempts to create producers' associations, scarcely eased the position of even a hundred German producers. But they promoted the awakening of the self-consciousness of those producers, and thereby did them a great deal of good. The same benefit, but this time directly and not in a roundabout way, was rendered by the educational activity of the German intellectuals: their schools, people's reading rooms, etc. The consequences of capitalist development which were harmful for the German people could be, at every particular moment, weakened or eliminated only to the extent to which the self-consciousness of the German producers developed. Marx understood this better than the Utopians, and therefore his activity proved more beneficial to the German people.

The same, undoubtedly, will be the case in Russia too. No later than in the October issue of *Russkoye Bogatstvo* for 1894, Mr. S. N. Krivenko "worries"—as we say—about the organization of Russian production. Mr. Krivenko will eliminate nothing and make no one happy by these "worries." His "worries" are clumsy, awkward, barren: but if they, in spite of all these negative qualities, awaken the self-consciousness of even one producer, they will prove beneficial—and then it will turn out that Mr. Krivenko has lived on this earth not only in order to make mistakes in logic, or to give wrong translations of extracts from foreign articles which he found "disagreeable." It will be possible in our country, too, to fight against the harmful consequences of our capitalism only to the extent that there develops the self-consciousness of the producer. And from these words of ours the subjectivist gentlemen can see that we are not at all "crude materialists." If we are "narrow," it is only in one sense: that we set before ourselves, first and foremost, a perfectly *idealistic aim.*

And now until we meet again, gentlemen opponents! We taste beforehand all that greatest of pleasures which your objections will bring us. Only, gentlemen, do keep an eye on Mr. Krivenko. Even though he doesn't write badly, and at any rate does so with feeling, yet "to put two and two together"—that has not been vouchsafed him!

APPENDIX I

ONCE AGAIN MR. MIKHAILOVSKY, ONCE MORE THE "TRIAD"

In the October issue of *Russkoye Bogatstvo*, Mr. Mikhailovsky, replying to Mr. P. Struve, again has made some observations on the philosophy of Hegel and on "economic" materialism.

According to him, the materialist conception of history and economic materialism are not one and the same thing. The economic materialists draw everything from economics. "Well, but if I seek the root or foundation not only of the legal and political institutions, of the philosophical and other views of society, but also of its economic structure, in the racial or tribal peculiarities of its members, in the proportions of the longitudinal and transverse diameters of their skulls, in the character of their facial angle, in the size and inclination of their jaws, in the size of their thorax, the strength of their muscles, etc.: or, on the other hand, in purely geographical factors—in the island position of England, in the steppe character of part of Asia, in the mountainous character of Switzerland, in the freezing of rivers in the north, etc.—will not this be the materialist conception of history? It is clear that economic materialism, as an historical theory, is only a particular case of the materialist conception of history...."*

---
* *Russkoye Bogatstvo*, October 1894, Part II, p. 50.

Montesquieu was inclined to explain the historical fate of peoples by "purely geographical factors." To the extent that he consistently upheld these factors, he was undoubtedly a materialist. Modern dialectical materialism does not ignore, as we have seen, the influence of geographical environment on the development of society. It only ascertains better in what way geographical factors influence "social man." It shows that the geographical environment provides men with a greater or lesser possibility of developing their productive forces, and thereby pushes them, more or less energetically, along the path of historical progress. Montesquieu argued thus: A certain geographical environment determines certain physical and psychical qualities of men, and these qualities bring in their train this or that structure of society. Dialectical materialism reveals that such an argument is unsatisfactory, and that the influence of geographical environment shows itself first of all, and in the strongest degree, in the character of *social relations*, which in their turn influence the views of men, their customs and even their physical development infinitely more strongly than, for example, climate. Modern geographical science (let us again recall the book of Mechnikov and its foreword by Elisée Reclus) fully agrees in this respect with dialectical materialism. This materialism is, of course, a particular case of the materialist view of history. But it explains it more fully, more universally, than could those other "particular cases." *Dialectical materialism is the highest development of the materialist conception of history*.

Holbach said that the historical fate of peoples is sometimes determined for a whole century ahead by the motion of an atom which has begun to play tricks in the brain of a powerful man. This was also a materialist view of history. But it was of no avail in explaining historical phenomena. Modern dialectical materialism is incomparably more fruitful in this respect. It is of course a particular case of the materialist view of history but precisely that particular case which alone corresponds to the modern condition of science. The impotence of Holbach's materialism showed itself in the return of its supporters to idealism: "Opinions govern the world." Dialectical materialism now drives idealism from its last positions.

Mr. Mikhailovsky imagines that only that man would be a consistent materialist who explains all phenomena with the help of molecular mechanics. Modern dialectical materialism cannot discover the *mechanical* explanation of history. This is, if you like, *its weakness*. But is modern biology able to give a mechanical explanation of the origin and development of species? It is not. That is *its weakness.** The genius of whom Laplace dreamed would have been, of course, above such weakness. But we simply don't know when that genius will appear, and we satisfy ourselves with such explanations of phenomena as best correspond to the science of our age. Such is *our* "particular case."

Dialectical materialism says that it is not the consciousness of men which determines their being, but, on the contrary, their social being that determines their consciousness; that it is not in the philosophy but in the eco-

---

* *Editor's Note*: Plekhanov's statement is radically at variance with the basic principles of Marxist-Leninist dialectics. Dialectical materialism has never aimed at reducing all natural and social phenomena to mechanics, at giving mechanical explanations of the origin and development of species and of the historic process. Mechanical motion is by no means the only form of motion. "... The motion of matter," Engels says, "is not merely crude mechanical motion, mere change of place, it is heat and light, electric and magnetic tension, chemical combination and dissociation, life and, finally, consciousness." (F. Engels, *Dialectics of Nature*, Moscow, 1954, p. 51.)

nomics of a particular society that one must seek the key to understanding its particular condition. Mr. Mikhailovsky makes several remarks on this subject. One of them reads as follows:

"... The negative halves" (!) "of the basic formula of the materialist sociologists contain a protest or a reaction not against philosophy in general, but evidently against that of Hegel. It is to the latter that belongs 'the explanation of being from consciousness.'... The founders of economic materialism are Hegelians and, in that capacity, insist so stubbornly 'not from philosophy,' 'not from consciousness,' that they cannot, and do not even attempt to, burst out of the circle of Hegelian thought."*

When we read these lines we thought that here our author, like Mr. Kareyev, was groping his way to the "synthesis." Of course, we said to ourselves, the synthesis of Mr. Mikhailovsky will be a little higher than that of Mr. Kareyev; Mr. Mikhailovsky will not confine himself to repeating that thought of the deacon in G. I. Uspensky's tale "The Incurable," that "the spirit is a thing apart" and that, "as matter has various spices for its benefit, so equally has the spirit." Still, Mr. Mikhailovsky too will not refrain from synthesis. Hegel is the thesis, economic materialism is the antithesis, and the eclecticism of the modern Russian subjectivists is the synthesis. How could one resist the temptation of such a "triad"? And then we began to remember what was the real relationship between the historical theory of Marx and the philosophy of Hegel.

First of all we "noted" that in Hegel historical movement is not at all explained *by the views of men or by their philosophy*. It was *the French materialists of the eighteenth century* who explained history by the views,

---

* *Russkoye Bogatstvo*, October 1894, Part II, pp. 51-52.

the "opinions" of men. Hegel ridiculed such an explanation: of course, he said, reason rules in history—but then it also rules the movement of the celestial bodies, and are they conscious of their movement? The historical development of mankind is reasonable in the sense that it is law-governed; but the law-governed nature of historical development does not yet prove at all that its ultimate cause must be sought in the views of men or in their opinions. Quite on the contrary: that conformity to law shows that men make their history unconsciously.

We don't remember, we continued, what the historical views of Hegel look like according to *Lewes*; but that we are not distorting them, anyone will agree who has read the famous *Philosophie der Geschichte* (*Philosophy of History* —Ed.). Consequently, in affirming that it is not the philosophy of men which determines their social existence, the supporters of "economic" materialism are not controverting Hegel at all, and consequently *in this respect* they represent no antithesis to him. And this means that Mr. Mikhailovsky's synthesis will not be successful, even should our author not confine himself to repeating the idea of the deacon.

In the opinion of Mr. Mikhailovsky, to affirm that philosophy, i.e., the views of men, does not explain their history, was possible only in Germany in the 40s, when a revolt against the Hegelian system was not yet noticeable. We now see that such an opinion is founded, at best, only on *Lewes*.

But how poorly *Lewes* acquaints Mr. Mikhailovsky with the course of development of philosophical thought in Germany is demonstrated, apart from the foregoing, by the following circumstance. Our author quotes with delight the well-known letter of Belinsky,[58] in which the latter makes his bow to the "philosophical nightcap" of Hegel. In this letter Belinsky says, among other things:

"The fate of a subject, an individual, a personality is more important than the fate of the world and the weal of the Chinese emperor, viz., the Hegelian Allgemeinheit" (Universality—*Ed.*). Mr. Mikhailovsky makes many remarks on the subject of this letter, but he does not *"remark"* that Belinsky has dragged in the Hegelian Allgemeinheit quite out of place. Mr. Mikhailovsky evidently thinks that the Hegelian Allgemeinheit is just the same as the spirit or the absolute idea. But Allgemeinheit does not constitute in Hegel even the main distinguishing feature of the absolute idea. Allgemeinheit occupies in his work a place no more honourable than, for example, Besonderheit or Einzelheit (Individuality or Singleness—*Ed.*). And in consequence of this it is incomprehensible why precisely Allgemeinheit is called the Chinese Emperor, and deserves—unlike its other sisters —an attentive and mocking bow. This may seem a detail, unworthy of attention at the present time; but it is not so. Hegel's Allgemeinheit, badly understood, still prevents Mr. Mikhailovsky, for example, from understanding the history of German philosophy—prevents him to such an extent that even *Lewes* does not rescue him from misfortune.

In the opinion of Mr. Mikhailovsky, worship of Allgemeinheit led Hegel to complete negation of the *rights of the individual*. "There is no system of philosophy," he says, "which treats the individual with such withering contempt and cold cruelty as the system of Hegel" (p. 55). This can be true only according to *Lewes*. Why did Hegel consider the history of the East to be the first, *lowest* stage in the development of mankind? Because in the East the *individual* was not developed, and had not up till then been developed. Why did Hegel speak with enthusiasm of ancient Greece, in the history of which modern man feels himself at last "at home"? Because in

Greece individual personality was developed ("beautiful individuality"—"schöne Individualität"). Why did Hegel speak with such admiration of Socrates? Why did he, almost first among the historians of philosophy, pay a just tribute even to the *sophists*? Was it really because he despised the individual?

Mr. Mikhailovsky has heard a bell, but where he cannot tell.

Hegel not only did not despise the individual, but created a whole cult of *heroes*, which was inherited in its entirety thereafter by Bruno Bauer. For Hegel heroes were the instruments of the universal spirit, and in that sense they themselves were *not free*. Bruno Bauer revolted against the *"spirit,"* and thereby set free his *"heroes."* For him the heroes of *"critical thought"* were the real demiurges of history, *as opposed to the "mass,"* which, although it does irritate its heroes almost to tears by its slow-wittedness and its sluggishness, still does finish up in the end by marching along the path marked out by the heroes' self-consciousness. The contrasting of *"heroes"* and *"mass"* ("mob") passed from Bruno Bauer to his Russian illegitimate children, and we now have the pleasure of contemplating it in the articles of Mr. Mikhailovsky. Mr. Mikhailovsky does not remember his philosophical kinship: that is not praiseworthy.

And so we have suddenly received the elements of a new "synthesis." The Hegelian cult of heroes, serving the universal spirit, is the *thesis*. The Bauer cult of heroes of "critical thought," guided only by their "self-consciousness," is the *antithesis*. Finally, the theory of Marx, which reconciles both extremes, eliminating the universal spirit and explaining the origin of the heroes' self-consciousness by the development of environment, is the *synthesis*.

Our opponents, so partial to "synthesis," must remember that the theory of Marx was not at all the first *direct* reaction against Hegel: that that first reaction—superficial on account of its one-sidedness—was constituted in Germany by the views of Feuerbach *and particularly of Bruno Bauer,* with whom our subjectivists should long ago have acknowledged their kinship.

Not a few other incongruities have also been piled up by Mr. Mikhailovsky about Hegel and about Marx in his article against Mr. P. Struve. Space does not permit us to enumerate them here. We will confine ourselves to offering our readers the following interesting problem.

We know Mr. Mikhailovsky; we know his complete ignorance of Hegel; we know his complete incomprehension of Marx; we know his irresistible striving to discuss Hegel, Marx and their mutual relations; the problem is, how many more mistakes will Mr. Mikhailovsky make thanks to his striving?

But it is hardly likely that anyone will succeed in solving this problem; it is an equation with too many unknowns. There is only one means of replacing *unknown* magnitudes in it by definite magnitudes; it is to read the articles of Mr. Mikhailovsky carefully and *notice his mistakes.* True, that is a far from joyful or easy task: there will be very many mistakes, if only Mr. Mikhailovsky does not get rid of his bad habit of discussing philosophy without consulting beforehand people who know more about it than he does.

We shall not deal here with the attacks made by Mr. Mikhailovsky on Mr. P. Struve. As far as these attacks are concerned, Mr. Mikhailovsky now belongs to the author of *Critical Remarks on the Question of the Economic Development of Russia,* and we do not wish to aspire to the property of another. However, Mr. P. Struve will perhaps forgive us if we permit ourselves to make two small "observations."

Mr. Mikhailovsky is insulted because Mr. P. Struve "struck at him" with a question-mark. He is so insulted that, not confining himself to pointing out faults of style in the language of Mr. Struve, he accuses him of being a "non-Russian," and even recalls the story of two Germans, one of whom said he had "shooted" a crow, and the other corrected him, saying that grammar required "shotted." Why did Mr. Struve, however, raise his hand, armed with a question-mark, against Mr. Mikhailovsky? It was because of his words: "The modern economic order in Europe began to come into existence at a time when the science which manages this sphere of phenomena was not yet in existence, etc." The question-mark accompanies the word "manages." Mr. Mikhailovsky says: "In German that may not perhaps sound well" (how biting: "in German"!), "but in Russian, I assure you, Mr. Struve, it arouses no question in any one, and requires no question-mark." The writer of these lines bears a purely Russian name, and possesses just as much of the Russian soul as Mr. Mikhailovsky: the most sarcastic critic will not venture to call him a German: and nevertheless the word "manages" arouses a question in him. He asks himself: if one can say that science *manages* a certain sphere of phenomena, could not one after this promote the technical arts to be *chiefs of particular units*? Could not one say, for example: the art of assaying commands alloys? In our opinion, this would be awkward, it would give the arts *too military an appearance*, in just the same way as the word *"manages"* gives science the appearance of a *bureaucrat*. Consequently, Mr. Mikhailovsky is wrong. Struve failed to react to the question; it is hard to say how he would have corrected Mikhailovsky's unhappy expression. Let us assume that he would have "shotted" a crow. But it is unfortunately an *accomplished fact* that Mikhailovsky has already "shooted" several crows. And yet he does not seem to be a "non-Russian."

Mr. Mikhailovsky in his article raised an amusing outcry about the words of Mr. Struve: "No, let us recognize our lack of culture and go into training by capitalism."[59] Mr. Mikhailovsky wants to represent affairs as though these words meant: *let us hand over the producer as a victim to the exploiter.*" It will be easy for Mr. P. Struve to demonstrate the vanity of Mr. Mikhailovsky's efforts, and it will probably be seen now by anyone who has carefully read the *Critical Remarks.* But Mr. Struve nevertheless did express himself very carelessly, whereby he probably led into temptation many simpletons and rejoiced the heart of some acrobats. *That will teach you a lesson,* we shall say to Mr. Struve, and we shall remind the acrobatic gentry how Belinsky, at the very end of his life, when he had long ago said good-bye to Allgemeinheit, expressed the idea in one of his letters that the cultural future of Russia can only be ensured by the *bourgeoisie.* In Belinsky this was also a very clumsy threat. But what was his clumsiness aroused by? *Generous fascination by the West.* It is the same fascination that brought about, we are convinced, the awkwardness of Mr. Struve. It is permissible to make a noise on the subject of that clumsiness only for those who have no reply, for example, to his economic arguments.

Mr. Krivenko too has declared war on Mr. P. Struve. He has his own cause of offence. He wrongly translated an extract from a German article by Mr. P. Struve, and the latter has exposed him. Mr. Krivenko justifies himself, and tries to show that the translation is almost correct; but his are lame excuses and he still remains guilty of distorting the words of his opponent. But you can't ask too much of Mr. Krivenko, in view of his undoubted resemblance to a certain bird, of whom it has been said:

> *Sirin, that heavenly bird,*
> *Its voice in singing is loudly heard;*
> *When the Lord's praise it sings,*
> *To forget its own self it begins.*[60]

When Mr. Krivenko is shaming the "disciples," to forget his own self he begins. Why can't you let him alone, Mr. Struve?

APPENDIX II

A FEW WORDS TO OUR OPPONENTS[61]

The question is again being raised in our literature: what path will the economic development of Russia follow? It is being discussed lengthily and passionately, so passionately that people who are known in common parlance as sensible minds are even perturbed by what would seem the excessive heat of the contending parties. Why, the sensible ones say, get excited and hurl proud challenges and bitter reproaches at your opponents? Why jeer at them? Would it not be better to examine dispassionately a question which is indeed of immense importance to our country, but which, just because of its immense importance, calls for dispassionate examination?

As always, the sensible minds are right and wrong at one and the same time. Why, indeed, such excitement and passion on the part of writers belonging to two different camps each of which—whatever its opponents might say—is striving to the best of its understanding, strength and ability to uphold the most important and most essential interests of the people? Evidently, the question has only to be put to have it answered immediately and once and for all with the help of two or three platitudes which might find a place in any copybook, such as: tolerance is a good thing; respect the opinions of others even if they radically differ from your own, and so on. All this is very true, and it has been "told the world" a very long time now. But it is no less true that human beings were, are, and will be inclined to get passionate wherever the issue affected, affects, or will affect their vital interests. Such is human nature—we might have said, if we did not know how often and how greatly this expression has been abused. Nor is this the whole matter. The chief thing is that we human beings have no reason to regret that such is our "nature." No great step in history has ever been taken without the aid of passion, which, multiplying as it does the moral strength and sharpening the intellectual faculties of people, is itself a great force of progress. Only such social questions are discussed dispassionately as are quite unimportant in themselves, or have not yet become *immediate* questions for the given country and the given period, and are therefore of interest only to a handful of arm-chair thinkers. But once a big social question has become an immediate question, it will infallibly arouse strong passions, no matter how earnestly the advocates of moderation may call for calmness.

The question of the economic development of our country is precisely that great social question which we cannot now discuss with moderation for the simple reason that it has become an *immediate question*. This of course does not mean that economics has only now acquired decisive importance in our social development. It has always and everywhere been of such importance. But in our country—as everywhere else—this importance has not always been consciously recognized by people interested in social matters, and their passion was therefore concentrated on questions that had only the most remote relation to economics. Recall, for instance, the 40s in our country. Not so now. Now the great and fundamental importance of economics is realized in our country even by those who passionately revolt against Marx's "*narrow*" theory of history. Now all thinking people realize that our whole future will be shaped by the way the question of our *economic* development is answered. That indeed is why even thinkers who are anything but "narrow" concentrate all their passion on this question. But if we cannot now discuss this question with *moderation,* we can and should see to it even now that there is no *licence* either in the defining of our own thoughts or in our polemical methods. This is a demand to which no objection can possibly be offered. Westerners know very well that earnest passion precludes all licence. In our country, to be sure, it is still sometimes believed that passion and licence are kin sisters, but it is time we too became civilized.

As far as the literary decencies are concerned, it is apparent that we are already civilized to quite a considerable degree—so considerable that our "progressive," Mr. Mikhailovsky, lectures the Germans (Marx, Engels, Dühring) because in their controversies one may allegedly find "things that are absolutely fruitless, or which distort things and repel by their rudeness." Mr. Mikhailovsky recalls Börne's remark that the Germans "have always been rude in controversy"! "And I am afraid," he adds, "that together with other German influences, this traditional German rudeness has also penetrated into our country, aggravated moreover by our own barbarousness, so that controversy becomes the tirade against Potok-Bogatyr which Count A. Tolstoi puts into the mouth of his princess:

> "*'You cadger, mumper, ignorant sot!*
> *Plague on your entrails, may you rot!*
> *You calf, pig, swine, you Ethiop,*
> *You devil's spawn, you dirty snob!*
> *Were it not that my virginal shame*
> *Forbids me stronger words to name,*

*'Tis not such oaths, you insolent cad,
I'd shower down upon your head.'* "*[62]

This is not the first time Mr. Mikhailovsky alludes to Tolstoi's coarse-mouthed princess. He has on many a previous occasion advised Russian writers not to resemble her in their controversies. Excellent advice, there's no denying. 'Tis only a pity that our author does not always follow it himself. We know, for example, that he called one of his opponents a *louse,* and another a *literary acrobat.* He ornamented his controversy with M. de la Cerda with the following remark: "Of all the European languages, it is only in the Spanish that the word la cerda has a definite signification, meaning in Russian pig." Why the author had to say this, it is hard to imagine.

"Nice, is it not?" M. de la Cerda observed in this connection. Yes, very nice, and quite in the spirit of Tolstoi's princess. But the princess was blunter, and when she felt like swearing she shouted simply: calf, pig, swine, etc., and did not do violence to foreign languages in order to say a rude word to her opponent.

Comparing Mr. Mikhailovsky with Tolstoi's princess, we find that he scorns such words as "Ethiop," "devil's spawn" and so on, and concentrates, if we may say so, on pachydermic epithets. We find him using "swine" and "pig," and pigs moreover of the most different kinds: Hamletized, green, etc. Very forcible this, if rather monotonous. Generally speaking, if we turn from the vituperative vocabulary of Tolstoi's princess to that of our subjective sociologist, we see that *the living charms bloom in different pattern,* but in power and expressiveness they are in no way inferior to the polemical charms of the

---

* *Russkoye Bogatstvo,* Vol. I, 1895, article, "Literature and Life."

lively princess. "Est modus in rebus (There is a measure in all things.—*Ed.*) or, as the Russian has it, you must know where to stop," says Mr. Mikhailovsky. Nothing could be truer, and we heartily regret that our worthy sociologist often forgets it. He might tragically exclaim:

> *Video meliora, proboque,*
> *Deteriora sequor!**

However, it is to be hoped that in time Mr. Mikhailovsky too will become civilized, that in the end his good intentions will prevail over "our own barbarousness," and he will cease hurling "swine" and "pig" at his opponents. Mr. Mikhailovsky himself rightly thinks that la raison finit toujours par avoir raison. ("Reason always triumphs in the end."—*Ed.*)

Our reading public no longer approves of virulent controversy. But, in its disapproval, it confuses virulence with rudeness, when they are very far from being the same. The vast difference between virulence and rudeness was explained by Pushkin:

> *Abuse at times, of course, is quite unseemly.*
> *You must not write, say: "This old dodderer's*
> *A goat in spectacles, a wretched slanderer,*
> *Vicious and vile."—These are personalities.*
> *But you may write and print, if so you will,*
> *That "this Parnassian Old Believer is*
> *(In his articles) a senseless jabberer,*
> *For ever languorous, for ever tedious,*
> *Ponderous, and even quite a dullard."*
> *For here there is no person, only an author.*[63]

If, like Tolstoi's princess or Mr. Mikhailovsky, you should think of calling your opponent a "swine" or a

---

* "I see the best and approve, but follow the worst!" From Ovid's *Metamorphoses.—Ed.*

"louse," these *"are personalities"*; but if you should argue that such-and-such a sociological or historical-sophistical or economic Old Believer is, in his articles, "works" or "essays," "for ever languorous, for ever tedious, ponderous and even" ... dull-witted, well "here there is no person, only an author," and it will be virulence, not rudeness. Your verdict, of course, may be mistaken, and your opponents will be doing well if they disclose your mistake. But they will have the right to accuse you only of a mistake, not of virulence, for without such virulence literature cannot develop. If literature should attempt to get along without virulence, it would at once become, as Belinsky expressed it, *a flattering reiterator of stale platitudes*, which only its enemies can wish it. Mr. Mikhailovsky's observation regarding the traditional German rudeness and our own barbarousness was provoked by Mr. N. Beltov's "interesting book," *The Development of the Monist View of History.* Many have accused Mr. Beltov of unnecessary virulence. For instance, a *Russkaya Mysl* reviewer has written in reference to his book: "Without sharing the, in our opinion one-sided, theory of economic materialism, we would be prepared in the interest of science and our social life to welcome the exponents of this theory, if some of them (Messrs. Struve and Beltov) did not introduce far too much virulence into their polemics, if they did not jeer at writers whose works are worthy of respect!"

This was written in the selfsame *Russkaya Mysl* which only a little while ago was calling the advocates of "economic" materialism "numskulls" and asserting that Mr. P. Struve's book was a product of undigested erudition and a total incapacity for logical thinking. *Russkaya Mysl* does not like excessive virulence and therefore, as the reader sees, spoke of the advocates of economic materialism in the mildest terms. Now it is prepared, in the interest of science and our social life, to welcome the exponents of this theory. But why? Can much be done for our social life by numskulls? Can science gain much from undigested erudition and a total incapacity for logical thinking? It seems to us that fear of excessive virulence is leading *Russkaya Mysl* too far and compelling it to say things that might induce the reader to suspect that it itself is incapable of digesting something, and of a certain incapacity for logical thinking.

Mr. P. Struve never resorts to virulence (to say nothing of excessive virulence), and if Mr. Beltov does, it is only to the kind of which Pushkin would probably have said that it refers only to writers and is therefore quite permissible. The *Russkaya Mysl* reviewer maintains that the works of the writers Mr. Beltov derides are worthy of respect. If Mr. Beltov shared this opinion, it would of course be wrong of him to deride them. But what if he is convinced of the contrary? What if the "works" of these gentlemen seem to him tedious and ponderous and quite vacuous, and even pernicious in our day, when social life has become so complicated and demands a new mental effort on the part of those who are not in the habit, to use Gogol's expression, of "picking their noses" as they look on the world. To the *Russkaya Mysl* reviewer these writers may probably seem regular torches of light, beacons of salvation. But what if Mr. Beltov considers them extinguishers and mind-druggers? The reviewer will say that Mr. Beltov is mistaken. That is his right; but he has to prove his opinion, and not content himself with simply condemning "excessive virulence." What is the reviewer's opinion of Grech and Bulgarin?[64] We are confident that if he were to express it, a certain section of our press would consider it excessively virulent. Would that mean that the *Russkaya Mysl* reviewer is not entitled to say frankly what he thinks of the literary activities of Grech and Bulgarin? We do not of course bracket the people with whom Messrs. P. Struve and N. Beltov are disputing in the same category as Grech and Bulgarin. But we would ask the *Russkaya Mysl* reviewer why literary decency permits one to speak virulently of Grech and Bulgarin, but forbids one to do so of Messrs. Mikhailovsky and Kareyev? The reviewer evidently thinks that there is no beast stronger than the cat, and that the cat, therefore, in distinction to other beasts, deserves particularly respectful treatment. But, after all, one has the right to doubt that. We, for instance, think that the subjective cat is not only a beast that is not very strong, but even one that has quite considerably degenerated, and is therefore not deserving of any particular respect. We are prepared to argue with the reviewer if he does not agree with us, but before entering into argument we would request him to ponder well on the difference which undoubtedly exists between *virulence of judgement* and *rudeness of literary expression*. Messrs. Struve and Beltov have expressed judgements which to very many may seem virulent. But has either of them ever resorted, in defence of his opinions, to such coarse abuse as that which has been resorted to time and again in his literary skirmishes by Mr. Mikhailovsky, that veritable Miles Gloriosus (Glorious warrior.—*Ed.*) of our "progressive" literature? Neither of them has done so, and the *Russkaya Mysl* reviewer would himself give them credit for this if he were to reflect on the difference we have indicated between virulence of judgement and coarseness of expression.

Incidentally, this *Russkaya Mysl* reviewer says: "Mr. Beltov unceremoniously, to say the least, scatters accusations to the effect that such-and-such a writer talks of Marx without having read his works, condemns the Hegelian philosophy without having acquainted himself with it personally, etc. It would be well, of course, if he did not at the same time commit blunders himself, especially on most essential points. Yet precisely about Hegel Mr. Beltov talks the wildest nonsense: 'If modern natural science,' we read on p. 86 of the book in question [p. 109 of this edition—*Ed.*], 'confirms at every step the idea expressed with such genius by Hegel, that quantity passes into quality, can we say that it has nothing in common with Hegelianism?' But the misfortune is, Mr. Beltov, that Hegel did not affirm this and argued the very opposite: with him, 'quality passes into quantity.' "

If we were to say what we thought of the reviewer's notion of Hegel's philosophy, our judgement would probably seem to him "excessively virulent." But the blame would not be ours. We can assure the reviewer that very virulent judgements of his philosophical knowledge were passed by all who read his review and have any acquaintance at all with the history of philosophy.

One cannot, of course, insist that every reviewer must have a thorough philosophical education, but one can insist that he does not take the liberty of arguing about matters of which he has no knowledge. Otherwise, very "virulent" things will be said of him by people who are acquainted with the subject.

In Part I of his *Encyclopaedia*, in an addendum to Section 108, on Measure, Hegel says: "To the extent that quality and quantity are still differentiated and are not altogether identical, these two definitions are to some degree independent of each other, so that, on the one hand, the quantity may change without the quality of the object changing, but, on the other, its increase or decrease, to which the object is at first indifferent, has a limit beyond which the quality changes. Thus, for example, alterations in the temperature of water at first do not affect its liquid state, but if the temperature is further increased or decreased, there comes a point when this state of cohesion undergoes a qualitative change and the water is transformed into steam or into ice. It seems at first that the quantitative change has no effect whatever on the essential nature of the object, but there is something else behind it, and this apparently simple change of quantity has the effect of changing the quality."

"The misfortune is, Mr. Beltov, that Hegel did not affirm this and argued the very opposite!" Do you still think that this is the misfortune, Mr. Reviewer?* Or perhaps you have now changed your opinion on this matter? And if you have, what is really the misfortune? We could tell you if we were not afraid that you would accuse us of excessive virulence.

We repeat that one cannot insist that every reviewer must be acquainted with the history of philosophy. The misfortune of the *Russkaya Mysl* reviewer is therefore not as great as might appear at the first glance. But "*the misfortune is*" that this *misfortune* is not the reviewer's last. There is a second which is the main and worse than the first: he did not take the trouble to read the book he was reviewing.

On pp. 75-76 of his book [pp. 96-97 in this edition] Mr. Beltov gives a rather long excerpt from Hegel's Greater Logic *Wissenschaft der Logik* (*The Science of Logic.— Ed.*). Here is the beginning of the excerpt: "Changes in being consist not only in the fact that one quantity passes into another quantity, but also that quality passes into quantity, and vice versa, etc." (p. 75).

If the reviewer had at least read this excerpt he would

---

* The reviewer continues to adhere to his opinion in the third issue of *Russkaya Mysl*, and advises those who do not agree with him to consult "at least" the Russian translation of Überweg-Heintze's *History of Modern Philosophy*. But why should not the reviewer consult "at least" Hegel himself?

not have fallen into misfortune, because then he would not have "affirmed" that "Hegel did not affirm this and argued the very opposite."

We know how the majority of reviews are written in Russia—and not only Russia, unfortunately. The reviewer runs through the book, rapidly scanning, say, every tenth or twentieth page and marking the passages which seem to him most characteristic. He then writes out these passages and accompanies them with expressions of censure or approval: he "is perplexed," he "very much regrets," or he "heartily welcomes"—and, hey presto! the review is ready. One can imagine how much nonsense is printed as a result, especially if (as not infrequently happens) the reviewer has no knowledge whatever of the subject discussed in the book he is examining!

It would not enter our heads to recommend reviewers to rid themselves of this bad habit *completely*: only the grave can cure the hunchback. All the same, they ought at least to take their business a little more seriously when—as in the dispute on Russia's economic development, for example—the vital interests of our country are concerned. Do they really propose to go on misleading the reading public on this subject, too, with their frivolous reviews? After all—as Mr. Mikhailovsky rightly says—one must know when to stop.

Mr. Mikhailovsky is likewise displeased with Mr. Beltov's polemical methods. "Mr. Beltov," he says, "is a man of talent and is not devoid of wit, but with him unfortunately it often passes into unpleasant buffoonery." Why buffoonery? And to whom, indeed, is Mr. Beltov's alleged buffoonery unpleasant?

When, in the 60s, *Sovremennik* scoffed at Pogodin,[65] say, it probably seemed to Pogodin that the journal was guilty of unpleasant buffoonery. And it seemed so not only to Pogodin alone, but to all who were accustomed to respect the Moscow historian. Was there any lack of attacks in those days on "the knights of the whistle"? Was there any lack of people who were outraged by the "schoolboyish pranks of the whistlers"? Well, in our opinion, the brilliant wit of the "whistlers" never passed into unpleasant buffoonery; and if the people they scoffed at thought otherwise, it was only because of that human weakness which led Ammos Fyodorovich Lyapkin-Tyapkin[66] to consider "*far too long*" the letter in which he was described as "very much of a boor."

"So that's it! You mean to suggest that Mr. Beltov possesses the wit of Dobrolyubov[67] and his fellow-contributors to *The Whistle*? Well, that's the limit!"— will exclaim those who find Mr. Beltov's polemical methods "not nice."

But wait a moment, sirs! We are not comparing Mr. Beltov with the "whistlers" of the 60s; we are only saying that it is not for Mr. Mikhailovsky to judge whether, and where exactly, Mr. Beltov's wit passes into unpleasant buffoonery. Who can be a judge in his own case?

But Mr. Mikhailovsky not only accuses Mr Beltov of "unpleasant buffoonery." He levels a very serious charge against him. To make it easier for the reader to understand what it is all about, we shall allow Mr. Mikhailovsky to formulate his charge in his own words:

"In one of my articles in *Russkaya Mysl* I recalled my acquaintance with the late N. I. Sieber and incidentally said that when discussing the future of capitalism that worthy savant 'used all possible arguments, but at the least danger hid behind the authority of the immutable and unquestionable tripartite dialectical development.' Citing these words of mine, Mr. Beltov writes: 'We had more than once to converse with the deceased, and never did we hear from him references to dialectical development; he himself said more than once that he was quite ignorant of the significance of Hegel in the development of modern economics. Of course, everything can be blamed on the dead, and therefore Mr. Mikhailovsky's evidence is irrefutable!' I would put it differently: everything cannot always be blamed on the dead, and Mr. Beltov's evidence is fully refutable....

"In 1879 an article of Sieber's was printed in the magazine *Slovo* entitled: 'The Application of Dialectics to Science.' This (unfinished) article was a paraphrase, even almost entirely a translation, of Engels's *Herrn Dühring's Umwälzung der Wissenschaft*.* Well, to remain, after having translated this book, 'quite ignorant of the significance of Hegel in the development of modern economics' would have been fairly difficult not only for Sieber but even for Potok-Bogatyr in the princess's polemical description quoted above. This, I think, must be clear to Mr. Beltov himself. In any case, I shall quote a few words from Sieber's brief foreword: 'Engels's book deserves particular attention both because of the consistency and aptness of the philosophical and socio-economic concepts it expounds, and because, in order to explain the practical application of the method of dialectical contradictions, it gives several new illustrations and factual examples which in no little degree facilitate a close acquaintance with this so strongly praised and at the same time so strongly deprecated method of investigating the truth. One might probably say that this is the first time in the existence of what is called dialectics that it is presented to the eyes of the reader in so realistic a light.'

"Hence Sieber was acquainted with the significance of

---

* *Herr Eugen Dühring's Revolution in Science (Anti-Dühring).*
—Ed.

Hegel in the development of modern economics; he was greatly interested in 'the method of dialectical contradictions.' Such is the truth, documentarily certified, and it fully decides the piquant question of who is lying for two."*

The truth, especially when documentarily certified, is an excellent thing! Also in the interest of truth we shall carry on just a little further the quotation given by Mr. Mikhailovsky from Sieber's article, "The Application of Dialectics to Science."

Right after the words that conclude the passage Mr. Mikhailovsky quoted, Sieber makes the following remark: "However, we for our part shall refrain from passing judgement as to the worth of this method in application to the various branches of science, and also as to whether it represents or does not represent—to the extent that actual significance may be attached to it—a mere variation or even prototype of the method of the theory of evolution or universal development. It is precisely in this latter sense that the author regards it; or, at least, he endeavours to indicate a confirmation of it with the help of the truths obtained by the theory of evolution—and it must be confessed that in a certain respect quite a considerable resemblance is here revealed."

We thus see that the late Russian economist, even after having translated Engels's *Herr Eugen Dühring's Revolution in Science*, still remained in ignorance of the significance of Hegel in the development of modern economics, and even, generally, whether dialectics could be suitably applied to the various branches of science. At all events, he was unwilling to pass judgement on it. And so we ask: is it likely that this selfsame Sieber, who did not venture to judge of the suitability of dialectics generally, yet in his disputes with Mr. Mikhai-

―――――――
* *Russkoye Bogatstvo*, January 1895, Part II, pp. 140-41.

lovsky "at the least danger hid behind the authority of the immutable and unquestionable dialectical development"? Why was it only in these cases that Sieber changed his usually irresolute opinion of dialectics? Was it because he stood in too great a "danger" of being demolished by his terrible opponent? Scarcely! Sieber, with his very weighty fund of knowledge, was the last person to whom such an opponent could have been "dangerous."

Yes, indeed, an excellent thing is truth documentarily certified! Mr. Mikhailovsky is absolutely right when he says that it fully decides the piquant question of who is lying for two!

But if the "Russian soul," having incarnated itself in the person of a certain individual, undoubtedly resorts to distorting the truth, it is not content with distorting it for two only once; for the late Sieber alone it distorts it *twice*: once when it asserts that Sieber hid behind the authority of the triad, and again when, with astonishing presumption, it cites the very statement that proves up to the hilt that Mr. Beltov is right.

Fie, fie, Mr. Mikhailovsky!

"It would be difficult to remain in ignorance of the significance of Hegel in the development of modern economics after having translated Engels's *Dühring's Revolution*," Mr. Mikhailovsky exclaims. Is it really so difficult? Not at all, in our opinion. It would really have been difficult for Sieber, having translated the said book, to remain in ignorance of *Engels's* (and, of course, Marx's) *opinion of the significance of Hegel in the development of the said science*. Of that opinion, Sieber was not ignorant, as is self-evident and as follows from his foreword. But Sieber might not be content with the *opinion of others*. As a serious scientist who does not rely on the opinion of others but is accustomed to studying a subject first-hand, he, though he knew Engels's opinion of Hegel, did not consider himself for all that entitled to say: "I am acquainted with Hegel and his role in the history of development of scientific concepts." This modesty of a scientist may perhaps be incomprehensible to Mr. Mikhailovsky; he himself tells us that he "does not claim" to be acquainted with Hegel's philosophy, yet he has the presumption to discuss it very freely. But quod licet bovi, non licet Jovi. Having all his life been nothing but a smart journalist, Mr. Mikhailovsky possesses the presumption natural to members of this calling. But he has forgotten the difference between him and men of science. Thanks to this forgetfulness, he ventured to say things that make it quite clear that the "soul" is certainly "lying for two."

Fie, fie, Mr. Mikhailovsky!

But is it only for two that the worthy "soul" is distorting the truth? The reader will perhaps remember the incident of Mr. Mikhailovsky's "omission" of the "moment of flowering." The omission of this "flowering" is of "vast significance"; it shows that he has distorted the truth also for Engels. Why has not Mr. Mikhailovsky said a single word about this instructive episode?

Fie, fie, Mr. Mikhailovsky!

But do you know what? Perhaps the "Russian soul" is not distorting the truth; perhaps, poor thing, it is telling the sheerest truth. Its veracity will be above all suspicion if we only assume that Sieber was just playing a joke on the young writer, was trying to frighten him with the *"triad."* Indeed, that looks like the truth: Mr. Mikhailovsky assures us that Sieber was familiar with the dialectical method; being familiar with this method, Sieber must have known very well that the celebrated triad never did play the role of an argument with Hegel. On the other hand, Mr. Mikhailovsky, not being familiar with

A FEW WORDS TO OUR OPPONENTS

Hegel, might in conversation with Sieber have expressed the thought—which later he expressed time and again—that the whole argumentation of Hegel and the Hegelians consisted in invoking the triad. This must have been amusing to Sieber, so he began calling in the triad to tease the excitable but ill-informed young man. Of course, if Sieber had foreseen into what a deplorable position his interlocutor would in time land as a result of his joke, he certainly would have refrained from it. But this he could not foresee, and so he allowed himself to joke at Mr. Mikhailovsky's expense. The latter's veracity is beyond all doubt if our assumption is correct. Let Mr. Mikhailovsky dig down into his memory: perhaps he will recall some circumstance which shows that our assumption is not altogether unfounded. We, for our part, would be heartily glad to hear of some such circumstance that would save the honour of the "Russian soul." Mr. Beltov would be glad too, of course.

Mr. Mikhailovsky is a very amusing fellow. He is much annoyed with Mr. Beltov for having said that in the "discoveries" of our subjective sociologist the "Russian mind and Russian soul repeats old stuff and lies for two." Mr. Mikhailovsky believes that, while Mr. Beltov is not responsible for the substance of the quotation, he may nevertheless be held responsible for choosing it. Only the rudeness of our polemical manners compels our worthy sociologist to admit that to level this rebuke at Mr. Beltov would be too much of a subtlety. But where did Mr. Beltov borrow this "quotation"? He borrowed it from Pushkin. Eugene Onegin was of the opinion that in all our journalism the Russian mind and Russian soul repeats old stuff and lies for two. Can Pushkin be held responsible for his hero's virulent opinion? Till now, as we know, nobody has ever thought—although it is very likely—that Onegin was expressing the opinion of the great poet himself. But now Mr. Mikhailovsky would like to hold Mr. Beltov responsible for not finding anything in his, Mr. Mikhailovsky's, writings save a repetition of old stuff and "lying for two." Why so? Why must this "quotation" not be applied to the "works" of our sociologist? Probably because these works, in the eyes of this sociologist, deserve far more respectful treatment. But, in Mr. Mikhailovsky's own words, "this is debatable."

"The fact is," says Mr. Mikhailovsky, "that in this passage Mr. Beltov has not convicted me of any lies; he just blethered, to make it sound hotter, and used the quotation as a fig leaf" (p. 140). Why "blethered," and not "expressed his firm conviction"? What is the meaning of the sentence: Mr. Mikhailovsky in his articles repeats old stuff and lies for two? It means that Mr. Mikhailovsky is only pronouncing old opinions that have long been refuted in the West, and in doing so, *adds to the errors of Westerners his own, home-grown errors.* Is it really absolutely necessary to use "a fig leaf" when expressing such an opinion of Mr. Mikhailovsky's literary activities? Mr. Mikhailovsky is convinced that such an opinion can only be "blether," and not the fruit of a serious and thoughtful evaluation. But—again to use his own words—this is debatable.

The writer of these lines declares quite calmly and deliberately, and without feeling the need for any fig leaf, that in his conviction *a not very high opinion of Mr. Mikhailovsky's "works" is the beginning of all wisdom.*

But if, when speaking of the "Russian soul," Mr. Beltov did not convict Mr. Mikhailovsky of any lie, why did our "sociologist" pick precisely on this "quotation" to start the luckless conflict over Sieber? Probably in order to make it sound "hotter." In reality, there is nothing hot at all about methods like these, but there are people to whom they seem very hot indeed. In one of G. I. Uspensky's sketches an official's wife is quarrelling with a janitor. The janitor happens to use the word *podlye* [near]. "What," cries the official's wife, "I'm *podlaya* [vile], am I? I'll show you! I have a son serving in Poland," etc., etc. Like the official's wife, Mr. Mikhailovsky pounces upon an individual word, and heatedly cries: "I'm lying for two, am I? You dare to doubt my veracity? Well, now I'll convict you of lying for many. Just look what you said about Sieber!" We look at what Mr. Beltov said about Sieber, and find that he spoke the honest truth. Die Moral von der Geschichte (The moral of the story.—*Ed.*) is that excessive heat can lead to no good either for officials' wives or for Mr. Mikhailovsky.

"Mr. Beltov undertook to prove that the final triumph of materialist monism was established by the so-called theory of economic materialism in history, which theory is held to stand in the closest connection with 'general philosophical materialism.' With this end in view, Mr. Beltov made an excursion into the history of philosophy. How desultory and incomplete this excursion is may be judged even from the titles of the chapters devoted to it: 'French Materialism of the Eighteenth Century,' 'French Historians of the Restoration,' 'Utopians,' 'Idealist German Philosophy,' 'Modern Materialism' " (p. 146). Again Mr. Mikhailovsky gets heated without any need, and again his heatedness leads him to no good. If Mr. Beltov had been writing even a brief sketch of the *history of philosophy*, an excursion in which he passed from French materialism of the eighteenth century to the French historians of the Restoration, from these historians to the Utopians, from the Utopians to the German idealists, etc., would indeed be desultory and incomprehensible. But the whole point is that it was not a history of philosophy that Mr. Beltov was writing. On the very first page of his book he said that he intended to give a brief sketch of the theory that is wrongly called *economic* materialism. He found some faint rudiments of this theory among the French materialists and showed that these rudiments were considerably developed by the French historical specialists of the Restoration; then he turned to men who were not historians by speciality, but who nevertheless had to give much thought to cardinal problems of man's historical development, that is, the Utopians and the German philosophers. He did not by a long way enumerate all the eighteenth-century materialists, Restoration historians, Utopians, or dialectical idealists. But he mentioned the chief of them, those who had contributed more than others to the question that interested him. He showed that all these richly endowed and highly informed men got themselves entangled in contradictions from which the only logical way out was Marx's theory of history. In a word, il prenait son bien où il le trouvait. (He took his goods wherever he found them.—*Ed.*) What objection can be raised to this method? And why doesn't Mr. Mikhailovsky like it?

If Mr. Mikhailovsky has not only *read* Engels's *Ludwig Feurbach* and *Dühring's Revolution in Science*, but also—which is more important—*understood* them, he knows for himself what importance the views of the French materialists of the last century, the French historians of the Restoration, the Utopians and the dialectical idealists had in the development of the ideas of Marx and Engels. Mr. Beltov underscored this importance by giving a brief description of what in this respect was most essential in the views of the first, the second, the third, and the fourth. Mr. Mikhailovsky contemptuously shrugs his shoulders at this description; he does not like Mr. Beltov's plan. To which we rejoin that every plan is a good plan if it helps its author to attain his end. And that Mr. Beltov's end was attained, is not, as far as we know, denied even by his opponents.

Mr. Mikhailovsky continues:

"Mr. Beltov speaks both of the French historians and the French 'Utopians,' and measures both by the extent of their understanding or non-understanding of economics as the foundation of the social edifice. But strangely enough, he makes no mention whatever of Louis Blanc, although the introduction to the *Histoire de dix ans* (*History of Ten Years.—Ed.*) is in itself enough to give him a place of honour in the ranks of the first teachers of so-called economic materialism. In it, of course, there is much with which Mr. Beltov cannot agree, but in it there is the struggle of classes, and a description of their economic earmarks, and economics as the hidden mainspring of politics, and much, generally, that was *later* incorporated into the doctrine which Mr. Beltov defends so ardently. I mention this omission because, firstly, it is astonishing in itself and hints at certain parallel aims which have nothing in common with impartiality" (p. 150).

Mr. Beltov spoke of Marx's *predecessors*, Louis Blanc was rather his *contemporary*. To be sure, the *Histoire de dix ans* appeared at a time when Marx's historical views had not yet finally evolved. But the book could not have had any decisive influence upon them, if only for the reason that Louis Blanc's views regarding the inner springs of social development contained absolutely nothing new compared, say, with the views of Augustin Thierry or Guizot. It is quite true that "in it there is the struggle of classes, and a description of their economic earmarks, and economics," etc. But all this was already in Thierry and Guizot and Mignet, as Mr. Beltov irrefutably showed. Guizot, who viewed things from the angle of the struggle of classes, sympathized with the struggle of the bourgeoisie against the aristocracy, but was very hostile to the struggle of the working class against the bourgeoisie, which had just begun in his time. Louis Blanc *did* sympathize with this struggle.* [In this he differed from Guizot. But the difference was not of an essential nature. It contributed nothing new to Louis Blanc's *view* of "economics as the hidden mainspring of politics."]**

Louis Blanc, like Guizot, would have said that political constitutions are rooted in the social being of a nation, and that social being is determined in the final analysis by property relations; but where these property relations spring from was as little known to Louis Blanc as to Guizot. That is why, despite his "economics," Louis Blanc, like Guizot, was compelled to revert to *idealism.* That he was an idealist in his views of philosophy and history is known to everyone, even if he has not attended a seminary.***

At the time the *Histoire de dix ans* appeared, the immediate problem of social science was the problem, solved *"later"* by Marx, *where property relations spring from.* On this question Louis Blanc had nothing new to say. It is natural to assume that it is precisely for this reason that Mr. Beltov said nothing about Louis Blanc. But Mr. Mikhailovsky prefers to make insinuations about parallel aims. Chacun a son goût! (Each has his own taste.—*Ed.*)

---

* But in his own peculiar manner, which accounted for the wretched role he played in 1848. A veritable gulf lies between the class struggle as it was *"later"* understood by Marx and the class struggle as Louis Blanc conceived it. Anyone who does not notice this gulf is like the sage who failed to notice the elephant in the menagerie.

** [Footnote to the 1905 edition.]

*** As an idealist of the lowest grade (i.e., non-dialectical), Louis Blanc naturally had his *"formula of progress,"* which, for all its *"theoretical insignificance,"* was at least no worse than Mr. Mikhailovsky's "formula of progress."

A FEW WORDS TO OUR OPPONENTS

In the opinion of Mr. Mikhailovsky, Mr. Beltov's excursion into the history of philosophy "is even weaker than might have been thought from these (above-enumerated) chapter heads." Why so? Why, because Mr. Beltov said that "Hegel called metaphysical the point of view of those thinkers—irrespective of whether they were idealists or materialists—who, not being able to understand the process of development of phenomena, willy-nilly represent them to themselves and others as petrified, disconnected, incapable of passing one into another. To this point of view he opposed *dialectics,* which studies phenomena precisely in their development and consequently, in their mutual connection." To this, Mr. Mikhailovsky slyly observes: "Mr. Beltov considers himself an expert in the philosophy of Hegel. I should be glad to learn from him, as from any well-informed person, and for a beginning I would request Mr. Beltov to name the place in Hegel's works from which he took this supposedly Hegelian definition of the 'metaphysical point of view.' I make bold to affirm that he will not be able to name it. To Hegel, metaphysics was the doctrine of the absolute essence of things, lying beyond the limits of experience and observation, of the innermost substratum of phenomena.... Mr. Beltov borrowed his supposedly Hegelian definition not from Hegel but from Engels (all in the same polemical work against Dühring), who quite arbitrarily divided metaphysics from dialectics by the earmark of immobility or fluidity" (p. 147).

We do not know what Mr. Beltov will say in reply to this. But, *"for a beginning,"* we shall take the liberty, without awaiting his explanation, to reply to the worthy subjectivist ourselves.

We turn to Part I of Hegel's *Encyclopaedia,* and there, in the addendum to paragraph 31 (p. 57 of Mr. V. Chizhov's Russian translation), we read: "The thinking of this metaphysics was not free and true in the objective sense, as it did not leave it to the object to develop freely out of itself and itself find its definitions, but took it as something ready-made.... This metaphysics is dogmatism, because, in accordance with the nature of final definitions, it had to assume that, of two antithetical assertions ... one was necessarily true, and the other necessarily false" (§ 32, p. 58, of the same translation).

Hegel is referring here to the old pre-Kantian metaphysics which, he observes, "has been torn out by the roots, has vanished from the ranks of science" (ist so zu sagen, mit Stumpf und Stiel ausgerottet worden, aus der Reihe der Wissenschaften verschwunden!).* To this metaphysics Hegel opposed his *dialectical philosophy,* which examines all phenomena in their development and in their interconnection, not as ready-made and separated from one another by a veritable gulf. "Only the whole is the truth," he says, "but the whole reveals itself in all its fulness only through its development" (Das Wahre ist das Ganze. Das Ganze aber ist nur das durch seine Entwicklung sich vollendende Wesen).** Mr. Mikhailovsky asserts that Hegel fused metaphysics with dialectics, but the person he heard this from did not explain the thing to him properly. With Hegel, the *dialectical factor* is supplemented by the *speculative factor*, owing to which his philosophy becomes an *idealist philosophy. As an idealist,* Hegel did *what all other idealists do*: he attached particular philosophical importance to such "results" (concepts) as the old "metaphysics" also prized. But with him, thanks to the "dialectical factor," these concepts (the Absolute in the various aspects of its de-

---

* *Wissenschaft der Logik,* Vorrede, S. 1.
** *Die Phänomenologie des Geistes,* Vorrede, S. XXIII.

velopment) appeared precisely *as results*, and not as original data. He dissolved metaphysics in logic, and for that reason he would have been very surprised to hear that he, a speculative thinker, was being called a metaphysician ohne Weiteres. He would have said that people who called him that "lassen sich mit Thieren vergleichen, welche alle Töne einer Musik mit durchgehört haben, an deren Sinn aber das Eine, die Harmonie dieser Töne, nicht gekommen ist" ("Might be compared to beasts who have heard all the sounds of a given piece of music, but have not grasped the whole, the harmony of these sounds."—*Ed.*) (the expression he himself used to brand learned pedants).

We repeat, this speculative thinker, who despised the *metaphysics of common sense* (his own expression again) was an *idealist,* and in this sense had his own *metaphysics of the reason*. But did Mr. Beltov forget this or fail to mention it in his book? He neither forgot it, nor did he fail to mention it. He quoted from *Die heilige Familie* of Marx and Engels long passages in which Hegel's "speculative" results are very mordantly criticized. We believe that these quoted passages bring out quite distinctly that dialectics must not be fused with what Mr. Mikhailovsky calls Hegel's *metaphysics*. Hence if Mr. Beltov forgot anything, it was only that, in view of the astonishing "indifference" of our "advanced" people to the history of philosophy, he should have taken care to explain how sharp was the distinction made in Hegel's time between *metaphysics* and *speculative philosophy*.* From all of

---

* Incidentally, if after all this Mr. Mikhailovsky should want to have at least a partial understanding of the historical significance of Hegel's "metaphysics," we would recommend him to read a very popular book that was quite well known in its time: *Die Posaune des jüngsten Gerichts über Hegel, den Atheisten und Antichristen* ("The Last of Judgement Over Hegel, the Atheist and Antichrist."—*Ed.*) A jolly little book.

which it follows that Mr. Mikhailovsky "makes bold to affirm" what cannot possibly be affirmed.

Mr. Beltov says that Hegel called metaphysical even the point of view of those materialists who were unable to examine phenomena in their interconnection. Is this true or not? Well, take the trouble to read this page of Section 27, Part I of Hegel's *Encyclopaedia:* "We find the fullest application of this point of view to philosophy in the old metaphysics, as expounded before Kant. However, the days of this metaphysics have passed only in respect to the history of philosophy; in itself, it continues to exist as always, representing the common sense view of objects." What is this common sense view of objects? It is the old metaphysical view of objects, as opposed to the dialectical. All the materialist philosophy of the eighteenth century was *essentially "common sense"* philosophy: it was able to examine phenomena solely from the standpoint of final definitions. That Hegel was very well aware of this weak side of French materialism, as of eighteenth century French philosophy generally, anyone can convince himself who takes the trouble to read the pertinent passages in Part III of his *Vorlesungen über die Geschichte der Philosophie.* ("Lectures on the History of Philosophy."—*Ed.*) Hence he could not but regard the view-point of the French materialists also as the old metaphysical view-point.* Well then, is Mr. Beltov right or

---

* [Footnote in the 1905 edition.] However, he said of materialism: "Dennoch muss man in dem Materialismus das begeisterungsvolle Streben anerkennen, über den zweierlei Welten als gleich substantiell und wahr annehmenden Dualismus hinauszugehen, diese Zerreissung des ursprünglich Einen aufzuheben." (*Enzyklopädie*, Theil III, S. 54). [We must nevertheless acknowledge the inspired desire of materialism to transcend the dualism which accepts the two worlds as equally substantial and true, and to eliminate this division of the original unity." (*Encyclopaedia*, Part III, p. 54.)—*Ed.*]

not? It is clear, we think, that he is absolutely right. Yet Mr. Mikhailovsky "makes bold to affirm."... However, neither Mr. Beltov nor the writer of these lines can do anything about that. Mr. Mikhailovsky's trouble is that, having entered into a controversy with the "Russian disciples" of Marx, he "made bold" to discuss things about which he knows absolutely nothing.

O, man of much experience, thy boldness is thy undoing!

Anyone acquainted with philosophy will have had no difficulty in observing that when Mr. Beltov expounds the philosophical views of Hegel or Schelling *he nearly always uses these thinkers' own words*. For example, his description of dialectical thinking is almost a word-forword translation of the *note* and first addendum to Section 81, Part I of the *Encyclopaedia*; next, he quotes almost word for word certain passages from the preface to the *Philosophie des Rechts* and from the *Philosophie der Geschichte*. But this author, who so very accurately quotes men like Helvetius, Enfantin, Oskar Peschel and so on, hardly ever indicates precisely which works of Schelling or Hegel, or which passages in these works, he is referring to in his exposition. Why, in this instance, did he depart from his general rule? It seems to us that Mr. Beltov was resorting to a military stratagem. His line of thought, we believe, was as follows: our subjectivists proclaim German idealist philosophy metaphysical, and rest content at that; they have not studied it, as the author of the comments on Mill, for instance, had. When I refer to certain remarkable thoughts of the German idealists, the subjectivist gentlemen, seeing no references to the works of these thinkers, will imagine that I invented these thoughts myself or borrowed them from Engels, and will cry: "That is debatable," "I make bold to affirm," etc. That's where I'll bring their ignorance into the light of day; that's where the fun will begin! If Mr. Beltov really did resort in his polemic to this little military stratagem, it must be confessed that it has eminently succeeded: there has indeed been quite a lot of fun!

But let us proceed. "Any philosophical system which, with Mr. Beltov, declares that 'the rights of reason are as boundless and unlimited as its powers,' and hence that it has disclosed the absolute essence of things—be it matter or spirit—is a metaphysical system.... Whether it has, or has not, arrived at the idea that its presumed essence of things develops, and, if it has, whether it ascribes to this development the dialectical or any other way, is of course very important in defining its place in the history of philosophy, but does not alter its metaphysical character" (*Russkoye Bogatstvo*, January 1895, p. 148). As far as can be gathered from these words, Mr. Mikhailovsky, shunning metaphysical thinking, does not believe that the rights of reason are unlimited. It is to be hoped that this will earn him the praises of Prince Meshchersky. Nor, apparently, does Mr. Mikhailovsky believe that the *powers* of reason are unlimited and unbounded either. This may seem astonishing in a man who has so often assured his readers that la raison finit toujours par avoir raison: with the powers (and even the rights!) of reason limited, this assurance seems hardly appropriate. But Mr. Mikhailovsky will say that he is assured of the ultimate triumph of reason only as far as practical affairs are concerned, but doubts its powers when it comes to cognizing the absolute essence of things ("be it matter or spirit"). Excellent! But what is this absolute essence of things?

It is, is it not, what Kant called the *thing in itself* (Ding an sich)? If so, then we categorically declare that we do know what the "thing in itself" is, and that it is to Hegel that we owe the knowledge. ("Help!" the "sober-minded philosophers" will cry, but we beg them not to get excited.)

"The thing in itself ... is the object from which knowledge, everything that can be definitely felt and thought about it, has been abstracted. It is easy to see what remains—a pure abstraction, a sheer emptiness, and that carried beyond the bounds of knowledge; the negation of all idea, feeling, definite thought, etc. But it is just as easy to judge that this caput mortuum (worthless residium—*Ed.*) is itself but a product of the thought which made this pure abstraction, of the empty *I* which makes an object of its empty identity. The negative definition which holds this abstract identity as an object is likewise included among the Kantian categories, and is just as well known. It is therefore surprising to read so often that it is not known [what the thing in itself is], when nothing is easier to know."*

We therefore repeat that we know very well what the absolute essence of things, or the thing in itself, is. It is a sheer abstraction. And Mr. Mikhailovsky wants to use this sheer abstraction to frighten people who follow Hegel in proudly saying: "Von der Grösse und Macht seines Geistes kann der Mensch nicht gross genug denken!"** The song is an old one, Mr. Mikhailovsky! Sie sind zu spät gekommen! (You have come too late!—*Ed.*)

We are certain that the lines we have just written will seem sheer sophistry to Mr. Mikhailovsky. "But pardon me," he will say, "what in that case do you mean by the materialist interpretation of nature and history?" This is what we mean.

When Schelling said that magnetism is the introduc-

---

* Hegel, *Encyclopaedia*, Part I, pp. 79-80, § 44.

** Man cannot think highly enough of the greatness and power of his mind.—*Ed.* (*Geschichte der Philosophie*, Part I, p. 6.)

tion of the subjective into the objective, that was an *idealist* interpretation of nature; but when magnetism is explained from the view-point of modern physics, its phenomena are given a *materialist* interpretation. When Hegel, or even our Slavophiles, attributed certain historical phenomena to the properties of the national spirit, they were regarding these phenomena from an *idealist* view-point, but when Marx attributed, say, the events of 1848-50 in France to the class struggle in French society, he was giving these events a *materialist* interpretation. Is that clear? We should say so! So clear, that it requires a considerable dose of obstinacy not to understand them.

"But there's something wrong here," Mr. Mikhailovsky conceives, his thoughts darting hither and thither (c'est bien le moment!). "Lange says...." But we shall take the liberty of interrupting Mr. Mikhailovsky. We know very well what Lange says, but we can assure Mr. Mikhailovsky that his authority is very much mistaken. In his *History of Materialism,* Lange forgot to cite, for example, the following characteristic remark of one of the most prominent of the French materialists: "Nous ne connaissons que l'écorce des phénomènes (we only know the skin of phenomena—*Ed.*). Other, and no less prominent, French materialists expressed themselves time and again in a similar vein. So you see, Mr. Mikhailovsky, the French materialists did not yet know that the thing in itself is only the caput mortuum of an abstraction, and held precisely to the view-point which is now called by many the *view-point of critical philosophy.*

All this, it need not be said, will seem to Mr. Mikhailovsky very novel and absolutely incredible. But we shall not tell him for the present to which French materialists and to which of their works we are referring. Let him first *"make bold to affirm,"* and then we shall have a word with him.

If Mr. Mikhailovsky is willing to know how we understand the relation between our sensations and external objects, we would refer him to the article of Mr. Sechenov, "Objective Thought and Reality," in the book *Aid to the Hungry*. We presume that Mr. Beltov and all other disciples of Marx, Russian and non-Russian, will fully agree with our celebrated physiologist. And this is what Mr. Sechenov says: "Whatever the external objects may be in themselves, independently of our consciousness—even if it be granted that our impressions of them are only conventional signs—the fact remains that the similarity or difference of the signs we perceive corresponds with a real similarity or difference. In other words: the similarities or differences man finds in the objects he perceives are real similarities or differences."*

When Mr. Mikhailovsky refutes Mr. Sechenov, we shall agree to recognize the limitation not only of the *powers,* but also of the *rights* of human reason.**

Mr. Beltov said that in the second half of our century there triumphed in science—with which meanwhile philosophy had been completely fused—materialistic monism. "I am afraid he is mistaken," Mr. Mikhailovsky observes. In justification of his fear, he appeals to Lange, in whose opinion "die gründliche Naturforschung durch ihre eignen Consequenzen über den Materialismus hinausführt." ("Sound natural research, by its own findings,

---

* *Aid to the Hungry*, p. 207.
** [Footnote in the 1905 edition.] Here is a very good opportunity for our opponents to convict us of contradicting ourselves: on the one hand we declare that the Kantian "thing in itself" is a sheer abstraction, on the other we cite with praise Mr. Sechenov who speaks of objects as they exist in themselves, independently of our consciousness. Of course, people who understand will see no contradiction, but are there many people of understanding among our opponents?

transcends materialism."—*Ed.*) If Mr. Beltov is mistaken, then materialistic monism has *not* triumphed in science. So, then, scientists to this day explain nature by means of the introduction of the subjective into the objective and the other subtleties of idealist natural philosophy? "We are afraid he would be mistaken" who assumed this, and the more afraid for the fact that a man of very great renown in science, the English *naturalist* Huxley, reasons as follows.

"Surely no one who is cognizant of the facts of the case, nowadays, doubts that the roots of psychology lie in the physiology of the nervous system. What we call the operations of the mind are functions of the brain, and the materials of consciousness are products of cerebral activity."* This, note, is said by a man who is what is known in England as an *agnostic*. He believes that the view he expresses on the activity of the mind is fully compatible with pure idealism. But we, who are familiar with the interpretations of natural phenomena consistent idealism is capable of giving, and who understand the reasons for the shamefacedness of the worthy Englishman, repeat with Mr. Beltov that *in the second half of the nineteenth century materialistic monism triumphed in science.*

Mr. Mikhailovsky is probably acquainted with Sechenov's psychological researches. This scientist's views were at one time passionately controverted by Kavelin.[68] We are afraid that the now deceased Liberal was very much mistaken. But perhaps Mr. Mikhailovsky agrees with Kavelin? Or perhaps he needs some further explanations on the point? Well, we withhold them for the event that he again begins to "affirm."

---

* Th. Huxley, *Hume. Sa vie, sa philosophie*, p. 108.

Mr. Beltov says that the point of view of "human nature" that prevailed in social science before Marx led to "an abuse of biological analogies which even up to the present day makes itself strongly felt in Western sociological, and particularly in Russian quasi-sociological, literature." This induces Mr. Mikhailovsky to accuse the author of the book on historical monism of outrageous injustice and once again to suspect the integrity of his polemical methods.

"I appeal to the reader, even though he be quite ill-disposed towards me but has some acquaintance with my writings—if not with all, at least with one article, say, 'The Analogical Method in Social Science' or 'What Is Progress?' It is not true that Russian literature particularly abuses biological analogies: in Europe, thanks to the good offices of Spencer, this stuff is far more extensive, to say nothing of the times of the comical analogies of Bluntschli and his fraternity. And if in our country the matter has gone no further than the analogical exercises of the late Stronin ('History and Method,' 'Politics as a Science'), Mr. Lilienfeld ('The Social Science of the Future'), and a few journalistic articles, a little of the credit presumably belongs to me. For nobody has spent as much effort combating biological analogies as I have. And at one time I suffered no little for this at the hands of the 'Spencerian lads.' I shall hope that the present storm will also pass in time..." (pp. 145-46). This peroration bears such an air of sincerity that indeed even a reader ill-disposed towards Mr. Mikhailovsky might think: "It does look as if Mr. Beltov has gone too far in his polemical ardour." But this is not so, and Mr. Mikhailovsky himself knows that it is not: if he pathetically appeals to the reader, it is solely for the same reason that Plautus's Tranion said to himself: "Pergam turbare porro: ita haec res postulat." ("I shall go on being riotous, for the case demands it."—*Ed.*)

What did Mr. Beltov really say? He said: "If the explanation of all historical social progress is to be sought in the nature of man, and if, as Saint-Simon himself justly remarks, society consists of individuals, then the nature of the individual has to provide the key to the explanation of history. The nature of the individual is the subject of physiology in the broad sense of the word, i.e., of a science which also covers *psychological* phenomena. That is why physiology, in the eyes of Saint-Simon and his followers, was the basis of sociology, which they called social physics. In the *Opinions philosophiques, littéraires et industrielles* published during Saint-Simon's lifetime and with his active participation, there was printed an extremely interesting but unfortunately unfinished article of an anonymous *doctor of medicine,* entitled: 'On Physiology Applied to the Improvement of Social Institutions.' The author considered the *science of society* to be a component part of *'general physiology,'* which, enriched by the observations and experiments of special physiology of the individual, devotes itself to considerations of a 'higher order.' Individuals are for it only 'organs of the social body,' the functions of which it studies, 'just as special physiology studies the functions of individuals.' General physiology studies (the author writes: 'expresses') the laws of social existence, with which the written laws should be accordingly co-ordinated. Later on the bourgeois sociologists, as for example Spencer, made use of the doctrine of the social organism to draw the most conservative conclusions. But the doctor of medicine whom we quote was first of all a *reformer.* He studied the social body with the object of social *reconstruction,* since only *social physiology* and the *hygiene* closely bound up with it provided the positive foundations on which it is possible to build the system of social organization required by the present state of the civilized world."

From these words alone it is apparent that, in Mr. Beltov's opinion, biological analogies may be abused not only in the sense of Spencer's bourgeois conservatism, but also *in the sense of utopian plans of social reform.* Here the likening of society to an organism is absolutely of *second-rate,* if not of tenth-rate, significance: the important thing is not the likening of society to an organism, but the desire to found *"sociology"* on *biological* conclusions. Mr. Mikhailovsky has passionately objected against likening society to an organism; in the struggle against this tendency "a little of the credit" does undoubtedly belong to *him.* But that is not of essential importance. The essentially important question is, did, or did not, Mr. Mikhailovsky, believe that sociology could be founded on biological conclusions? And on this point no doubt is possible, as anyone can see by reading, for example, the article, "The Darwinian Theory and Social Science." In this article Mr. Mikhailovsky says, in part: "Under the general heading 'The Darwinian Theory and Social Science,' we shall speak of various questions dealt with, settled or resettled by the Darwinian theory or by one or another of its supporters, whose numbers are swelling from day to day. Our chief task, however, will consist in determining, from the standpoint of the Darwinian theory, the interrelation between physiological division of labour, i.e., division of labour between the organs of one indivisible whole, and economic division of labour, i.e., division of labour between whole indivisible species, races, peoples or societies. In our view, this task resolves itself into a search for the basic laws of co-operation, i.e., the foundation of social science."* To search

---

* Mikhailovsky, *Works,* Vol. V, p. 2.

for the basic laws of co-operation, i.e., the *foundation of social science, in biology* is to adopt the view-point of the French Saint-Simonists of the 20s—in other words, "to repeat old stuff and lie for two."

Here Mr. Mikhailovsky might exclaim: "But, you know, the Darwinian theory didn't exist in the 20s!" The reader, however, will understand that the point here is not the Darwinian theory, but the utopian tendency—common to Mr. Mikhailovsky and the Saint-Simonists—*to apply physiology to the improvement of social institutions.* In the article referred to Mr. Mikhailovsky entirely agrees with Haeckel ("Haeckel is absolutely right") when he says that future statesmen, economists and historians will have to turn their attention chiefly to comparative zoology, that is, to the comparative morphology and physiology of animals, if they want to have a true conception of their special subject. Say what you like, but if Haeckel is "absolutely right," that is, if sociologists (and even historians!) must turn their attention "*chiefly*" to the morphology and physiology of animals, then there is bound to be abuse of biological analogies *in one direction or another.* And is it not clear that Mr. Mikhailovsky's view of sociology is the old Saint-Simonist view?

Well, that is all Mr. Beltov said, and it is in vain that Mr. Mikhailovsky tries, so to speak, to disavow responsibility for the sociological ideas of Bukhartsev-Nozhin. In his own sociological inquiries he has not retreated very far from the views of his late friend and teacher. Mr. Mikhailovsky has not grasped what Marx's discovery consists in, and he has therefore remained an incorrigible Utopian. That is a very deplorable situation, but our author might escape from it only by another effort of thought; fearful appeals to the reader, even the quite ill-disposed reader, will not help our poor "sociologist" at all.

Mr. Beltov said a couple of words in defence of Mr. P. Struve. This induced Messrs. Mikhailovsky and N. —on to say that Beltov had taken Mr. Struve under his *"protection."* We have said a great deal in defence of Mr. Beltov. What will Mr. Mikhailovsky and Mr. N. —on say about us? They will probably consider Mr. Beltov our vassal. Apologizing in advance to Mr. Beltov for anticipating his retort to Messrs. the subjectivists, we shall ask the latter: does agreeing with an author necessarily mean taking him under one's protection? Mr. Mikhailovsky is in agreement with Mr. N. —on on certain current questions of Russian life. Must we understand their agreement to mean that Mr. Mikhailovsky has taken Mr. N. —on under his protection? Or, perhaps, that Mr. N. —on is the protector of Mr. Mikhailovsky? What would the late Dobrolyubov have said on hearing this strange language of our present-day "progressive" literature?

It seems to Mr. Mikhailovsky that Mr. Beltov has misrepresented his doctrine of heroes and the crowd. Again we think that Mr. Beltov is quite right and that, in controverting him, Mr. Mikhailovsky is playing the role of Tranion. But before supporting this opinion of ours, we think it necessary to say a few words about Mr. N. —on's note—"What Does Economic Necessity Really Mean?"—in the March issue of *Russkoye Bogatstvo*.

In this note Mr. N. —on sets up two batteries against Mr. Beltov. We shall consider them one by one.

The target of the first battery is Mr. Beltov's statement that "in order to reply to the question—will Russia follow the path of capitalist development, or not?—one must turn to a study of the actual position of the country, to an analysis of its present-day internal life. On the basis of such an analysis, the Russian disciples of Marx say: there are no data allowing one to hope that Russia will soon leave the path of capitalist development." Mr. N.

—on slyly repeats: "There is *no* such analysis." Really not, Mr. N. —on? First of all, let us agree on terminology. What do you call an *analysis*? Does an analysis provide new data for forming a judgement on a subject, or does it operate with already existing data, obtained in other ways? At the risk of incurring the charge of being "metaphysical," we adhere to the old definition which holds that an analysis does not provide new data for forming a judgement on a subject, but operates with ready-made data. From this definition it follows that the Russian disciples of Marx, in their analysis of Russian internal life, might not offer any independent observations of that life, but content themselves with material collected, say, in Narodist literature. If from this material they drew a new conclusion, that in itself implies that they subjected these data to a new analysis. Hence the question arises: what data on the development of capitalism is to be found in Narodist literature, and did the Russian disciples of Marx really draw a new conclusion from these data? In order to answer this question we shall take, if only for one, Mr. Dementyev's book, *The Factory, What It Gives to, and What It Takes from, the Population*. In this book (pp. 241 et seq.) we read: "Our industry, before it assumed the form of capitalist factory production in which we find it now, passed through all the same stages of development as in the West.... One of the strongest reasons why we are now lagging behind the West was serfdom. Because of it, our industry passed through a far longer period of handicraft and home production. It was only in 1861 that capital acquired the possibility of instituting that form of production to which, in the West, it had passed nearly a century and a half earlier, and only from that year on did there begin a more rapid decline of handicraft and home production and their conversion into factory production.... But in the thirty years (since the abolition of serfdom) everything has changed. Having embarked on the same path of economic development as Western Europe, our industry had inevitably, fatally to assume—and did assume—the form into which it had evolved in the West. The possession of land by the popular masses, to which there is such a fondness to refer in proof of the impossibility in our country of a special class of workers who are free from everything—a class that is an inevitable concomitant of the modern form of industry—undoubtedly has been, and still is, a strong retarding factor, but by no means so strong as is usually thought. The very frequent inadequacy of the land allotment and the complete decline of agriculture, on the one hand, and the deep concern of the government to develop the manufacturing industries as an essential element in maintaining the economic equilibrium of the country, on the other, are conditions that eminently tended, and still tend, to detract from the importance of land possession. We have seen the result of this state of things: the formation of a special class of factory workers, a class which continues to bear the name of 'peasant,' but which has practically nothing in common with the peasant tillers, has retained to only an insignificant degree its association with the land, and half of which, already in the third generation, never quits the factory and has no property whatever in the countryside, save a legal and practically almost unrealizable right to land."

The *objective data* given by Mr. Dementyev show very eloquently that capitalism, with all its consequences, is developing fast in Russia. These data Mr. Dementyev supplements with reflections which would imply that the further advance of capitalist production can be halted, and that to do so, all that is necessary is to recall the maxim: gouverner—c'est prévoir (to govern is to foresee—*Ed.*) (p. 246). The Russian disciples of Marx subject this conclusion of Mr. Dementyev's to their *own* analysis, and find that *in this matter nothing can be halted*, that Mr. Dementyev is mistaken, like the whole *crowd* of Narodniks who, in their researches, communicate a whole mass of objective data quite similar to those he, Mr. Dementyev, communicates.* Mr. N. —on asks where this analysis is to be found. What he apparently wants to say is, when, and where, did such an analysis appear in the Russian press. To this question we can give him at least two answers.

First, in the book of Mr. Struve which he finds so disagreeable there is a competent discussion of *the limits to which government interference in the economic life of Russia is possible at this time.* This discussion is already, in part, the analysis which Mr. N. —on demands, and against this analysis Mr. N. —on has nothing competent to offer.

Second, does Mr. N. —on remember the dispute which took place in the 40s between the Slavophiles and the

* "Among the several hundred statistical and other inquiries made in the last twenty years or thereabouts," says Mr. N. —on, "we have not met any works whose conclusions agreed in any respect with the economic conclusions of the Beltovs, Struves and Skvortsovs." The authors of the inquiries to which you, Mr. N. —on, refer usually draw two kinds of conclusion: one which accords with objective truth and says that capitalism is developing and the ancient "foundations" are crumbling; the other, a *"subjective"* conclusion, which holds that the development of capitalism might be halted, if etc., etc. *But no data are ever adduced in confirmation of this latter conclusion, so that it remains literally unsupported*, notwithstanding the more or less abundant statistical material contained in the inquiries which it adorns. Mr. N. —on's *Essays* suffer from a similar weakness—what might be called the *anaemia of "subjective" conclusion.* What "analysis," indeed, confirms Mr. N. —on's idea that our society can organize production already at this stage? *There is no such analysis.*

Westernists? In this dispute, too, an "analysis of internal Russian life" played a very important part, but in the press this analysis was applied almost exclusively to purely literary themes. For this there were historical reasons, which Mr. N. —on must certainly take into account if he does not want to be reputed a ridiculous pedant. Will Mr. N. —on say that these reasons have no bearing today on the analysis of the "Russian disciples"?

So far the "disciples" have not published any independent investigations of Russian economic life. The explanation is that the trend to which they belong is extremely new in Russia. It is the *Narodist* trend that has until now predominated in Russian literature, thanks to which investigators, when communicating objective data testifying to the crumbling of the ancient "foundations," have always drowned them in the waters of their *"subjective"* hopes. But it is precisely the abundance of the data communicated by the Narodniks that has impelled the appearance of a new view of Russian life. This new view will unquestionably become the basis of new, independent observations. Even now we can draw Mr. N. —on's attention, for example, to the writings of Mr. Kharizomenov, which strongly contradict the Narodist catechism, as was duly sensed by Mr. V. V., who tried often and vainly to refute the worthy investigator. The author of *The South-Russian Peasant Economy* is anything but a Marxist, but Mr. N. —on will scarcely say that Mr. Postnikov's views on the present state of the village community, and peasant land tenure generally, in Novorossia agree with the customary views of our Narodniks.

Then there is Mr. Borodin, the author of a remarkable investigation of the Urals Cossack organization, who already stands foursquare on the point of view which we uphold and which has the misfortune of not being agreeable to Mr. N. —on. Our Narodist publicists paid no attention to this investigation, not because it is devoid of intrinsic value, but solely because these publicists are imbued with a specific "subjective" spirit. And there will be more of them, Mr. N. —on, as time goes on: the era of Marxist research is only beginning in Russia.*

Mr. N. —on also considers himself a Marxist. He is mistaken. He is nothing but an *illicit* offspring of the great thinker. His world outlook is the fruit of an illegitimate cohabitation of the Marxian theory with Mr. V. V. From "Mütterchen" Mr. N. —on derived his terminology and several economic theorems which, incidentally, he understands very abstractly, and therefore incorrectly. From "Väterchen" he inherited a utopian attitude to social reform, and it is with its help that he set up his second battery against Mr. Beltov.

Mr. Beltov says that social relations, by the very logic of their development, bring man to a realization of the causes of his enslavement by economic necessity. "Having realized that the cause of his enslavement lies in the anarchy of production, the producer ('social man') organizes that production and thereby subjects it to his will. Then terminates the kingdom of necessity, and there begins the reign of freedom, which itself proves a necessity." It the opinion of Mr. N. —on, all this is quite true. But to Mr. Beltov's true words he adds the following remark: "Consequently, the task is that society, instead of passively observing the manifestation of the given law which retards the development of its productive forces,

---

* We say nothing of Mr. P. Struve's book, because Mr. N. —on finds it disagreeable. But it is in vain that Mr. N. —on so decidedly stamps this book as worthless. In controversy with Mr. N. —on, Mr. P. Struve is quite capable of taking care of himself. And as to Mr. N. —on's own "analysis," when somebody undertakes to *"analyze"* it from the Marxian standpoint, nothing will remain of it but general platitudes. And it is to be hoped that this analysis will not be long in forthcoming.

should, with the help of the existing material economic conditions, find a means of bringing this law under its power, by surrounding its manifestation with such conditions as would not only not retard, but facilitate the development of the productive forces of the labour [forces of labour!] of all society taken as a whole."

Without himself noticing it, Mr. N. —on has drawn from the "quite true" words of Mr. Beltov an extremely confused conclusion.

Mr. Beltov is talking of social man, of the sum-total of producers, before whom there really does lie the task of vanquishing economic necessity. But for the *producers* Mr. N. —on substitutes *society,* which "as a producing whole, cannot look on indifferently, 'objectively,' at the development of such social and economic relations as condemn the majority of its members to progressive impoverishment."

"Society as a producing whole." ... Marx's "analysis," to which Mr. N. —on allegedly adheres, did not stop at the idea of society being a producing *whole*. It *divided* society, in accordance with its true nature, into separate *classes,* each of which has its own economic interest and its own special task. Why does not Mr. N. —on's "analysis" do likewise? Why, instead of speaking of the task of the Russian producers, does Mr. N. —on speak of the task of society as a whole? This society, taken as a whole, is usually, and not without reason, contrasted to the people, and it then turns out to be, despite its "wholeness," only a small part, only an insignificant minority of the Russian population. When Mr. N. —on assures us that this tiny minority will organize production, we can only shrug our shoulders and say: it is not from Marx Mr. N. —on has taken this; he has inherited it from his "Väterchen," from Mr. V. V.

According to Marx, organization of production presumes a conscious attitude to it on the part of the producers, whose economic emancipation must therefore be the work of their own hands. With Mr. N. —on, organization of production presumes a conscious attitude to it on the part of society. If this is Marxism, then surely Marx was never a Marxist.

But let us assume that society does really act as the organizer of production. In what relation does it then stand to the producers? It *organizes them*. Society is the *hero;* the producers are the *crowd*.

We ask Mr. Mikhailovsky, who "affirms" that Mr. Beltov has misrepresented his doctrine of heroes and the crowd, does he, like Mr. N. —on, think that society can organize production? If he does, then he in fact holds to the view that society, the *"intelligentsia,"* is the *hero*, the demiurge of our future historical development, while the millions of producers are the *crowd,* out of which the hero will mould whatever he considers necessary in accordance with his ideals. Now let the impartial reader say: was Mr. Beltov right when he said that the "subjective" view regarded the people as a crowd?

Mr. Mikhailovsky declares that he, too, and those who think like him are not opposed to the development of the self-consciousness of the producers. "It only seems to me," he says, "that for so simple and clear a programme there was no need to rise above the clouds of the Hegelian philosophy and sink down to a hotch-potch of the subjective and objective." But the fact of the matter is, Mr. Mikhailovsky, that in the eyes of people of your type of thought the self-consciousness of the producers cannot have the same meaning as it has in the eyes of your opponents. From your point of view production can be organized by "society"; from the point of view of your opponents it can be organized only by the producers themselves. From your point of view society acts, and the producer assists. From the point of view of your opponents the producers do not assist, they just act. It stands to reason that assistants need a smaller degree of consciousness than actors, for it has been said long ago and very justly: "there is one glory of the sun, and another glory of the moon, and another glory of the stars: for one star differeth from another star in glory." *Your attitude to the producers is that of the French and German Utopians of of the 30s and 40s.* Your opponents condemn *any and every utopian attitude to the producers.* If you were better acquainted with the history of economic literature, Mr. Mikhailovsky, you would have known that in order to get rid of the utopian attitude to the producers, it was indeed necessary to rise to the clouds of the Hegelian philosophy and then sink down to the prose of political economy.

Mr. Mikhailovsky does not like the word "producer": it smacks, don't you see, of the stable.* Well, all we can say is that he is welcome to the best we have. The word *"producer,"* as far as we know, was first used by Saint-Simon and the Saint-Simonists. Since the existence of the journal, *Le Producteur,* that is, since 1825, it has been used in Western Europe countless numbers of times, and has never reminded anyone of the stables. Then the Russian *repentant nobleman* began to speak of producers, and the stables came to his mind at once. To what are we to attribute this strange phenomenon? Evidently, to the memories and traditions of the repentant nobleman.

Mr. N. —on, with an air of deep slyness, cites the following words of Mr. Beltov: "Of course one of them" [the Russian disciples of Marx] "may have greater and another less extensive economic knowledge, but what matters here is not the amount of knowledge of individual

---

* Russian proizvoditel (producer) also means "stallion."—*Tr.*

persons, but the point of view itself." Mr. N. —on asks: "What has become of all the demands to adhere to the ground of reality, of the necessity for a detailed study of the course of economic development?" ("Demands of the necessity for a detailed study"—that doesn't sound very lucid, Mr. N. —on.) Now it appears that all this is something secondary, that "what matters is not the amount of knowledge but the point of view."

Mr. N. —on, as we see, likes to say something funny every now and again. But we would advise him, when he wants to make people laugh, not to forget common sense. Otherwise the laugh will not be on his side.

Mr. N. —on has not understood Mr. Beltov. Let us try to rescue him from his difficulty. In the same issue of *Russkoye Bogatstvo* in which Mr. N. —on's note appeared, we find in an article by Mr. Mokievsky called "What Is an Educated Man?" (p. 33, note) some lines that might be very instructive to Mr. N. —on: "An Arab savant once said to his disciples: 'If anyone should tell you that the laws of mathematics are erroneous and, in proof, should transform a stick into a snake, do not regard such a proof as convincing.' This is a typical example. An educated man will reject such proof, even if (unlike the savant) he is not acquainted with the laws of mathematics. He will say that the transformation of a stick into a snake is an extraordinary miracle, but it does not follow from it that the laws of mathematics are erroneous. On the other hand, it is not to be doubted that uneducated people would at once lay all their convictions and beliefs at the feet of the miracle-worker."

One of the disciples of the wise Arab may have had greater and another less extensive mathematical knowledge, but neither of them, probably, would have fallen at the feet of the miracle-worker. Why? Because both had had a good schooling; because what matters here is not the amount of knowledge, but *that point of view* from which the transformation of a stick into a snake cannot serve as a refutation of mathematical truths. Is that clear to you, Mr. N. —on? We hope so, for it is so very simple, quite elementary in fact. Well, then, if it is clear, you should now see yourself that what Mr. Beltov says about the point of view, etc., does not do away with what he also says about the necessity of adhering to the ground of reality.

But we are afraid you are not clear on the matter, after all. Let us give another example. God knows, you haven't much economic knowledge, but you do have more than Mr. V. V. That, however, does not prevent you from holding to the same point of view. *You are both Utopians.* And when anyone undertakes to describe your common views, he will leave aside the amount of your respective knowledge, and will say: What matters is these people's point of view, which they have borrowed from the Utopians of the days of Old King Cole.

Now it should be quite clear to you, Mr. N. —on, that you were quite off the mark when you implied that Mr. Beltov had resorted to the subjective method, that you blundered egregiously.

At all events, let us put the same thing in different words. However much the Russian followers of Marx may differ in the extent of their knowledge, not one of them, if he remains true to himself, will believe you, or Mr. V. V., when you assert that "society"—whatever that is—will organize our production. Their point of view will prevent them from *laying their convictions* at the feet of social miracle-workers.*

Enough of this. But once we have touched upon the sub-

---

* [*Footnote in the 1905 edition.*] "Let me refer again to the above-mentioned statement of Feuerbach that it is the point of view which distinguishes man from the ape."

jective method, let us remark how contemptuously Mr. N. —on treats it. It follows from what he says that this method did not have the slightest grain of science in it, but was only furnished with a sort of cloak that "lent it the mere tinge of a 'scientific' exterior." Excellent, Mr. N. —on! But what will your "protector," Mr. Mikhailovsky, say of you?

Generally speaking, Mr. N. —on deals very discourteously with his subjectivist "protectors." His article, "Apologia of the Power of Money as the Sign of the Times," bears the epigraph: L'ignorance est moins éloignée de la vérité que la préjugé. (Ignorance is less far from the truth than prejudice.—*Ed.*) The Truth is undoubtedly Mr. N. —on himself. He says as much: "If anybody should really follow the subjective method of investigation unswervingly, one may be quite certain that he would arrive at conclusions akin to, if not identical with, those we have arrived at." (*Russkoye Bogatstvo,* March, p. 54.) Prejudice is of course Mr. Struve, against whom Truth directs the sting of its "analysis." And who is Ignorance, which is nearer to Truth (i.e., Mr. N. —on) than Prejudice, i.e., Mr. Struve? Ignorance, evidently, is Mr. N. —on's present subjectivist allies. Excellent, Mr. N. —on! You have hit the weak spot of your allies to a nicety. But again, what will Mr. Mikhailovsky say of you? He will surely recall the moral of the well-known fable:

> *Though help in time of need we highly prize,*
> *Not everyone knows how to give it....*

But enough of argument! We think we have left none of our opponents' objections unanswered. And if we have by chance lost sight of any of them, we shall certainly have plenty of occasion to return to the dispute. So we may lay down the pen. But before parting with it, we should like to say another word or two to our opponents.

Now you, sirs, are always "exerting yourselves" to do away with capitalism. But just see what comes of it: capitalism goes sweetly on and does not even notice your "exertions," while you, with your "ideals" and your splendid intentions, keep marking time in one spot. And to what purpose? Neither you benefit, nor anyone else! What can be the reason? The reason is that you are Utopians, you nourish *utopian* plans of social reform and fail to see those direct and urgent tasks which, excuse the expression, lie under your very noses. Ponder well on it. Then, perhaps, you will say yourselves that we are right. However, on this subject we shall talk to you on another occasion. Meanwhile—Dominus vobiscum.

NOTES

¹ *N. K. Mikhailovsky* (1842-1904)—Russian publicist, one of the principal theoreticians of Liberal Narodism, subjective sociologist.
p. 5

² *Russkoye Bogatstvo*—monthly magazine published from 1876 to 1918. Organ of Liberal Narodniks in the 90s. It waged a bitter struggle against Marxism. N. K. Mikhailovsky was one of its editors.
p. 5

³ *Kudrin*—pseudonym of N. S. Rusanov, Russian publicist, opponent of Marxism.
p. 10

⁴ *V. V.*—pseudonym of V. P. Vorontsov (1847-1918) one of the principal theoreticians of Liberal Narodism.
p. 20

⁵ The reference is to *N. G. Chernyshevsky* (1828-89), great revolutionary democrat, scientist and writer, who headed the revolutionary and democratic movement of the 60s. He was born into the family of a clergyman residing in Saratov. In 1850 Chernyshevsky graduated from St. Petersburg University. From 1854 to 1862 he was one of the editors of *Sovremennik* (see note 8). In 1862 he was arrested and sentenced to exile in Siberia, where he spent over eighteen years. Chernyshevsky's scientific and literary work was many-sided: he dealt with problems of philosophy, sociology, political economy, ethics, aesthetics and education. Chernyshevsky's novel *What Is To Be Done?* which expressed his idea of a real revolutionary, had a tremendous influence on generations of Russian revolutionaries. Marx spoke of Chernyshevsky as a great Russian scholar and critic who masterly exposed the bankruptcy of bourgeois political economy.

A theorist of revolutionary democracy, Chernyshevsky was at the same time a brilliant leader of the popular masses in the struggle against autocracy and serfdom.

Chernyshevsky translated into Russian Mill's *Principles of Political Economy* and provided the translation with comprehensive comments. p. 48

⁶ *N. I. Sieber* (1844-88)—Russian economist. He was among the first Russian writers who popularized the economic theories of Marx and opposed his critics, Y. Zhukovsky in particular. p. 60

⁷ *Y. G. Zhukovsky* (1822-1907)—Russian bourgeois economist, author of the pseudoscientific and slanderous article "Karl Marx and His Book on Capital" in which he attempted to disprove the economic theory of Marx. The article gave rise to a lively discussion on Marx's *Capital*, Vol. I. Mikhailovsky's "Karl Marx Before the Judgement of Mr. Zhukovsky" appeared in this connection. p. 61

⁸ *Sovremennik*—a political and literary monthly, founded by A. S. Pushkin. It was published in St. Petersburg from 1836 to 1866. From 1847 it came out under the editorship of N. A. Nekrasov and I. I. Panayev. Among the contributors to the magazine were the outstanding figures of Russian revolutionary democracy V. G. Belinsky, N. G. Chernyshevsky, N. A. Dobrolyubov and M. E. Saltykov-Shchedrin. *Sovremennik* was the most progressive magazine of its time, the mouthpiece of Russian revolutionary democrats. It was suppressed by the tsarist government in 1866. p. 61

⁹ *N. I. Kareyev*—Russian bourgeois historian and publicist. Polemized with Marxists as a "subjective sociologist." p. 64

¹⁰ This is a slightly changed phrase from the Manifesto issued by Nicholas I in 1848 in connection with the revolutions in Vienna, Paris and Berlin. The original phrase read: "Hear, O tongues and be stilled, since the Lord Himself is with us." The Manifesto was intended to restrain the liberal elements of Russian society and to intimidate revolutionary Europe. p. 64

¹¹ *Shchedrin*—pen-name of M. E. Saltykov (1829-89), great Russian satirist and revolutionary democrat. The words of a "Moscow historian" freely rendered by G. V. Plekhanov (Shchedrin mentions Mstislav and Rostislav) are borrowed from Shchedrin's "Modern Idyll" which describes the feuds of Russian dukes in the twelfth and thirteenth centuries. p. 66

¹² *Kostanjoglo*—character from Gogol's *Dead Souls*, incarnation of a model businessman who makes "every piece of rubbish pay"

and tries to adapt new, capitalist methods of economy to a patriarchal and feudal form of economy. p. 69

[13] Land village communities are implied here. p. 74

[14] *N. —on*—pseudonym of N. F. Danielson (1844-1918), Russian economist, ideologist of Liberal Narodism. He was the first to translate Marx's *Capital* into Russian. p. 76

[15] The reference is to the founders of scientific socialism, K. Marx and F. Engels. p. 76

[16] *N. Nozhin* (1843-66)—Russian publicist and biologist, advocate of subjective sociology. p. 85

[17] *Russkaya Mysl*—a monthly of a Liberal and Narodnik trend. Started publication in 1880. p. 85

[18] A line from the unfinished poem *Ilya Muromets* by N. M. Karamzin (1786-1826). p. 88

[19] Evidently Plekhanov has in mind the following passage from Goethe's *Poetry and Truth:* "We did not understand how such a book (*System de la Nature.—Tr.*) could be dangerous; it seemed to us so gloomy, so Cimmerian, so deathlike, that we found it difficult to endure its presence..." (Part III, Book XI). p. 92

[20] *Karonin*—pseudonym of the Narodnik author *N. E. Petropavlovsky* (1857-92). p. 100

[21] *V. G. Belinsky*—great Russian revolutionary democrat and literary critic. Belinsky jokingly called Hegel Yegor Fedorovich. p. 112

[22] Somewhat changed words of a character from A. G. Griboyedov's *Wit Works Woe*. p. 117

[23] Plekhanov has in mind the following passage from Hegel's *Philosophy of History:* "When philosophy begins to paint in grey colours on the grey background of reality its youth cannot be restored, it can only be cognized; Minerva's owl flies only at night." p. 126

[24] At one time Mikhailovsky contributed to *Otechestvenniye Zapiski* of which magazine Shchedrin was an editor (from 1868 to 1884). p. 141

[25] Plekhanov has in view P. L. Lavrov (1823-1900), Russian publicist and Narodnik theorist, founder of the "subjective school" in sociology. His *Historical Letters* produced a strong influence

upon Russian intellectuals of the 70s. Lavrov believed that the "critically thinking personalities" were the motive forces of history. p. 148

[26] *Suzdal*—from Suzdal locality in Russia where icon painting was widespread. Icon prints produced in Suzdal in great quantities were cheap and inartistic. Hence, the adjective *Suzdal* has come to denote something that is cheap and inartistic. p. 151

[27] *G. I. Uspensky* (1843-1902)—famous Russian writer. In his sketches of Russian life (in particular in "Ruin" mentioned by Plekhanov) he vividly described the process of decline of feudalism and growth of capitalism in the Russian countryside. p. 152

[28] *Vestnik Yevropy*—historical and political monthly of a Liberal trend, published in St. Petersburg from 1866 to 1918. It opposed Marxism since the early 90s of the last century. p. 167

[29] *L. I. Mechnikov*—Russian geographer and sociologist. Brother of I. I. Mechnikov, a well-known biologist. p. 199

[30] In the 18th-century Russia, to pronounce "word and deed" meant to accuse one of high treason and immediately take him into custody. p. 204

[31] *Prince Meshchersky*—reactionary publicist and writer, extreme monarchist. p. 242

[32] See note 25. p. 244

[33] The quoted words are from Nekrasov's "Knight for an Hour." The relevant passage reads:

> *From the jubilant crowd of idlers*
> *Whose hands are stained with blood*
> *Lead me on to the camp of fighters*
> *For the great cause of love.* p. 247

[34] See note 19. p. 248

[35] *Chatsky* and *Famusov*—characters in Griboyedov's comedy *Wit Works Woe*. *Chatsky* personifies the progressive section of the Russian noble youth in the first quarter of the nineteenth century. He is a man of lofty ideals and advanced views. *Famusov* is a domineering obscurantist and hypocrite. p. 249

[36] *Skalozub*—in Griboyedov's *Wit Works Woe*, ignorant and presumptuous officer, opponent of free thinking. p. 249

³⁷ The reference is to *The Communist Manifesto* by K. Marx and F. Engels. p. 251

³⁸ This refers to K. Marx's letter to the editor of *Otechestvenniye Zapiski* written at the end of 1877 in reply to Mikhailovsky's article "Karl Marx Before the Judgement of Mr. Zhukovsky" (see note 7). Marx had not sent this letter. It was found by F. Engels after Marx's death and forwarded to Russia. The letter is discussed on pages 294-301 of this edition. p. 252

³⁹ From the Russian soldiers' song which derided Russian incapable generals (General Réad among them) during the Crimean War (1853-56). The author of the song is Lev Tolstoi, then an officer in the field. p. 260

⁴⁰ The man earned his living by letting violin strings to travelling fiddlers. "I can breathe only with the string"—he used to say.
p. 264

⁴¹ The quoted words are taken from Pushkin's draft copy of one of the chapters in *Eugene Onegin*. p. 267

⁴² From I. A. Krylov's fable "Tom-tit." p. 271

⁴³ Another character in Griboyedov's *Wit Works Woe*, a careerist and toady. p. 275

⁴⁴ *N. A. Polevoi* (1796-1846)—Russian publicist, critic and historian. p. 286

⁴⁵ *Kolupayevs and Razuvayevs*—names symbolizing the Russian capitalist sharks, heroes of the "primitive accumulation," portrayed by Saltykov-Shchedrin in his sketch of provincial life, "My Refuge Mon Repos." p. 290

⁴⁶ *Molchalinism*—from Molchalin (see note 43) synonymous of servility and adaptability. p. 293

⁴⁷ *S. N. Krivenko* (1847-1907)—publicist. He was one of the first Narodniks to come out against Marxism in the legal press.
p. 294

⁴⁸ *P. B. Struve* (1870-1944)—prominent exponent of "Legal Marxism"—a Liberal-bourgeois trend that appeared in the 90s and was, in fact, a distortion of Marxism. Struve finished up as a monarchist and whiteguard émigré.

"Legal Marxists"—they were called "Legal Marxists" because they published their articles in legal periodicals, i.e., periodicals licensed by the tsarist government—had their own methods of fighting against the Narodniks, seeking to subjugate the working-class movement to the interest of the bourgeoisie. At one time Marxists entered into an alliance with "Legal Marxists" in combating the Narodniks. p. 294

[49] Plekhanov does not quote the exact words of K. Marx. Below we give the French original and the exact translation of this passage:

"Si la Russie tend à devenir une nation capitaliste, à l'instar, des nations de l'Europe occidentale—et pendant les dernières années elle s'est donnée beaucoup de mal dans ce sens—elle n'y réussira pas sans avoir préalablement transformé une bonne partie de ses paysans en prolétaires; et après cela, une fois amenée au giron du régime capitaliste, elle en subira les lois impitoyables, comme d'autres peuples profanes. Voilà tout." Karl Marx, Friedrich Engels. *Ausgewählte Briefe.* Berlin 1953.

"If Russia is tending to become a capitalist nation after the example of the West-European countries—and during the last few years she has been taking a lot of trouble in this direction—she will not succeed without having first transformed a good part of her peasants into proletarians; and after that, once taken to the bosom of the capitalist regime, she will experience its pitiless laws like other profane peoples. That is all." K. Marx and F. Engels, *Selected Correspondence,* Moscow 1955, p. 379. p. 302

[50] See note 26. p. 309

[51] The reference is to G. I. Uspensky's story "Nothing." The hero of the story breaks up with his village community and abandons the plot of land allotted to him because of the inordinate taxation. He prefers to pay the pall tax, i.e., to "pay for nothing." Uspensky's story exemplifies the process of Russian peasants fleeing from the village community. p. 310

[52] *P. Y. Chaadayev* (1794-1856)—Russian idealist philosopher. He became known in 1836 when he published his *Philosophical Letter*—a sharp criticism of the backward and stagnant system of serfdom in Russia. He hoped that the West, in particular Catholicism, would help to destroy serfdom and ensure progress.

p. 310

[53] *S. N. Yuzhakov* (1849-1910)—publicist, ideologist of Liberal Narodism. p. 310

[54] A character in Tolstoi's *War and Peace.* p. 311

[55] *Moskovskiye Vedomosti*—a reactionary and monarchist newspaper published in Moscow from 1756 to 1918 (except the years from 1779 to 1789 when it was produced by N. I. Novikov, a progressive publisher). p. 311

[56] *List, Friedrich* (1789-1846)—German bourgeois economist, advocate of protective tariffs. p. 312

[57] Danielson's book *Sketches of Our Social Economy Since the Reform* appeared in 1893. It expounded the economic views of the Narodniks. p. 322

[58] This refers to V. G. Belinsky's letter to V. P. Botkin (March 1, 1841), in which letter Belinsky broke with the philosophical system of Hegel (see also note 21). p. 332

[59] See note 48. Struve's *Critical Remarks on the Question of the Economic Development of Russia* was the object of profound criticism by Vladimir Ilyich Lenin in his *Economic Content of Narodism and Its Criticism in Mr. Struve's Book* published in 1894. Lenin exposed the Liberal views of Struve and advanced the viewpoint of the revolutionary Marxism. Struve's call "to go into training to capitalism" was defined by Lenin as a purely bourgeois slogan. p. 337

[60] The heavenly bird Sirin—an image of a mythical heavenly bird with woman's face and breast used in old Russian manuscripts and legends. p. 338

[61] Plekhanov's article "A Few Words to Our Opponents" was published in 1895 under the signature of Utis in the symposium *Materials Characterizing Our Economic Development*, which was arrested and committed to flame. Later on, the article was appended to the third edition of *The Development of the Monist View of History*, which came out in 1906. p. 339

[62] *A. K. Tolstoi* (1817-75)—Russian poet and playwright. The poem in question is entitled *Potok-Bogatyr*. p. 342

[63] Excerpt from Pushkin's epigram on M. T. Kachenovsky, critic and historian. p. 343

[64] *N. I. Grech* (1787-1867) and *F. V. Bulgarin* (1789-1859) —reactionary journalists and writers, secret police agents. Their names symbolized political corruption and dishonesty. p. 345

[65] *M. P. Pogodin* (1800-1875)—a reactionary historian and publicist, apologist of autocracy. p. 349

[66] *Lyapkin-Tyapkin*—a personage in Gogol's *Inspector General*.
p. 350

[67] *N. A. Dobrolyubov* (1836-61)—revolutionary democrat, prominent critic and publicist, close associate of Chernyshevsky. In 1859-61 Dobrolyubov supplied the copy and edited the satirical supplement to *Sovremennik* (See note 8) entitled *The Whistle*. *The Whistle* scathingly ridiculed the Liberals' complacency and inactiveness. It was extremely popular with the democratically-minded intellectuals and aroused hatred and fury among the conservative people who called its editorial workers "Whistlers." p. 350

[68] *K. D. Kavelin* (1818-85)—liberal publicist, scientist and public figure; advocate of subjective idealism. p. 370

NAME INDEX

A

Aeschylus—219
Archimedes—164, 166
Archytas—164
Aristotle—102, 213, 269
Arnaud F.—42

B

Bacon F.—123
Balzac H. De—265
Barth P.—200-03, 207
Bastiat F.—213
Bauer Bruno—144, 147-50, 244, 247, 267, 334
Bauer Edgar—144-48
Bazard A.—33, 34, 39
Belinsky V.—111, 332, 333, 337, 344, 389, 390, 394
Beltov N. (Plekhanov)—10, 344-51, 353, 355-61, 363-66, 369-75, 380-85
Berkeley G.—14
Blanc L.—359-61
Blos W.—262
Bluntschli J.-K.—371
Börne K.-L.—341
Borodin—379
Botkin V.—394
Bourbon—75

Brandes G.—237
Brunetière F.—222, 223, 230, 231, 236, 239
Büchner Georg—80, 194, 195, 275
Büchner Ludwig—13
Buhl L.—316-23
Bulgarin F.—345, 346, 395

C

Cabet E.—46
Caesar Gaius Julius—272
Cato the Censor—186
Cerda, de la—342
Chateaubriand F. R.—238
Chaadayev P.—310, 393
Chernyshevsky—61, 104, 105, 240, 243, 287, 388, 389, 395
Comte Aug.—83, 84
Condorcet G.-A.—41, 43, 47
Considérant V.—46, 47
Copernicus N.—193, 194, 243, 244
Corroyer E.—239
Cousin V.—286

D

D'Alembert J. R.—322, 323
Dahlmann F. Chr.—244
Darwin Ch.—109, 152, 154, 158,

168, 193, 250, 253, 254-58, 269, 274, 275
Descartes R.—15, 102, 124
Dementyev—376-78
Diderot D.—124, 238
Dobrolyubov N.—350, 375, 389, 395
Dumas A.—230
Dühring E.—114, 341, 351, 361

E

Edison Th. A.—164
Enfantin B. P.—53, 57-60, 365
Engels F.—7, 76, 109, 112, 114-15, 118, 119, 122, 150, 151, 153, 156, 167, 168, 170-73, 190, 196, 216, 244, 258, 263, 267-69, 276, 288-90, 292-93, 298, 314, 315, 330, 341, 351-54, 358, 361, 363, 365, 390, 392, 393
Eudoxus—164
Euripides—219

F

Feuerbach L.—144, 248, 335, 385
Fichte J.-G.—100, 102, 142, 143
Filippov—140, 141
Flint R.—51
Fourier F. M. Ch.—46, 47, 69, 70, 73, 77, 78
Fox Ch. J.—32
Franklin B.—154
Frazer P.—141, 142
Fustel de Coulanges N. D.—261

G

Galvani L.—142
Geiger L.—162, 163
Gervinus G. G.—244
Giraud-Teulon—171, 173, 261

Godwin W.—48
Goethe J. W.—55, 92, 93, 229, 248, 276, 277, 390
Gogol N.—69, 345, 389, 395
Gorsse H.—47
Grech—345, 346, 395
Griboyedov—390-92
Grimm F. M.—20, 42
Grün K.—315
Guibert—208, 209
Guizot F.—29-31, 34-37, 40, 49, 198, 359, 360
Gumplowicz L.—213
Guyau J. M.—239

H

Haeckel E.—111, 254, 258, 374
Harvey W.—96
Hegel G. W. F.—21, 28, 45, 55, 92, 94, 96, 99, 100, 101, 102-03, 105-07, 109-13, 116-19, 122-23, 126, 128, 135, 136, 139-44, 149, 150, 153, 159, 180, 190, 192, 199, 204, 228, 238, 242, 250, 279, 285, 328, 331-35, 347-49, 351-55, 361-65, 367, 368, 390, 394
Heinzen K. P.—288-91, 294, 304, 311, 316, 325
Heliogabalus—22
Helvetius C. A.—15, 17, 20, 25, 40, 45, 48, 71, 81, 90, 91, 158, 214, 215, 226, 248, 276, 365
Heraclitus—141
Hess M.—80, 315
Hobbes Th.—202
Holbach P. H.—14, 15, 20, 23, 41, 81, 227, 248, 276, 329, 330
Hubbard N. G.—51
Hugo V.—230
Hume D.—227, 228, 242, 243, 370
Huxley Th.—370

NAME INDEX

I

Ibsen Henrik—265
Inama-Sternegg—200, 201

K

Kachenovsky M.—394
Kant I.—16, 21, 102-03, 125, 215, 216, 228, 364, 367
Karamzin N.—390
Kareyev N.—64, 65, 66, 167, 170, 173, 174, 177, 188, 193, 197, 198, 200, 202-10, 247, 257, 262, 310, 331, 346, 389
Karonin (Petropavlovsky N.)— 100, 390
Kautsky K.—263
Kavelin K.—370, 395
Kharizomenov S.—379
Kovalevsky M.—180, 181, 183, 185, 190, 196
Krivenko S.—294, 295, 304-07, 310, 323-25, 327, 337, 338, 392
Kudrin N.—10, 388
Krylov I.—392

L

Lamarck J.-B.—217, 274
La Mothe le Vayer, F., de—25
Lange F.-A.—45, 368
Laplace P.-S.—330
Lassalle F.—101, 102, 105, 173
Lavrov P.—391
Leibniz G.-W.—128-31
Lenin V.—6, 7, 8, 394
Lenormant F.—199
Lermina—181
Lewes G.—110, 250, 332, 333
Titus Livy—269
Lilienfeld—371

Lippert T.—172
List F.—312, 314, 394
Littre M.-P.-E.—51
Locke J.—15, 19, 40, 91, 123, 202, 226, 227
Louis-Philippe—69, 237
Louis XIV—220
Titus Lucretius Carus—132
Lyelle Ch.—95

M

Malthus, Thomas Robert—48, 57-60
Martius K. F. Ph., von—159, 184
Marx K.—6, 7, 61, 62, 99, 122, 139, 144, 148, 150-54, 156, 160, 161, 173, 190-96, 199-203, 205, 206, 207, 210, 212, 215-16, 218-19, 221, 222, 225, 237, 243, 269, 271, 272, 274-76, 278, 280-90, 292-302, 304, 306, 311, 312, 314, 321, 323-26, 334, 335, 341, 346, 358-60, 365, 368, 369, 371, 374-75, 378, 382, 383, 385, 388-90, 392, 393
McLennan J. F.—171-72
Mechnikov I.—199, 329, 391
Meshchersky V.—242, 366, 391
Mignet F. A.—31, 32, 33, 34, 40, 49, 359
Mikhailovsky N.—8, 9, 13, 61-62, 71, 72, 77, 85-87, 95, 99, 100, 105-06, 109-12, 114-18, 120, 121, 122, 124, 125, 140-43, 146, 167, 170, 189, 190, 193, 195, 242, 244, 247, 252-57, 259-70, 281-88, 290, 295-99, 304, 310, 325, 328, 330-37, 341-44, 346, 349-71, 373-75, 382, 383, 386, 388, 390, 392
Mill J. S.—48, 61, 62, 212, 243, 286, 365

Mokievsky P.—384
Moleschott J.—13
Molière—163
Montesquieu Ch.-L.—23, 48, 272, 273, 329
Morgan L. H.—167, 172, 199, 267, 269

N

Nekrasov N.—72, 310, 389, 391
Newton I.—109
Nicholas I.—389
Nikolai —on /N. —on; Danielson N./—76-78, 320, 323, 325, 326, 376, 378-86, 390, 394
Novikov N.—394
Nozhin N.—85-87, 374, 390

O

Offenbach J.—115
Opitz Th.—247
Ovid Publius, Naso—343
Owen R.—46, 47

P

Panayev I.—389
Pecchio—212
Peschel O.—184, 189, 190, 206, 261, 365
Plato—116, 165, 212
Plautus—371
Playfair J.—95
Plutarch—10, 164-66, 212
Pogodin M.—350, 395
Polevoi N.—286, 392
Polybius—269
Post Alb.-Herm—187, 188
Postnikov V.—379

Proudhon P.-J.—52, 299
Prugavin V.—77
Puchta G. F.—176, 177, 179, 183
Pushkin A.—343, 345, 355, 389, 392, 394

Q

Quinault Ph.—230

R

Racine J.—225, 230
Ratzel F.—159-61
Raynal G.—121
Reclus Elisee—199, 329
Ricardo D.—57-60, 62, 213
Rink H.—178, 179, 185
Rodbertus K. J.—78, 186
Rothschild—94
Rousseau J.-J.—23, 117-22, 124, 202

S

Saint-Simon C. H.—39, 46, 47-54, 67, 68, 74, 75, 82, 231, 232, 299, 372, 383
Savigny F. C., von—175-76, 178
Say J. B.—57, 67, 127, 243
Schelling F.—125, 128, 133, 139, 141, 142, 166, 180, 183, 190, 192, 365, 367
Schlosser Friedrich—244
Sechenov I.—369, 370
Shakespeare W.—94
Sieber—60, 99, 181, 279-81, 350-55, 357, 389
Shchedrin—66, 100, 141, 205, 389, 392
Sismondi J. Ch. L.—26-27, 29
Skvortsov A.—378

NAME INDEX

Smith A.—59, 61, 213
Socrates—334
Sophocles—219
Spartacus—166
Spasovich V.—99, 110
Spencer H.—82, 109, 172, 371-73
Spinoza B.—124, 128, 198
Steinen K.-von den—9
Stronin A.—371
Struve P.—294, 328, 335-38, 344-46, 375, 378, 380, 386, 392, 394
Suard J. B. A.—18, 19
Szeliga—244, 267

T

Taine H.—219, 221
Thierry Aug.—31, 32, 34, 37-39, 49, 359
Thucydides—269
Tolstoi A. K.—341, 342, 343, 394
Tolstoi L. N.—311, 342, 392, 394

U

Überweg Fr.; Heintze Max—348
Uspensky G.—152, 264, 310, 331, 357, 391, 393

V

Vanderbilt—94
van-der-Hoeven—86
Van Tieghem—116, 117
Vico G. B.—28, 30, 212
Virchow R.—258
Vollgraf—321-23
Volta A.—142
Voltaire F. M.—20, 28, 122, 124, 230, 238, 273
V. V. (Vorontsov V.)—20, 21, 62-65, 105, 180, 198, 203, 294, 379-81, 385, 388

W

Weisengrün P.—167, 170
Wilson—154

X

Xenophon—213, 243, 269

Y

Yuzhakov S.—310, 394

Z

Zhukovsky Y.—61, 122, 279-85, 296, 297, 323, 389, 392

INDEX*

Allgemeine Volksblatt (1845), proposals for saving Germany from capitalism, 315-16
Arnaud, Abbé, art of speech determined by social needs, 42
Art connected with conditions of its age, 219-21

BARTH, P., essay on Hegelian philosophy of history, 200-01
on Rousseau, 202
Bauer, E. and B., their revolt against Hegel's "Absolute Idea," 145-47
theory of "critical spirit" and "mass," 147-48
exposed by Marx and Engels, 148-51
their followers' views on objectivity in history, 244
Bazard, St. A., on relationship between classes and revolutions, 33-34
criticism of Thierry, 39
Berkeley, Bishop, a monist, 14
Biological analogies arise in sociology through starting

* Compiled by Andrew Rothstein.

from "human nature," 81-82
Brunetière, F., influence of environment, 222
contradiction as a motive in literary development, 230-31
Büchner, G., his despair at "fatalism of history," 194-95
Buhl, L., suggestions in 1845 for eliminating capitalism from Germany, 316-19

CABET, E., on influence of education, 46
"Capital," accepting its definition of value implies admitting Marx's historical theory, 251-52
began study of real history of mankind, 256
its fate in German universities, 258
Capitalism, impossibility of arresting its development in Germany, 292
its consequences in Russia, 301-02
impotence of subjectivist ideals to arrest its development, 302-03
insufficient development in Germany in 1840's, 312

INDEX

Chernyshevsky, N. G., utopian views on economic questions, 62

Chernyshevsky, N. G., exposition of Hegel's principles, 102-04
his illustrations of principle that "truth is concrete," 104-105
mistaken use of the "triad," 106-07
material basis of aesthetic standards, 240-41

Classes, their struggle gives rise to political theories, 214
their psychology, 217-218
in ancient Greece and Rome, 269

Comte, A., his theory of "social physics," 83-84

Condorcet, M.J.A. de, on origin of ideas, 41

Contradiction, the motive force of progress, 21-22
in development of monetary theory, 231-32
in French philosophy, 232
in ideology of English and French Revolutions, 233-34
influence on ideas in class society, 239
leads to objective truth, 242-43

Coulanges, F. de, confirms Marx in spite of himself, 261-62

DARWIN, CHARLES, on animals' use of embryonic tools, 154, 168-69
man dependent on his hands, 158

Dialectical materialism solves the problem of influence of environment, 273-74
eliminates fatalism inherent in metaphysical materialism, 275
the only accurate description of Marx's philosophy, 276
the philosophy of action, 276
strives for elimination of classes, 279
doesn't point a way inevitable for all nations at all times, 297-98
its advance from materialism of Montesquieu and Holbach, 329-30

Dialectics studies phenomena in their development, 92
the principle of life, 92-93
illustrations, 93-94
cannot rely on abstract conclusions from abstract principles, 101
Chernyshevsky's definition of its distinguishing feature, 107
in thought, according to Engels, 122-24

Dualism almost always existed, 14

ECONOMICS, definition of, 300

Enfantin, B. P., importance of his economic works in history of Socialist thought, 57
used subjective method in political economy, 58-59
on Malthus, 59-60

Engels, F., on negation of negation, 114
on dialectical thinking, 122-24
on "critical history," 150-51

Environment, influence on man,

according to eighteenth-century French materialists, 16-18
their view of its origin, 19
its interaction with opinion, 23-25
depends on human nature, according to nineteenth-century Utopian Socialists, 45-46
geographical, its influence on human development, 158-61
social, determined by productive forces, 222-23
influence of historical environment upon societies, 224-25
dispute of Montesquieu and Voltaire, 272-73
Eskimos, their forms of property, 178-79, 182-83
Evolution, French materialists unable to explain it in human or social life, 89-92
regarded by metaphysicians as growth or quantitative change, 95-96
leaps no less essential a part of it, according to Hegel, 96-97
illustrations in physics and chemistry, 97-98
Haeckel on various branches of its history, 253-54

Family, its history, 169-170
Fatalism arises in history through regarding progress as due to successes of knowledge, 54-55
outcome of idealist philosophy, 132
Fourier, F.M.C., based his proposals on analysis of human passions, 46
his efforts to enlist support of all classes, 69-70
Fox, Charles James, on Whigs' view of popery, 32
French materialists followed Locke, 15
fearless sensationalists, 15-16
considered man's notions the result of his social environment, 16-17, 24-25
their fundamental contradiction, 24
on legislation, 27-28
unable to explain questions of evolution, 89-91
French tragedy linked with monarchy of Louis XIV, 220-21

Geiger, L., tools discovered by accident, 162-63
Genius, a, his rôle in ideology, 239-41
Geographical environment, influence on man's development, 158-59
influence on social development, 160-61
German idealists regarded phenomena from standpoint of their evolution, 95-97
weak side of their philosophy, 144-45
Germany, conditions of workers and peasants in the 1840's, 312-14
Giraud-Teulon on formation of primitive family, 171
Goethe on materialism, 92
on dialectics, 93

on things becoming their opposite, 229
on action preceding reason, 276
Gothic architecture, its connection with feudalism, 219-20
Greek tragedy, its connection with the city States, 219
Grimm, F. M. von, on history of literature, 42
Guizot, F.P.G., society the basis of political institutions, 29-30
property relations and class struggles in the English Revolution, 30-31
property relations after the fall of the Roman Empire, 35-36
an eclectic, 37
Gumplowicz, L., origin of public law in class struggles, 213-14

HAECKEL, E., on interdependence of all branches of history of evolution, 253-54
Hegel, G.F.W., on contradiction as motive force of progress, 21-22
opposed dialectics to metaphysics, 92
on leaps in evolution, 96-97
didn't depend on "triad," 98-101
Lassalle's view of his philosophy, 101-02
influence on German thought, 110-11
his theory of the "Idea" of each people, 136-37
expressed materialist views on historical questions, 139-40
Edgar Bauer's revolt against his theory, 145
his explanation of development of German philosophy, 228-29
his cult of the individual, 333-34
Heinzen, K., his utopian attacks on Marx and Engels in 1848, 288-91
Helvetius, C. A., man as fruit of his environment, 17-18
on opinion, 20
on perfect system of laws, 45
relied upon accident for mankind's future happiness, 71
on evolution, 90
on mankind's ideals, 214-15
Holbach, P.H.T. d', a monist, 14
his *Politique naturelle*, 23
attempt to explain the development of knowledge, 25
view of human nature presupposed existence of bourgeois society, 41-42
condemnation of capitalism in England, 81
showed Hume his first atheists, 227-228
Human nature as explanation of "knotty cases," 37, 39-42
Suard on, 43-44
Utopian Socialists on, 46, 54-55, 91
bearing upon economic problems, 57
Hume, D., differed from his French fellow-thinkers in attitude of religion, 227-28
his revolt against the Mercantilists, 231

IDEALISM DEFINED, 13-14
  its brilliant revival in the nineteenth century, 89
  leads to fatalism, 132
  and materialism, 275-77
  the subjective method its *reductio ad absurdum,* 244-45
Inama-Sternegg, K.T. von, interaction between politics and economics in the Carolingian period, 200-01
Individual, dialectical materialists "idealistic" in their attitude to him, 277
Innate ideas, Locke on, 15
Interaction as explanation of social life, 23-24
  as reply to Marx, 200-04

KAREYEV, N. I., his exposition of "subjective" view of history, 65-66
  its dualist nature, 67
  on Engels, 167-68
  on German historical school of law, 173-74
  on relations of body and soul, 198, 207-10
  on interaction between politics and economics, 201
Kovalevsky, M. M., on individual and social appropriation in primitive society, 180-83
Krivenko, S. N., what Marxists should do if capitalism inevitable in Russia, 294-95
  alleged desire of Marxists to see horrors of capitalism, 304-09

LAMARCK, J. B., influence of environment on animals, 217
La Mothe Le Vayer on enlightenment, 25
Law in social development, 53-55
  conformity to, in Nature, 126-28
  examples of this given by Leibniz and Spinoza, 128-29
  origin of, according to idealist historians, 173-80
  difference between general and particular, 235-38
Literature of one country, its influence on that of another depends on their respective social relations, 225-27
Locke, John, opinions determined by interests, 19

MACLENNAN, J. F., on primitive infanticide, 172
Man, his evolution the study first of naturalist then of historian, 169-70
Manners and constitutions, French materialists on, 22-24
  Sismondi on, 27
Marx, K., criticism of Hegel's speculative philosophy, 137-39, 148-49
  on Bruno Bauer, 149-50
  caricatures of his theory of history, 152, 215
  short statement of his views on the State, 153
  on man's relationship with Nature, 153-54
  on men's relations in production, 156-57, 190

geographical factors spur on man's economic efforts, 160-61

on causes of social revolution, 196

importance of political institutions in economic development, 201-02

on relationship between social relations and ideological superstructure, 216-19

his theory the most idealistic of all, 246-47

on chief defect of earlier materialism, 248

his investigation begins where Darwin's ends, 274-75

his letter on Mikhailovsky, 296-301

views on the consequences of Russia's becoming capitalist, 302

Martius, C. F. von, primitive society in Brazil, 159, 184

Mignet, F. A., class struggles the mainspring of political events, 32-33

thought landownership depended on conquest, 40

Mikhailovsky, N. K., his tributes to Zhukovsky and Chernyshevsky, 61

utopian views on economics, 61-62

utopian proposals for industrial development of Russia, 71-72

on "physiology of society," 85-86

Mikhailovsky, N. K., his "formula of progress" states how history *ought* to have advanced, 87

on Hegel's "triad," 99

on Hegel and later evolutionary theory, 109-11

on Rousseau, 118-19

galvanism the basis of Hegel's theory, 141-42

capitalism the basis of metaphysics, 142-43

comparison of Marx and Darwin, 254-58

on Marx's "Capital," 258-59

on class struggles in antiquity, 268-69

on necessity, 269-70

views in 1877 and in 1894 on alleged formalism of Marx, 282-86

on "economic materialism," 328

on Hegel's "contempt" for the individual, 333-34

Mill, J. S., origin of political economy in practice, 212-13

Monism defined, 14-15

NARODNIKS, the utopians of the end of the nineteenth century, 71

their illusions about the Peasant Bank, 73-74

Necessity, consciousness of, the basis of freedom, 130-35, 194-95

in gradual conquest by man, 271-75

Negation in Nature, according to Mikhailovsky, 112-13

in Nature, according to Engels, 114

according to van Tieghem, 116

Nikolai—on (N. F. Danielson), lament that "society" did

not prevent development of capitalism in Russia, 75-76
a full-blooded Utopian, 78
attempted to terrify Russian society with the example of Western Europe, 78
Similarity of his views and those of German Utopians in 1845, 320-23

OPINIONS, French materialists' views on, 19-20, 28-29
Suard on, 19
and environment, 21-22
Oppositeness in dialectical process, 108-109, 293
Owen, R., on human nature as basis of rational government, 46

PECCHIO, G., origin of political economy in experience, 212
Peschel, O., means of procuring food determined forms of early society, 189-90
Philosophy, its varying subjects of study, from age to age, 125
its successes in Germany, their causes, 228-29
Plutarch, his apology for Archimedes' inventions, 164
on origin of mechanics, 164-65
Productive forces, influence of their development on man's social relations, 156-57, 189-91
come into conflict with property relations, 196
condition external as well as internal relations of society, 199-200
Property, relations of, their influence on history, 30-35
origin of property relations, according to Guizot, Thierry and Mignet, 35-40
their rôle admitted by Hegel, 139-40
influence of, on development of the family, 171-73
origin of, according to Kovalevsky, 180-82, 185
of primitive hunter in his weapons, 184
Proudhon, P. J., borrowed ideas on rôle of authority from Saint-Simon, 52
Prugavin, V. S., an example of utopian economic views of the Narodniks, 77
Psychology of society, changed with its economy, 205-07, 210-11
of classes, requires an artist to describe, 265
Puchta, G. F., on origin of law, 176-77

RATZEL, F., rôle of the sea in history, 159
rôle of sources of energy in history, 161
Religion, its different rôles in France, Germany and England in the eighteenth century, 227-28
Revolution, French, effect of on historians, 29
Rink, H. J., on property relations of the Eskimo, 178-79
Rousseau, J. J., connection be-

tween moral retrogression and intellectual progress, 120-22

SAINT-SIMON, C. H. de, inconsistent views on history, 39, 49-53
views of his followers on human nature, 46-47
seeks conformity to law in man's history, 48-49, 52-53
production the object of social organization, 49-50
on diminution of principle of authority in social life, 51-52
Saint-Simon, C. H. de, fatalist view of economic development, 56
contradictory attitude to government, 68-69
tried to frighten the government into adopting his proposals, 74
tried to reconcile Bourbons and industrialists, 75
considered physiology the basis of sociology, 82-83
differences with French eighteenth-century philosophers on religious questions, 232
Savigny, F. C. von, on origin of law, 175-76
Say, J. B., on unimportance of political systems, 67
Schelling, F. W. von, on freedom and necessity, 125, 133
on magnetism, 139
Science preceded by practice (views of Pecchio and Mill), 212-13
Sensationalism defined, 15
French materialists and, 15-16

Sieber, N. I., reply to Zhukovsky's criticism of Marx, 279-81
Sismondi, J. C. L., governments the cause of changes in national character, 26-27
Slavery, its origin, historical advantages and limitations, 164-66
Specialists, scientific, their research confirms Marx's theory, 260-62
Struve, P. B., his advice to Russia to "go into training by capitalism," 337
Suard, J. B. A., on opinion and interest, 19
on human nature, 43-44
Szeliga, ridicule of historical objectivity, 244

TAINE, H., influence of environment on the arts, 219-22
Thierry, A., on class struggle in the English Revolution, 31-32
on conquest as the origin of class distinctions, 37-39
Tieghem, P. van, on life of plants, 116-17
Tools, used exclusively by man, 154
their rôle in man's development, 155
their discovery by accident, 162-63
Greek views on, conditioned by system of slavery, 164-65
their use the province of historian, not of naturalist, 169-70
Triad, its nature, 100

mistaken use by Chernyshevsky, 106-07

USURY, views of ancient Romans on, 186-87
Utopians, French, their attempts to invent a perfect legislation, 45
explained man by his environment, and environment by human nature, 46-47
attempts to break away from formal abstractions, 47-48
historical laws became Fate in their writings, 54-55
recipes for reorganization of society their chief concern, 56-57
fallacy of their view of politics, 67-69
their search for a happy accident, 69-71
their appeals to governments to "correct their mistakes," 74-75
tried to terrify contemporaries with the example of England, 78, 81

Utopians, German, hoped to avoid capitalism as the product of "Western Europe," 78-81
better unconstitutional government than development of capitalism, 80
thought intellectuals could eliminate capitalism from Germany, 314-19, 321, 324-25, 326
forgot to investigate social forces, 324-25
Utopians, Russian, becoming accomplices of capitalism, 309-11

VICO, J. B., on origin of civil law, 28, 30
Vollgraf, K., his belief in 40s that growth of German capitalism had stopped, 321-22
"V. V." (V. P. Vorontsov), his works, 20-21
views on economic development of Russia, 62-63
how affected by capitalist development of Russia, 63-65

Printed in the Union of Soviet Socialist Republics